LIBRARY OF HEBREW BIBLE/
OLD TESTAMENT STUDIES

726

Formerly Journal for the Study of the Old Testament Supplement Series

Editors
Laura Quick, Oxford University, UK
Jacqueline Vayntrub, Yale University, USA

Founding Editors
David J. A. Clines, Philip R. Davies and David M. Gunn

FROM CREATION TO ABRAHAM

Further Studies in Genesis 1–11

John Day

LONDON · NEW YORK · OXFORD · NEW DELHI · SYDNEY

T&T CLARK
Bloomsbury Publishing Plc
50 Bedford Square, London, WC1B 3DP, UK
1385 Broadway, New York, NY 10018, USA
29 Earlsfort Terrace, Dublin 2, Ireland

BLOOMSBURY, T&T CLARK and the T&T Clark logo
are trademarks of Bloomsbury Publishing Plc

First published in Great Britain 2022
Reprinted in 2022

Cover design: Top cover image: *Adam and Eve*, 1526 by Lucas Cranach the Elder (1472–1553)
© Courtauld Gallery / Bridgeman Images
Bottom cover image: *Abraham's Journey from Ur to Canaan*, 1850, painting by Jozsef Molnar
(1821–1899) © DeAgostini / Getty Images

A catalogue record for this book is available from the British Library.

Library of Congress Control Number: 2021945548.

ISBN: HB: 978-0-5677-0310-1
         ePDF: 978-0-5677-0311-8

Series: Library of Hebrew Bible/Old Testament Studies, volume 726
ISSN 2513-8758

Typeset by Trans.form.ed SAS
Printed and bound in Great Britain

To find out more about our authors and books visit www.bloomsbury.com
and sign up for our newsletters.

CONTENTS

PREFACE

This is the second volume of essays that I have written on Genesis 1–11, both constituting spin-offs from my ongoing work for the forthcoming ICC commentary on these chapters. The first volume, *From Creation to Babel: Studies in Genesis 1–11*, appeared in 2013 and apparently sold so well that the editor at that time, Dr Andrew Mein, asked if I could produce a second volume, which I was intending to do anyway. Those impatient to see my ICC commentary – and I know from correspondence that there are indeed such people – may gain some idea of my approach by perusing the 22 essays in these two volumes.

As has been usual in my previous work, in this volume I continually strive to get to the bottom of disputed problems, in so far as this is possible, to find the most natural interpretation of the texts with which I deal, and to read them in the light of their surrounding ancient Near Eastern background. In the case of Genesis 1–11 this most often, but certainly not exclusively, involves reading them in the light of Mesopotamian sources (see especially Chapters 6, 10, 11, but also occasionally in virtually every other chapter). At the same time, in keeping with recent trends, I have been devoting more attention to the history of interpretation and reception history of these chapters, and have learnt a lot in the process (see especially Chapters 2, 6, 8, 11, but also occasionally elsewhere). However, I have remained unconvinced by the attempts of some recent scholars to overturn the Documentary Hypothesis, which still seems to me the most satisfactory way of accounting for the formation of the text, more specifically of Genesis 1–11, which is my focus here (see especially Chapter 7). At the same time I have come to conclude that the Yahwistic source was not all written at one go (see especially Chapter 7 but also Chapter 5).

Overall, I hope that this volume will make a significant contribution to our understanding of Genesis 1–11, and that the reader will enjoy reading it as much as I have enjoyed researching and writing it. As on many previous occasions, I am enormously indebted to the copy-editor and typesetter, Dr Duncan Burns, for his great care in attention to detail and for undertaking the laborious task of compiling the indexes.

John Day

ACKNOWLEDGEMENTS
AND STATUS OF THE CHAPTERS

Chapter 1
GENESIS 1.1-5: THE FIRST DAY OF CREATION
  Previously unpublished.

Chapter 2
'SO GOD CREATED HUMANITY IN HIS OWN IMAGE' (GENESIS 1.27):
WHAT DOES THE BIBLE MEAN AND WHAT HAVE PEOPLE
THOUGHT IT MEANT?
  Revised and expanded version of an essay previously published
  in John Loughlin (ed.), *Human Dignity in the Judaeo-Christian
  Tradition: Catholic, Orthodox, Anglican and Protestant Perspectives*
  (London: Bloomsbury, 2019), pp. 15-35. Overlapping parts reprinted
  by kind permission of Bloomsbury.

Chapter 3
THE SERPENT IN THE GARDEN OF EDEN: ITS BACKGROUND AND ROLE
  Previously unpublished.

Chapter 4
WISDOM AND THE GARDEN OF EDEN
  Revised and expanded version of an essay previously published in
  John Jarick (ed.), *Perspectives on Israelite Wisdom: Proceedings of the
  Oxford Old Testament Seminar* (LHBOTS, 618; London: Bloomsbury
  T&T Clark, 2016), pp. 336-52. Overlapping parts reprinted by kind
  permission of Bloomsbury T&T Clark.

Chapter 5
PROBLEMS IN THE INTERPRETATION OF THE STORY OF CAIN AND ABEL
  Previously unpublished.

Chapter 6
THE ENOCHS OF GENESIS 4 AND 5 AND THE EMERGENCE
OF THE APOCALYPTIC ENOCH TRADITION
> Revised and expanded version of an article previously published
> in Joel Baden, Hindy Najman and Eibert Tigchelaar (eds.), *Sibyls,*
> *Scriptures, and Scrolls: John Collins at Seventy*, I (2 vols.; JSJ, 175;
> Leiden: Brill, 2017), pp. 293-313. Overlapping parts reprinted by kind
> permission of Brill.

Chapter 7
THE SOURCE ANALYSIS AND REDACTION OF THE GENESIS FLOOD STORY
> Previously unpublished.

Chapter 8
THE COVENANT WITH NOAH AND THE NOACHIC COMMANDMENTS
> Previously unpublished.

Chapter 9
THE TABLE OF THE NATIONS IN GENESIS 10
> Previously unpublished.

Chapter 10
IN SEARCH OF NIMROD:
PROBLEMS IN THE INTERPRETATION OF GENESIS 10.8-12
> Revised and expanded version of an article previously published in
> Dennis Mizzi, Nicholas C. Vella and Martin R. Zammit (eds.), *"What*
> *Mean These Stones?" (Joshua 4:6, 21): Essays on Text, Philology,*
> *and Archaeology in Honour of Anthony J. Frendo* (Ancient Near
> Eastern Studies, Supplement 40; Leuven: Peeters, 2017), pp. 95-110.
> Overlapping parts reprinted by kind permission of Peeters.

Chapter 11
FROM ABRAHAM OF UR TO ABRAHAM IN THE FIERY FURNACE
> Previously unpublished.

ABBREVIATIONS

AB	Anchor Bible
AfO	*Archiv für Orientforschung*
ArRel	*Archiv für Religionswissenschaft*
AJA	*American Journal of Archaeology*
AJSL	*American Journal of Semitic Languages and Literatures*
AnBib	Analecta Biblica
ANET	J.B. Pritchard (ed.), *Ancient Near Eastern Texts relating to the Old Testament* (Princeton: Princeton University Press, 3rd edn with Supplement, 1969)
AnSt	*Anatolian Studies*
AOAT	Alter Orient und Altes Testament
AOS	American Oriental Society
ArOr	*Archiv Orientální*
ArRel	*Archiv für Religionswissenschaft*
ATANT	Abhandlungen zur Theologie des Alten und Neuen Testaments
ATD	Das Alte Testament Deutsch
AUSS	*Andrews University Seminary Studies*
AV	Authorized Version
AYB	Anchor Yale Bible
BARev	*Biblical Archaeology Review*
BDB	Francis Brown, S.R. Driver and Charles A. Briggs, *A Hebrew and English Lexicon of the Old Testament* (Oxford: Clarendon Press, 1907)
BETL	Bibliotheca ephemeridum theologicarum lovaniensium
Bib	*Biblica*
BJRL	*Bulletin of the John Rylands Library*
BKAT	Biblischer Kommentar: Altes Testament
BN	*Biblische Notizen*
BASOR	*Bulletin of the American Schools of Oriental Research*
BSOAS	*Bulletin of the School of Oriental and African Studies*
BWANT	Beiträge zur Wissenschaft vom Alten und Neuen Testament
BZ	*Biblische Zeitschrift*
BZAW	Beihefte zur *ZAW*
CAD	I.J. Gelb *et al.* (eds.), *The Assyrian Dictionary of the Oriental Institute of the University of Chicago* (21 vols.; Chicago, IL: Oriental Institute, 1956–2010)
CBC	Cambridge Bible Commentary
CBQ	*Catholic Biblical Quarterly*

CBQM	Catholic Biblical Quarterly Monograph Series
CBSC	Cambridge Bible for Schools and Colleges
CHANE	Culture and History of the Ancient Near East
ConBOT	Coniectanea biblica, Old Testament
DJD	Discoveries in the Judaean Desert
EstBib	*Estudios Bíblicos*
ET	English Translation
ExpTim	*Expository Times*
FAT	Forschungen zum Alten Testament
FRLANT	Forschungen zur Religion und Literatur des Alten und Neuen Testaments
FzB	Forschung zur Bibel
GKC	Gesenius' *Hebrew Grammar* (ed. E. Kautzsch, revised and trans. A.E. Cowley; Oxford: Clarendon Press, 1910)
HALAT	L. Koehler *et al.* (eds.), *Hebräisches und aramäisches Lexikon zum Alten Testament* (5 vols.; Leiden: Brill, 1967–95)
HALOT	L. Koeher, W. Baumgartner, J.J. Stamm *et al.* (eds.), *Hebrew and Aramaic Lexicon of the Old Testament* (trans. and ed. M.E.J. Richardson; 5 vols.; Leiden: Brill, 1994–2000)
HAT	Göttinger Handkommentar zum Alten Testament
HBAI	*Hebrew Bible and Ancient Israel*
HBM	Hebrew Bible Monographs
HKAT	Göttinger Handkommentar zum Alten Testament
HM	Heythrop Monographs
HSM	Harvard Semitic Monographs
HTR	*Harvard Theological Review*
HThKAT	Herders theologischer Kommentar zum Alten Testament
ICC	International Critical Commentary
IDB	George Arthur Buttrick (ed.), *The Interpreter's Dictionary of the Bible* (4 vols.; Nashville, TN: Abingdon Press, 1962)
IEJ	*Israel Exploration Journal*
IJS	Institute of Jewish Studies
Int	*Interpretation*
IVP	Inter-Varsity Press
JAJ	*Journal of Ancient Judaism*
JANES	*Journal of the Ancient Near Eastern Society*
JAOS	*Journal of the American Oriental Society*
JB	Jerusalem Bible
JBL	*Journal of Biblical Literature*
JBTh	*Jahrbuch für biblische Theologie*
JCS	*Journal of Cuneiform Studies*
JETS	*Journal of the Evangelical Theological Society*
JHS	*Journal of Hebrew Scriptures*
JJS	*Journal of Jewish Studies*
JNES	*Journal of Near Eastern Studies*
JNSL	*Journal of Northwest Semitic Languages*
JPS	Jewish Publication Society

JPSV	Jewish Publication Society Version
JQR	*Jewish Quarterly Review*
JRAS	*Journal of the Royal Asiatic Society*
JSJSup	Journal for the Study of Judaism Supplement Series
JSOT	*Journal for the Study of the Old Testament*
JSOTSup	*Journal for the Study of the Old Testament*, Supplement Series
JSP	*Journal for the Study of the Pseudepigrapha*
JSS	*Journal of Semitic Studies*
JTS	*Journal of Theological Studies*
KAI	H. Donner and W. Röllig (eds.), *Kanaanäische und aramäische Inschriften* (3 vols.; Wiesbaden: Otto Harrassowitz, 1962–64)
KEHAT	Kurzgefasstes exegetisches Handbuch zum Alten Testament
KHAT	Kurzer Hand-Commentar zum Alten Testament
KTU³	M. Dietrich, O. Loretz and J. Sanmartín, *Die keilalphabetischen Texte aus Ugarit, Ras Ibn Hani and anderen Orten/The Cuneiform Alphabetic Texts from Ugarit, Ras Ibn Hani and Other Places* (*KTU³*, 3rd Enlarged edition, Münster: Ugarit Verlag, 2013)
LHBOT	Library of Hebrew Bible/Old Testament Studies
LXX	Septuagint
MT	Masoretic Text
NAB	New American Bible
NCB	New Century Bible
NCBC	New Cambridge Bible Commentary
NEB	New English Bible
NETS	A. Pietersma and B.J. Wright (eds.), *New English Translation of the Septuagint* (New York: Oxford University Press, 2007)
NF	Neue Folge
NICOT	New International Commentary on the Old Testament
NIV	New International Version
NJB	New Jerusalem Bible
NJPSV	New Jewish Publication Society Version
NRSV	New Revised Standard Version
NS	New Series
NTS	*New Testament Studies*
OBO	Orbis biblicus et orientalis
OLP	*Orientalia Lovaniensia Periodica*
OLZ	*Orientalische Literaturzeitung*
Or	*Orientalia*
OT	Old Testament
OTG	Old Testament Guides
OTL	Old Testament Library
OTS	*Oudtestamentische Studiën*
PL	J.-P. Migne, *Patrologia Latina* (221 vols., Paris: J.-P. Migne, 1844–65)
RA	*Revue d'Assyriologie et d'archéologie orientale*
RB	*Revue biblique*
REB	Revised English Bible
REg	*Revue d'Egyptologie*

RevQ	*Revue de Qumran*
*RGG*³	*Die Religion in Geschichte und Gegenwart*, 3rd edn
*RGG*⁴	*Die Religion in Geschichte und Gegenwart*, 4th edn
RHR	*Revue de l'histore des religions*
RS	Ras Shamra
RSR	*Recherches de science religieuse*
RSV	Revised Standard Version
RV	Revised Version
SBL	Society of Biblical Literature
SBLSCS	Society of Biblical Literature Septuagint and Cognate Studies
SBLWAW	Society of Biblical Literature Writings from the Ancient World
SBS	Stuttgarter Bibelstudien
SCM	Student Christian Movement
SBT	Studies in Bibical Theology
SJOT	*Scandinavian Journal of the Old Testament*
SJT	*Scottish Journal of Theology*
SOTS	*Society for Old Testament Study*
STDJ	Studies on the Texts of the Desert of Judah
SVTP	Studia in Veteris Testamenti Pseudepigrapha
TBü	Theologische Bücherei
TLZ	*Theologische Literaturzeitung*
TOTC	Tyndale Old Testament Commentaries
TSAJ	Texts & Studies in Ancient Judaism/Texte und Studien zum Alten Judentum
TSBA	*Transactions of the Society of Biblical Archaeology*
TynBul	*Tyndale Bulletin*
TZ	*Theologische Zeitschrift*
UCOP	University of Cambridge Oriental Publications
UF	*Ugarit-Forschungen*
VT	*Vetus Testamentum*
VTSup	Supplements to Vetus Testamentum Supplements
WBC	Word Biblical Commentary
WBWSBL	Writings from the Biblical World, Society of Biblical Literature
WMANT	Wissenschaftliche Monographien zum Alten und Neuen Testament
WO	*Die Welt des Orients*
WTJ	*Westminster Theological Journal*
ZAH	*Zeitschrift für Althebraistik*
ZAW	*Zeitschrift für die alttestamentliche Wissenschaft*
ZBK	Zürcher Bibelkommentare
ZDMG	*Zeitschrift der deutschen morgenländischen Gesellschaft*

Chapter 1

GENESIS 1.1-5:
THE FIRST DAY OF CREATION

Introduction

One of the major purposes of the present chapter is to argue, contrary to the current general consensus, that Gen. 1.1-5 as a whole, and not merely vv. 3-5, constitute the first day of creation in the understanding of the Priestly writer of the creation account in Gen. 1.1–2.3(4a). This was, in fact, the universal view of both Jews and Christians over many centuries. As a consequence of this view, I shall also be arguing that throughout Genesis 1 the day is envisaged as beginning in the evening, not the morning as most modern commentators tend to suppose, and that the darkness over the face of the deep in Gen. 1.2 represents the first part of the first day, rather than the creation of light in Gen. 1.3. I shall also consider other important questions raised by this passage as a whole.

When it comes to v. 1 there are three main interpretations. The first view translates it as a sentence, 'In the beginning God created the heavens and the earth', and understands this as God's first creative act, prior to the events in vv. 2ff. The second view follows the same translation of v. 1 but regards it as either a heading or summary of the entire Priestly creation account which follows. The third view understands v. 1 as a temporal clause, 'In the beginning, when God created the heavens and the earth', with v. 2 in parenthesis and the apodosis in v. 3, or less commonly v. 2 is seen as the apodosis.

Verse 1 as Opening Temporal Clause or Simple Sentence?

First we must discuss the view that v. 1 functions as a temporal clause, treating *bᵉrē'šît* as in the construct, lit. 'in the beginning of God's creating the heavens and the earth …', i.e. 'When God began to create the heavens and the earth …' This view was first suggested in the mediaeval period by the rabbinic commentator Rashi (died 1105), followed by another rabbinic commentator, Ibn Ezra (died *c.* 1167). However, whereas Rashi saw the apodosis as in v. 3, v. 2 serving as a parenthesis, Ibn Ezra understood v. 2 as the apodosis. The former of these views has become particularly dominant in American scholarship in recent decades,[1] for example, 'When God began to create heaven and earth – the earth being unformed and void, with darkness over the surface of the deep and a wind from God sweeping over the water – God said, "Let there be light"; and there was light' (N.M. Sarna). It is reflected in several modern Bible translations, the NAB, NJPSV and NRSV, as well as the NEB, but not in the revision of the latter in the REB, or in the RSV, JB, NJB or NIV. If it is in the construct we might more naturally have expected the text to read *berē'šît berō'*, with the infinitive construct, rather than *berē'šit bārā'* with the perfect. However, there are occasionally instances of a construct before a perfect, for example, Hos. 1.2; Exod. 6.20. This interpretation is therefore not impossible. It has also been argued in support that the word *rē'šît* is elsewhere in the construct, though there is an exception in Isa. 46.10, which speaks of God 'declaring the end from the beginning (*mērē'šît*)'.[2]

However, it should be noted that *rē'šît* in the construct is nowhere else followed by a verb, unlike what is proposed in Gen. 1.1. Furthermore, it is important to note that it is actually normal for expressions of time in biblical Hebrew to lack the definite article. In addition to *mērē'šît* already noted above, biblical Hebrew also regularly has *mērō'š*, not *mēhārō'š*, 'from the beginning' (cf. Isa. 40.21; 41.4, 26; 48.16; Eccl. 3.11). Further, the Hebrew Bible regularly has *miqqedem*, 'from of old' (cf. Isa. 46.10; Hab. 1.12; Ps. 74.12; Neh. 12.46), as well as *mē'ôlām*, 'from of old' (cf. Gen. 6.4; Josh. 24.2; Isa. 46.9; Prov. 8.23) and *le'ôlām* or *le'ōlām*, 'forever'

---

1. Those following the temporal-clause view include E.A. Speiser, *Genesis* (AB, 1; Garden City, NY: Doubleday, 1964), pp. 12-13; N.M. Sarna, *Genesis* (JPS Torah Commentary; Philadelphia, PA: JPS, 1989), p. 5; J.D. Levenson, *Creation and the Persistence of Evil* (San Francisco: Harper & Row, 1988), p. 5; B.T. Arnold, *Genesis* (NCBC; Cambridge: Cambridge University Press, 2009), pp. 34-36; M.S. Smith, *The Priestly Vision of Genesis 1* (Minneapolis, MN: Fortress Press, 2010), pp. 44-46; J. Blenkinsopp, *Creation, Un-Creation, Re-Creation: A Discursive Commentary on Genesis 1–11* (London: T&T Clark, 2011), pp. 30-31. R.D. Holmstedt, 'The Restrictive Syntax of Genesis i 1', *VT* 58 (2008), pp. 56-67, also renders in a similar manner but understands it in terms of an unmarked relative clause, 'In the initial period that/ in which God created the heavens and the earth'.

2. Already Rashi had noted Hos. 1.2, and claimed that *rē'šît* always comes elsewhere in the construct.

(Gen. 3.22; 6.3; Ps. 103.9), all without the article. It is important to note that these references encompass prose as well as poetic texts (including three instances of the former in Gen. 1–11), so the omission of the definite article cannot simply be dismissed as poetic style. Accordingly, there is no reason to suppose that *bᵉrē'šît* in Gen. 1.1 represents a construct, 'in the beginning of …' It is precisely what we should expect for 'in the beginning'. We may perhaps compare the omission of the definite article to American English saying 'in light of', whereas British English has 'in the light of'.

Secondly, another argument claimed in support of taking v. 1 as a temporal clause is that it would parallel other creation accounts which begin with 'when', for example, Gen. 2.4b-7 and *Enuma elish*. However, it should be noted that the parallels with *Enuma elish* and Gen. 2.4b-7 are far from exact. As for Gen. 2.4b-7 (J), this lacks the words 'In the beginning', and vv. 5-6 refer parenthetically to what was not yet created, whereas Gen. 1.2 refers to precisely what did exist at that point. *Enuma elish* likewise lacks the words 'In the beginning', it does not start with a construct, and begins by recounting a time when there was no heaven and earth rather than describing their initial creation as Genesis 1 does. Then it continues with a theogony of the gods, and we have to wait till tablets 4 and 5 of *Enuma elish* before we can read about the creation of heaven and earth.

In favour of the traditional rendering,[3] 'In the beginning God created the heavens and the earth', a view accepted particularly by European scholars, the following points should also be noted. First, this was the universal

---

3. The traditional rendering of Gen. 1.1 is supported, for example, by AV, RV, RSV, JPSV, NIV, JB, NJB; G. von Rad, *Das erste Buch Mose: Genesis* (ATD, 2.4; Göttingen: Vandenhoeck & Ruprecht, 5th edn, 1958), pp. 34, 36-37, ET *Genesis*, Genesis (trans. J.H. Marks; OTL; London: SCM Press, 2nd edn, 1963), pp. 44, 46-47; C. Westermann, *Genesis 1–11* (BKAT, 1.1; Neukirchen-Vluyn: Neukirchener Verlag, 1974), pp. 107, 108-109, 139-36, ET *Genesis 1–11* (trans. J.J. Scullion; London: SPCK, 1974), pp. 76, 78, 93-98; G.J. Wenham, *Genesis 1–15* (WBC, 1; Waco, TX: Word Books, 1987), pp. 2, 11-13; H. Seebass, *Genesis. I. Urgeschichte (1,1–11,26)* (Neukirchen-Vluyn: Neukirchener Verlag, 3rd edn, 2009), pp. 58, 64-65; H.-J. Stipp, 'Gen 1,1 und asyndetische Relativsätze im Bibelhebräischen', in *Alttestamentliche Studien. Arbeiten zu Priesterschrift, Deuteronomischen Geschichtswerk und Prophetie* (BZAW, 442; Berlin: W. de Gruyter, 2013), pp. 3-51; J. L'Hour, *Genèse 1-2,4a. Commentaire* (Etudes bibliques, NS 71; Leuven: Peeters, 2016), pp. 32, 54-63; J.C. Gertz, *Das erste Buch Mose, Genesis. I. Die Urgeschichte Gen 1–11* (ATD, 1; Göttingen: Vandenhoeck & Ruprecht, 2018), pp. 26, 34-37. G. Fischer, *Genesis 1–11* (HThKAT; Freiburg: Herder, 2018), pp. 115, 118, translates 'In a beginning', but this rendering is awkward and unnecessary.

understanding of antiquity for over one thousand years up to the time of Rashi. Without exception all the ancient Versions support rendering 'In the beginning God created the heavens and the earth' (cf. too John 1.1), the earliest of these, the Septuagint, dating from the third century BCE, a time when other parts of the Hebrew Bible were still being written. So if the temporal-clause understanding is correct, the Priestly author totally failed to convey his meaning clearly and it was early forgotten. That does not seem very plausible.

Secondly, the longwinded, convoluted parenthesis, which the temporal clause rendering presupposes in v. 2, is not typical of P's style throughout Genesis 1. A short, snappy sentence 'In the beginning God created the heavens and the earth' is far more typical of P's style. Occasionally in the Old Testament we do find more complicated sentences, e.g. Gen. 2.4b-7, but this is from J, not P.

Thirdly, it should be noted that on the temporal-clause view there is a contradiction between vv. 1 and 2. Whereas v. 1 supposedly states that God was beginning to create the heavens and the earth, v. 2 seems to imply that the earth was already present in inchoate form before God's effective creative work could start in v. 3. But is it really plausible that P, with his great emphasis on God's transcendent omnipotence, could tolerate a belief in a pre-existent inchoate earth?[4]

Genesis 1.1: Heading, Summary Statement or God's First Act of Creation?

Granted that Gen. 1.1 should be rendered as an independent sentence, 'In the beginning God created the heavens and the earth', the question then arises whether these words constitute a heading to or summary of the whole Priestly creation account, or whether they rather represent God's first creative act prior to his subsequent creative acts from v. 3 onwards.

The suggestion that the words are a heading[5] is unacceptable, since they read like a complete sentence. A heading would simply say something like *rēʼšît bᵉrōʼ ʼet-haššāmayim wᵉʼet hāʼāreṣ*, 'The beginning of the creation of the heavens and the earth'. As for the second suggestion, that the

---

4. Cf. B.S. Childs, *Myth and Reality in the Old Testament* (SBT, 17; London: SCM Press, 1960), pp. 40-41.

5. E.g. Seebass, *Genesis. I. Urgeschichte*, p. 65, 'Überschrift'. Seebass refers to W. von Soden, 'Mottoverse zu Beginn babylonischer und antiker Epen, Mottosätze in der Bibel', in H.-P. Müller (ed.), *Bibel und alter Orient. Altorientalische Beiträge zum Alten Testament von Wolfram von Soden* (BZAW, 162; Berlin: W. de Bruyter, 1985), pp. 206-12 (209), though von Soden has a preference for 'Mottosatz' to 'Überschrift'.

words are a summary of all that follows in the P creation account, this has actually been the most widely accepted view in Europe, including Britain, for quite some time.[6] Its proponents emphasize that elsewhere in the Old Testament 'the heavens and the earth' means the total universe as the Israelites knew it. Further, it is argued that if v. 1 is God's first act, then the heavens and earth are unaccountably made twice, since the heavens (in the form of the firmament) are subsequently made on day 2 (vv. 6-8) and the earth in the form of the dry land is made on day 3 (vv. 9-10). However, these arguments are not compelling. So far as the earth allegedly being made twice is concerned, we should observe that the earth in inchoate form (but not a chaos, as we shall see below) is already in existence prior to vv. 9-10 in v. 2; what emerges in vv. 9-10 is specifically the dry ground, the land in its final form following its separation from the waters. Further, with regard to the heavens, it is simply the solid firmament or dome which is created in vv. 6-8. The term 'the heavens' is not confined to this but in the Old Testament includes everything above the earth: it could be used of God's dwelling and also of the atmosphere.[7] The wind already existed in v. 2 ('the wind of God was blowing to and fro over the waters'; see defence of this translation below), which implies the existence of the air. Having thought of this last point, I subsequently discovered that it is already present in Philo, *De Opificio Mundi* 7(.29)–8(.30), who equates the 'breath of God' with the air, and in the Babylonian Talmud, *Ḥagiga* 12a, where the wind/air is created on the first day. Josephus (*Ant*. 1.1) also implies that the wind (and hence the air) was already in existence immediately following the initial creation of the heavens and the earth. And *Jubilees* states that on the very first day, along with the abyss, darkness and light (cf. Gen. 1.2) God created 'the angels of the spirit of the winds' (*Jub*. 2.2). We recall further that birds are sometimes called literally 'birds

6. E.g. S.R. Driver, *The Book of Genesis* (Westminster Commentaries; London: Methuen, 1904), p. 3; J. Barr, 'Was Everything that God Created Really Good? A Question in the First Verse of the Bible', in T. Linafelt and T.K. Beal (eds.), *God in the Fray: A Tribute to Walter Brueggemann* (Minneapolis, MN: Fortress Press, 1998), pp. 55-65 (55-60), reprinted in J. Barton (ed.), *Bible and Interpretation: The Collected Essays of James Barr*. II. *Biblical Studies* (3 vols.; Oxford: Oxford University Press, 2013), pp. 178-87 (178-82); Seebass, *Genesis*. I. *Urgeschichte*, p. 62; Westermann, *Genesis 1–11*, p. 131, ET *Genesis 1–11*, p. 94; Gertz, *Das erste Buch Mose*, I, p. 36.

7. Cf. L.I.J. Stadelmann, *The Hebrew Concept of the World* (AnBib, 39; Rome: Pontifical Biblical Institute Press, 1970), p. 61. N. Chambers, 'Genesis 1.1 as the First Act of Creation', *JSOT* 43 (2019), pp. 385-94, sees 'heaven' in Gen. 1.1 as simply referring to God's dwelling place. But Gen. 1 appears to be confining itself to a description of the creation of the physical universe.

of the heavens' (cf. Gen. 1.26, 28, 30; 2.19, 20; 7.3; Job 12.7; Eccl. 10.20; Hos. 2.20 [ET 18]), which clearly means 'birds of the air', since the Israelites could surely see that they did not fly as high as the firmament, where the sun, moon and stars were conceived to be.

Since the inchoate earth and the heavens in the sense of the air/wind were already in existence in Gen. 1.2, it is most natural to assume that Gen. 1.1 refers to God's creative act in making them. The fact that elsewhere 'the heavens and the earth' means the total universe is not a compelling argument to the contrary in this instance, since what we have in Gen. 1.1 is a unique situation, the very beginning of creation.

Such an understanding is also supported by Gen. 2.4a, 'These are the generations of the heavens and the earth when they were created'.[8] Other examples of 'these are the generations of ...' in Genesis clearly imply that the generations are what emerged subsequent to what has been mentioned, not what preceded what is mentioned (e.g. 'the generations of Noah' in Gen. 6.9). Consequently, the phrase implies that the heavens and earth came first, and that the fulness of creation within the heavens and earth emerged from them, 'the heavens and earth ... and all their multitude' referred to in Gen. 2.1. Thus, following the creation of the inchoate earth in Gen. 1.1 (cf. v. 2), in Gen. 1.11, 20, 24, the earth is said to bring forth vegetation and subsequently various living creatures. Again, the heavens in the sense of the atmosphere above the earth is envisaged as being created in Gen. 1.1, the solid dome of the firmament is added in vv. 6-8, and finally the sun, moon and stars come into existence, having been set in the firmament in vv. 14-18.

A problem with the summary interpretation of Gen. 1.1 is that this verse implies that God created the earth, but the supposed beginning of the narrative in v. 2 states that the earth (in inchoate form) was already in existence. Holders of the summary interpretation commonly assume that v. 2 refers to pre-existent matter from the time before God's creative work commenced in v. 3. However, it does not make sense for v. 1 to say in a summary statement that God created the earth and then not tell the story of

---

8. On the problems of interpretation of Gen. 2.4a, see my discussion in J. Day, *From Creation to Babel: Studies in Genesis 1–11* (LHBOTS, 592; London: Blooms-bury T&T Clark, 2013), pp. 18-19. I accept that Gen. 2.4a is redactional, but unlike some recent scholars I adhere to the traditional view that it refers back to Gen. 1.1–2.3, since 'the generations of the heavens and the earth', as well as employing P-like language, forms an admirable summary of the creation story there. However, it would constitute a very poor summary of Gen. 2.4b–3.24, where hardly anything is said about the generation of the heavens.

its original creation but rather assume its pre-creation existence. Verse 1, therefore, most naturally relates to God's creation of the earth, along with the heavens, immediately preceding v. 2. This was, in fact, the universal view in antiquity. Just to cite some of the earliest examples, the Septuagint in the third century BCE clearly implied by its wording that v. 2 followed on chronologically directly after v. 1: 'In the beginning God made the heaven and the earth. Yet the earth was invisible and unformed, and darkness was over the abyss, and a divine wind was carried along over the water' (*NETS*). Josephus (*Ant.* 1.1), echoing the Septuagint, also clearly implies that the earth shrouded in darkness (Gen. 1.2) is the earth previously made by God in Gen. 1.1. Again, the second-century BCE book of *Jubilees* (2.2), explicitly states that on the first day God created the heavens and the earth and the various items listed in Gen. 1.2. Similarly, Philo, *De Opificio Mundi* 7(.29) holds that God made first the heavens and the earth, as well as the other things mentioned in Gen. 1.2 (air, water, the deep, darkness and light). Later on the same is true in the Babylonian Talmud, *Ḥagiga* 12a. We may also recall even earlier, Ps. 148.7, which seems to imply that 'all deeps' (*tᵉhōmôt*; cf. the *tᵉhōm* in Gen. 1.2) were created by God (cf. v. 5). Even more significantly, Jer. 4.23, which seems to know the tradition behind Genesis 1, if not Genesis 1 itself, depicts the reversal of creation and declares, 'I looked on the earth, and lo, it was desolate and empty (*tōhû wābōhû*); and to the heavens, and they had no light'. Why this is significant is because it implies the existence of the heavens and earth prior to the creation of light and when it was *tōhû wābōhû*. If those are right who claim that Gen. 1.1 is merely a summary heading, with the heavens and earth denoting the completed universe, then there ought not to be a heaven in existence prior to the creation of light. This supports the thesis argued here, that Gen. 1.1 is indeed God's first act of creation,[9] not merely a summary heading.

So in my view, the first day of creation started in Gen. 1.1, not 1.3. In keeping with this, the darkness of Gen. 1.2 may be seen as the evening of the first day, while the creation of light in v. 3 corresponds to the

9. Similarly J. Wellhausen, *Prolegomena zur Geschichte Israels* (Berlin: G. Reimer, 2nd edn, 1883), pp. 313, 411 n. 1, ET *Prolegomena to the History of Israel* (trans. J.S. Black and A. Menzies; Edinburgh: A. & C. Black, 1885), pp. 298, 387 n. 1; N.H. Ridderbos, 'Gen 1:1 und 2', *OTS* 12 (1958), pp. 214-60; Childs, *Myth and Reality*, pp. 31-43; Wenham, *Genesis 1–15*, pp. 11-13. V. Notter, *Biblischer Schöpfungsbericht und ägyptische Schöpfungsmythen* (SBS, 68; Stuttgart: KBW Verlag, 1974), pp. 23-26, notes that there are many Egyptian parallels to the notion that a god first created matter, the primaeval ocean, and subsequently organized it.

subsequent dawning of the first morning. This would cohere well with the statement in Gen. 1.5, 'And there was evening and there was morning, the first day' (lit. 'day one'). However, the majority of modern commentators[10] suppose that the first day only starts with the creation of light in v. 3, and hold that 'morning' refers to the dawning of the next day. But in that case, the morning would effectively be the first part of the next day, whereas the language used strongly suggests that it constitutes a significant part of the latter half of day one: 'And there was evening and there was morning, the first day'. However, holders of the view that the first day started with the creation of the light in v. 3 cannot admit this, since for them this already inaugurated the morning of the first day, so there is no room within that day for a full morning after the evening.

A further supporting argument for the day starting in the evening in Genesis 1 is the fact that on the seventh day God rested and sanctified that day (Gen. 2.1-3), clearly implying that this constituted a prototype for the Sabbath. Now in the post-exilic period the Sabbath certainly started in the evening (cf. Neh. 13.19; Lev. 23.32). We should therefore expect P likewise to have understood God's seventh-day rest in Genesis as proceeding from the beginning of one evening to just before the beginning of the following evening. The general situation in the Old Testament is that pre-exilic sources tend to presuppose the day as beginning in the morning (cf. Gen. 19.33-34; Judg. 21.4; 1 Sam. 19.11), while post-exilic sources presuppose that it starts in the evening (Neh. 3.19; Dan. 8.14; Est. 4.16; Jdt. 11.17; cf. Ps. 55.18, ET 17).[11] What brought about the change? Clearly it must have been a consequence of the Babylonian conquest and exile, for the Babylonians started the day in the evening (unlike say, the Egyptians, who started in the morning). Babylonian influence on the Priestly calendar is already seen in P's following the spring new year calendar in contrast to the earlier autumnal calendar (cf. Exod. 12.2-3, 18; Lev. 23.5-6, 26; Num. 9.1-5; 28.16; contrast non-P Exod. 23.16; 34.22), so it would be

10. E.g. H. Gunkel, *Genesis* (HKAT, 1.1; Göttingen: Vandenhoeck & Ruprecht, 3rd edn, 1910), p. 106, ET *Genesis* (trans. Mark Biddle; Macon, GA: Mercer University Press, 1997), p. 108; U.(M.D.) Cassuto, *A Commentary on the Book of Genesis*. I. *From Adam to Noah* (ET, I. Abrahams; Jerusalem: Magnes Press, 1961), pp. 28-30; von Rad, *Das erste Buch Mose: Genesis*, p. 33, ET *Genesis*, p. 51; Sarna, *Genesis*, p. 8; V.P. Hamilton, *The Book of Genesis: Chapters 1–17* (NICOT; Grand Rapids, MI: Eerdmans, 1990), p. 121; Fischer, *Genesis 1–11*, p. 131. This view was already supported centuries earlier by the mediaeval commentator Rashbam.

11. Cf. R. de Vaux, *Les institutions de l'Ancien Testament* (2 vols.; Paris: Cerf, 1958–60), I, pp. 275-78, ET *Ancient Israel* (trans. J. McHugh; London: Darton, Longman & Todd, 2nd edn, 1965), pp. 180-82.

in keeping with this that P should also reflect the Babylonian practice for the start of the day (cf. Lev. 23.32).[12] All this holds true whether one ultimately sees P as exilic or post-exilic.[13]

Bārā', 'to Create' or 'to Separate'?

So far I have been assuming that *bārā'* means 'to create'. This is almost universally accepted and has been so throughout history. However, a modern Dutch scholar, Ellen van Wolde,[14] has been insistent in several articles during the last few years that it means rather 'to separate' throughout the Old Testament, including in Gen. 1.1–2.4a. Van Wolde's radical new rendering was sensationally publicized by a British newspaper, *The Daily Telegraph*, on October 8, 2009, with the dramatic headline, 'God is not the Creator, says academic'! It should be noted that the translation 'create' is supported by all the ancient Versions. This includes the Septuagint Genesis, probably dating from the first half of the third century BCE, when the writing of some other parts of the Hebrew

---

12. The argument above, that evening preceded morning in Gen. 1 and that the evidence of the Sabbath supports this, was previously argued by D. Hoffmann, 'Probleme der Pentateuchexegese', *Jeschurun* 1 (1914), pp. 114-19 (114-16), but his argument has been largely overlooked.

13. Although P makes use of earlier traditions, in its final form it cannot be pre-exilic. For example, P's clear distinction between priests and subordinate Levites, the former being equated with the sons of Aaron, corresponds with the post-exilic reality (cf. Chronicles), and stands in advance not only of D, where all Levites are priests, but also of Ezek. 44, where the priests are called the sons of Zadok (a somewhat narrower group than the sons of Aaron). Again, the Day of Atonement, which P is aware of (cf. Lev. 16), is something still unattested in the exilic Ezekiel, even though in Ezek. 45 he knows the spring calendar, including the spring New Year's day. We should also note that P's overwhelming preference for *'ⁿnî* over against *'ānōkî* for 'I' corresponds to both the dominant exilic and post-exilic usage but not that of pre-exilic times.

14. E. van Wolde, *Reframing Biblical Studies: When Language and Text Meet Culture, Cognition and Context* (Winona Lake, IN: Eisenbrauns, 2009), pp. 184-200; *eadem*, 'Why the Verb ברא Does Not Mean "To Create" in Genesis 1.1–2.4a', *JSOT* 34 (2009), pp. 3-23; *eadem* (with R. Rezetko), 'Semantics and the Semantics of ברא: A Rejoinder to the Arguments Advanced by B. Becking and M. Korpel', *JHS* 11 (2011), article 9; *eadem*, 'Separation and Creation in Genesis 1 and Psalm 104, A Continuation of the Discussion of the Verb ברא', *VT* 67 (2017), pp. 611-47. The last but one contribution above was a reply to B. Becking and M.C.A. Korpel, 'To Create, to Separate or to Construct: An Alternative for a Recent Proposal as to the Interpretation of ברא in Genesis 1.1–2.4a', *JHS* 10 (2010), article 3.

Bible was still taking place. It should further be noted that the translation 'create', or occasionally something close to it, makes excellent sense in every instance of *bārā'* in the Old Testament, unlike 'separate', both in the qal and niphal. (The piel means 'to cut down' in Josh. 17.15, 18, and 'to mark out' in Ezek. 21.24.) Just to give one example, why would Qohelet say, 'Remember also your Separator in the days of your youth' rather than 'Remember your Creator in the days of your youth' (Eccl. 12.1)? Moreover, it is highly significant that there are many instances in which *bārā'* appears in close parallelism with the verbs *'āśâ*, 'to make, do', and *yāṣar*, 'to form', as well as occasionally with *yāsad*, 'to found', and *kōnēn*, 'to establish' (cf. Gen. 1.26-27; 2.3; Exod. 34.10; Isa. 41.20; 43.1, 7; 45.7, 18; 65.17//66.22; Amos 4.13; Ps. 89.12-13, ET 11-12). These offer a very clear indication of the broad, general meaning of *bārā'*, and support the meaning 'create' rather than 'separate'. It is difficult to believe, for example, in the light of God's reference in Isa. 66.22 to 'the new heaven and the new earth which I am *making ('ōśeh)*', that Isa. 65.17 is not similarly declaring, 'Behold I am *creating (bôrē')* a new heaven and a new earth'. To think with van Wolde that it means rather 'Behold, I am separating a new heaven and a new earth' would be distinctly odd. It should also be noted that in Ezek. 21.35 (ET 30) 'in the place *nibrē'tā* [traditionally, "we were created"]' stands in parallelism with 'the land of your origin', and in Mal. 2.10 *bᵉrā'ēnû* (traditionally, 'our creator') stands parallel to a reference to God as 'father', both of which further support 'create' rather than 'separate' as the basic meaning of *bārā'*.

The pattern throughout the days of creation in Genesis 1 is that God declares 'Let something be …' and then we read that it was so or God caused it to be so. Several of these instances do not involve the verb *bārā'* (days 1-4), so van Wolde does not dispute the usual translations there. Accordingly, when on day 6 God declares in Gen. 1.26, 'Let us *make* humanity in our image, after our likeness', it is natural to assume that v. 27 goes on to say, as traditionally rendered, 'So God *created* humanity in his own image, in the image of God he *created* them', rather than 'And God *separated* humanity in his own image, in the image of God he *separated* them'. Van Wolde, supporting the latter rendering, claims that it refers rather to the division of humanity into male and female, something actually referred to later on in that verse. However, this is to jump ahead. First of all in v. 27 we expect a reference to God's accomplishing what he had just commanded in v. 26, namely the making or creation of humanity.

Again, in v. 20 we read that God said, 'Let the waters bring forth swarms of living creatures, and let birds fly above the earth across the firmament of the heavens'. Accordingly, by analogy with other verses, we expect v. 21 to say, as traditionally rendered, 'So God *created* the great sea monsters and every living creature that moves, with which the waters swarm, according to their kinds, and every winged bird according to its kind', not 'And God *separated* the great sea monsters ...' Van Wolde uniquely sees here a threefold division of sea monsters in the deep sea, other sea creatures higher up in the earth's seas, and birds in the air'. But it is the creatures themselves to which the verb *bārā'* relates, not their habitat, and there are various indications that sea monsters were sometimes visible in the earth's seas (e.g. Ps. 104.26). Further, van Wolde thinks that the sea monsters already existed before God's creative work, and claims that this is why they are not specifically mentioned in v. 20, as they already existed. But there is no evidence to support that, and it is more natural to assume that the sea monsters are singled out for mention as a specially noteworthy kind of creature swarming the seas, rather than that they dwelt at a lower level.

Consequently, the other three more general references to *bārā'* in Gen. 1.1–2.4a (Gen. 1.1; 2.3, 4a) must likewise refer to God's *creation*, not separation, of heaven and earth. Furthermore, as I have already pointed out[15] – and van Wolde has offered no response to this point – in biblical Hebrew one does not simply separate things but separates between them, as illustrated by the verb *hibdîl* (hiphil of *bādal*). Indeed, it is interesting to note that five clear acts of separation are mentioned in Gen. 1.4, 6, 7, 14, 18 and in each case the verb employed is *hibdîl*, rather than *bārā'*.

The verb *bārā'* in the qal and niphal is used only of divine creation and we are never told of any material used in the creation of anything. As with our argument above that Gen. 1.1 describes God's first creative act, so this is compatible with a belief in *Creatio ex Nihilo*, but it is not proved thereby that Genesis intended it. The first explicit statement of *Creatio ex Nihilo* appears to have come centuries later. Some have found it in 2 Macc. 7.28, but even that is debated, and some hold that it was only in second-century CE Christianity (arising from its conflict with Gnosticism) that we find it finally and definitively spelled out.[16]

15. Day, *From Creation to Babel*, p. 6.

16. For differing views on the earliest attestation of belief in *Creatio ex Nihilo*, see G. May, *Schöpfung aus dem Nichts: Die Entstehung der Lehre von der Creatio ex Nihilo* (Arbeiten zur Kirchengeschichte, 48; Berlin: W. de Gruyter, 1978), ET *Creatio ex Nihilo: The Doctrine of 'Creation out of Nothing' in Early Christian Thought* (trans. A.S. Worrall; Edinburgh: T. & T. Clark, 1994); J.C. O'Neill, 'How Early is the Doctrine of *Creatio ex Nihilo*?', *JTS* 53 NS (2002), pp. 449-65; M. Bockmuehl, '*Creatio ex Nihilo* in Palestinian Judaism and Early Christianity', *SJT* 65 (2012),

Tōhû wābōhû: *'Without Form and Void' or 'Desolate and Empty',*
or a Description of Chaos?

Verse 2 declares, 'Now (lit. "and") the earth was *tōhû wābōhû*'. The earth is clearly here in existence but in inchoate form, not the earth as it later became. On the interpretation offered here, this is the earth that has just been created in v. 1. The word *tōhû* occurs twenty times in the Old Testament (Gen. 1.2; Deut. 32.10; 1 Sam. 12.21 [×2]; Job 6.12; 12.24; 26.7; Ps. 107.40; Isa. 24.10; 29.21; 34.11; 40.17, 23; 41.29; 44.9; 45.18, 19; 49.4; 59.4; Jer. 4.23). From these passages it is clear that the word's meaning can extend from the concrete 'desert' or 'wasteland' (cf. Deut. 32.10; Job 6.18; 12.24; Ps. 107.40; perhaps also in Ugaritic in *KTU³* 1.5.I.15), through the desolation of a destroyed city or country (Isa. 24.10; 34.11) to the abstract 'non-entity' (cf. 1 Sam. 12.21 [×2]; Isa. 41.29; 44.9). Its central meaning, uniting these extremes, is that of being 'empty' (cf. Jer. 4.23; Isa. 29.21; 45.18; 59.4) or 'nothing' (cf. Job 26.7; Isa. 40.17, 23; 49.4). Emptiness seems to be the idea in view in Gen. 1.2.

The second term, *bōhû*, only occurs alongside *tōhû* and was perhaps modelled on it. Apart from here *bōhû* occurs with *tōhû* in Isa. 34.11 and Jer. 4.23. The second passage is particularly interesting, since it is part of a passage describing the reversal of creation, and seems to know the tradition behind Genesis 1. The word *bōhû* is plausibly connected with Arabic *bahiya*, 'to be empty', and one may assume that it also means 'emptiness', thus providing a good parallel to *tōhû*.

There is no good reason to derive the word *bōhû* from the name of Ba'u, a Mesopotamian goddess of birth and fertility.[17] The name of the goddess in the first millennium BCE was probably spelled Babu (originally Baba), and there is nothing in common with the Hebrew *bōhû*. The lack of any divine overtones in *bōhû* also makes unlikely any connection with the Phoenician goddess Baau (meaning 'night'), wife of Colpia (the wind) in Philo of Byblos (cited by Eusebius, *Praeparatio evangelica* 1.10.7).[18]

The sense in Gen. 1.2 is therefore that the primaeval earth was 'desolate and empty'. The two words constitute a hendiadys (cf. 'assault

pp. 253-70; N.J. Chambers, *Reconsidering Creatio ex Nihilo in Genesis 1* (Journal of Theological Interpretation Supplement, 19; University Park: Pennsylvania State University Press [Eisenbrauns], 2020).

17. On this goddess, see E. Ebeling, 'Ba'u', in E. Ebeling and B. Meissner (eds.), *Reallexikon der Assyriologie*, I (Berlin: de W. Gruyter, 1932), pp. 432-33.

18. See R.A. Oden and H.W. Attridge, *Philo of Byblos, The Phoenician History: Introduction, Critical Text, Translation, Notes* (CBQMS, 9; Washington, DC: Catholic Biblical Association of America, 1961), pp. 40-41.

and battery'). There was nothing on the earth (apart, of course, from the waters of the deep that submerged it). The earth still awaited the creation of its scenery and inhabitants which are described subsequently in Genesis 1.

Contrary to what has sometimes been supposed, it is a mistake to think of *tōhû wābōhû* as meaning chaos. Chaos suggests disorder, but the use of these words elsewhere in the Old Testament indicates rather desolation and emptiness (the words are both nouns), but it would be more natural in English to translate them here adjectivally, 'desolate and empty'.[19] If one wishes to convey the word play of the Hebrew in English one could render the phrase as 'desolate and deserted'. (Mark Smith has alternatively suggested 'void and vacuum'.[20]) One therefore cannot object, as is sometimes done, to Gen. 1.1 being God's first act of creation on the grounds that God's first act would strangely have been to create a chaos, since *tōhû wābōhû* does not actually denote chaos. Rather, the earth's being *tōhû wābōhû* constituted the first stage in the ongoing step-by-step process of creation, which Genesis 1 describes.

Although *tōhû wābōhû* does not denote chaos, the term 'chaos' is not inappropriate of the raging waters that God is said to have defeated at the time of creation in some Old Testament poetic passages (e.g. Ps. 104.6-9), and which ultimately lie behind the waters of the deep in Gen. 1.2.

Rûaḥ *'ᵉlōhîm*: *'The Spirit of God', 'the Wind of God', 'the Breath of God', or a Mighty Wind?*

There has been much discussion over the precise translation of *rûaḥ 'ᵉlōhîm* in v. 2. Does it refer to the Spirit of God,[21] the wind of God,[22] a

---

19. See D.T. Tsumura, *Creation and Destruction: A Reappraisal of the* Chaoskampf *Theory in the Old Testament* (Winona Lake, IN: Eisenbrauns, 2005), pp. 9-35; T. Fenton, 'Chaos in the Bible? Tohu vabohu', in G. Abramson and T. Parfitt (eds.), *Jewish Education and Learning: Published in Honour of Dr David Patterson on the Occasion of His Seventieth Birthday* (London: Harwood Academic Publishers, 1994), pp. 203-19.

20. Smith, *The Priestly Vision of Genesis 1*, pp. 50, 51, 52, 57.

21. This has been the traditional Christian view and is followed in AV, RV, RSV, REB, NIV, as well as Hamilton, *The Book of Genesis: Chapters 1–17*, pp. 113-14; Fischer, *Genesis 1–11*, pp. 115, 128. Amongst Jewish scholars it is followed by Cassuto, *A Commentary on the Book of Genesis*, I, pp. 21, 24.

22. Cf. NRSV, NJB; H.M. Orlinsky, 'The Plain Meaning of Ruaḥ in Gen. 1.2', *JQR* 48 (1957–58), pp. 174-82; B. Janowski and A. Krüger, 'Gottes Sturm und Gottes Atem. Zum Verständnis von רוח אלהים in Gen 1,2 und Ps 104,29f', *JBTh* 24

mighty wind,[23] or the breath of God?[24] It is easiest to dismiss the rendering 'mighty wind', since not only is the occurrence of the divine name in an intensive sense in the Old Testament dubious,[25] but the 34 other refer-ences to Elohim in the Priestly creation narrative all clearly refer to the deity. Moreover, the idea of a mighty wind could have been more clearly expressed by using an expression like *rûaḥ s^e 'ārâ* or *rûaḥ s^e 'ārôt*, 'strong wind' (Pss. 107.25; 148.8), or *rûaḥ qādîm*, 'east wind' (Ps. 48.8, ET 7; Jer. 18.17).

So we are left with a choice between 'the Spirit of God', 'the wind of God', and 'the breath of God'. One problem in deciding is that, whatever it is, the expression occurs in no other place in the Genesis 1 creation narrative. This is particularly surprising if it is the creative Spirit of God, since we might have expected a mention of it in connection with the subse-quent creative acts of God in Genesis 1. Of course, it might be objected that the wind or breath of God also plays no further role in Genesis 1. But in the course of the flood story Gen. 8.1 (likewise P) does state that 'God made a wind blow over the earth, and the waters subsided', and the flood represents a re-emergence of the primordial earth submerged in water in Gen. 1.2, in which context the *rûaḥ ^{e}lōhîm* is mentioned. Although Genesis 1 does not say that God's *rûaḥ* blew away the waters, it is likely that a more mythological version of the story underlying our creation narrative did so. Psalm 104 is particularly telling, since it has the same order of creation as Genesis 1,[26] and in v. 3 God rides on the wings of the

---

(2009), 3-29 (3-19). Cf. M. Bauks, *Die Welt am Anfang. Zur Verständnis von Vorwelt und Weltentstehung in Gen 1 und in der altorientalischen Literatur* (WMANT, 74; Neukirchen-Vluyn: Neukirchener Verlag, 1977), p. 147, who renders 'ein Windhauch Gottes', i.e. 'a breath of wind/breeze of God'.

23. Cf. NEB, NAB; von Rad, *Das erste Buch Mose*, p. 37, ET *Genesis*, p. 47 renders 'storm of God', taking it to mean 'a terrible storm', but the text translation in ET, p. 44 misleadingly has 'the Spirit of God' in spite of the German, p. 34 'ein Gottessturm'; Speiser, *Genesis*, pp. 3, 5 ('an awesome wind'); B. Vawter, *On Genesis: A New Reading* (London: Geoffrey Chapman, 1977), pp. 40-41; J.J. Scullion, *Genesis* (Collegeville, MN: Liturgical Press, 1992), pp. 10, 16.

24. Cf. Seebass, *Genesis. I. Urgeschichte*, pp. 58, 60-61, and Gertz, *Das erste Buch Mose*, I, pp. 26, 44.

25. See J. Day, *The Recovery of the Ancient Hebrew Language: The Lexicograph-ical Writings of D. Winton Thomas* (HBM, 20; Sheffield: Sheffield Phoenix Press, 2013), pp. 11-13, where I critically examined all of D.W. Thomas's alleged examples.

26. See J. Day, *God's Conflict with the Dragon and the Sea: Echoes of a Canaanite God in the Old Testament* (UCOP, 35; Cambridge: Cambridge University Press, 1985), pp. 51-53; *idem, From Creation to Babel*, pp. 21-22.

wind prior to the battle with the waters – the birdlike imagery paralleling the use of the verb *rḥp* used in connection with the *rûaḥ* in Gen. 1.2 (see below). Moreover, in another passage where Yahweh rides on the wings of the wind prior to a battle with the waters (Ps. 18.11, ET 10//2 Sam. 22.11), he actually rebukes the waters with what the psalmist calls 'the blast of the breath of your nostrils' (Ps. 18.16, ET 15//2 Sam. 22.16), i.e. the wind (the context is meteorological). This implies that the wind of God can also be understood as his breath. However, both Seebass and Gertz, who render 'breath' here (cf. n. 24) relate it to God's subsequent speaking (v. 3 onwards), dissociating it from the wind. Another noteworthy passage is Job 26.13, where Yahweh's wind is again mentioned in connection with the divine conflict with the sea, here at the time of creation, as in Psalm 104. We may also recall Marduk in his battle with the sea monster Tiamat at the time of creation, who rides a storm chariot in *Enuma elish* 4.50, and employs his wind against Tiamat in 4.32, 42-49, 96-99, 132. However, although something like this doubtless lies *behind* the reference to the wind of God blowing to and fro over the waters in Gen. 1.2 (see below for this translation), in the text as we have it this is simply left as part of the primordial state of things; the wind plays no further role.[27] It is a relic of an earlier mythological construct.

Finally, it may be noted that the rendering 'wind' also has important support in some of the ancient Versions. Thus, the earliest, the Septuagint, translates 'and a divine wind was being carried along over the water' (NETS), Targum Pseudo-Jonathan renders, 'a merciful wind from before God was blowing over the surface of the water',[28] Targum Onqelos translates 'a wind from before the Lord was blowing on the surface of the water',[29] and Targum Neofiti has 'and a wind of mercy from before the Lord was blowing over the surface of the waters'.[30] Some mediaeval

27. G. Darshan, '*Ruaḥ 'Elohim* in Genesis 1:2 in Light of Phoenician Cosmogonies: A Tradition's History', *JNSL* 45.2 (2019), pp. 51-78, offers fascinating information about what can be gleaned about Phoenician cosmogony from various classical sources, and this reflects belief in the creative power of the primordial wind. However, unlike Darshan, I do not believe this to be relevant to Gen. 1.2, whose background I see rather in the conflict myth referred to above, though the reference to the wind is now simply a relic of this.

28. M. Maher, *Targum Pseudo-Jonathan: Genesis* (The Aramaic Bible, 2; Edinburgh: T. & T. Clark, 1992), p. 16.

29. B. Grossfeld, *Targum Onqelos: Genesis* (The Aramaic Bible, 6; Edinburgh: T. & T. Clark, 1988), p. 42.

30. M. McNamara, *Targum Neofiti I: Genesis* (The Aramaic Bible, 1A; Edinburgh: T. & T. Clark, 1992), p. 52, renders 'a spirit of mercy', but as Maher, *Targum*

Jewish writers also supported 'wind', including Saadia, Ibn Ezra and especially Rashbam.

Mᵉraḥepet: 'Hovering', 'Sweeping', or 'Blowing to and fro'?

At one time, including up to and including H. Gunkel and J. Skinner,[31] it was sometimes thought that *mᵉraḥepet* in Gen. 1.2 meant that God's *rûaḥ* was brooding over the waters of the earth, the earth being conceived as a world-egg. This was based on the fact that Syriac *raḥep* could mean 'to brood'. However, even within Syriac this was only a secondary meaning, and all the ancient Versions implied that *mᵉraḥepet* was rather a verb of motion. The only other instance of the piel of *rḥp* in the Hebrew Bible means 'to flutter' or 'to hover' of an eagle over its young when teaching them to fly (Deut. 32.11), the same meaning as is attested of Ugaritic *rḥp* with regard to eagles in the Aqhat legend (*KTU³* 1.18.IV.20, 21, 31, 32). (Cf. Yahweh riding on the wings of the wind in Ps. 104.3 and Ps. 18.11, ET 10//2 Sam. 22.11 referred to above.) The qal of *rḥp* is also attested and means 'to shake' in Jer. 23.9. Coming to the translation in Gen. 1.2, a number of scholars render 'hovered', though this tends to be favoured now by those preferring 'Spirit' to 'wind' (e.g. REB, NIV), and in English we do not speak of the wind as hovering. Others favour 'swept' (e.g. NEB, NAB, NRSV),[32] a word more appropriate for wind, but the overtones suggested elsewhere for the verb *rḥp* seem to favour a fluttering or vibratory movement of some kind, so we can perhaps best render it as 'the wind was blowing to and fro'.[33]

Pseudo-Jonathan, p. 16 n. 5, notes in his translation of the comparable words in Targum Pseudo-Jonathan, the occurrence of the verb 'to blow' in connection with it supports the meaning 'wind'.

31. Gunkel, *Genesis*, p. 104, ET *Genesis*, pp. 103-104; J. Skinner, *Genesis* (ICC; Edinburgh: T. & T. Clark, 1910, reprinted 1930), p. 18. Some earlier scholars also took this view.

32. Also von Rad, *Das erste Buch Mose*, p. 34, but ET *Genesis*, p. 44, has 'was moving', not reflecting von Rad's true understanding; Arnold, *Genesis*, p. 27; Gertz, *Das erste Buch Mose*, I, p. 42.

33. Westermann, *Genesis*, p. 107, ET *Genesis 1–11*, p. 76, and Scullion, *Genesis*, p. 10, rendered 'was moving to and fro', which gives the right idea, except it seems more natural to speak of the wind blowing to and fro, rather than moving to and fro. But on p. 148 (ET, p. 107) Westermann inconsistently states that the best translation is 'hover', 'flutter' or 'flap'.

Tᵉhōm, *'Deep'*

The word *tᵉhōm* has provoked a lot of discussion. In general, the term is used in the Old Testament of the waters under the earth (hence 'the deep'), but in the primordial era here described these waters also submerged the earth. Much discussion has turned on the question whether the word *tᵉhōm* reflects the Babylonian female sea monster Tiamat, who was defeated at the time of creation by the god Marduk in *Enuma elish* (so Gunkel[34] and many subsequently). Certainly in Gen. 1.2 *tᵉhōm* is a name for the cosmic waters; but there is no personification whatsoever, and God's subsequent division of the waters by means of the firmament (vv. 6-7) is simply a job of work, not a battle. Moreover, whereas in *Enuma elish* heaven is made out of one half of Tiamat and earth out of the other, in Genesis 1 the earth is already in existence when the cosmic waters are split in two, which become respectively the waters above the firmament and the waters below the firmament. The order of creation is also quite different; the claims of Heidel and Speiser[35] to the contrary were overturned by the discovery of the missing part of tablet 5 of *Enuma elish*,[36] which completely upset the parallels.[37] It is now apparent that in *Enuma elish* the order of creation was the division of Tiamat, the making of the firmament, luminaries, meteorological phenomena [no strict equivalent in Genesis], Euphrates/Tigris/mountains/springs [no equivalent in Genesis], and dry land, whereas in Genesis 1 it is heaven and earth [inchoate], light [no strict equivalent in *Enuma elish*], firmament, division of waters, dry land, and luminaries. Subsequently, though both conclude with the creation of humanity, prior to that *Enuma elish* lacks any equivalent to the creation of sea creatures and birds, and beasts of the earth on days 5 and 6 in Genesis 1. Nevertheless, coming back to *tᵉhōm*, the two words Tiamat and *tᵉhōm* are philologically cognate (both mean 'sea'), and it is noteworthy that *tᵉhōm* is almost

34. H. Gunkel, *Schöpfung und Chaos in Urzeit und Endzeit* (Göttingen: Vandenhoeck & Ruprecht, 1895), ET *Creation and Chaos in the Primeval Era and the Eschaton* (trans. K.W. Whitney Jr; Grand Rapids, MI: Eerdmans, 2006). I shall not document all the many supporters of this view subsequent to Gunkel.

35. A. Heidel, *The Babylonian Genesis* (Chicago, IL: University of Chicago Press, 2nd edn, 1951), pp. 128-30; Speiser, *Genesis*, p. 10.

36. See B. Landsberger and J.V. Kinnier Wilson, 'The Fifth Tablet of Enuma eliš', *JNES* 20 (1961), pp. 154-79.

37. Speiser's commentary was published in 1964, subsequent to the publication of the missing part of tablet 5 in 1961, and the Preface is dated August 25th, 1962, so he ought to have known of it.

always spelled without the definite article (except in the plural instances in Isa. 63.13; Ps. 106.9). There is also a hint of the personification of *tᵉhōm* in Gen. 49.25 and Deut. 33.13, 'the deep that couches beneath' (the verb *rbṣ*, 'couch',[38] is elsewhere used of animals). It is possible therefore that ultimately a mythical being lies behind *tᵉhōm*; but if so, it was probably Canaanite rather than Babylonian (cf. personified *thm* in the phrase *bt. šmm wthm*, 'the daughter of Heavens and Deep', in the Ugaritic text *KTU³* 1.100.1).

Underlying Genesis 1 in my view is Psalm 104 (see below), which has a similar order of creation, but seems more mythological. Interestingly, in v. 6 'the deep' (*tᵉhōm*) covered it [the earth] like a garment, the waters stood above the mountains', and in v. 7 the waters flee at the sound of God's thunder. The idea of a divine conflict with the waters at the time of creation is also attested in poetic passages like Pss. 74.13-14; 89.10-11 (ET 9-10); Job 26.12-13; 38.8-11. This is demythologized in Genesis 1 so that God's control of the waters is now simply but a job of work (Gen. 1.6-7).[39]

The Creation of Light

In Gen. 1.3 we read the famous words, 'And God said, "Let there be light", and there was light'. We have here what is called creation by divine fiat, a term derived from the Latin Vulgate rendering of 'Let there be light', *fiat lux*. The impression is given that God's command was fulfilled instantaneously, as if by magic. This event has often been referred to as God's first act of creation, but as we have seen above, the first act of

38. Not 'crouch'. See R.P. Gordon, '"Couch" or "Crouch"? Genesis 4:7 and the Temptation of Cain', in J.K. Aitken, K.J. Dell and B.A. Mastin (eds.), *On Stone and Scroll: Essays in Honour of Graham Ivor Davies* (BZAW, 420; Berlin: W. de Gruyter, 2011), pp. 195-209 (200-203).

39. See Day, *God's Conflict with the Dragon and the Sea, passim*, where I argued that the Old Testament's divine conflict with the dragon and the sea imagery, which is demythologized in Gen. 1 by becoming merely a job of work, utilizes Canaanite imagery, not Babylonian. For example, Leviathan, the *tannîn* (dragon), and 'twisting serpent' are attested in Ugaritic, and Rahab (unattested in Ugaritic) is an alternative name for Leviathan, since both are called 'twisting serpent' in the Old Testament. Cf. too W.G. Lambert, 'A New Look at the Babylonian Background of Genesis', *JTS* NS 16 (1965), pp. 287-300 (290), reprinted in expanded format in R.S. Hess and D.T. Tsumura (eds.), *"I Studied Inscriptions from before the Flood: Ancient Near Eastern, Literary, and Linguistic Approaches to Genesis 1–11* (Winona Lake, IN: Eisenbrauns, 1994), pp. 96-113 (99-100).

creation is actually described in v. 1, the formation of the inchoate heaven and earth, together with the consequences referred to in v. 2.

One scholar, however, Mark Smith,[40] has argued that Gen. 1.3 does not actually describe the creation of light. Rather, he maintains that the light was deemed to be something primordial, divine and uncreated. However, as presented in Gen. 1.3 it certainly sounds as if light is a new thing. God declares, 'Let there be light', and there was light'. Surely this is a case of the creation of something new, as in all the other 'Let ... be' declarations by God in the Genesis 1 creation account. At first there was no light (only darkness, v. 2) and then suddenly light appeared. Further, it is to be noted that immediately afterwards we read, 'And God saw that the light was good'. This sounds like a new observation on God's part, not something that he was already familiar with. Smith seeks to defend his position by appealing to various passages which imply that light was something primordial and divine that already existed behind the scenes. Thus, in 2 Esd. 6.40, Ezra says to God, 'Then you commanded that a ray of light be brought forth from your treasuries, so that your works might then appear'. Again, in Philo, *De Opificio Mundi* 8(.31) light is the image of the divine Logos, an invisible light preceding the divine word in Gen. 1.3, and in John 1.4-5 the light is God's own light, located in the Logos which became incarnate in Christ. Finally, the Zohar, in commenting on Gen. 1.3, declares, 'And there was light – light that already was'. But these are all much later sources, more than five or six hundred years after the time of the Priestly writer of Genesis 1, and in the case of the Zohar about two thousand years later. Can they really be appealed to in order to overthrow the straightforward meaning seemingly implied by Gen. 1.3? It is true that Smith does appeal to one source which I understand as being prior to Genesis 1, namely Ps. 104.2, which declares to God, 'you cover yourself with light as with a garment'. However, as I have argued elsewhere,[41] there are good grounds for believing that Psalm 104 was a major source behind Genesis 1. As noted earlier, they have the same order of creation, but Psalm 104 is clearly more mythological than Genesis 1, having a divine battle with the waters, not merely control of the waters

---

40. M.S. Smith, 'Light in Genesis 1:3 – Created or Uncreated: A Question of Priestly Mysticism?', in C. Cohen *et al.* (eds.), *Birkat Shalom: Studies in Bible, Ancient Near Eastern Literature, and Postbiblical Judaism Presented to Shalom M. Paul on the Occasion of his Seventieth Birthday*, I (2 vols.; Winona Lake, IN: Eisenbrauns, 2008), pp. 125-34; *idem, The Priestly Vision of Genesis 1*, pp. 71-79.

41. Day, *God's Conflict with the Dragon and the Sea*, pp. 51-53; *idem, From Creation to Babel*, pp. 21-22.

as in Genesis, speaking of 'Leviathan' rather than 'great sea monsters', and of Yahweh 'riding on the wings of the wind' rather than simply 'the wind of God was blowing to and fro'. In addition, Gen. 1.24 employs the poetic form *ḥayetō*, 'beasts', unattested elsewhere in prose, but occurring in Ps. 104.11, 20. Consequently, it is likely that Ps. 104.2 lies behind Gen. 1.3, and therefore the latter has transformed the pre-existent divine light into something made at the beginning of creation.

For us today, and indeed throughout history, it has been deemed odd that light was already created prior to the creation of the heavenly luminaries that bestow light from day 4. (Day 4 parallels day 1, just as days 5 and 6 parallel days 2 and 3.[42]) However, it appears that the ancient Hebrews could envisage the light as having its own existence apart from the luminaries. As God says to Job, 'Where is the way to the dwelling of light, and where is the place of darkness, that you may take it to its territory and that you may discern the paths to its home?' (Job 38.19-20; cf. Job 26.10).

Unlike the light, it is not explicitly stated that God created the darkness, and some scholars deny that it was so created, envisaging it as pre-existent to God's creative activity in Genesis 1. But if, as we have argued above, everything in Gen. 1.2 was created by God in Gen. 1.1, then the darkness too was created. In Isa. 45.7, God actually declares, 'I form light and create darkness, I make weal and create woe'. Contrary to what some suppose, what is stated about the darkness in Isa. 45.7 may be in keeping with Genesis 1.

---

42. See Day, *From Creation to Babel*, pp. 1-2.

Chapter 2

'SO GOD CREATED HUMANITY IN HIS OWN IMAGE' (GENESIS 1.27): WHAT DOES THE BIBLE MEAN AND WHAT HAVE PEOPLE THOUGHT IT MEANT?

Introduction

One way in which the dignity of human beings has been grounded is in the belief that we are all created in the image of God. For example, during the Renaissance H.C. Agrippa von Nettesheim[1] appealed to this belief in the very first paragraph of his book in defence of the status of women. Again, more recently, Archbishop Desmond Tutu[2] frequently appealed to this notion as a basis of his opposition to Apartheid and racism in South Africa. This belief has played a larger role within Christianity than Judaism, even though it is rooted in the Hebrew Bible. But within the Hebrew Bible it is somewhat unusual, for it affirms the Godlikeness of human beings, whereas so much of the Old Testament emphasizes God's otherness over against humanity.

But in what sense are human beings Godlike? What does humanity's creation in God's image actually mean? This has been a most disputed topic and has given rise to a vast literature in Old Testament studies[3] as

---

1. H.C. Agrippa von Nettesheim, *De nobilitate et praecellentia foeminei sexus* (Geneva: Droz, 1529, reprinted 1990), p. 49, ET *Female Pre-eminence: Or the Dignity and Excellency of that Sex, above the Male* (London: Million, 1670), p. 1.

2. D. Tutu, *In God's Hands* (London: Bloomsbury, 2014), pp. 19-21.

3. In addition to the many works cited below, see J. Jervell, *Imago Dei: Gen 1, 26f im Spätjudentum, in der Gnosis und in den paulinischen Briefen* (FRLANT, NF 58; Göttingen: Vandenhoeck & Ruprecht, 1960); O. Loretz, *Die Gottebenbildlichkeit des Menschen* (Munich: Kösel-Verlag, 1969); T.N.D. Mettinger, 'Abbild oder Urbild?

well as in theology more generally.[4] Over the centuries theologians have made many suggestions which are essentially guesswork. As one Old Testament scholar put it, 'Many "orthodox" theologians right through the centuries have lifted the phrase "the image of God" (*imago dei*) right out of its context, and like Humpty-Dumpty, they have made the word mean just what they choose it to mean'.[5] This is certainly true, but it also has to be admitted that working out exactly what the Bible does mean is not that simple, since it does not offer an explanation.

Curiously, in view of its later importance in Christian theology, there are only three passages alluding to the image of God in humanity in the Old Testament, though it is referred back to occasionally in the Apocrypha and New Testament. These three Old Testament passages are all from the Priestly source in the early chapters of Genesis. First and best known, in connection with God's creation of humanity, is Gen. 1.26-27, 'And God said, "Let us make humanity[6] in our image, after our likeness; and let them have dominion over the fish of the sea and over the birds of the air, and over the cattle, and over all the earth, and over every creeping thing that creeps upon the earth". So God created humanity in his own image; in the image of God he created them; male and female he created them.' This is later referred back to in Gen. 5.1-3, 'When God created humanity, he made them in the likeness of God. Male and female he created them, and he blessed them and called their name humanity when they were created.

»Imago Dei« in traditionsgeschichtlicher Sicht', *ZAW* 86 (1974), pp. 403-24; G.A. Jónsson, *The Image of God: Genesis 1:26-28 in a Century of Old Testament Research* (ConBOT, 26; Lund: Almqvist & Wiksel, 1988); W.R. Garr, *In His Own Image and Likeness: Humanity, Divinity, and Monotheism* (CHANE, 15; Leiden: Brill, 2003); A. Schellenberg, *Der Mensch das Bild Gottes* (ATANT, 101; Zurich: Theologischer Verlag, 2011).

4. For works by modern systematic theologians see C.G. Berkouwer, *Man: The Image of God* (Grand Rapids, MI: Eerdmans, 1962); D. Cairns, *The Image of God in Man* (London: Collins, rev. edn, 1973); A. Hoekema, *Created in God's Image* (Grand Rapids, MI: Eerdmans, 1986); I.A. McFarland, *The Divine Image: Envisioning the Invisible God* (Minneapolis, MN: Fortress Press, 2005), in addition to the work by D.J. Hall cited below in n. 20.

5. N.H. Snaith, 'The Image of God', *ExpTim* 86 (1974), p. 24. Not that Snaith's own view – that it refers to humanity's dominion over the earth – is right either. See below.

6. Here the Hebrew word *'ādām* means 'humanity' rather than an individual person. This is shown by the plural verb that follows on afterwards, 'and let *them* have dominion'. Furthermore, v. 27 makes clear that *hā'ādām* includes both male and female. Again, Gen. 5.2 states, 'Male and female he created them, and blessed them and called *their* name humanity (*'ādām*)'.

When Adam had lived 130 years he became the father of a son in his own likeness, after his image, and named him Seth.' Finally, the last reference is in Gen. 9.6, where following the flood God declares to Noah, 'Whoever sheds the blood of a human, by a human shall their blood be shed; for God made humanity in his own image'.

The Nature of the Image

Spiritual Views

Traditionally in Christian theology the idea of people being made in the image of God has been understood as referring to humanity's reason, soul, spirituality or suchlike: some internal aspect of the human person that sets us apart from animals and makes us resemble God. This is probably the best known kind of interpretation for many people, even though most modern Old Testament scholars believe it to be either mistaken, or only partially true. For example, Augustine of Hippo (*De Trinitate*, esp. books 7–15)[7] saw an analogy between the Trinity and the threefold division of human memory, intellect and will. But this is purely fanciful, and of course the Old Testament knew nothing of the Trinity. Many like Athanasius (*De Incarnatione* 3)[8] and Aquinas (*Summa Theologiae* part 1, Question 13; *De Veritate* 10) envisaged the image as specifically referring to human reason, whereas Ambrose (*Hexaemeron* 6.7-8) and Calvin (*Institutes* 1.15.3) believed it alluded to the human soul. But in suggesting these various ideas Christian theologians were clearly simply speculating when endeavouring to calculate what it was that humanity had in common with God (in contrast to the animals), rather than relying on biblical evidence.

A further Christian reading distorting the original biblical meaning is to be found in the second-century Church Father Irenaeus (*Adversus Haereses* 5.6.1; 5.16.1-2),[9] who made a distinction between the image and likeness of God. He thought the image referred to the permanent features of the human persona, like reason, whereas the likeness of God alluded to human qualities lost at the Fall, but which could be regained through Christ. This view persisted till the Reformers rightly questioned

7. See J.E. Sullivan, *The Image of God: The Doctrine of St. Augustine and its Influence* (Dubuque, IA: Priory, 1963).

8. See R. Bernard, *L'image de Dieu d'après saint Athanasius* (Paris: Aubier, 1952).

9. See T. Holsinger-Friesen, *Irenaeus and Genesis* (Journal of Theological Interpretation, Supplements 1; Winona Lake, IN: Eisenbrauns, 2009).

its exegetical viability. The evidence of the Bible suggests that there is no essential difference between the image and likeness of God; the two terms are used interchangeably. Thus, whereas Gen. 1.26 declares that God made humanity in the image and likeness of God, the very next verse as well as Gen. 9.6 say that he made humans simply in the image of God, while Gen. 5.1 only says that God made humanity in the likeness of God.

Another misguided idea is found in the Protestant Reformers Luther and Calvin, who tended to speak of the image and likeness of God in humanity as something that was marred or obliterated as a result of the Fall.[10] However, in Gen. 9.6 we still read of humans possessing the image of God long after the Fall, in the time of Noah; similarly, the New Testament letter of James declares that we are made in the image of God (Jas 3.9). It is somewhat puzzling that the Reformers, who claimed to give priority to Scripture, adopted such a manifestly unbiblical view.

The view that the image of God in humanity refers purely to some kind of spiritual resemblance between God and human beings persisted among Old Testament scholars throughout the nineteenth century and among some even into the twentieth century (e.g. S.R. Driver, W. Eichrodt, H.H. Rowley),[11] but it now has virtually no support. However, the situation is different among systematic theologians. In addition to some modern systematic theologians who reiterate older purely spiritual views mentioned above, there have been newer suggestions such as that humans being in the image of God refers to their freedom[12] or self-transcendence,[13] in addition to reciprocal views to be considered below. None of these can claim support from Genesis.

Nevertheless, as we shall see later, although not the whole truth, humanity being in the image of God does *partly* imply some kind of spiritual resemblance between God and humans.

10. See J. Pelikan (ed.), *Luther's Works*. I. *Lectures on Genesis Chapters 1–5* (St Louis, MO: Concordia, 1958), p. 61; J. Calvin, *Commentaries on the First Book of Moses*, I (trans. J. King; Edinburgh: Calvin Translation Society, 1847), pp. 94-95.

11. Driver, *The Book of Genesis*, pp. 14-15, 'self-conscious reason'; W. Eichrodt, *Theologie des Alten Testaments*, II (2 vols.; Stuttgart: Klotz, 1957), pp. 60-65, ET *Theology of the Old Testament*, II (trans. J.A. Baker; 2 vols.; London: SCM Press, 1961), pp. 122-31, originally a physical likeness but P has spiritualized the concept; H.H. Rowley, *The Faith of Israel* (London: SCM Press, 1956), pp. 78-79, 'man's spiritual nature'.

12. R. Seeberg, *Christliche Dogmatik*, I (2 vols.; Erlangen; A. Deichert, 1924–25), p. 499.

13. R. Niebuhr, *The Nature and Destiny of Man*, I (2 vols.; London: Nisbet, 1941-43), pp. 176-78.

The Functional View

In contrast, a very different interpretation of the meaning of human beings bearing the divine image has been dominant amongst Old Testament scholars since the 1960s. This is the so-called functional view. By this is meant the understanding that it alludes to humanity's position as God's viceroy, having dominion over the earth and its living creatures.

This functional view was already occasionally held among the early Church Fathers, for example by John Chrysostom (*Homilies on Genesis* 8.3) and Theodoret of Cyrrhus (*Questions on Genesis* 20). It was also maintained later by some early Socinians (Unitarians), who incorporated this doctrine in their Racovian Catechism of 1605,[14] as well as by some early Remonstrants (Dutch Arminians). It was also held by the prominent tenth-century Jewish rabbi Saadia.[15] Additionally, a few nineteenth- and early twentieth-century scholars followed this view.[16] All these held this position because in Gen. 1.26-28 the reference to humanity's ruling the animals and the earth follows shortly after the allusion to humanity's being made in the image of God. However – and this is very important – it is more natural to suppose that humanity's lordship over the animals and the earth is a consequence of its having been made in God's image, rather than what the image itself denotes. This is made clear by v. 28, where God's command to humanity to rule over animals and the earth takes place only after God's blessing of them and commanding them to be fruitful and multiply and fill the earth, whereas humanity has already been made in God's image in v. 27. This important point is often overlooked by defenders of the functional interpretation.

The conclusion that God's image in humanity refers to something other than humanity's rule over the animals and the earth is also supported by a consideration of the other Genesis passages which refer to the image of God. Thus, in Gen. 5.1-2, the statement is repeated that 'When God created humanity, he made them in the image of God. Male and female he created them, and he blessed them and called their name humanity when they were created.' Then v. 3 continues, 'When Adam had lived 130 years, he became the father of a son in his own likeness, after his image, and named him Seth.' Note that the same language is used of Seth's resemblance to Adam as is used of Adam's resemblance to God. This resemblance clearly includes a physical resemblance and cannot have anything to do with

14. G.L. Oederus, *Catechismus Racoviensis* (Frankfurt: J.A. Schmidt, 1739), p. 48.

15. M. Zucker (ed.), *Saadya's Commentary on Genesis* (Hebrew; New York: Jewish Theological Seminary of America, 1984), pp. 257-58.

16. E.g. H. Holzinger, *Genesis* (KHAT, 1; Freiburg: J.C.B. Mohr [Paul Siebeck], 1898), p. 12.

ruling over animals and the earth. Again, in Gen. 9.6 we read, 'Whoever sheds the blood of a human, by a human shall their blood be shed; for God made humanity in his own image'. These words are surely implying something about the inherent dignity and worth of human life, rather than referring to humans having dominion over the animals and the earth.

In spite of all this important counter-evidence, the most common view among Old Testament scholars since the 1960s has been that the image of God in humanity refers to humans ruling over the world.[17] Why should this be? The continued repetition of this view probably owes something to intellectual fashion. Just as someone said that history does not repeat itself, but historians repeat one another, so there is an undoubted tendency for commentators to repeat one another. But the original impetus for the popularity of this view came in the 1960s, when two Old Testament scholars, Hans Wildberger and W.H. Schmidt,[18] independently presented evidence that in ancient Egypt and Assyria the king could be spoken of as being the image of a god. They further suggested that in Genesis 1 the idea that human beings generally are created in the image and likeness of God is a democratization of this concept. As stated, this view has become very popular in Old Testament circles. There is a particularly thorough defence of it by J. Richard Middleton.[19] In contrast, only a minority of systematic theologians have taken this view.[20]

17. Apart from scholars listed below, see, e.g., R. Davidson, *Genesis 1–11* (CBC; Cambridge: Cambridge University Press, 1973), p. 25; W. Brueggemann, *Genesis* (Interpretation; Atlanta: John Knox Press, 1982), p. 32; J.D. Levenson, *Creation and the Persistence of Evil* (San Francisco: Harper & Row, 1988), pp. 111-16; C. Amos, *The Book of Genesis* (Epworth Commentaries; Werrington: Epworth Press, 2004), p. 11; Arnold, *Genesis*, p. 45.

18. See H. Wildberger, 'Das Abbild Gottes. Gen. 1,26-30', *TZ* 21 (1965), pp. 245-59, 481-501, reprinted in Wildberger, *Jahwe und sein Volk: Gesammelte Aufsätze zum Alten Testament* (eds. H.H. Schmid and O.H. Steck; TBü, 66; Munich: Chr. Kaiser, 1979), pp. 110-45; W.H. Schmidt, *Die Schöpfungsgeschichte der Priesterschrift* (WMANT, 17, Neukirchen-Vluyn: Neukirchener Verlag, 1964), pp. 127-49. However, this subject was first raised by J. Hehn, 'Zum Terminus „Bild Gottes"', in G. Weil (ed.), *Festschrift Eduard Sachau zum siebzigsten Geburtstage* (Berlin: G. Reimer, 1915), pp. 36-52, primarily citing Mesopotamian sources. Specifically on Egyptian kingship and its alleged relationship with Gen. 1.26-7, see B. Ockinga, *Die Gottebenbildlichkeit im alten Ägypten und im Alten Testament* (Ägypten und Altes Testament, 7; Wiesbaden: Harrassowitz, 1984).

19. J.R. Middleton, *The Liberating Image: The* Imago Dei *in Genesis 1* (Grand Rapids, MI: Brazos Press, 2005).

20. E.g. D.J. Hall, *Imaging God: Dominion as Stewardship* (Grand Rapids, MI: Eerdmans, 1986).

There are, however, some problems with this view. First, we have no evidence that the Israelite kings themselves were ever spoken of as being in the image of a god. The assumption has to be made that the Israelites borrowed the imagery either from Egyptian or Assyrian kingship and then democratized it to refer to humanity. But with regard to Assyria, it must be noted that the imagery is rare: only six references are known,[21] and of those four come from a single scribe about three individuals in two letters from the time of Esar-haddon (681–669 BCE) and a fifth comes from the reign of his successor Ashurbanipal (668–c. 627 BCE), while the other is from the time of Tukulti-Ninurta I (c. 1243–1207 BCE). It does not seem very likely, therefore, that P's language was adopted from the Assyrians. What then of ancient Egypt? It is true that there are far more occurrences of the concept in Egypt, but although there are occasional allusions down to Ptolemaic times, they are overwhelmingly from the eighteenth dynasty (c. 1550–1290 BCE), about 800–1050 years prior to the time of the Priestly writer. Incidentally, although the Priestly writer probably wrote in the exilic or early post-exilic period, either during or not long after the Babylonian exile, no references to the king as the image of a god are attested in Babylonia at any period.[22]

A popular variant of the functional view maintains that it was the custom of placing actual images of foreign kings in conquered territory as representations of their authority in absence that lies behind the alleged democratized representation of humans as images of the invisible God in Genesis.[23] However, as noted earlier, the fundamental objection to any functional understanding of the image of God is that it does not fit any of the three passages in Genesis very well. Even in Gen. 1.26-28 humanity's rule over the earth is more naturally a consequence of its being in the divine image, not what the image itself is.

Finally, those who adopt the functional view tend to argue that human beings are not said to be made in (or after) the image and likeness of God but rather as an image and likeness of God. This involves taking the preposition *beth* as so-called *beth essentiae*,[24] 'as', hence 'as the image

---

21. See A. Angerstorfer, 'Ebenbild eines Gottes in babylonischen und assyrischen Keilschrifttexten', *BN* 88 (1997), pp. 47-58.

22. Merely of one Neo-Babylonian priest do we read this. See Angerstorfer, 'Ebenbild eines Gottes', p. 54.

23. E.g. Brueggemann, *Genesis*, p. 32.

24. With D.J.A. Clines, 'The Image of God in Man', *TynBul* 19 (1967), pp. 53-103 (75-80), reprinted as 'Humanity as the Image of God', in Clines, *On the Way to the Postmodern: Old Testament Essays 1967–1998* (JSOTSup, 293, Sheffield: Sheffield Academic Press, 1998), II, pp. 447-97 (470-75); W. Gross, 'Die Gottebenbildlichkeit

and likeness of God', not 'in (i.e. after/according to) the image and likeness of God'. However, as J. Maxwell Miller[25] aptly pointed out, this is improbable since the preposition *beth* is used here interchangeably with the preposition *kaph*, 'after/according to', but there is no *kaph essentiae* in biblical Hebrew. We thus have to conclude that humans are said to be made in (i.e. according to) the image of God (cf. Septuagint *kata*, Vulgate *ad*), not merely as an image of God.

Karl Barth and the Reciprocal View

We shall now consider what might be called the reciprocal view of the nature of the divine image in humans. It was made famous by Karl Barth,[26] who argued that the key to understanding the meaning of humanity's being made in the image of God is to be found in Gen. 1.27, which declares, 'So God created humanity in his own image, in the image of God he created them; male and female he created them'. From this he deduced that the image of God consists of the reciprocal relationship of male and female. In this he sees a reflection of God himself, who says 'Let us make humanity', implying (he supposes) a plurality within the Deity himself (though not explicitly the Trinity, as the Church Fathers and some later Christians supposed). But Old Testament scholars generally find this unconvincing. Thus first, 'Let us make humanity' is generally understood as God addressing the heavenly beings or angels around him (cf. Gen. 3.22; 11.7; Isa. 6.8), rather than implying a plurality within God himself. We can rule out a royal plural or a plural of exhortation here, as these are unattested elsewhere with verbs in biblical Hebrew.[27] We may assume

des Menschen nach Gen 1,26.27 in der Diskussion des letzten Jahrzehnts', *BN* 68 (1993), pp. 35-48; (35, 37); B. Janowski, 'Gottebenbildlichkeit', in *RGG*[4], III (Tübingen: Mohr Siebeck, 2000), cols. 1159-60, ET 'Image of God', *Religion Past & Present*, VI (Leiden: Brill, 2009), pp. 414-15 (414).

25. J.M. Miller, 'In the "Image" and "Likeness" of God', *JBL* 91 (1972), pp. 289-304 (296).

26. K. Barth, *Kirchliche Dogmatik* 3.1 (Zollikon: Evangelischer Verlag, 1945), pp. 205-26, ET *Church Dogmatics* 3.1 (trans. G.W. Bromiley; Edinburgh: T. & T. Clark, 1958), pp. 183-201.

27. A majority of scholars today see a reference to the heavenly court here. For a defence of this view see especially P.D. Miller, *Genesis 1–11: Studies in Structure & Theme* (JSOTSup, 8; Sheffield: JSOT Press, 1978), pp. 9-20. This view follows in the train of an ancient and mediaeval Jewish interpretation attested in Philo, Targum Pseudo-Jonathan, Rashi and Ibn Ezra. Interestingly, early Jewish rabbinic sources seem more concerned in Gen. 1.26 with the interpretation of 'Let *us* make humanity' than with the precise nature of the divine image borne by humans.

that God includes the heavenly court in the momentous decision to create humanity, even though it is God alone who finally enacts it (Gen. 1.27). Secondly, it is much more natural to suppose that male and female both bear the divine image individually, rather than that the image consists in their reciprocal relationship. Thirdly, animals too consist of both male and female, but we should expect humanity's being in the image of God to be something distinguishing them from the animals, which would not be so on Barth's interpretation. Fourthly, it is difficult on Barth's understanding to make sense of Gen. 5.3, where Seth is said to be made in the likeness and image of his father Adam, implying a resemblance in appearance, so the same logically ought to be the case with Adam's being in the likeness and image of God mentioned only two verses earlier (Gen. 5.1). Fifthly, Barth's understanding does not fit Gen. 9.6, where God's making humanity in his own image is cited as the reason for forbidding the murder of a human being. The mutuality of the sexes seems quite irrelevant here. Rather, the words seem to be highlighting the value and dignity of human life which its Godlikeness betokens.

Karl Barth was neither the first nor the last scholar to put forward a relational view of the image of God. He appears to have been dependent on Dietrich Bonhoeffer,[28] who asserted that part of being in God's image was the freedom to exist in relationship with other human beings, including between men and women. A number of other scholars who understood the image of God in relational terms were (prior to Barth) the systematic theologian Emil Brunner and the Old Testament scholars W. Riedel and (subsequent to Barth) the Old Testament scholars F. Horst, J. J. Stamm and C. Westermann.[29] However, these scholars understood the mutuality not to be that between a man and a woman but the fact that God and humans can speak to each other. But it is difficult to find anything in Genesis that implies this as the meaning.

28. D. Bonhoeffer, *Schöpfung und Fall* (Dietrich Bonhoeffer Werke, 3; Munich: Chr. Kaiser, [1933] 1989), pp. 58-60, ET *Creation and Fall: A Theological Exposition of Genesis 1–3* (Dietrich Bonhoeffer Works, 3; Minneapolis, MN: Fortress Press, 1988), pp. 52-57.

29. E. Brunner, *Der Mensch im Widerspruch* (Berlin: Furche-Verlag, 1937), pp. 92-96, ET *Man in Revolt* (London: Lutterworth Press, 1939), pp. 102-105; W. Riedel, 'Die Gottesebenbildlichkeit des Menschen', in *Alttestamentliche Untersuchungen*, I (Leipzig: A. Deichert, 1902), pp. 42-47; F. Horst, 'Face to Face: The Biblical Doctrine of the Image of God', *Int* 4 (1950), pp. 259-70; J.J. Stamm, *Die Gottebenbildlichkeit des Menschen im Alten Testament* (Theologische Studien, 54; Zollikon: Evangelischer Verlag, 1959); Westermann, *Genesis 1–11*, p. 157.

Physical Likeness

We have now to consider the idea that humanity's being in the image of God refers to a physical resemblance between God and humans. Though this might seem rather crude to the modern sophisticated person, there is good evidence that this is at least part of what Genesis envisaged, even if finally we conclude that both a physical and a spiritual likeness are intended.

First, it should be noted that the word used for image, Hebrew *ṣelem*, is regularly employed elsewhere in the Old Testament to denote the physical representation of something, most frequently images of pagan gods (Num. 33.52; 2 Kgs 11.18; 2 Chron. 23.17; Ezek. 7.20; 16.17; Amos 5.26). The only other examples are images of the Chaldaeans (Ezek. 23.14) and of tumours and mice (1 Sam. 6.5 [×2]; 6.11).[30] Further, the biblical Aramaic cognate *ṣᵉlēm, ṣalmā'* is used eleven times in Dan. 3.1-8 of the statue of a pagan god that the people are commanded to worship by Nebuchadrezzar, and the same Aramaic word occurs several times in Dan. 2.31-35 of the statue symbolizing the four world empires in Nebuchadrezzar's dream. It may seem surprising that a word which is used overwhelmingly of pagan images should be employed in Genesis of humanity's high dignity. However, the fact that its meaning was not confined to idols but could refer to an image generally, meant that it was acceptable.

The word 'likeness' (Hebrew *dᵉmût*) tends to be more abstract in meaning. Sometimes it means 'appearance, form', though on occasion it is used in the comparison of two things. Most frequently it is used in Ezekiel's visions, where it sometimes seems to make the comparison more approximate and less definite (e.g. Ezek. 1.5, 26; 8.2; 10.1). So some think that in Genesis it is used to make humanity's physical resemblance to God a bit more approximate and less definite. However, there are three places in the Old Testament where the word *dᵉmût* is not abstract but a physical depiction of some kind; cf. 2 Kgs 16.10, 'a model (*dᵉmût*) of the altar', 2 Chron. 4.3, 'figures (*dᵉmût*) of oxen', and Ezek. 23.15, 'a picture (*dᵉmût*) of Babylonians'. (Note that in Ezek. 23.14 *ṣelem*, 'image', is likewise used of the Chaldeans [Babylonians].) Interestingly, in a bilingual Aramaic–Akkadian inscription on a ninth-century statue of Hadad-yis'i,

---

30. The occurrences of *ṣelem* in Pss. 39.7 (ET 6) and 73.20 probably mean something like 'shadow' or 'phantom', and appear to be an extension in meaning of *ṣelem*, 'image', i.e. *mere* images as opposed to reality. One recalls the shadowy images in Plato's famous allegory of the cave. This is more likely than the view that *ṣelem* here means 'darkness'.

king of Gozan, discovered at Tell Fekheriyeh in Syria,[31] the Aramaic cognates *ṣelēm* and *demûtā'* are both employed to render the Akkadian word *ṣalmu*, 'image', used of the statue. Ultimately, it is likely that there is no great difference between the 'likeness' and 'image' of God in Genesis, seeing that both terms are used interchangeably, as noted earlier.

Secondly, very tellingly, in Gen. 5.3 we read that 'Adam ... became the father of a son in his likeness, after his image, and named him Seth'. It will be noted that the identical terminology of Gen. 1.26-27 about humanity being made in the image and likeness of God is employed here. Moreover, just two verses before Gen. 5.3 in v. 1, we read that 'When God created humanity, he made them in the likeness of God'. Since Seth's likeness to Adam undoubtedly implies a physical resemblance, the natural conclusion is that there is similarly a physical likeness between God and human beings.

Thirdly, in addition to frequent references to Yahweh's body parts,[32] it ought to be noted that the Old Testament sometimes envisages God as appearing in human form (cf. Gen. 18.1-2; 32.24-25, 30). Perhaps the most well-known example is Isaiah's famous vision in Isaiah 6, where the prophet 'saw the Lord sitting upon a throne, high and lifted up; and his train filled the temple'. But most relevant for our present purpose is Ezek. 1.26, where the prophet states that in his vision of God he 'saw a likeness as the appearance of a human being'.[33] It is significant that Ezekiel was a

31. A. Abou-Assaf, P. Bordreuil and A.R. Millard, *La statue de Tell Fekherye et son inscription assyro-araméenne* (Etudes assyriologiques, 7; Paris: Editions Recherche sur les civilisations, 1982), pp. 23-25, lines 1, 12, 15, 16 of the inscription.

32. E.g., note the references to Yahweh's face (Exod. 33.11, 20, 23), back (Exod. 33.23), loins (Ezek. 1.27; 8.2) and eyes (Prov. 15.3; 2 Chron. 16.9). On this subject generally, see B.D. Sommer, *The Bodies of God and the World of Ancient Israel* (New York: Cambridge University Press, 2009), *passim*.

33. Similarly, in Ezek. 8.2, referring to God, the prophet says he saw 'the likeness (*demût*) as the appearance of a man'. It is generally accepted that the LXX preserves the original reading, 'man', and that the last word in the Hebrew text, *'ēš*, 'fire', should be emended to *'îš*, 'man'. The parallel description in Ezek. 1.27 confines the fire to the lower part of the divine body, which supports this emendation in Ezek. 8.2, as does the personal possessive in 'his loins', later in the verse. The occurrence of 'fire' later in Ezek. 8.2 could well have given rise to the confusion. Alternatively, A. Geiger, *Urschrift und Übersetzungen der Bibel* (Frankfurt: Madda, 2nd edn, 1928), p. 343, and W. Zimmerli, *Ezechiel*, I (BKAT, 13.1, Neukirchen-Vluyn: Neukirchener Verlag, 1969), p. 191, ET *Ezekiel*, I (Hermeneia; Philadelphia, PA: Fortress Press, 1979), p. 216, held that the original Hebrew text was changed out of reverence for the divine appearance.

priest, not so long before the Priestly account of creation in Genesis 1 was written. Moreover, the word 'likeness' (Hebrew *dᵉmût*), which Ezekiel uses in Ezek. 1.26 (cf. 8.2), is the same word that the Priestly source employs in Gen. 1.26 to denote humanity's likeness to God. Ezekiel's statement that God had 'a likeness as the appearance of human being/ man' and Genesis's statement that humanity was made in the likeness of God sound like the obverse and reverse of each other.[34]

Fourthly, it should be noted that God says, 'Let *us* make humanity in our image ...' There is general agreement amongst Old Testament scholars that God is here addressing his heavenly court, the angels, since, as already noted, in Hebrew the verb has no royal plural, and there is no evidence for a plural of exhortation. Accordingly, a point often overlooked is that humanity is made in the image of the angels, and not merely of God. Now there is good evidence that angels were envisaged as being in human form. Compare, for example, the angel Gabriel, who is described in Dan. 8.15 and 10.18 as 'one having the appearance of a man' and in Dan. 10.16 as 'one in the likeness of the sons of men'. Again, in Genesis 19, those referred to as angels in v. 1 are called men in v. 5.

So it seems likely that human beings were thought to have a similar physical appearance to God, and that this is at least part of what the image of God in humanity includes. To the objection that men and women do not have an identical appearance, L. Koehler[35] argued that we could think more generally of human beings sharing upright form as what constitutes their resemblance to God. With him we may compare Ovid's *Metamorphoses* 1.83-86, where Prometheus 'moulded them into the image of all-controlling gods' and in contrast to the animals, 'gave human beings an upturned aspect ... and upright'.

Conclusion: Both a Physical and Spiritual Likeness

In the light of the above discussion, it would appear that a strong case can be made that the notion of humanity's being in the image of God did imply a physical resemblance between God and human beings. Within the

34. Incidentally, Sommer, *The Bodies of God*, p. 225 n. 72, notes that, apart from the Hellenistically influenced Philo, the Jews tended to envision God as having a body right up till the time of Saadia in the tenth century.

35. L. Koehler, 'Die Grundstelle der Imago-Dei-Lehre', *TZ* 4 (1948), pp. 16-22. The case for the physical nature of the divine image was made most forcefully by P. Humbert, 'L'«Imago Dei» dans l'Ancien Testament', in *Etudes sur le récit du Paradis et de la chute dans la Genèse* (Neuchâtel: University of Neuchâtel, 1940), pp. 153-75.

early chapters of Genesis this is most clearly evident in Gen. 5.1-3, where Adam's being in the likeness of God seems analogous to Seth's being in the image and likeness of Adam.

However, it is to be noted that within the three passages in Genesis 1, 5 and 9 it is repeatedly implied that it is humans in their totality who are made in God's image and likeness, not just their physical exterior. So logically this ought to include not only the physical form of humanity but also the inner spiritual reality within them – humans' mind and intelligence. This latter side of things would appear to be more in evidence in Gen. 9.6, where the reason given for prohibiting murder of a human being is that 'God made humanity in his own image'. The fact that humans have a similar physical form to God would not appear to be very relevant here. Rather the inviolability of human life must surely have to do with the innate dignity and worth of human beings in their inner being.

Again, as we have seen earlier, humans being made in the image of God provided the foundation for their being given lordship over the animals and the world in Gen. 1.26-28. One may grant that humanity's mastery of the world was partly a consequence of its considerable physical strength. However, it was also humanity's superior intelligence and creative ability that enabled it to take charge of animals and the world. So this must also be a part of what is implied in humanity's being in God's image, distinct from the animals. We may again compare Ovid (*Metamorphoses* 1.76-78), who similarly declared, 'And yet there was no animal capable of higher thought that could have dominion over all the rest. Then humanity was born.'

This view of the image as including both a physical and spiritual resemblance between God and humanity, which I am advocating, has previously been proposed by a number of other scholars in the past, but mainly before the functional view became popular. Some of these scholars emphasized more the physical side of the resemblance and others more the spiritual side.[36]

36. E.g., with varying degrees of emphasis, A. Dillmann, *Die Genesis* (KEHAT; Leipzig: S. Hirzel, 5th edn, 1886), p. 31, ET *Genesis Critically and Exegetically Expounded*, I (2 vols.; Edinburgh: T. & T. Clark, 1897), pp. 81-82; Skinner, *Genesis*, p. 32; C.A. Simpson, 'Genesis', in *Interpreter's Bible*, I (New York: Abingdon-Cokesbury Press, 1952), pp. 437-829 (484); von Rad, *Das erste Buch Mose*, pp. 45-46, ET *Genesis*, pp. 56-57.

Later Biblical References to the Image (Real and Alleged)

Alleged Echoes of Genesis 1.26-28 Elsewhere in the Old Testament

It has often been supposed that Ps. 8.4-9 (ET 3-8) is dependent on Gen. 1.26-28. The text reads as follows:

> When I look at your heavens, the work of your fingers,
> The moon and the stars which you have established,
> What is man that you are mindful of him,
> And the son of man that you care for him?
> Yet you have made him little less than the gods (or angels),
> And crown him with glory and honour.
> You have given him dominion over the works of your hands,
> You have put all things under his feet,
> All sheep and oxen,
> and also the beasts of the field,
> the birds of the air, and the fish of the sea,
> whatever passes along the paths of the sea.

There is undoubtedly a close similarity here with Gen. 1.26-28, in that both combine a confident belief in the high status of humanity with an allusion to the God-given rule of human beings over the animals. The royal language is more marked than in Gen. 1.26-28, for the psalm speaks not merely of giving humanity dominion over the works of God's hands but also of crowning humans with glory and honour. However, it is important to note that the psalm does not actually speak of humanity being made in the image or likeness of God. Rather humans are said to be little less than the gods (or angels). Elsewhere in this psalm God is referred to as Yahweh (vv. 2, 10, ET 1, 9), so the reference to humanity being a little less than the *'elōhîm* more naturally refers to the gods or angels. This was already perceived in the principal ancient Versions (the Septuagint, Vulgate, Targum and Peshitta), which all rendered 'angels' here.[37] Rather than being dependent on Gen. 1.26-28, it is possible that Psalm 8 lies behind Gen. 1.26-28, or is at least less theologically advanced than it[38] – note, e.g., creation by Yahweh's fingers rather than

---

37. Though Aquila, Symmachus and Theodotion altered the LXX to read 'God'.

38. So J. Barr, 'The Image of God in the Book of Genesis: A Study in Terminology', *BJRL* 51 (1968–69), pp. 11-26 (12), reprinted in Barton (ed.), *Bible and Interpretation: The Collected Essays of James Barr*, II, pp. 66-77 (67); B.W. Anderson, 'Human Dominion over Nature', in M. Ward (ed.), *Biblical Studies in Contemporary Thought* (Burlington: Trinity College Bible Institute, 1975), pp. 27-45 (43).

divine fiat – just as I have argued elsewhere that Psalm 104 lies behind Genesis 1.[39]

We turn now to the prophet known as Second Isaiah (Isa. 40–55). The view was first put forward by Moshe Weinfeld, and subsequently followed by Michael Fishbane and Benjamin Sommer,[40] that there are various verses in Second Isaiah which reject particular points of the Priestly account of creation (Gen. 1.1–2.4a). Although superficially the various points made might at first seem enticing, when carefully analysed individually we find that they do not bear out Weinfeld's position. But here we need only consider Weinfeld's arguments in so far as they concern Gen. 1.26. In this connection Weinfeld claimed that Isa. 40.18 (cf. 40.25) is a deliberate rejection of Gen. 1.26's notion that humanity was made in the image of God. In Isa. 40.18 the prophet declares, 'To whom will you liken God, or what likeness compare with him?'. However, the very next verse makes clear that Second Isaiah was emphasizing Yahweh's uniqueness over against idols, rather than opposing Gen. 1.26, for he says, 'An idol? A workman casts it, and a goldsmith overlays it with gold'. Then v. 20, which is somewhat obscure, says more about idolatry. Isaiah 46.5 repeats the question, 'To whom will you liken me and make me equal, and compare me, as though we were alike?'. And just as after Isa. 40.18 the prophet again goes on to speak of idolatry: 'Those who lavish gold from the purse and weigh out silver in the scales – they hire a goldsmith, who makes it into a god; then they fall down and worship. They lift it to their shoulders, they carry it, they set it in its place, and it stands there, it cannot move from its place. If one cries out to it, it does not answer, or save anyone from trouble' (Isa. 46.6-7). Further, Isa. 46.1-2 makes it clear that Second Isaiah was thinking in terms of Babylonian idolatry (he mentions Bel [Marduk] and Nebo [Nabu] in v. 1.) So it is clear that in raising the question to whom one might compare God Second Isaiah is rejecting the view that other gods, such as the Babylonian ones, can compete with Yahweh in power or importance. He is not alluding to Gen. 1.26's implication that there is a certain physical or spiritual resemblance between Yahweh and humans in appearance or inner psyche.

39. Day, *God's Conflict with the Dragon and the* Sea, pp. 51-53.

40. M. Weinfeld, 'God the Creator in the Priestly Source and Deutero-Isaiah' (Hebrew), *Tarbiz* 37 (1967–68), pp. 105-32, ET *The Place of the Law in the Religion of Ancient Israel* (VTSup, 100; Leiden: Brill, 2004), pp. 95-117; M.A. Fishbane, *Biblical Interpretation in Ancient Israel* (Oxford: Clarendon Press, 1985), pp. 322-26; B.D. Sommer, *A Prophet Reads Scripture: Allusion in Isaiah 40–66* (Stanford, CA: Stanford University Press, 1998), pp. 142-45. I previously followed this view in Day, *God's Conflict with the Dragon and the Sea*, pp. 54-55, but am no longer convinced.

But there is another verse of Second Isaiah which Weinfeld thinks is also countering Gen. 1.26. We have already seen that the words 'Let us make humanity' imply that God addressed his heavenly court, the angels, when creating humanity. Weinfeld thinks that this idea is being countered in Isa. 40.13-14, 'Who has directed the spirit of the Lord, or as his counsellor instructed him …?' He also points to Isa. 44.24, 'I am the Lord, who made all things, who alone stretched out the heavens, and spread out the earth. Who was with me?' However, this last verse is speaking of the creation of heaven and earth, not of humanity, and as for Isa. 40.13-14 it is not clear that the prophet is speaking of creation at all. It sounds rather as if he is speaking generally of Yahweh's not needing anyone to instruct him in wisdom (cf. Isa. 40.14, 'who taught him the path of justice?').

The Apocrypha

Before we come to the New Testament there are three references in the Apocrypha that we need to consider. The earliest of these is in Ecclus 17.3-4, which declares 'He [God] endowed them [humans] with a strength like his own, and made them in his own image. He put the fear of him in all living beings, and gave them dominance over beasts and birds.' So on the one hand humans being in God's image is taken to imply that they are strong, and on the other hand it is associated with humanity's domination over the beasts. But this is not the peaceful, harmonious rule over the animals to which Genesis 1 refers, but rather the fear-ridden rule of Genesis 9, after humanity has been given permission to eat meat following the Flood.

    Another apocryphal reference is in Wis. 2.23, where we read, 'for God created us for incorruption, and made us in the image of his own eternity'. The book of Wisdom was much influenced by Middle Platonism, and continually emphasizes human immortality, so it is in keeping with this that the image of God in humans is taken to refer to their immortal spirit. Somewhat similarly, another Alexandrian Jew, Philo, explains the image of God in humans as 'the most important part of the soul, the mind' (*De Opificio Mundi* 69), thereby anticipating some later Christian ideas.

    Finally, 2 Esd. 8.44 refers to 'people who have been formed by your [God's] hands and are called your own image because they are made like you, and for whose sake you have formed all things'. This both emphasizes humanity's resemblance to God and also refers to the consequent human domination of the earth.

The New Testament

What is said about humanity being in the image of God in the New Testament? First, we should note the Letter of James, where the writer says of the tongue, 'With it we bless the Lord and Father, and with it we curse those who are made in the image of God' (Jas 3.9).

But the most interesting passage is in one of Paul's letters, in 1 Cor. 11.7, where in the course of a discussion of what headdress is appropriate when praying or prophesying in Church, Paul declares, 'For a man ought not to have his head veiled, since he is the image and glory of God, but woman is the glory of man'. This is explained by the continuation in v. 8, where Paul says, 'Indeed, man was not made from woman, but woman from man'. For those of us who are accustomed to the view expressed in Gen. 1.26 that both men and women are made in the image of God, Paul's words here will come as a shock. The explanation for what he says lies in the fact that whereas we read Gen. 1.1–2.4a and 2.4b–3.24 as two separate stories (from the P and J sources respectively), Paul read them as a unity. In addition, he understood *hā'ādām* in Gen. 1.26-27 to mean '(an individual) man' rather than 'humanity', a meaning which it has in Genesis 2–3. Accordingly, the words 'male and female he created them' at the end of Gen. 1.27 are understood to be partly proleptic, i.e. 'male (and later) female he created them', corresponding to the Garden of Eden story in Genesis 2, where the woman is made from the side (traditionally rib) of the man. Woman would thus be in the image of God but only indirectly so for Paul, via the man.[41]

But there are also other Pauline references to the image of God of a different character, and these are probably not dependent on Gen. 1.26-27. In particular, Col. 1.15 refers to Christ as 'the image of the invisible God' and 2 Cor. 4.4 speaks of Christ as 'the image of God'. Although it is true that Paul calls Christ 'the last Adam' (1 Cor. 14.45), there is probably no direct connection with Gen. 1.26-27 in these cases where Christ is called the image of God. Rather, as is the case with Heb. 1.3 stating that Christ 'reflects the glory of God and bears the very stamp of his nature', it seems more natural to detect Wisdom influence here. Compare Wis. 7.26, 'For she (Wisdom) is a reflection of eternal light, a spotless mirror of the

---

41. See J. Barr, *Biblical Faith and Natural Theology* (Oxford: Clarendon Press, 1993), pp. 165-67. We should also note Barr's conclusion (p. 167) regarding the nature of the image in Paul here: '… it seems to side with a *physical* understanding of the image in Genesis more than with any other. The image is a sort of luminosity which radiates from the man.'

working of God, and an *image* of his goodness'. The role of Christ in the creation of the world in Col. 1.15-17 also supports this background, since Wisdom was active in creation, the phrase 'the first-born of creation' that follows on after 'the image of the invisible God' being taken from Prov. 8.22, where it refers to pre-existent Wisdom.

Further Pauline passages refer to Christians being transformed into Christ's image or likeness; for example, they are 'to be conformed to the image of his Son' (Rom. 8.29). Again, 'we all ... are being changed into his likeness from one degree of glory to another' (2 Cor. 3.18), and 'you have put on the new nature, which is being renewed in knowledge after the image of its creator' (Col. 3.10).[42] For Paul, unlike the later Reformers, this transformation into the likeness of Christ is not to be understood as a restoration of the image of God in Gen. 1.26-27, since as we have seen above, for Paul all men (and by extension women) are already in the image of God referred to there (1 Cor. 11.7).

Theological Consequences of Humanity Being Made in the Image and Likeness of God

What theological consequences might one draw from the fact that human beings are described as being made in the image and likeness of God? First, it clearly indicates that humans have enormous dignity, since there is something Godlike about them. Psalm 8 puts it in a different way when it declares that humans are a little lower than the angels or gods. Because of humanity's Godlikeness Gen. 9.6 deems it inappropriate to murder a human being. However, many nowadays would expand the biblical writer's vision and argue that the judicial murder of the murderer should also be outlawed. This is in line with the New Testament's reversal of the book of Exodus's doctrine of an 'eye for an eye and tooth for a tooth', which follows on 'a life for a life' (Exod. 21.23-24; cf. Mt. 5.38-42). The idea of the Godlike dignity of human beings is expressed elsewhere in Prov. 17.5, which declares, 'He who mocks the poor mocks his maker'. Somewhat comparable are Jesus's words at the last judgment, 'Truly, I say to you, as you did it to one of the least of these my brethren, you did it to me' (Mt. 25.40, cf. v. 45).

Interestingly, both men and women are said to be created in the image of God. This seems undeniable from Gen. 1.27 and 5.1-2. Genesis 1.27 states, 'So God created humanity in his own image, in the image of

---

42. Similarly the Deutero-Pauline Eph. 4.24, 'put on the new nature, created after the likeness of God in true righteousness and holiness'.

God he created them, male and female he created them', and Gen. 5.1-2 declares, 'When God created humanity, he made them in the likeness of God. Male and female he created them.' From this we should draw the conclusion that men and women are deemed equal in the sight of God, something generally accepted throughout the history of Judaism and Christianity, though M.C. Horowitz[43] has also noted a minority of dissenters. Men and women are thus subsequently both given dominion over the earth and the animals (Gen. 1.26, 28). Whilst this is generally accepted, it has curiously been denied by one feminist scholar, Phyllis Bird,[44] who maintains that the dominion is understood as confined to men. However, it is explicitly stated in v. 28 that the command to rule over the animals and the earth was given by God 'to them', which can only mean to both male and female just referred to. But this does not mean that the Priestly writer had thought through the full implications of this in terms of social equality. For example, the Priestly writer of Genesis 1 later on tends to list almost entirely men in his genealogies, and he has only men, not women, performing a priestly role within the cult. We may compare the fact that Paul in Gal. 3.28 declares that 'There is neither Jew nor Greek, there is neither slave nor free, there is neither male nor female; for you are all one in Christ Jesus', but it took hundreds of years for slavery to be abolished, and there are still some branches of the Christian church which exclude women from the priesthood, just as Orthodox Judaism still rejects women as rabbis.

In Genesis 1 humans being made in the image of God is something that distinguishes them from the animals. Subsequently, humans are commanded to have lordship over the earth, including the animals. Lynn White[45] famously declared that the modern environmental crisis can be blamed on this passage. However, this is not the case. First, if one goes on to read the next few verses one discovers that at the end of Genesis 1 the food of human beings is limited to a vegetarian diet (Gen. 1.29). Accordingly, the lordship over the world implied here can only be meant

43. M.C. Horowitz, 'The Image of God in Man – Is Woman Included?', *HTR* 72 (1979), pp. 175-206.

44. P. Bird, '"Male and Female He Created Them": Gen 1:27b in the Context of the Priestly Account of Creation', *HTR* 74 (1981), pp. 129-59 (151), reprinted in P. Bird, *Missing Persons and Mistaken Identities: Women and Gender in Ancient Israel* (Minneapolis, MN: Fortress Press, 1997), pp. 123-54 (145). Contrast, for example, P. Trible, *God and the Rhetoric of Spirituality* (Philadelphia, PA: Fortress Press, 1978), p. 19.

45. L. White, 'The Historical Roots of our Ecologic Crisis', *Science* 155, no. 3767 (1967), pp. 1203-207.

in a benign sense, more akin to stewardship.[46] We are reminded of the lovely biblical image of the king as a shepherd (Isa. 44.28; Jer. 23.4; Ezek. 34.23; 37.24; Mic. 5.3, ET 4). Secondly, there is little evidence that this passage was later misunderstood to justify the ruthless exploitation of nature.[47] The allusion to having dominion over (*rādâ*) the animals and the earth (Gen. 1.26, 28) seems to appropriate royal terminology (cf. Pss. 72.8; 110.2; 1 Kgs 5.4, ET 4.24; Isa. 14.6; Ezek. 34.4), though this language is not exclusively royal. But in the current context it lacks all harshness. Further, the reference to subduing (*kābaš*) the earth (not animals!) in v. 28 is probably basically the same as having dominion over the earth. It most likely refers to humanity establishing territorial authority over the earth, as later implied in the table of the nations in Genesis 10. This coheres with the usage of the verb *kābaš* in a number of other Old Testament passages, including some others from the Priestly writer (Num. 32.22, 29; Josh. 18.1), as well as elsewhere (2 Sam. 8.11; 1 Chron. 22.18), though unlike these the initial settling down would not have been understood violently. It is also possible that the establishment of agricultural order on the world, tilling the soil, might be included, as James Barr proposed.[48] This is not to deny that since the flood a harsher regime is regarded as having been in operation, with humans being given permission to eat meat (Gen. 9.1-7).[49]

---

46. This is rightly emphasized by J. Barr, 'Man and Nature – The Ecological Controversy and the Old Testament', *BJRL* 55 (1972), pp. 9-32, reprinted in Barton (ed.), *Bible and Interpretation*, II, pp. 344-60; J.W. Rogerson, 'The Creation Stories: Their Ecological Potential and Problems', in D.G. Horrell, C. Hunt, C. Southgate and F. Stavrakopoulou (eds), *Ecological Hermeneutics: Biblical, Theological Perspectives* (London: T&T Clark, 2010), pp. 21-31. Other important studies are U. Rutersworden, *Dominium Terrae: Studien zur Genese einer alttestamentlichen Vorstellung* (BZAW, 215; Berlin: W. de Gruyter, 1993), pp. 81-130; U. Neumann-Gersolke, *Herrschen in den Grenzen der Schöpfung. Ein Beitrag zur alttestamentlichen Anthropologie am Beispiel von Psalm 8, Genesis 1 und verwandten Texten* (WMANT, 101; Neukirchen-Vluyn: Neukirchener Verlag, 2004).

47. Barr, 'Man and Nature', pp. 23-24, reprinted version, pp. 354-55.

48. Barr, 'Man and Nature', p. 22, reprinted version, p. 353.

49. A. Schellenberg, 'Humankind as "Image of God"', *TZ* 97 (2009), pp. 87-111 (102), curiously maintains that after the flood humanity is no longer God's viceroy, deputed to rule the world. She emphasizes that Gen. 9.1-7, which recapitulates much of what God says to the first humans in Gen. 1.26-30, fails to employ the verb *rādâ*, 'to have dominion over', in connection with humanity's role. However, it is stated that God delivers the animals into human hands and that the fear of humanity will be upon them (Gen. 9.2). This surely betokens divinely sanctioned human rule, albeit on a harsher level than previously, as a concession to human weakness. The absence of the verb *rādâ* is not significant, any more than the absence of the verb *kābaš* with

But with Paradise restored the ultimate biblical eschatological hope is for the restoration of harmony in nature, including between humans and animals (Isa. 11.6-9).[50]

reference to subduing the earth. Furthermore, the table of the nations in Gen. 10 reflects human territorial authority over the earth, which fulfils an aspect of the human dominion over the world commanded by God in Gen. 1. If Schellenberg is right that humans no longer exercise God-given authority over the world following the flood, this point would surely be expressed clearly in Gen. 9.1-7, which is not the case.

50. As a final aside I should add that C.L. Crouch, 'Genesis 1:26-7 as a Statement of Humanity's Divine Parentage', *JTS* NS 61 (2010), pp. 1-15, has argued that the notion that humans are made in the image of God is a way of asserting their divine parentage. Now it is true that in the Bible all humans have God as their father just as they are all in the image of God, so there is clearly some overlap in conception. But are they absolutely identical in meaning? Having God as father is surely an affirmation of having God as one's creator and protector, while being in the image of God asserts a certain resemblance (in my view physical and spiritual) between God and humans. It should also be noted that though God is the father of all, not all are spoken of his sons; this language in the Old Testament is limited to the Judahite kings and Israel itself, but these are never specifically singled out as being in the image of God.

Chapter 3

The Serpent in the Garden of Eden: Its Background and Role

Introduction

For Adam and Eve the serpent in the Garden of Eden represented the voice of temptation but it needs to be noted that for the original writer, the Yahwist (or J) source, the serpent was not equated with Satan (the Devil). The concept of Satan developed only later (first attested as a personal name *c.* 300 BCE in 1 Chron. 21.1).[1] Earlier references in Zech. 3.1-2 and Job 1–2 speak of 'the Satan' (or the Adversary) but these do not allude to the fully fledged concept of the Devil, the leader of all the host of evil over against God, but refer to the figure in an earlier stage of its development.

---

1. That Satan is mentioned in 1 Chron. 21.1 is the most common view. However, P.L. Day, *An Adversary in Heaven: śāṭān in the Hebrew Bible* (HSM, 43; Atlanta, GA: Scholars Press, 1988), pp. 127-43 argued against *śāṭān* being a personal name in 1 Chron. 21.1 because she dated Chronicles to the sixth century BCE and the next reference to Satan would not be till the second-century BCE book of *Jubilees*. Similarly, R. Stokes, *Satan: How God's Executioner Became the Enemy* (Grand Rapids, MI: Eerdmans, 2019), pp. 18-21, who also sees the Chronicler as prior to Job (p. 20 n. 34). But there are good grounds for rejecting a very early date for Chronicles; see H.G.M. Williamson, *Israel in the Books of Chronicles* (Cambridge: Cambridge University Press, 1977), pp. 83-86. The time gap between Chronicles and *Jubilees* would then be much less. Both Peggy Day and Ryan Stokes curiously sees *śāṭān* in 1 Chron. 21.1 as a celestial figure but distinct from Satan. However, if Chronicles dates from *c.* 300 BCE it would be simpler to see it as Satan. It appears that the Chronicler understandably found it difficult to conceive how Yahweh, as recorded in his underlying source in 2 Sam. 24, could justifiably both inspire David to conduct a census (v. 1) and then punish him for doing so (vv. 10-17). He thus substituted a reference to Satan.

Thus, in Job 1–2 the Satan mingles with the sons of God (a part of God's heavenly court) and appears as God's public prosecutor. Anyway, we first find Satan equated with the Eden serpent about the turn of the era in the apocryphal book of Wisdom (Wis. 2.24), 'but through the Devil's envy death entered the world'. Sometimes this verse has been understood instead as referring to Cain's murder of Abel in Genesis 4.[2] However, it is more natural to see the reference as alluding to Adam, Eve and the serpent in Genesis 3, since it was already then that death for humanity was formally confirmed: 'you are dust and to dust you shall return' (Gen. 3.19; cf. Paul in Rom. 5.12 [Adam]; Ecclus 25.24[3] [Eve]). Adam and Eve were, of course, already destined for mortality as long as they failed to eat of the tree of life in the garden. The tree of life had not been barred to them by Yahweh, so the chance of immortality was there for them. However, it was their disobedience in eating of the tree of knowledge which finally sealed their destiny, and it is this which Gen. 3.19 confirms and to which Wis. 2.24 refers. It should further be noted that the Septuagint regularly uses *diabolos*, 'Devil', found in Wis. 2.24, as a translation of Satan (in 1 Chron. 1.1 without the definite article, as in Wis. 2.24), with whom the serpent became equated. Again, it is significant that Josephus, *Ant.* 1.1.4 similarly attributes the serpent's temptation of Eve to jealousy, namely jealousy of the blessings which he thought Adam and Eve would receive if they obeyed God. Cain's murder of Abel was the first murder, not the institution of death. Towards the end of the first century CE we further find the serpent and Satan equated in the references to 'that ancient serpent, who is [called] the Devil and Satan' (Rev. 12.9; 20.2). Less well known is the

2. E.g. J.A.F. Gregg, *The Wisdom of Solomon* (CBSC; Cambridge: Cambridge University Press, 1909), pp. 22-23. The view that the reference is to Cain, already found in 1 Clem. 3.4–4.7, is still regarded as a possibility by J. Byron, *Cain and Abel in Text and Tradition: Jewish and Christian Interpretations of the First Sibling Rivalry* (Themes in Biblical Narrative: Jewish and Christian Traditions, 14; Leiden: Brill, 2011), pp. 221-24, but on the assumption that *diabolos* refers to an 'enemy', i.e. Cain, rather than to the Devil. It has sometimes been argued against an Adamic reference in Wis. 2.24 that Wis. 10.1-2 appears to minimize Adam's sin, but it nevertheless still does refer to 'his fall' (v. 1).

3. There is a tension between Ecclus 25.24 and 17.7, the latter seeing the knowledge of good and evil as a divine gift, contrary to a natural reading of Gen. 3 and the implications of Ecclus 25.24. However, the view of J.R. Levison, 'Is Eve to Blame? A Contextual Study of Sirach 24:24', *CBQ* 47 (1985), pp. 617-23, that Ecclus 25.24 does not allude to Eve is unconvincing. Levison claims that we should understand the verse to be saying, 'From the [evil] wife is the beginning of sin, and because of her we [husbands] all die', death being a hyperbolical allusion to the devastating effect a wife has on her husband!

fact that the Eden serpent is equated in *1 En.* 69.6 with Gader'el, one of the wicked angels who descended from heaven to have sex with women on the earth (elaborating the story in Gen. 6.1-4).

Genesis 3.1, however, refers to the Eden serpent as one of Yahweh's earthly creatures, a 'beast of the field'. It is certainly the case that it is the ancestor of later ordinary serpents known to humanity (cf. Gen. 3.14-15), but in its original pre-cursed state the serpent not only has the capacity to speak but also to have supernormal knowledge, which makes it more than an ordinary serpent at that point, a kind of magical animal.[4] We may recall Balaam's ass in Num. 22.28-30 for the only other example of a talking animal in the Old Testament, one moreover with comparable supernatural awareness, a passage which has likewise been traditionally ascribed to the J source. However, it should be noted that in v. 28 it is God who opened the mouth of Balaam, unlike with the serpent in Genesis 3. But the attribution to J gains further support from the fact that the Balaam narrative in Num. 24.17, 22 similarly knows a Cain [Kain] and a Seth [Sheth], here with clear ethnic overtones, the names of figures who also appear in the J source in Genesis 4.

Charlesworth's View of a Positive Serpent

In 2010, James Charlesworth wrote a massive and learned book entitled *The Good and Evil Serpent*[5] in which he argued that in the ancient Near East and classical world the serpent was mostly viewed positively, not negatively, and he claims this is also true of the serpent of Genesis 3.[6] However, without going into all his ancient Near Eastern and classical material, I would argue that most references in the Hebrew Bible clearly indicate that the serpent was viewed negatively in ancient Israel, and this is certainly the case in Genesis 3. Most frequently we read of serpents biting people (Gen. 49.17;[7] Prov. 23.32; Eccl. 10.8, 11; Jer. 8.17; Amos 5.19; 9.3); they also symbolize the wicked (Pss. 40.5, ET 3; 58.5, ET 4) and are mentioned in connection with the dreadful wilderness and

---

4. Cf. T.C. Vriezen, *Onderzoek naar de Paradijsvoorstelling bij de oude Semietischen Volken* (Wageningen: H. Veenman, 1937), p. 177.

5. J.H. Charlesworth, *The Good and Evil Serpent* (AYB Reference Library; New Haven, CT: Yale University Press, 2010).

6. For Gen. 3, see Charlesworth, *The Good and Evil Serpent*, pp. 275-324, with endnotes on pp. 562-73.

7. Charlesworth, *The Good and Evil Serpent*, p. 217, regards Gen. 49.17 as a positive reference to the serpent. It is true that the serpent acts on behalf of the Israelite tribe of Dan, but it acts harmfully against its enemies by biting.

scorpions (Deut. 8.15). In addition, the sea monster (Rahab, Leviathan) defeated by Yahweh is depicted as a serpent (Job 26.13; Isa. 27.1). The only positive references to the serpent in the Hebrew Bible which I see are the bronze serpent Nehushtan in Num. 21.8-9 (unlike in 2 Kgs 18.4, when it had become idolatrous), and the apparently partially serpentine heavenly seraphim which surround Yahweh in Isaiah 6 (cf. Isa. 30.6). Against this generally strong negative background we would require strong evidence to be persuaded that the Eden serpent is viewed positively, but Charlesworth fails to provide this.

Specifically with regard to the serpent in Genesis 3 Charlesworth claims that it does not tempt Eve (it merely asks her a question![8]), it tells the truth (unlike God), is described as clever (not crafty), and is not a symbol of evil. However, if all this is true it becomes difficult to understand why the serpent should be so thoroughly cursed towards the end of the story so as to become the lowliest of creatures (Gen. 3.14-15). Again, Eve declares that 'the serpent beguiled me' (Gen. 3.13); Charlesworth claims that Eve is just making excuses, but it is clearly an assertion accepted by God (Gen. 3.14) and which the reader too is therefore meant to accept. It is difficult, therefore, to believe that there is no element of temptation in the serpent's questioning of Eve. This indicates that the negative meaning 'crafty' or 'cunning' (such as is found in Job 5.12; 15.5)[9] rather than the positive meaning 'wise, clever, prudent, sensible, shrewd' or the like (such as is attested in Prov. 12.16, 23; 13.16; 14.8, 15, 18; 22.3; 27.12) is a more likely translation of the Hebrew word *'ārûm* used to describe the serpent in Gen. 3.1. There is also a noun *'ōrem*, 'craftiness' (Job 5.13), a noun *'ormâ* that can mean 'craftiness' (Exod. 21.14; Josh. 9.4) as well as 'good sense, prudence' (Prov. 1.4; 8.5, 12), and a verb *'ārōm*, that can mean 'to be cunning' (1 Sam. 23.22), or 'to plan craftily' (hiphil, Ps. 83.4, ET 3), in addition to 'to be shrewd' (Prov. 15.5; 19.25). On the basis of the context, therefore, we should render, 'Now the serpent was more crafty (or cunning) than any other wild creature that the Lord God had made'.[10]

8. Though in fact the serpent's words to Eve in Gen. 3.1 are not strictly a question, since *'ap kî*, lit. 'indeed that', never carries interrogative force elsewhere in the Hebrew Bible. It would be better to render, 'Indeed, to think that God said "You shall not eat of any tree of the garden!"'. The words thus constitute an insinuation and provoke a response, even though not strictly a question. Cf. Skinner, *Genesis*, p. 74.

9. 4QGen[k] actually has the interrogative particle before *'ap* here, but the Samaritan Pentateuch supports MT.

10. In the previous verse (Gen. 2.24) Adam and Eve are described as *'ărummîm*, 'naked'; there is clearly here a wordplay between this and *'ārûm*, 'crafty', in Gen. 3.1. (Contrast the spellings *'êrōm* and *'êrummîm*, 'naked', in Gen. 3.7, 10, 12.) This is in

As for the claim that the serpent tells the truth, unlike God, it is clear that the serpent does not speak the whole truth. While the eyes of Adam and Eve are indeed opened so as to know good and evil and become like gods as a result of eating the forbidden fruit, just as the serpent had predicted, it fails to inform them that they will also be expelled from the Garden of Eden as a consequence of their disobedience to God, thereby denying them access to the tree of life and ensuring their eventual death, even if they do not die immediately (the latter seemingly a result of the divine compassion).[11]

Although it is not central to his argument, Charlesworth also holds that, in being cursed so that it had to crawl on its belly and seemingly eat dust (Gen. 3.14), the serpent was deprived of its feet and legs by God. This suggestion goes back to antiquity (cf. Josephus, *Ant.* 1.1.4; Targum Pseudo-Jonathan on Gen. 3.14; Midrash *Genesis Rabbah* 20.5), and serpents with feet and legs are also attested elsewhere in ancient Near Eastern iconography.[12] However, since nothing explicitly is said in Genesis 3 about the serpent actually having had feet and legs and being deprived of them it is perhaps preferable to think of the serpent as originally having a good sense of balance so that it could move upright without legs.

The Background of the Serpent

Turning now to the ancient Near Eastern background, it should be noted that a few scholars have tried to see the Eden serpent as symbolic of Canaanite religion. Thus, F.F. Hvidberg saw it as symbolic of the god Baal, a view more recently adopted by B.T. Arnold,[13] while Nick Wyatt once understood it rather as symbolic of the god El, but has since retracted this view.[14] Both views are unconvincing. Baal was never symbolized by

keeping with J's well-known liking for wordplays. But P. Kübel, 'Ein Wortspiel in Genesis 3 und sein Hintergrund: Die „kluge" Schlange und die „nackten" Menschen. Überlegungen zur Vorgeschichte von Gen 2–3', *BN* 93 (1998), pp. 11-22 (16-18), thinks there is also a hint of the serpent's nakedness in the light of the fact that snakes shed their skins. This is possible but not certain.

11. For this conclusion see Day, *From Creation to Babel*, pp. 38-41.

12. See picture in Z. Zevit, *What Really Happened in the Garden of Eden?* (New Haven, CT: Yale University Press, 2013), p. 198.

13. F.F. Hvidberg, 'The Canaanitic Background of Gen. i–iii', *VT* 10 (1960), pp. 285-94 (287-90); Arnold, *Genesis*, pp. 62-63.

14. N. Wyatt, 'Interpreting the Creation and Fall Story in Genesis 2–3', *ZAW* 93 (1981), pp. 10-21 (18-20). Recently, Wyatt has informed me that he no longer sees the need to posit any deity behind the serpent.

a serpent in Canaanite religion (or anywhere else in the Old Testament) – indeed, it was Baal who defeated the sea serpent Leviathan in Canaanite mythology – and nor is El, who is universally viewed positively throughout the Old Testament, and is actually equated with Yahweh. More generally, J. Coppens, J.A. Soggin and K. Jaroš have seen the serpent as symbolic of the Canaanite fertility cult, Jaroš[15] even suggesting that the serpent approached Eve rather than Adam because women were allegedly more prone to the fertility cult. It is true that there is evidence suggesting that the serpent could symbolize fertility in Canaanite religion: in iconography it is associated with the Canaanite nude goddess Qedeshet (not Qudshu, as frequently claimed), in addition to bulls and water, all of which were symbolic of fertility or life.[16] However, there is no particular reason to find that meaning in Genesis 3; the knowledge of good and evil which the serpent tempts the first humans to acquire is quite unrelated to the fertility cult.[17] Moreover, the fertility cult is not depicted as an important concern of the Yahwist source elsewhere, so it would be surprising to find it represented as the archetypal sin at the time of creation.

15. J. Coppens, *La connaissance du bien et du mal et la péché du Paradis* (Gembloux: J. Duculot, 1948), *passim*; J.A. Soggin, 'The Fall of Man in the Third Chapter of Genesis', in *idem, Old Testament and Oriental Studies* (Rome: Biblical Institute Press, 1975), pp. 88-111 (94-100); K. Jaroš, 'Die Motive der heiligen Bäume und der Schlange in Gen 2–3', *ZAW* 92 (1980), pp. 204-15. R. Gnuse, *Misunderstood Stories: Theological Commentary on Genesis 1–11* (Eugene OR: Wipf & Stock [Cascade Books], 2014), p. 122, sees a connection between the Eden serpent and fertility, as well as healing, but without specifically mentioning a Canaanite background.

16. On the serpent's association with fertility see the data presented in K.R. Joines, 'The Bronze Serpent in the Israelite Cult', *JBL* 87 (1965), pp. 245-58 (246-50); *idem, Serpent Symbolism in the Old Testament* (Haddonfield, NJ: Haddonfield House, 1974), pp. 63-73. However, note that the 'serpents' rolled round the legs of a goddess at Tell Beit Mirsim and Shechem are in reality coils from her clothing; cf. R. Merhav, 'The Stele of the "Serpent Goddess" from Tell Beit Mirsim and the Plaque from Shechem Reconsidered', *The Israel Museum Journal* 4 (1985), pp. 27-42. On Qedeshet rather than Qudshu, see S.A. Wiggins, 'The Myth of Asherah: Lion Lady and Serpent Goddess', *UF* 23 (1991), pp. 383-94. Of the three instances of the word *qdš* found in close association with Athirat in the Ugaritic texts (leading some scholars to equate them), one actually means 'sanctuary' (*KTU³* 1.14.IV.34) and the other two constitute rather an epithet of El (*KTU³* 1.16.I.11, 22).

17. On the meaning of the knowledge of good and evil, see Day, *From Creation to Babel*, pp. 41-44, as well as in Chapter 4 below.

Over the last decade several new theories about the origin of the serpent in the Garden of Eden have been put forward. However, as I hope to demonstrate here, they are all wrong. First, in a BBC TV programme broadcast in 2011 (episode 3 of *The Bible's Buried Secrets*), Francesca Stavrakopoulou claimed that the serpent in the Garden of Eden symbolized snake worship; she seems to be thinking of the bronze serpent Nehushtan. She follows Nick Wyatt[18] in thinking that the expulsion of Adam and Eve symbolized the exile of 597 or 586 BCE. But Nehushtan, which was allegedly made by Moses (cf. Num. 21.4-9), had already been destroyed by King Hezekiah a century earlier than the exile (2 Kgs 18.4). It should also be noted that the Hebrew Bible never attributes the exile to snake worship. Furthermore, Genesis 3 does not speak of actual worship of the serpent. Finally, it is unlikely that the Garden of Eden story constitutes an allegory of the exile of 597 or 586 BCE. It is far more natural to hold that the Eden story is rather what it appears to be, namely an explanation of the human condition. Although the text refers to the river Gihon emerging from Eden (Gen. 2.13), this cannot refer to the Gihon spring in Jerusalem (though there may be some symbolic connection), since it is said to traverse the whole land of Kush (Nubia), which can only refer to the river Nile, as in LXX Jer. 2.18; Ecclus 24.27; Josephus, *Ant.* 1.1.3; and probably Genesis Apocryphon 21.15, 18. Furthermore, we actually possess a variant of the Eden myth coming from the exilic period in Ezek. 28.12-19, but this does not relate it to the Jewish exile in Babylon but rather to the expected downfall of the king of Tyre.

Finally, although I will not go into this in detail here, there are good grounds for continuing to maintain a pre-exilic date for the Eden story and the J narrative generally. I will simply mention some linguistic points. First, J's preference for *'ānōkî* rather than *'ᵃni* for 'I', including in the Eden narrative (Gen. 3.10), is greater than most other parts of the Old

---

18. Wyatt, 'Interpreting the Creation and Fall Story', pp. 19-21. Here Wyatt argued that the story originally related to the exile of the last Northern Israelite king, Hoshea, in 722 BCE, but later became applied to the Judaean king in 586 BCE. However, Wyatt has recently informed me that he now simply relates the Eden story to 586 (or 597) BCE. Cf. his more recent article, 'A Royal Garden: The Ideology of Eden', *SJOT* 28 (2014), pp. 1-35 (29). It should be noted that F. Stavrakopoulou, 'Tree-Hogging in Eden: Divine Restriction and Royal Rejection in Genesis 2–3', in M. Higton, J. Law and C. Rowland (eds.), *Theology and Human Flourishing: Essays in Honor of Timothy J. Gorringe* (Eugene, OR: Wipf & Stock [Cascade Books], 2011), pp. 41-53, similarly argues for the Eden story as a reflection of the exile of the Judaean monarch in 597 BCE. However, she says nothing there of serpent worship.

Testament, and therefore suggestive of a pre-exilic date; contrast P, likely from the sixth century BCE, which already overwhelmingly uses *'anî*.[19] Again, on a number of occasions, J has a liking for the earlier passive qal form, including in the Eden narrative (Gen. 3.19, 23), whereas the sixth-century P source uniformly uses the later standard niphal form for the passive in Genesis 1–11. Moreover, J several times employs the archaic 3rd p.s.m. suffix in *-ōh* (cf. Gen. 9.21; 12.8; 13.3; 35.21),[20] and a plausible case can be made for its occurrence also in the Eden narrative. Thus, in Gen. 2.15 we read that God set the man in the garden 'to till it and keep it' (MT *le'obdāh ûle šomrāh*), but the feminine verbal suffixes in *-āh* here do not agree with the masculine referent, *gan*, 'garden'. This problem would be easily solved if we were to read the archaic 3rd p.s.m. suffix *-ōh* instead of *-āh* with both these verbs. Finally, although not found in the Eden narrative, J's consistent preference for the qal rather than the later dominant hiphil of *yld*, 'to give birth' (e.g. Gen. 4.17-18, 20, 22, 26), again in contrast to P, also indicates an earlier rather than a later date for the J source.[21] In conclusion, the fact that the Eden narrative (in common with J more generally) has multiple examples of earlier linguistic forms, in contrast to P, is a strong argument for its pre-exilic date, and rules out its being symbolic of the Babylonian exile.

My second example concerns a highly original attempt to find a Canaanite background to the serpent in Genesis 3, indeed to the Garden of Eden story more generally, by Marjo Korpel and Johannes de Moor in

---

19. See the useful comparative chart in R.S. Hendel and J. Joosten, *How Old Is the Hebrew Bible?* (AYB Reference Library; New Haven, CT: Yale University Press, 2018), p. 18.

20. See J.S. Baden, '"His Tent": Pitched at the Intersection of Orthography and Source Criticism', in J. Lam, E. Reymond and H.H. Hardy (eds.), *Dennis Pardee Festschrift* (forthcoming), who makes many interesting observations about the *-ōh* suffix. For example, all the occurrences of this suffix in Genesis occur in passages traditionally ascribed to the J source, thereby tending to support the existence of that source. Again, whilst the *-ōh* 3rd p.s.m. suffix reappears much later at Qumran from the second century BCE onwards (cf. Dan. 11.10), it never replaces *-ô* in its versions of biblical texts.

21. See Day, *From Creation to Babel*, pp. 48-49. More recently, cf. Hendel and Joosten, *How Old Is the Hebrew Bible?*, pp. 16-18. More generally, cf. J.A. Emerton, 'The Date of the Yahwist', in J. Day (ed.), *In Search of Pre-Exilic Israel* (JSOTSup, 406; London: T&T Clark, 2004), pp. 107-29. Specifically on the evidence for the qal of *yld* being predominant in an earlier period than the hiphil, see R.S. Hendel, '"Begetting" and "Being Born" in the Pentateuch: Notes on Historical Linguistics and Source Criticism', *VT* 50 (2000), pp. 38-46.

a book entitled *Adam, Eve, and the Devil*.[22] Basing themselves on their interpretation of the Ugaritic texts *KTU*[3] 1.100 and 1.107, they conclude, in the words of their book's blurb, that 'El, the creator deity, and his wife Asherah lived in a vineyard or garden on the slopes of Mt Ararat, known in the Bible as the mountain where Noah's ark came to rest. The first sinner was not a human being but an evil god called Horon who wanted to depose El. Horon was thrown down from the mountain of the gods, and in revenge he transformed the tree of life in the garden into the tree of death and enveloped the whole world in a poisonous fog. Adam was sent down to restore life on earth, but failed because Horon in the form of a huge serpent bit him. As a result, Adam and his wife lost their immortality.' Their book is erudite and makes fascinating reading, but Korpel and De Moor themselves admit that the basis of their thesis is somewhat fragile. In fact, anyone who reads through the Ugaritic texts in question, say in Dennis Pardee's excellent edition,[23] will see how virtually everything in Korpel and De Moor's summary account given above is not explicitly in our preserved texts but has to be reconstructed in the gaps of the fragmentary text. For example, the idea that Horon wished to depose El and in consequence was thrown down from the mountain of the gods is pure supposition, based on what Korpel and De Moor think was referred to in a hypothetical missing tablet preceding *KTU*[3] 1.107. Again, it should be noted that though *KTU*[3] 1.100.65 refers to a 'tree of death', nothing in the actual text implies that this had been transformed from a tree of life. I would also note that the word *'adm*, which Korpel and De Moor understand as a reference to Adam, occurs only once in the whole of the preserved texts, in *KTU*[3] 1.107.3, and the only other reference to Adam that Korpel and De Moor find has to be reconstructed (*KTU*[3] 1.107.21). Korpel and De Moor also find a personal name *'adm* in *KTU*[3] 1.179.9, but this also requires textual reconstruction. Moreover, since *'adm* occurs everywhere else in Ugaritic simply as a word for 'man', rather than as a personal name, this is most likely the case here too (though, of course,

---

22. M.C.A. Korpel and J.C. de Moor, *Adam, Eve, and the Devil: A New Beginning* (Hebrew Bible Monographs, 65; Sheffield: Sheffield Phoenix Press, 2014). There was also a subsequent revised Dutch edition, *Adam, Eva en de Duivel: Kanaänitische Mythen en de Bijbel* (Vught: Skandalon, 2016). An earlier version of the rudiments of this thesis was put forward by De Moor in 'East of Eden', *ZAW* 100 (1988), pp. 105-11.

23. See D. Pardee, *Les textes para-mythologiques de la 24e campagne (1961)* (Ras Shamra-Ougarit, IV; Paris: Editions Recherche sur les Civilisations, 1988), pp. 193-226, 227-56; *idem, Ritual and Cult at Ugarit* (WBWSBL; Atlanta, GA: SBL, 2002), pp. 172-79, 179-91.

'*ādām* in Gen. 2–3 is also not a personal name, but that is another matter). As a consequence of all this, I do not feel we can have confidence in Korpel and De Moor's reconstruction, so it is unlikely that it lies behind Genesis 3. Accordingly, the Genesis serpent does not derive from the Canaanite god Horon. We cannot even be certain that Horon could take the form of a serpent.

I would, however, agree with Korpel and De Moor that the Canaanite god El was thought to dwell on a mountain in Armenia (not necessarily the mountain in the far east of Turkey called Mt Ararat since mediaeval times), and that this is the location of the Garden of Eden in Gen. 2.10-14, which derives from El's dwelling. The Ugaritic texts repeatedly speak of El's mountain dwelling as being 'at the source of the two rivers, amidst the source of the deeps' without indicating precisely where this was. The Canaanite–Hittite Elkunirsha myth, however, specifies that Elkunirsha (= El creator of the earth) dwelt at the source of the river Mala, i.e. the Hittite name of the river Euphrates.[24] This can only be the western end of the Euphrates in Armenia, which is mountainous, unlike the flat eastern end (cf. Ezek 28.13, 14, 16, where Eden is set on a mountain, though here seemingly in Phoenicia[25]). Similarly, in Gen. 2.10-14 the Garden of Eden is set in Armenia, since it is located at the source of four headwaters (*rā'šîm*), including the Tigris and Euphrates, both of which rise in Armenia.[26]

My third example is as follows. In 2015 Duane Smith[27] suggested that the Eden serpent could have a background in Mesopotamian ophiomancy, that is, divination based on the observation of serpents. He claims that God's mind (if not his will) is revealed through the Eden serpent, which provides a kind of analogy, if very imprecise, to the Mesopotamian practice of divining by means of serpents. In addition, he suggests that the

24. See *ANET*, p. 519.

25. Cf. too Ezek. 31.16, which refers to 'all the trees of Eden, the choicest and best of Lebanon', and Ezek. 31.8, which alludes to 'the cedars in the garden of God'. We may compare the dwelling of the gods on the cedar mountain forest in the Old Babylonian Ishchali version of the Gilgamesh epic, rev. line 38; see A.R. George, *The Babylonian Gilgamesh Epic: Introduction, Critical Edition and Cuneiform Texts*, I (2 vols.; Oxford: Oxford University Press, 2003), pp. 264-65. It was not a normal Mesopotamian viewpoint that gods dwelt on mountains, so this location surely represents a Canaanite viewpoint.

26. See Day, *From Creation to Babel*, pp. 27-32, on the location of Eden and the rivers flowing from it.

27. D.E. Smith, 'The Divining Snake: Reading Genesis 3 in the Context of Mesopotamian Ophiomancy', *JBL* 134 (2015), pp. 31-49.

word *'ārûm* used to denote the serpent in Gen. 3.1 means 'portentous' and that the knowledge of good and evil which the serpent encourages Adam and Eve to acquire refers to knowledge of good and bad fortune. However, I do not find any of this convincing. First, the word *'ārûm* never means 'portentous' but rather 'crafty' (or alternatively 'clever', though this is less appropriate here, as we have already seen above). Secondly, the parallels to the expression elsewhere in the Hebrew Bible indicate that 'knowledge of good and evil' means a state of maturity and ethical awareness of right and wrong, something which children acquire on growing up (cf. Deut. 1.39; Isa. 7.16, and below, Chapter 4), not knowledge of future good and bad fortune. Thirdly, the differences from Mesopotamian ophiomancy seem too great. Adam and Eve were not seeking out divinatory knowledge through observing the serpent but were being misled into temptation through the words of the serpent, which does not, in fact, convey the mind of God perfectly.

A fourth recent proposal is by Robert D. Miller,[28] who suggests that we should equate the Eden serpent with a chaos dragon. He does not specify precisely which one, but mentions Yam, Iluyanka, Aži Dahāka or Ḫedammu as possibilities. These are respectively Canaanite, Hittite, Persian and Hurrian, of which only Canaanite Yam seems culturally close enough to be a likely possibility. However, Yam was not actually a dragon; it was his associate, Leviathan, who is called a dragon,[29] though Miller assumes they were identical. Both dwelt in the sea, but whereas Yam seems to have had only one head, Leviathan had seven (contrast the one head of the serpent in Gen. 3.15). In any case, nothing that is said of the serpent in Genesis 3 is particularly suggestive of a chaos dragon. The Eden tempter is simply called a serpent or snake, not a dragon (*tannîn*), and it is already reduced to the lowest of creatures from the time of the beginning of humanity (Gen. 3.14), becoming the kind of snake that humans can tread on (Gen. 3.15). This does not sound like a chaos dragon.

28. Robert D. Miller, *The Dragon, the Mountain, and the Nations: An Old Testament Myth, its Origins, and its Afterlives* (University Park, PA: Eisenbrauns, 2018), pp. 202-208. A connection of the Eden serpent with the chaos serpent had earlier been proposed prior to this last decade by T.N.D. Mettinger, *The Eden Narrative: A Literary and Religio-Historical Study of Genesis 2–3* (Winona Lake, IN: Eisenbrauns, 2007), pp. 80-83, but unlike Miller he was thinking only in terms of Leviathan. Within the last decade a connection with the chaos serpent was also proposed by I. Provan, *Seriously Dangerous Religion: What the Old Testament Really Says and Why it Matters* (Waco, TX: Baylor University Press, 2014), pp. 110-11.

29. See Day, *God's Conflict with the Dragon and the* Sea, p. 14. Contrast Miller, *The Dragon, the Mountain, and the Nations*, p. 117.

Finally, I should briefly mention a fifth view put forward in 2010 by Walter R. Mattfeld, a self-styled amateur scholar, in his book *Eden's Serpent: Its Mesopotamian Origins*.[30] The most valuable part of this book is his thorough recounting of scholarly views on the origin of the Eden serpent from 1854–2010. However, his own positive proposals are unconvincing. He maintains that the Eden serpent is derived from no less than ten different Mesopotamian figures, including the deities Ea, Ningishzida, Dumuzi, Anu, Enlil, Marduk, Ishtar, Nergal, the hunter Sadu, and even the prostitute Shamhat! However, most of these have no connection with a serpent. Furthermore, this proposal seriously violates the principle of Occam's razor, according to which the simplest hypothesis is to be preferred.

If none of the above views are likely, is it still possible that the ancient Near Eastern background can shed light on the origin of the Eden serpent? Possibly it can. In tablet 11 of the Mesopotamian Gilgamesh epic (Standard Version) we read that it was a serpent[31] that snatched and ate the plant of life (lit. 'plant of heartbeat [or pulsating life]'[32]) which Gilgamesh had been seeking, thereby depriving Gilgamesh of rejuvenation and gaining it himself (Gilgamesh 11.305-307), just as it was a serpent that tempted Adam and Eve to eat of the forbidden fruit, thereby denying them access to the tree of life which granted immortality. But in addition to a life-depriving serpent and a life-giving plant or tree of life, both works imply that immortality in this life is beyond the grasp of humans. It is thus possible that the Garden of Eden narrative represents a reworking of similar elements in the Gilgamesh epic.[33] We have

30. W.R. Mattfeld, *Eden's Serpent: Its Mesopotamian Origins* (n.p.; Walter R. Mattfeld, 2010).

31. A.W. Sjöberg, 'Eve and the Chameleon', in W.B. Barrick and J.R. Spencer (eds.), *In the Shelter of Elyon: Essays on Ancient Palestinian Life and Literature in Honor of G.W. Ahlström* (JSOTSup, 31; Sheffield: JSOT Press, 1984), pp. 217-25 (221-23), claimed that the Gilgamesh epic and perhaps Gen. 3 referred to a chameleon rather than a serpent, but this view has rightly failed to gain acceptance.

32. Akkadian *šam-mu ni-kit-ti*. Cf. George, *The Babylonian Gilgamesh Epic*, II, pp. 895-96.

33. Apparently first suggested as a possibility by P. Jensen, *Die Kosmologie der Babylonier: Studien und Materiallen* (Strasbourg: Trübner, 1890), p. 227 n. 1. More recently its supporters have included S.G.F. Brandon, *Creation Legends of the Ancient Near East* (London: Hodder & Stoughton, 1963), pp. 130, 135, 139; J. Blenkinsopp, 'Gilgamesh and Adam: Wisdom through Experience in *Gilgamesh* and in the Biblical Story of the Man, the Woman, and the Snake', in *Treasures Old and New: Essays in the Theology of the Pentateuch* (Grand Rapids, MI: Eerdmans, 2004), pp. 85-101; Charlesworth, *The Good and Evil Serpent*, pp. 294-96.

evidence that the Gilgamesh epic was known in Palestine and the Levant from a Late Bronze Age fragment found at Megiddo (but originally from Gezer according to scientific analysis[34]), as well as other Late Bronze Age fragments discovered at Ugarit and Emar in Syria (not to mention a bit further away at Hattusha in Anatolia),[35] and even as late as the third century BCE we find in Eccl. 9.7-9 a virtual paraphrase of the words of the divine barmaid Shiduri in the Old Babylonian version of the Gilgamesh epic (10.3.6-14) about the purpose of life, with six parallels occurring in identical order.[36] (However, as I have argued elsewhere, I hold that the biblical flood story is dependent on Atrahasis rather than Gilgamesh.[37]) But if Genesis 3 is a reworking of Gilgamesh we must grant that it is a radical reworking, since the plant of life was a source of rejuvenation, not immortality,[38] and was to be found under water, as was the serpent, rather than on land. The dependence of Genesis 3 on the Gilgamesh epic must therefore remain an interesting possibility rather than a certainty. But even if the Eden narrative is not directly dependent on the Gilgamesh epic, the two works are utilizing some similar motifs.

Is there a Connection between the Serpent and Eve?

Already in antiquity some detected the similarity of the name Eve (*ḥawwâ*) and the Aramaic word for serpent, *ḥewyâ*. Thus, in *Genesis Rabbah* 20 we read, 'the serpent is your [Eve's] serpent and you are Adam's serpent'.

34. Y. Goren, H. Mommsen, I. Finkelstein and N. Na'aman, 'A Provenance Study of the Gilgamesh Fragment from Megiddo', *Archaeometry* 51 (2009), pp. 763-73.

35. See George, *The Babylonian Gilgamesh Epic*, I, pp. 306-47.

36. See J. Day, 'Foreign Semitic Influence on the Wisdom of Israel and its Appropriation in the Book of Proverbs', in J. Day, R.P. Gordon and H.G.M. Williamson (eds.), *Wisdom in Ancient Israel: Essays in Honour of J.A. Emerton* (Cambridge: Cambridge University Press, 1995), pp. 55-70 (59-60).

37. See J. Day, 'The Biblical Flood Narrative in Relation to Ancient Near Eastern Flood Accounts', in K.J. Dell and P.M. Joyce (eds.), *Biblical Interpretation and Method: Essays in Honour of Professor John Barton* (Oxford: Oxford University Press, 2013), pp. 74-78, reprinted in Day, *From Creation to Babel*, pp. 98-112.

38. Although not all Old Testament scholars seem fully aware of this, most Assyriologists are generally agreed about this. Cf. W.G. Lambert, 'Trees, Snakes and Gods in Ancient Syria and Anatolia', *BSOAS* 48 (1985), pp. 435-51 (440 n. 34). Note Gilgamesh 11.298-300, where Gilgamesh says of the plant, 'I will feed some to an old man and put the plant to the test. Its (or his) name will be "The old man has grown young", I will eat some myself and go back to how I was in my youth!"' However, even though the plant offered simply rejuvenation, it is quite clear that, following the death of Enkidu, Gilgamesh was actually on a quest for immortality.

But this is simply a word play on the name of Eve, implying that just as the serpent seduced Eve, so Eve seduced Adam, acting like the serpent. Again, although it has sometimes been claimed that Philo of Alexandria in *De Agricultura Noe* 21-22 explains the name Eve as meaning 'serpent',[39] this is not the case: he clearly takes it to mean 'life' but allegorically speaks of Eve's serpent as denoting pleasure.[40] However, in the nineteenth century certain scholars such as T. Nöldeke and J. Wellhausen[41] actually went so far as to suggest that Eve was originally a serpent goddess, and subsequently M. Lidzbarski and H. Gressmann[42] argued that the goddess in question, *Ḥwt*, was an underworld serpent goddess. Impetus for this latter view was given by the publication by Lidzbarski[43] in 1902 of a third- or second-century BCE Punic text from Carthage, which appeared to mention 'Lady *Ḥwt*, goddess, queen'. Although *Ḥwt* may be an underworld serpent goddess here, since inscriptions of this type tend to involve underworld deities, there is nothing in the text of Genesis to suggest that Eve had such an origin.

More recently, Howard Wallace[44] has claimed that *Ḥwt* (which he thinks means either 'life' or 'serpent') is an epithet of the goddess Tannit, which, following F.M. Cross, he thinks means '(the one of) the serpent' and whom he equates with Asherah. Furthermore, Wallace argues that it is this goddess who ultimately lies behind the figure of Eve. However, this whole train of thought is highly speculative. First, the name Tannit is unlikely to mean 'the one of the Serpent'. Tannin means 'dragon' or 'serpent' and the feminine form of this, if it were to exist, would be expected to be Tannin(i)t, not Tannit, which in any case would be expected to mean 'female dragon or serpent', not 'the one of the Serpent'.

39. J. Wellhausen, *Prolegomena zur Geschichte Israels* (Berlin: G. Reimer, 2nd edn, 1883), p. 324 n. 1, ET *Prolegomena to the History of Israel* (trans. J.S. Black and A. Menzies; Edinburgh: A. & C. Black, 1885), p. 308 n. 1.

40. So rightly A.J. Williams, 'The Relationship of Genesis 3 20 to the Serpent', *ZAW* 89 (1977), pp. 357-74 (360-61).

41. T. Nöldeke, review of F. Baethgen, *Beiträge zur semitischen Religionsgeschichte*, in *ZDMG* 42 (1888), pp. 470-87 (487); Wellhausen, *Prolegomena zur Geschichte Israels*, p. 324 n. 1, ET *Prolegomena to the History of Israel*, p. 308 n. 1.

42. M. Lidzbarski, 'Eine punische *tabella devotionis*', in his *Ephemeris für semitische Epigraphik* (Giessen: J. Ricker, 1902), pp. 26-34 (30); H. Gressmann, 'Mythische Reste in der Paradieserzählung', *ArRel* 10 (1907), pp. 345-67 (357-61).

43. M. Lidzbarski, 'Eine punische *tabella devotionis*', pp. 26-34. For a more recent edition of this text, see *KAI* 89.

44. H.N. Wallace, *The Eden Narrative* (HSM, 32; Atlanta, GA: Scholars Press, 1985), pp. 147-61.

Secondly, Tannit was the wife of Baal-Ḥammon, whom there is good reason to see as a form of Baal rather than El,[45] so Tannit may be more analogous to Astarte (with whom she is actually equated in an inscription from Sarepta[46]), rather than Asherah, and there is no compelling reason to associate Eve with Asherah.

We do not know for certain what the etymology of the name Eve was. Although 'serpent' is not impossible (cf. the Hebrew personal name Nahash with this meaning), there is nothing in particular to encourage such a view. Certainly the current biblical text shows no awareness of it. Genesis 3.20 declares, 'The man called his wife's name Eve, because she was the mother of all living (*ḥay*)'. This suggests a connection with the verb 'to live'. Most likely, as Scott Layton has suggested,[47] the meaning derives from the piel of *ḥwh* (*ḥwy*), an older form of *ḥyh*, 'to live', the piel meaning 'cause to live', a form attested in Ugaritic, Phoenician and Punic. Although J's etymologies are typically unscientific and often appear forced, in this instance 'life-giver' is rather appropriate for the ancestress of the human race, and certainly more plausible than some other sugges- tions for the meaning of Eve's name, such as 'tent dweller', 'Hivite' or the Hurrian goddess Ḥepat.[48]

The Serpent and the Divine Name

In the interaction between the serpent and Eve in Gen. 3.1-5, which has been called 'the first conversation *about* God' (Dietrich Bonhoeffer[49]), the serpent uses the general word Elohim for God, and this is taken up by Eve in the ensuing discussion. As its name betokens, the Yahwist source generally uses Yahweh for the divine name, and throughout the Garden of Eden story except here we find the combined form Yahweh Elohim (seemingly the work of a redactor making clear the identity of the Yahweh of Gen. 2–3 with the Elohim of Gen. 1). Why, therefore, should we find just Elohim here? Among the suggestions that have been made are that the

45. See the arguments in J. Day, *Molech: A God of Human Sacrifice in the Old Testament* (UCOP, 41; Cambridge: Cambridge University Press, 1989), pp. 37-40.

46. See J.B. Pritchard, *Recovering Sarepta: A Phoenician City* (Princeton, NJ: Princeton University Press, 1978), pp. 104-106.

47. S. Layton, 'Remarks on the Canaanite Origin of Eve', *CBQ* 59 (1997), pp. 22-32.

48. *HALOT*, I, p. 296, lists seven possibilities altogether. Cf. Vriezen, *Onderzoek*, pp. 192-93; J. Heller, 'Der Name *Eva*', *ArOr* 26 (1958), pp. 634-56.

49. D. Bonhoeffer, *Schöpfung und Fall* (Munich: Chr. Kaiser Verlag, 1933), p. 63, ET *Creation and Fall* (London: SCM Press, 1959), p. 70.

serpent was keeping its distance from Yahweh or that it was felt inappropriate by the writer for one giving evil counsel to mention God's personal name,[50] but neither of these suggestions seems very plausible. What needs to be noted is that, while Yahweh is found throughout the J narrative, there are occasions of speeches of individuals in J, in addition to Gen. 3.1-5, in which Elohim occurs, including Gen. 4.25; 9.27; 27.28. But why should the serpent and Eve avoid the name Yahweh in this particular passage, Gen. 3.1-5? It would seem plausible to suppose that the reason is that the specific name Yahweh had not yet been revealed. This would be consistent with the fact that Gen. 4.26 states it was not till the days of Enosh that people started calling on the name of Yahweh. In keeping with that, Eve still uses the word Elohim just prior to this in Gen. 4.25, declaring 'God has set in place[51] another child for me instead of Abel, because Cain killed him'. It might be objected that the name Yahweh is already known to Eve in Gen. 4.1 and that Cain and Abel are said to have brought offerings to Yahweh (Gen. 4.3-4). However, this may be countered by pointing out that the Cain narrative, in which these references occur, must originally have been set in a later context, since unlike the current context, it presupposes that there were other people around who might slay Cain (Gen. 4.14-15), as well as women from whom Cain could acquire a wife (Gen. 4.17). As I argue below in Chapter 5, it is a later addition to the original Yahwistic narrative, as many previously have also detected.

The So-Called Protoevangelium in Genesis 3.15

As noted earlier, the serpent was eventually cursed by God for tempting the woman into disobeying him, and is destined to become the lowest of wild beats, crawling on its belly (Gen. 3.14). In so doing it is said to eat dust (cf. Mic. 7.17; Isa. 65.25), though serpents do not actually do so, but merely appear to. At the conclusion of the cursing of the serpent in Gen. 3.15 God declares to the serpent, 'I will put enmity between you and the woman, and between your offspring and her offspring; they shall strike your head, and you will strike their heel'. In its original meaning, cohering with the character of Gen. 3.14-19 as an aetiology of the state of the world as the Israelites knew it, this is clearly referring to the enmity between snakes and human beings, with snakes biting the heels of human

50. For these two views see respectively P.J. Titus, *The Second Story of Creation (Gen 2:4–3:24): A Prologue to the Concept of the Enneateuch?* (European University Studies, 23.912; Frankfurt: Peter Lang, 2011), p. 326; Cassuto, *Genesis*, I, p. 88.

51. Or 'appointed', but 'set' (Hebrew *šāt*) preserves the Hebrew word play on the name of Seth (*šēt*).

beings and humans treading on snakes' heads. The same Hebrew verb
(*šûp*) is used for both humans treading on the head of the serpent and for
the serpent biting the heels of humans. The traditional rendering 'bruise'
(AV, RV, RSV) does not seem quite appropriate for the latter action. The
best way to reproduce the meaning of the Hebrew here is to render by
'strike' or 'strike at' in both places, as it is appropriate for the action of
both humans and snakes, as several modern Bible translations recognize
(NRSV, NEB, REB, NAB). The same Hebrew verb is used in Job 9.17,
where Job complains of God, 'For he *crushes* me with a tempest, and
multiplies my wounds without cause'. In Exod. 32.20 this verb means 'to
grind'. All this is in keeping with the parallel Aramaic verb *šûp*, which
means 'to pound, crush, grind'. Since 'to pound' means 'to strike heavily
or repeatedly', translating the verb *šûp* in Gen. 3.15 as 'strike' or 'strike
at' seems quite appropriate. Anyway, what is here translated 'they shall
strike' is literally 'he shall strike', the 'he' being a collective singular,
referring to Eve's offspring or seed (Hebrew *zera‘*, a masculine word).
There is no indication that one side would be victorious over the other in
the ongoing hostilities (even if striking the head sounds more severe than
striking the heel), and an eschatological meaning would be completely
out of place in this aetiological context. However, for centuries a popular
Christian understanding of these words understood them as a prediction
of Christ's victory over Satan, a view first attested *c.* 180 CE in Irenaeus's
Against Heresies 3.23.7 and 5.21.1. This passage of Genesis thus became
known as the *Protoevangelium*, the first declaration of the Gospel. While
this is an interpretation that very few serious scholars today would
entertain, this passage is still read out at some Christmas services with the
traditional understanding in view, for example, at the annual service of
carols and lessons from King's College, Cambridge.[52]

It has, however, been suggested by R.A. Martin that the Greek
Septuagint in the third century BCE, which rendered 'he will watch
your head, and you will watch his heel', already equated the 'he' with
the Messiah, in which case this would be the earliest known Messianic
interpretation of Gen. 3.15.[53] The evidence presented for this view is

---

52. For a useful historical survey of the *Protoevangelium* interpretation throughout the centuries, see J.P. Lewis, 'The Woman's Seed (Gen 3:15)', *JETS* 34 (1991),
pp. 299-319.

53. R.A. Martin, 'The Earliest Messianic Interpretation of Genesis 3 15', *JBL* 84
(1965), pp. 425-27. J. Becker also thinks this is possible; see his *Messiaserwartung
im Alten Testament* (SBS, 83; Stuttgart: Katholisches Bibelwerk, 1977), p. 29, ET
Messianic Expectation in the Old Testament (trans. D.E. Green; Edinburgh: T. & T.
Clark, 1980), p. 35.

that the Septuagint still speaks of 'he', although rendering 'offspring' or 'seed' by the Greek word *sperma*, which is neuter, despite the fact that everywhere else in the Septuagint of Genesis the Hebrew word *hû'*, 'he', is translated by a word of the appropriate gender in Greek, whether *autos*, 'he', *aute*, 'she', or *auto*, 'it'. The Septuagint's 'he', it has therefore been argued, most naturally does not refer to Eve's offspring generally but to a specific masculine individual and it has been proposed that this is the Messiah. There is, however, a problem with this view. This is that it would be remarkable if the Septuagint understood the 'he' as referring to the Messiah, when such an understanding is completely lacking in subsequent Jewish understanding of the verse. Even though the fulfilment of Gen. 3.15 in the Messianic age is attested several centuries later in the Neofiti, Pseudo-Jonathan and Fragment Targums, the 'he' is there still interpreted collectively (of the righteous Jews) and not of the Messiah.[54] In the light of all this it seems more likely that the Septuagint's 'he' is simply an over-literal translation of the Hebrew.[55] Nevertheless, the idea of the *Protoevangelium* did eventually emerge from it in the early church.[56]

Finally, it is interesting to note that in Gen. 3.15 the Latin Vulgate reads 'she' (*ipsa*) rather than 'he' (*ipse*) for whoever is to strike the head of the serpent. This is surprising, since Jerome was generally very concerned to adhere closely to the original Hebrew in his Vulgate translation. Indeed, in his *Quaestiones Hebraicae in Genesim*, when commenting on Gen. 3.15, Jerome clearly presupposes the reading *ipse*, 'he', and makes no reference to the *ipsa*, 'she', reading. The 'she' of the Vulgate must therefore be seen as a later scribal alteration of the text, probably undertaken by someone who felt it more appropriate that the one striking the head of the serpent (Satan) should be equated with Eve, who has just been mentioned earlier in the verse as being at enmity with the serpent. However, many mediaeval and later exegetes within the Roman Catholic

---

54. See M. McNamara, *The New Testament and the Palestinian Targum to the Pentateuch* (AnBib, 27; Rome: Pontifical Biblical Institute, 1966), pp. 217-21.

55. J.W. Wevers, *Notes on the Greek Text of Genesis* (SBLSCS, 35; Atlanta, GA: Scholars Press, 1993), p. 44, likewise understands the LXX's 'he' as not referring to a literal individual but prefers to put it this way: 'What the translator has done is to personify the seed, i.e. the αὐτός is an ad sensum reference to the seed, not as a collective but as individual offspring of the woman. The sense of the Greek would be better conveyed by the plural: "they shall carefully watch your head".'

56. Modern critical scholars generally reject the Messianic interpretation of Gen. 3.15. It is, however, still defended by A.O. Ojewole, *The Seed in Genesis 3:15* (Berrien Springs, MI: Adventist Theological Society, 2002).

Church subsequently understood the Vulgate's 'she' as referring to the Virgin Mary, who is to join with Jesus in vanquishing the serpent Satan.[57] However, modern Catholic critical scholars now rightly reject this understanding of Gen. 3.15 and follow the Hebrew text (cf. NAB, JB, NJB).

57. See T. Gallus, *Interpretatio Mariologica Protoevangelii* (3 vols.; Rome: Edizioni di storia e letteratura, 1949–54); cf. *idem, Die "Frau" in Gen 3,15* (Klagenfurt: Carinthia, 1979).

Chapter 4

WISDOM AND THE GARDEN OF EDEN

The Two Special Trees in the Garden of Eden
and the Meaning of the Knowledge of Good and Evil

One way of reading the story of the Garden of Eden is to see it as explaining how it came to be that the first humans acquired a degree of wisdom but were deprived of the chance of immortality (in this life). Wisdom and immortality are symbolized by two trees, the tree of the knowledge of good and evil (wisdom) and the tree of life (immortality), the first humans eating of the former but eventually being deprived of the latter. This reminds one of the Babylonian myth of Adapa, the first sage, who similarly obtained wisdom but not immortality.[1] As one of the first lines of the text declares, 'To him he (Ea) gave wisdom, he did not give him eternal life' (Adapa A, col. 1, line 4).[2] Moreover, just as with the first humans in Eden, so Adapa's fate has repercussions for humanity generally. This is made clear by the god Anu's words immediately after Adapa's refusal to eat the bread of life and drink the water of life offered to him (in keeping with the god Ea's misleading advice to him[3]), 'Come,

---

1. There does not appear to be any etymological connection between Adam and Adapa, contrary to what has occasionally been claimed, e.g. by Layton, 'Remarks on the Canaanite Origin of Eve', pp. 30-31.

2. Cf. S. Izre'el, *Adapa and the South Wind: Language has the Power of Life and Death* (Winona Lake, IN: Eisenbrauns, 2001), pp. 10-11. However, a different recension of the myth in fragment D may imply that Adapa was allowed to stay in heaven. See Izre'el, *Adapa*, pp. 38-39, 42.

3. Probably it was Ea rather than Anu who was tricking Adapa, since Ea was noted for his craftiness. See T.N.D. Mettinger, *The Eden Narrative: A Literary and Religio-Historical Study of Genesis 2–3* (Winona Lake, IN: Eisenbrauns, 2007), pp. 99-107.

Adapa, why did you not eat or drink! Hence you shall not live. Alas for inferior humanity' (Adapa B, lines 67-68).[4] It is therefore entirely natural that we find two special trees in the Garden of Eden, one symbolizing wisdom and the other representing immortality, and attempts to claim that there was originally only one (usually the tree of knowledge) are unnecessary.[5]

Whereas the meaning of the tree of life is clear – its fruit conveyed immortality,[6] reminding one of the plant of life (lit. 'plant of heart beat [or pulsating life]') in the Babylonian Gilgamesh epic (which is said to look like a box-thorn, Gilgamesh 11.283-84), which conveyed rejuvenation – the precise meaning of the tree of the knowledge of good and evil is debated. That the tree of knowledge bestowed wisdom of some

---

4. Cf. Izre'el, *Adapa*, pp. 20-21.

5. K. Budde, *Die biblische Urgeschichte (Gen. 1–12,5)* (Giessen: J. Ricker, 1883), pp. 46-65, and others following him have claimed that the references to the tree of life are secondary, both in Gen. 2.9 and 3.22, 24, but most recent scholars have defended their authenticity as crucial to the story, e.g. Mettinger, *The Eden Narrative*, pp. 5-11. However, in Gen. 2.9, superficially it may sound rather as if the tree of knowledge is an addition, but few scholars advocate that. Moreover, long ago S.R. Driver, 'Grammatical Notes. I. On Genesis II., 9b', *Hebraica* 2 (1885), p. 33 pointed out that *we*, 'and' can also mean 'as also'. So we can translate, 'Out of the ground the Lord God caused to grow ... and the tree of life in the middle of the garden, as also the tree of the knowledge of good and evil'. Driver further notes that it would have been 'inelegant and heavy' to have written 'and in the middle of the garden the tree of life and the tree of the knowledge of good and evil' or 'and the tree of life and the tree of the knowledge of good and evil in the middle of the garden'. The fact that Eve later refers only to the tree of knowledge as 'the tree that is in the middle of the garden' (Gen. 3.3) does not mean that it is the only tree there; rather it is the tree to which God has specifically drawn attention as forbidden.

Nick Wyatt, 'A Royal Garden: The Ideology of Eden', pp. 19-20 claims that even the Eden narrative as we now have it has only one special tree, since he equates the tree of life with the tree of knowledge by finding explicative *waw* in Gen. 2.9: 'the tree of life in the middle of the garden, that is, the tree of knowing all things'. But it is quite clear that the first humans had eaten of the tree of knowledge but were cast out of Eden so they could not eat of the tree of life too. It is therefore impossible to equate them. Wyatt also fails to explain why the same tree should be called by different names in different parts of the narrative.

6. For a wide-ranging study of the tree of life, ranging from ancient Near Eastern literature and iconography, through the Bible and centuries of reception history, right up to modern theology, see the valuable collection of essays in D. Estes (ed.), *The Tree of Life* (Themes in Biblical Literature, 27; Leiden: Brill, 2020). See too M. Bauks, 'Sacred Trees in the Garden of Eden and their Ancient Near Eastern Precursors', *JAJ* 3 (2012), pp. 267-301.

kind is made clear by Gen. 3.6, which states that 'the woman saw ... that the tree was to be desired to make one wise (*lᵉhaśkîl*)'. Eve's awareness of this follows on from the words of the serpent, 'your eyes will be opened, and you will be like gods,[7] knowing good and evil' (Gen. 3.6). However, there is debate as to the precise nature of this wisdom. Three main views have been advanced by modern scholars about the nature of the knowledge of good and evil. These are (1) that it alludes to the ethical discernment of good and evil and associated maturity;[8] (2) that it means omniscience, knowledge of everything, 'good and evil' constituting a merism;[9] and (3) that the knowledge referred to is sexual knowledge.[10] In this connection Engnell regarded it specifically as knowledge of procreation.[11]

Option 3 is the easiest to refute. It is true that the verb 'to know' can be used of carnal knowledge, as in Gen. 4.1, 'Now the man knew Eve, his wife, and she conceived and bore Cain ...' However, there is no evidence from anywhere in the Hebrew Bible that the phrase 'knowledge of good and evil' was ever used to denote simply sexual knowledge. Robert Gordis[12] attempted to show that it could have this meaning by appealing

---

7. Elohim is more likely 'gods' than 'God' here: this has the support of all the ancient Versions as well as Gen. 3.22, where God subsequently declares, 'See, the man has become like *one of us*, knowing good and evil', referring to the heavenly court as well as to God himself.

8. E.g. Budde, *Die biblische Urgeschichte*, pp. 65-70; S.R. Driver, *Genesis*, p. 41; J. Barr, *The Garden of Eden and the Hope of Immortality* (London: SCM Press, 1992), p. 62; R. Albertz, '„Ihr werdet sein wie Gott". Gen 3, 1-7 auf dem Hintergrund des alttestamentlichen und des sumerisch-babylonischen Menschenbildes', *WO* 24 (1993), pp. 89-111 (91-96); Zevit, *What Really Happened in the Garden of Eden?*, p. 264.

9. E.g. P. Humbert, *Etudes sur le récit du Paradis et de la chute dans la Genèse* (Neuchâtel: Secrétariat de l'université, 1940), pp. 82-94, 113-14; von Rad, *Das erste Buch Mose*, p. 65, ET *Genesis*, p. 79; Wallace, *The Eden Narrative*, pp. 115-30; C.H. Gordon and G.A. Rendsburg, *The Bible and the Ancient Near East* (New York: W.W. Norton, 4th edn, 1997), p. 36.

10. E.g. H. Schmidt, *Die Erzählung von Paradies und Sündenfall* (Tübingen: J.C.B. Mohr [Paul Siebeck], 1931), pp. 26-28; J. Coppens, *La connaissance du bien et du mal et le péché du Paradis* (Gembloux: J. Duculot, 1948), *passim*; B. Reicke, 'The Knowledge Hidden in the Tree of Paradise', *JSS* 1 (1956), pp. 193-202; R. Gordis, 'The Knowledge of Good and Evil in the Old Testament and the Qumran Scrolls', *JBL* 76 (1957), pp. 123-38; L. Hartman, 'Sin in Paradise', *CBQ* 20 (1958), pp. 26-40.

11. I. Engnell 1955), '"Knowledge" and "Life" in the Creation Story', in M. Noth and D.W. Thomas (eds.), *Wisdom in Israel and in the Ancient Near East Presented to Professor Harold Henry Rowley* (VTSup, 3; Leiden: Brill), pp. 103-19 (116).

12. Gordis, 'The Knowledge of Good and Evil', pp. 136-37.

to the Qumran text 1QSa 1.9-11, 'He shall not approach a woman to have intercourse with her until he has attained the age of twenty when he knows good and evil'. However, knowledge of good and evil is here the precondition for sexual intercourse, not a consequence of it, and clearly refers to a state of maturity generally, thereby supporting option 1 (see below). Moreover, the view that the tree of knowledge conveyed simply sexual knowledge is also unlikely on the grounds that the man and woman are already implied to be one flesh in Gen. 2.24, the aetiology of marriage and sexual union being given at this point, before the knowledge of good and evil is acquired in Genesis 3. Again, God, whom the first humans become like after acquiring the knowledge of good and evil (Gen. 3.22), is not a sexual being in the view of the biblical writers.[13] But one can understand how the view arose that it referred to sexual knowledge, since we are informed that after the human couple had eaten of the tree they became aware of their nakedness. T.L. Thompson's view[14] that knowledge of their nakedness is all they learnt is surely inadequate, since it would be very strange for this thing alone to make them like God or the gods! Rather the consciousness of nakedness must be simply one aspect of some greater awareness, as we shall see presently.[15]

Anyway, the notion that the tree of knowledge conveyed wisdom has sometimes led to the second view, the idea that the wisdom conveyed omniscience. This view tends to assume that 'good and evil' are a merism, 'good and evil' together denoting the totality of things. This meaning is found, for example, in Gen. 24.50; 31.24, 29, but it is never attested with the verb 'to know' with this meaning. However, it might be supposed that this view can be supported by extrapolating 2 Sam. 14.17 and 20. In 2 Sam. 14.17 the wise woman of Tekoa flatters King David by saying

---

13. Admittedly the sons of God in Gen. 6.1-4 participate in sexual intercourse, but this is never said of Yahweh himself in the Old Testament.

14. T.L. Thompson, *The Bible in History: How Writers Create a Past* (London: Jonathan Cape, 1999), p. 86; also published as *The Mythic Past: Biblical Archaeology and the Myth of Israel* (New York: Basic Books, 1999), p. 86.

15. It has sometimes been argued that support for the sexual interpretation is provided by the Gilgamesh epic, e.g. by Gordis, 'The Knowledge of Good and Evil', pp. 134-35. After Gilgamesh's companion Enkidu has had sexual intercourse with a prostitute, the latter says (on a hitherto common translation), 'You are wise (*[en]-qa-ta*), Enkidu, like a god' (Gilgamesh 1.207). The assumption has been that being introduced to civilization by the prostitute has made him wise like a god. However, it has become clear that the more likely rendering is 'You are handsome (*[dam]-qa-ta*), Enkidu, like a god' (cf. *CAD* D: 70b; George, *The Babylonian Gilgamesh Epic*, I, p. 551), since in Babylonian Akkadian 'you are wise' should be *en-qē-ta*.

that he 'is like the angel of God, discerning good and evil', while in 2 Sam. 14.20 she declares that he has 'wisdom like the wisdom of the angel of God to know all things that are on the earth'. However, these are clearly complementary, not identical things. Whereas the latter does indeed exaggeratingly ascribe omniscience to David, following David's expression of his justified suspicion to the wise woman of Tekoa that Joab was behind her attempt to get Absalom freed from banishment, the former more naturally refers to the king's fine moral judgment. This was important for his judicial role, which makes sense here in a context in which the wise woman of Tekoa has just been attempting to persuade David to make the right decision regarding Absalom. This meaning is further illustrated by 1 Kgs 3.9, where Solomon specifically prays for wisdom to discern between good and evil so that he might be able to judge God's people (cf. 1 Kgs 3.11, 28).

It might be argued that the idea that the first man was omniscient can claim support from Job 15.7-8 and Ezek. 28.12 (cf. v. 3), which suggest that he was superlatively wise (for more on which, see below). However, if so here, it would be completely out of keeping with everything else that transpires in Genesis 3, where aetiologies are provided of the state of humanity as the Israelites actually knew it, which was not at all omniscient.[16] So while this view may well represent one strand of understanding of the first man in ancient Israel, it cannot represent the viewpoint of the author of Genesis 3, where it would be out of place.

So this brings us to the first view, the idea that the tree of knowledge conveyed the ability to distinguish ethically between good and evil. This acquisition may be seen as symbolizing the wisdom of a mature adult as opposed to a child, as already noted in the Qumran text 1QSa 1.9-11 above. Compare Deut. 1.39, which refers to 'your children who as yet do not know good and evil', with Isa. 7.16, which explicates the meaning of this with the words 'Before the child knows how to refuse the evil and choose the good ...' In keeping with this, the 80-year-old

---

16. It may be for this reason that some scholars attempt to redefine 'knowledge of everything' to mean not literal 'omniscience' but rather simply the general knowledge that early humans actually had. For example, R.A. Oden, 'Divine Aspirations in Atrahasis and in Genesis 1–11', *ZAW* 93 (1981), pp. 197-216 (211-13), takes it to refer in particular to the cultural knowledge that developed in the subsequent chapters of Genesis. But if Adam and Eve already had all this knowledge, it is surprising that it took so many further generations to take effect (cf. Gen. 4.17, 20-22, 26; 9.20-21). Also, it is doubtful that the first two humans' general knowledge, or specifically cultural knowledge, could in any meaningful way be called 'knowledge of everything' in the way that the merism view requires.

Barzillai declares, 'I am now eighty years old. Can I distinguish between good and evil? Can your servant taste what he eats or drinks, or still appreciate the voices of singers and songstresses?' (2 Sam. 19.36, ET 35). We recognize here what has been called second childhood! If the knowledge of good and evil refers to the wisdom of a mature adult, this would explain why the first humans became aware of their nakedness in contrast to their previous childlike state of innocence (Gen. 3.10; contrast 2.25). Some Church Fathers such as Theophilus of Antioch and Irenaeus already envisaged Adam and Eve as being children,[17] a view also shared by modern scholars such as H. Gunkel.[18] However, L. Bechtel[19] surely goes too far in her analysis in claiming that Gen. 2.7-9 specifically depicts infancy, 2.16-23 early and middle childhood, 3.1-19 adolescence, and 3.20-24 the transition to adulthood. Rather there seems to be but one transition from childlike innocence to a state of mature adult wisdom, even though they had not literally been children.

Anyway, the view that the acquisition of the knowledge of good and evil refers to the ability to distinguish between good and evil, and human maturity more generally, has the distinct advantage of taking the phrase 'knowledge of good and evil' in the sense that it is employed elsewhere in the Old Testament. However, it raises the question why God should want humans to remain ignorant of basic, mature wisdom. Elsewhere in the Old Testament the acquisition of wisdom is thought of as a good thing, as throughout the book of Proverbs, for example (even if the limits of wisdom are also recognized; cf. Prov. 15.3; 16.1, 9; 19.21; 20.24; 21.30). Indeed, in the light of the Old Testament as a whole, it is difficult to see why God should want humans to remain ignorant of the knowledge of good and evil for ever. The most likely explanation is that God disapproves of the first humans acquiring the knowledge of good and evil by the assertion of their human autonomy in disobedience to his explicit command not to eat of the tree of knowledge.[20] Rather this knowledge

17. So Theophilus of Antioch, *Ad Autolycum* 2.24-25; Irenaeus, *Adversus haereses* 3.22.4-5; 4.38.1-2; *Epideixis* 12, 14. Cf. M.C. Steenberg, 'Children in Paradise: Adam and Eve as "Infants" in Irenaeus of Lyons', *Journal of Early Christian Studies* 12 (2004), pp. 1-22.

18. Gunkel, *Genesis*, p. 30, ET *Genesis*, p. 30.

19. L.M. Bechtel, 'Genesis 2.4b–3.24: A Myth about Human Maturation', *JSOT* 67 (1995), pp. 3-26.

20. W.A.M. Clark, 'A Legal Background to the Yahwist's Use of "Good and Evil" in Genesis 2–3', *JBL* 88 (1969), pp. 266-78 (277); J. Van Seters, *Prologue to History: The Yahwist as Historian in Genesis* (Louisville: Westminster/John Knox, 1992), pp. 126, 133 n. 71.

should be acquired through humble obedience to God. 'The fear of the Lord is the beginning of knowledge/wisdom', as Prov. 1.7 and 9.10 later assert. We are reminded of the words of Jesus in Mt. 18.3-4, where he declares, 'Truly I tell you, unless you turn and become like children, you will never enter the kingdom of heaven. Whoever humbles himself like this child is the greatest in the kingdom of heaven.'[21]

Wisdom and the Man in Eden in Ezekiel 28

Ezekiel 28.12-19 and Genesis 2–3 sound like different versions of the same myth.[22] The variant account in Ezekiel occurs as part of the prophet's oracle against the king of Tyre:

> You were the signet[23] of perfection,
> full of wisdom and perfect in beauty.
> You were in Eden, the garden of God;
> every precious stone was your covering,
> carnelian, chrysolite, and moonstone,
> beryl, onyx, and jasper,
> sapphire, turquoise, and emerald;
> and worked in gold were your settings
> and your engravings.
> On the day that you were created
> they were prepared.
> With[24] an anointed cherub as guardian I placed you;[25]
> you were on the holy mountain of God;
> you walked among the stones of fire.
> You were blameless in your ways
> from the day that you were created,
> until iniquity was found in you.

21. Cf. Skinner, *Genesis*, pp. 96-97.

22. The myth in Ezek. 28.12-19 has also sometimes been equated with that in Isa. 14.12-15, but they are certainly different myths. Whereas the figure of Ezek. 28 is human, perfect until the time of his fall, and dwells on the sacred mountain from the beginning, the figure of Isa. 14.12-15 is a star (even if used to symbolize the king of Babylon), arrogant from the beginning, and fails in its goal of ascending the sacred mountain so as to rival the deity.

23. Reading *ḥôtam* with a few MSS, LXX, Aquila, Peshitta and Vulgate for MT *ḥôtem*.

24. Reading *'et* with LXX and Peshitta for MT *'att*. See the discussion in the main body of this chapter.

25. Reading *ûnᵉtattîkā* with LXX and Arabic version for MT *nᵉtattîkā*.

In the abundance of your trade
you were filled[26] with violence, and you sinned;
so I cast you as a profane thing from the mountain of God,
and the guardian cherub drove you out[27]
from among the stones of fire.
Your heart was proud because of your beauty;
you corrupted your wisdom for the sake of your splendour.
I cast you to the ground;
I exposed you before kings,
to feast their eyes on you.
By the multitude of your iniquities,
in the unrighteousness of your trade,
you profaned your sanctuaries.
So I brought out fire within you;
it consumed you,
and I turned you to ashes on the earth
in the sight of all who saw you.
All who know you among the peoples are appalled at you;
you have come to a dreadful end
and you shall be no more for ever.

In both Ezekiel 28 and Genesis 2–3 we read of a man who was in the Garden of Eden, but who was subsequently cast out by God because of disobedience.[28] In Gen. 3.24 the cherubim guard the way to the tree of life after the man's expulsion, while in Ezek. 28.16 it is a cherub who

---

26. Reading *millē'tā* with LXX and Peshitta for MT *mālû*, the *t* having fallen out through haplography with the *t* at the beginning of the following word.

27. Reading *wᵉ'ibbadᵉkā* for MT *wā'abbedᵉkā*.

28. Some scholars in recent years have argued that there is no sin in Gen. 3 because the word is not used there, e.g. Barr, *The Garden of Eden*, p. 6; K. Schmid, 'The Ambivalence of Wisdom: Genesis 2–3 as a Sapiential Text', in S.C. Jones and C.R. Yoder (eds.), *"When the Morning Stars Sang": Essays in Honor of Choon Leong Seow on the Occasion of his Sixty-fifth Birthday* (BZAW, 500; Berlin: W. de Gruyter, 2018), pp. 275-86 (280, 283-84; not present in the German redaction of this article); M.S. Smith, *The Genesis of Good and Evil: The Fall(out) and Original Sin in the Bible* (Louisville, KY: Westminster/John Knox, 2019), pp. 35-38 and *passim*. However, one can surely have the concept of sin without the word, and if sin is understood as disobedience to God it manifestly is present, since the couple transgressed the explicit command of the deity, and the subsequent divine punishments meted out on the humans also imply it. If one were simply to judge the presence of sin within Gen. 1–11 by the occurrence of the word, it would be confined to the story of Cain (Gen. 4.7), which would be ridiculous. One should also note that in Ezek. 28.16 it is explicitly stated that the man in Eden 'sinned', and v. 15 declares that 'iniquity' was found in him. Of course, from a modern perspective the action

casts the man out. There is also an association of the man with wisdom in both versions: in Ezekiel the man is already wise in the garden from the beginning until he is cast out because of pride, whereas in Genesis 3 the man acquires wisdom as a result of eating the forbidden fruit, immediately prior to his expulsion from the garden.[29]

Among the points listed above is that of a cherub casting out the man from Eden in Ezek. 28.16. This is the view that we find in the Septuagint and Peshitta, whereas the Masoretic text rather equates the man with the cherub. Similarly, the Septuagint and Peshitta of Ezek. 28.14 imply that the man is 'with (Hebrew *'et*) the cherub', whereas the Masoretic text addresses the man, 'you (Hebrew *'att*) are a ... cherub'. The following reasons may be given for supporting the Septuagint and Peshitta understanding. First, the parallels between Genesis 2–3 and Ezekiel 28 are in general such that it is most likely that they are alternative versions of the same myth, in which case the cherub would not be identical with the man but set over against him. Secondly, it is unparalleled in the whole of the Old Testament and Jewish literature for there to be a wicked cherub or a cherub who is cast out of Eden. On the other hand, J. Barr[30] has argued that it is easier to understand how the Masoretic text's *'att*, 'you', was corrupted to *'et*, 'with', rather than the other way round. However, this view is open to question. In both the previous and succeeding verses of Ezekiel 28 the king is addressed in the second person, and it is, moreover, rare to start a sentence with *'et*, 'with', so it is quite easy to imagine how a scribe might have misunderstood *'et* as *'att*, 'you'.

The idea of the man in Eden's pre-eminent wisdom, which the above passage associates with the king of Tyre to whom the oracle is addressed, is further paralleled in Ezek. 28.3, which declares of the king of Tyre, 'You are wiser than Daniel, no secret is hidden from you'. This same Daniel is further mentioned in Ezek. 14.14, 20, where he is cited as a

of Adam and Eve may be interpreted as an assertion of autonomy that made further human progress possible ('a fall upward'), but that is not the viewpoint expressed by the writer of Gen. 3.

29. This particular point is rightly emphasized by K. Schmid, 'Die Unteilbarkeit der Weisheit. Überlegungen zur sogenannten Paradieserzählung Gen 2f. und ihrer theologischen Tendenz', *ZAW* 114 (2002), pp. 21-39 (36-37). (Not present in the English redaction of this article.)

30. J. Barr, '"Thou art the Cherub": Ezekiel 28.14 and the Post-Ezekiel Understanding of Genesis 2–3', in E.C. Ulrich *et al.* (eds.), *Priests, Prophets and Scribes: Essays on the Formation and Heritage of Second Temple Judaism in Honour of Joseph Blenkinsopp* (JSOTSup, 140: JSOT Press, 1992), pp. 213-22, reprinted in Barton (ed.), *Bible and Interpretation: The Collected Essays of James Barr*, II, pp. 220-28.

person of exemplary righteousness alongside Noah and Job, two figures of hoary antiquity, suggesting that Daniel was a comparable person. This, together with the fact that Ezekiel expects the king of Tyre (a Phoenician, and therefore a kind of Canaanite) to have heard of him, lends credence to the idea that he is to be identified with the Daniel (or Danel) known from the Ugaritic Aqhat epic, where he is referred to as a righteous judge, dispensing justice to widows and orphans at the city gate (*KTU*[3] 1.17.V.4-8; 1.19.I.19-25). Wisdom was, of course, essential for the administration of justice (cf. 1 Kgs 3.9, 12, 28; Prov. 8.15-16). Is it a coincidence that a figure called Daniel exercises judicial wisdom in the apocryphal book of Susannah, where he exposes the lies and attempted adultery of the two elders towards her? From this comes the phrase 'a Daniel come to judgment' found in Shakespeare's *The Merchant of Venice*, 4.1.222.[31]

It would appear that a reflection of the same variant tradition about the first man as being superlatively wise that we find in Ezekiel 28 is also present in Job 15.7-9. In the second cycle of speeches, Eliphaz there says to Job:

> Are you the firstborn of the human race?
> Were you brought forth before the hills?
> Have you listened in the council of God?
> And do you limit wisdom to yourself?
> What do you know that we do not know?
> What do you understand that is not clear to us?

It seems that both Ezek. 28.12-19 and Job 15.7-9 reflect an earlier and more mythological version of the story of the first man in Eden, even though, as I argue later in this chapter, Genesis 3 is chronologically earlier. We may compare the fact that the book of Job similarly has a more primitive mythological depiction of God's battle with the primaeval waters at the time of creation (cf. Job 9.13; 26.12-13; 38.8-11), even though the account in Genesis 1, where God merely controls the waters as a job of work (vv. 2, 6-10), is chronologically earlier.

The Serpent: Wise or Crafty?

In Genesis 3 the serpent is described as '*ārûm* (Gen. 3.1), which is language characteristic of the Wisdom literature that can mean either 'wise, clever, prudent, sensible, shrewd' or 'crafty, cunning', the former

---

31. On all this and more, see J. Day, 'The Daniel of Ugarit and Ezekiel and the Hero of the Book of Daniel', *VT* 30 (1980), pp. 174-84.

meaning being found in Proverbs and the latter in Job. I have already argued above in detail in Chapter 3 that the intended meaning in Gen. 3.1 is 'crafty, cunning', so I refer the reader to there and will not repeat all my arguments here. The basic point is that in keeping with the general Old Testament view of serpents, the narrator depicts the serpent in negative terms, since it leads to the first man and woman disobeying God and thereby being punished and ultimately expelled from Paradise, while the serpent itself ends up being cursed by God to become the lowliest of creatures. Accordingly, we should render, 'Now the serpent was more crafty (or cunning) than any other wild animal that the Lord God had made' (Gen. 3.1).

The Tree of Life in the Book of Proverbs

Interestingly the tree of life of Genesis 2–3 is mentioned on four other occasions in the Old Testament, each time in a wisdom book, the book of Proverbs (Prov. 3.18; 11.30; 13.12; 15.4). In all four instances 'the tree of life' seems to be used metaphorically as a symbol of life or long life (not eternal life, unlike Gen. 3). Now in Prov. 3.18 the tree of life is explicitly equated with wisdom, in contrast to Genesis 3 where it is rather the tree of knowledge that symbolizes wisdom. Proverbs 3.18 declares, 'She [wisdom] is a tree of life to those who grasp her', which reiterates the message found two verses earlier in Prov. 3.16, 'In her [wisdom's] right hand is long life'. Mark Smith[32] has attempted to relate the tree of life here to the Asherah sacred tree, and holds that the personification of wisdom derives from the goddess Asherah. However, this is unlikely, since we have no evidence that the goddess Asherah was ever associated with wisdom, unlike her consort, the god El. The motivation for Smith's view comes from the occurrence of the reference to the tree of life in the same context as the use of the word *'ašrê*, 'blessed', in Prov. 3.13 as well as *me'uššār*, 'blessed', in Prov. 3.18, which he sees as word plays on Asherah. However, the word *'ašrê* is common elsewhere in Proverbs (Prov. 8.32, 34; 13.21; 16.20; 20.7; 28.14; 29.18) where there is no reason to suspect any allusion to Asherah.

In the Masoretic text the second reference to the tree of life in Prov. 11.30 also alludes to the root *ḥkm*, 'wise', but most scholars think the text is corrupt and read *ḥāmās*, 'violence', instead of *ḥākām*, 'wise man', possibly with the support of the Septuagint: 'The fruit of the righteous

---

32. M.S. Smith, *The Early History of God* (San Francisco: Harper & Row, 1990), pp. 94-95.

is a tree of life, but violence (*ḥāmās*) results in the taking of lives'. This makes a nice contrast between righteousness extending life and violence taking life away. A minority of scholars attempt to retain the Masoretic text, translating 'the wise man wins souls', but it is doubtful whether the Hebrew can bear this meaning. Elsewhere *lqḥ nepeš*, lit. 'to take life', means 'to take away life', i.e. kill (cf. Ezek. 33.6; Jon. 4.3; Ps. 31.14, ET 13; Prov. 1.19).

As for the other two references, Prov. 13.12 declares 'Hope deferred makes the heart sick, but a desire fulfilled is a tree of life', and Prov. 15.4 states, 'A gentle tongue is a tree of life, but perverseness in it breaks the spirit'. The meaning of both is pretty clear and in each instance the tree of life seems to denote that which is life-enhancing.

The Relation of Wisdom to the Garden of Eden Story
More Generally

Over the last half-century, some scholars claim to have detected wisdom influence on Genesis 3, whereas others have detected rather an anti-wisdom *Tendenz*. Those envisaging wisdom influence include A.M. Dubarle, L. Alonso-Schökel, G.E. Mendenhall and E. Otto. A.M. Dubarle's arguments[33] were very brief, and formed the basis for Alonso-Schökel's more extended discussion[34] in an article originally in Spanish. Like others subsequently, he identified wisdom language in the story (e.g. *leḥaśkîl*, 'to make wise', and *'ārûm*, 'crafty' [of the serpent]). He particularly saw the knowledge of good and evil as a wisdom theme, but also compared Adam's naming of the animals with List wisdom and noted word play as something found in wisdom. He also states that the section on the four rivers in Gen. 2.10-14 has a wisdom flavour. Going against the consensus of the day he (like some others below) thought the story was late. One may agree that the vocabulary cited is suggestive of wisdom, and the fact that the knowledge of good and evil is explicitly related to wisdom (Gen. 3.6) is relevant, but Alonso-Schökel does not get to grips with the problem that this wisdom is forbidden to the first humans, whereas the

33. A.M. Dubarle, *Les Sages d'Israël* (Lectio Divina, 1; Paris: Cerf, 1946).

34. L. Alonso-Schökel, 'Motivos sapienciales y de alianza en Gn 2–3', *Bib* 43 (1962), pp. 295-316, ET 'Sapiential and Covenant Themes in Genesis 2–3', in J.L. Crenshaw (ed.), *Studies in Ancient Israelite Wisdom* (New York: Ktav, 1976), pp. 468-80. Although this author usually wrote under the name of Alonso Schökel without a hyphen, in this article his name is spelled with a hyphen.

wisdom books tend to see the pursuit of wisdom as a good thing. Further, it should be noted that the idea of the knowledge of good and evil is in no way late (cf. Isa. 7.16; 2 Sam. 14.17; 19.36; 1 Kgs 3.9; Deut. 1.39). It is also doubtful whether Adam's naming of the animals has anything to do with List wisdom (it is unlikely that the Old Testament ever alludes to such wisdom; 1 Kgs 5.13, ET 4.33, which has often been seen as attesting knowledge of List wisdom, more likely alludes to fables[35]). Moreover, word plays are found all over the Old Testament, including frequently in J where there is no obvious wisdom connection. It is also difficult to see what the four rivers have to do with wisdom.

Another early contribution to the debate was that of G.E. Mendenhall, who wrote on 'The Shady Side of Wisdom: The Date and Purpose of Genesis 3'.[36] Against the consensus of the time he argued that Genesis 3 should be regarded as a wisdom story, a *mashal* or parable written in the sixth century BCE after the fall of Jerusalem. It thereby provides an analogy to the fall and exile of the kingdom of Judah. Apart from connecting the expulsion of the first couple to the Judaean exile, Mendenhall related the prominence of Eve to the prophetic condemnation of upper-class women from Jezebel onwards, while the seeking after the knowledge of good and evil he inconsistently relates to Solomon's pursuit of wisdom, leading (according to Mendenhall) to schism and Shishak's invasion, long before the 586 BCE fall of the state. While accepting that the narrative is basically written in classical Hebrew, which he attributes to sixth-century archaizing, he notes various examples of wisdom language in the narrative and claims it is all late, but this is not clear, since a number of the parallels in Proverbs, for example, could be pre-exilic. Since Mendenhall's article a number of other scholars have seen the Garden of Eden story as an allegory of the exile, but the arguments are not compelling, as I have shown elsewhere.[37]

35. See J. Day, 'Foreign Semitic Influence on the Wisdom of Israel and its Appropriation in the Book of Proverbs', in J. Day, R.P. Gordon and H.G.M. Williamson (eds.), *Wisdom in Ancient Israel: Essays in Honour of J.A. Emerton* (Cambridge: Cambridge University Press, 1995), pp. 55-70 (61-62).

36. G.E. Mendenhall, 'The Shady Side of Wisdom: The Date and Purpose of Genesis 3', in H.N. Bream, R.D. Heim and C.A. Moore (eds.), *A Light Unto My Path: Old Testament Studies in Honor of Jacob M. Myers* (Philadelphia, PA: Temple University Press, 1974), pp. 319-34.

37. Day, *From Creation to Babel*, pp. 46-47, as well as above in Chapter 3, towards the end of my critique of the view of F. Stavrakopoulou, pp. 48-49.

A more recent argument for wisdom influence on the Eden narrative comes from E. Otto,[38] but his position is quite different. Unlike the scholars whose views will be considered below, he understands Gen. 2.4b–3.24 to be a literary unity. He sees it as combining late wisdom theology with Deuteronomic covenant theology (cf. Deut. 4.6), and like other scholars envisaging wisdom influence he bases himself partly on alleged wisdom vocabulary, e.g. '*ārûm, ta'ªwâ, neḥmād, 'ēṣeb, ṭôb,* and *ra'.* He also identifies the concern with the question of humans' ability to know good and evil as a late wisdom theme (cf. Ecclus 7.12; 17.6-7 and Eccl. 8.6-7 for contrasting optimistic and pessimistic approaches), compares the 16 word plays in Genesis 2–3 to word plays in the book of Proverbs, and Adam's naming of the animals in Gen. 2.19 to so-called List wisdom. Otto understands this narrative imbued with wisdom and Deuteronomic theology to be a post-Priestly supplement, the work of the redactor of the Pentateuch who added this narrative to the already existing Creation story of P in Gen. 1.1–2.3 in order to show how human disobedience led to the corruption of God's good creation of Genesis 1 (a view also held by some other recent, especially European, scholars). However, writing from within the European tradition itself Walter Bührer has demonstrated at length that the Eden narrative shows no knowledge of P, which one would have expected if it were a post-P supplement.[39] Moreover, I would argue that there are good grounds for continuing to hold that J generally is older than P.[40] On linguistic grounds alone, the J Eden narrative is clearly earlier

38. E. Otto, 'Die Paradieserzählung Genesis 2–3. Eine nachpriesterschriftliche Lehrerzählung in ihrem religionshistorischen Kontext', in A.A. Diesel, R.G. Lehmann, E. Otto and A. Wagner (eds.), *„Jedes Ding hat seine Zeit ... " Studien zur israelitischen und altorientalischen Weisheit. Diethelm Michel zum 65. Geburtstag* (BZAW, 241; Belin: W. de Gruyter, 1996), pp. 167-92.

39. W. Bührer, *Am Anfang... Untersuchungen zur Textgenese und zur relativ-chronologischen Einordnung von Gen 1–3* (FRLANT, 256; Göttingen: Vandenhoeck & Ruprecht, 2014), pp. 313-54. The whole of Chapter 4 (pp. 275-375) argues well for the priority of Gen. 2–3 to Gen. 1. See too Bührer's briefer defence of his views in his article 'The Relative Dating of *Gen 2–3', *VT* 65 (2015), pp. 365-76.

40. For powerful defences of J as a pre-exilic source see E.W. Nicholson, *The Pentateuch in the Twentieth Century: The Legacy of Julius Wellhausen* (Oxford: Clarendon Press, 1998), pp. 132-60; R.S. Hendel, '"Begetting" and "Being Born" in the Pentateuch: Notes on Historical Linguistics and Source Criticism', *VT* 50 (2000), pp. 38-46; *idem*, 'Historical Context', in C.A. Evans, J.N. Lohr and D.L. Petersen (eds.), *The Book of Genesis: Composition, Reception, and Interpretation* (VTSup, 152; Leiden: Brill, 2012), pp. 51-81; J.A. Emerton, 'The Date of the Yahwist', in J. Day (ed.), *In Search of Pre-Exilic Israel: Proceedings of the Oxford Old Testament Seminar* (JSOTSup, 406; London: T&T Clark, 2004), pp. 107-29; R.M. Wright,

than P, as I have shown in the previous chapter. I also remain doubtful whether one should see Deuteronomic covenant theology in Genesis 2–3; not only does the word 'covenant' never appear there, but the theme of sin and divine punishment is surely too widespread in the thought of the Old Testament to require specifically Deuteronomistic influence. It is even found outside Israel in the neighbouring country of Moab in the ninth-century stele of King Mesha. Moreover, in Deut. 4.6, which Otto compares, wisdom is equated with obedience to Yahweh's covenant law, whereas in Genesis 2–3 the first humans' seeking out the forbidden tree of wisdom is seen as a sign of disobedience. As for wisdom influence, one may grant that some of the vocabulary of the narrative is suggestive of this, but as already noted, it seems far-fetched to connect Adam's naming of the animals with so-called List wisdom, and word plays are common all over the Old Testament, not merely in wisdom, and are a particular love of the J source, including in many places with no obvious wisdom connection, as has again already been noted. Finally, it should be pointed out that knowledge of good and evil was far from being merely a late wisdom theme, as it is already attested in Isaiah, Samuel, Kings and Deuteronomy, as noted earlier.

Among those envisaging rather an anti-wisdom *Tendenz* in Genesis 3 are D. Carr and J.-M. Husser. Carr[41] has argued that originally Genesis 2–3 consisted of simply a truncated Creation story in Genesis 2 (vv. 2.4b-5, 7-8, 15bβ, 18-24). Other parts of Genesis 2 are redactional, while a later anti-wisdom writer added Genesis 3. In its final form, therefore, the Eden story is an anti-wisdom tale, opposed to humans seeking wisdom on the basis of their own autonomy. In addition, Carr sees further specific pieces of anti-wisdom polemic in Genesis 3 which strike me as highly speculative and not particularly convincing. For example, he sees a polemic against the wisdom tradition in the description of the serpent as *'ārûm*, 'clever, wise', for in Proverbs this quality leads to success whereas the serpent brought disaster. However, this overlooks the fact that the word *'ārûm* could also have negative overtones in the wisdom tradition in the book of Job, and that is more naturally the meaning in Gen. 3.1, since the author of Genesis 3 clearly views the serpent negatively. He further claims that the failure of God's threat of the immediate death of Adam and Eve to take place

Linguistic Evidence for the Pre-Exilic Date of the Yahwistic Source (LHBOTS, 419; London: T&T Clark, 2005); Day, *From Creation to Babel*, pp. 48-49, and above, Chapter 3, pp. 48-49.

41. D.M. Carr, 'The Politics of Textual Subversion: A Diachronic Perspective on the Garden of Eden Story', *JBL* 112 (1993), pp. 577-95. But it should be noted that Carr told me in 2019 that he now sees Gen. 2.4b–3.24 as a unity.

should be understood in the light of Job and Ecclesiastes' grappling with the problem of the discrepancy between traditional religious belief and observed reality. But in Genesis 3 the non-death of Adam and Eve should probably be seen as a generous manifestation of the divine compassion,[42] which was not a particular problem for the wisdom literature. Again, Carr maintains that the wisdom-seeking Eve is to be seen as a deliberate contrast to the personified wisdom of Proverbs 8, the former bringing disaster in contrast to the latter, who brings success. However, this seems fanciful.

J.-M. Husser[43] likewise sees within Genesis 2–3 an original Creation story (which he dates to the pre-exilic period) that was extended by a Paradise narrative coming from the hand of a subsequent redactor (dated to the exile). However, the verses ascribed to each are not the same as in Carr's analysis. Moreover, Husser ascribes a significant third and final redaction of the Eden narrative to a wisdom redactor, which he holds dates from the post-exilic period. To the wisdom redactor Husser ascribes all the references to the knowledge of good and evil, including the tree of the knowledge of good and evil, as well as the allusions to Adam and Eve's awareness of their nudity which goes with this. He holds that the original Paradise narrative spoke of only one tree, the tree of life (in contrast to the many who have seen the tree of knowledge as original and the tree of life as redactional). Husser envisages this wisdom redactor as having a tragic view of reality, emphasizing humanity's mortality in the face of his longing for immortality, while the references to Adam and Eve's nudity he understands as emphasizing humanity's closeness to the animals. For Husser both of these themes recall Ecclesiastes, so he regards the post-exilic wisdom redaction as coming from a redactor sharing similar views to Qohelet. Husser argues his case well but to me this all seems far too hypothetical.

Clearly many different views of the precise relation between wisdom and the Garden of Eden story have been put forward in recent decades. The reason for this is the apparently ambiguous attitude of the story to wisdom. As Konrad Schmid[44] says, 'the Paradise story argues for the fundamental ambivalence of wisdom. Genesis 2–3 narrates how the human species became "adult", that is, "knowledgeable", at the beginning of time, and it explains at the same time why their achievement of

42. Cf. Day, *From Creation to Babel*, pp. 38-41.

43. J.-M. Husser, 'Entre mythe et philosophie. La relecture sapientielle de Genèse 2-3', *RB* 107 (2000), pp. 232-59.

44. Schmid, 'The Ambivalence of Wisdom', p. 279. (These words are not present in the German redaction of the article.)

knowledge and wisdom produced a fundamental and inevitable distance from God.' On the one hand, the narrative employs a number of words indicating indebtedness to the wisdom tradition (e.g. *lᵉhaśkîl*, *'ārûm*) and the first humans acquire a degree of wisdom, but on the other hand the first humans are punished for eating of the tree of the knowledge of good and evil which conveyed this wisdom. This latter contrasts with the Old Testament elsewhere, in which human beings are encouraged rather to pursue wisdom. It would appear that God disapproves of Adam and Eve because they seek out wisdom on the basis of their own human autonomy, in disobedience to God's explicit command. However, it would be strange if J uniquely held that God wanted humans to remain in ignorance of wisdom for ever. Rather, one imagines that it should be sought out in obedience to God: as Proverbs later put it, the fear of the Lord is the beginning of wisdom (Prov. 9.10; cf. 1.7).

Chapter 5

PROBLEMS IN THE INTERPRETATION
OF THE STORY OF CAIN AND ABEL

Genesis 4.1

The story of Cain and Abel is full of problems of interpretation, and they start in the very first verse. At the end of v. 1 Eve declares *qānîtî 'îš 'et-yhwh*. This raises the question whether *qānîtî* should be rendered 'I have created' or 'I have acquired'. That is, should we render 'I have created a man with the Lord' or 'I have acquired a man with the Lord'? The verb *qnh* in biblical Hebrew is certainly capable of both meanings. The more common meaning is 'to acquire'. However, *qnh* not only occurs with the meaning 'to create' in Ugaritic, Phoenician and Neo-Punic (cf. *KTU*³ 1.4.I.22 and often; *KAI* 26AIII.18; 129.1), but there is a general consensus that there are a number of passages in the Hebrew Bible where this meaning is also found. This is the case in Gen. 14.19, 22; Deut. 32.6; Ps. 139.13, and Prov. 8.22, as well as in the name Elqanah (e.g. 1 Sam. 1.1), while the noun *qinyān* in Ps. 104.24, apparently meaning 'creatures', also most naturally derives from this root. Now Ps. 139.13 actually speaks of God's creating (*qnh*) a human being in the womb. We might also recall Ugaritic *qnyt 'ilm*, 'creatress of the gods' (*KTU*³ 1.4.I.22, etc.), a term used of the goddess Athirat (Asherah). In contrast, the verb *qnh*, 'to acquire', is never attested elsewhere in connection with a woman giving birth to a child. Accordingly, we should render, 'I have created a man with the Lord'. Although it might be objected that the verb *qnh*, 'create', is elsewhere used only of God,[1] the fact that in Gen. 4.1 Eve claims to share

---

1. So P. Humbert, '*Qānā* en hébreu biblique', in W. Baumgartner, O. Eissfeldt, K. Elliger and L. Rost (eds.), *Festschrift Alfred Bertholet zum 80. Geburtstag* (Tübingen: J.C.B. Mohr [Paul Siebeck], 1950), pp. 259-66, reprinted in *idem, Opuscules d'un Hébraïsant* (Neuchâtel: Secrétariat de l'Université, 1958), pp. 166-74.

the creative activity with God makes its use here appropriate. What Eve says reminds one of the statement in the Babylonian Talmud that 'There are three partners in the production of a human being; the Holy One, blessed be He, his father and his mother' (*b. Nid.* 31a).[2]

Some Akkadian parallels for the use of *'et*, 'with', in a creation context have been suggested (Akkadian *itti*, cognate with Hebrew *'et*, means 'with'). The most appropriate parallel was proposed already over a century ago by John Skinner[3] in a bilingual version of the creation of the world (BM 93014), in which the creation of humanity is attributed to the joint work of Marduk and the goddess Aruru (= Ninhursag). Obverse line 21 reads, 'Aruru *with him* (i.e. Marduk) created the seed of mankind' (ᵈMIN *ze-er a-me-lu-ti it-ti-šu ib-ta-na*). A more recently proposed parallel, however, is not cogent. Isaac M. Kikawada[4] has suggested as a parallel a passage in a creation context in the Atrahasis epic (1.201) *it-ti ᵈen-ki-ma i-ba-aš-ši ši-ip-ru*, which Kikawada translates as 'Together with Enki lies the task'. However, against this it needs to be noted that the previous line (1.200) reads *it-ti-ia-ma*, but the meaning has to be 'with me' in the sense of 'for me', not 'together with me'. As Lambert and Millard[5] translate line 200, 'It is not possible for me to make things'. Hence line 201 should be rendered, 'The task lies with Enki'. The use of *itti* here does not therefore provide a parallel to the use of *'et* in Gen. 4.1.

A perverse way to translate *qānîtî 'îš 'et-yhwh* would be to render it as 'I've acquired a man, Yahweh', understanding *'et* as the sign of the accusative. Although perverse, it was actually proposed by a modern German scholar, Friedemann Golka.[6] But more importantly, it also lies behind the rabbinic view reflected in the Targums that Cain was the offspring of the evil angel Sammael or Satan. How did this come about? Well, starting with the mistranslation, 'I've acquired a man, Yahweh',

---

2. For a recent defence of 'create' or rather 'procreate' in Gen. 4.1, see D.E. Bokovoky, 'Did Eve Acquire, Create, or Procreate with Yahweh? A Grammatical and Contextual Reassessment of קנה in Genesis 4:1', *VT* 63 (2013), pp. 19-35.

3. Skinner, *Genesis*, p. 102. In his recent edition of the text W.G. Lambert, *Babylonian Creation Myths* (Winona Lake, IN: Eisenbrauns, 2013), pp. 366-75, names the text 'The Founding of Eridu' (Eridu here referring to Babylon).

4. I.M. Kikawada, 'Two Notes on Eve', *JBL* 91 (1972), pp. 33-37 (esp. 35-37).

5. W.G. Lambert and A.R. Millard, *Atra-ḥasīs: The Babylonian Story of the Flood* (Oxford: Clarendon Press, 1969), p. 57.

6. F.W. Golka, 'Keine Gnade für Kain', in R. Albertz, H.-P. Müller, H.W. Wolff and W. Zimmerli (eds.), *Werden und Wesen des Alten Testaments. Festschrift für Claus Westermann zum 70. Geburtstag* (Göttingen: Vandenhoeck & Ruprecht; Neukirchen-Vluyn: Neukirchener Verlag, 1980), pp. 58-73 (61).

it became felt that if Eve was to have Yahweh as a husband he would have to be in the form of the angel of the Lord. And because Cain was a bad fellow, the angel subsequently became regarded as an evil angel, or Sammael. That this is the case is supported by the fact that the *editio princeps* of Targum Pseudo-Jonathan of Gen. 4.1 reads, 'And Adam knew Eve his wife who lusted after the angel; and she conceived and bore Cain, and said. 'I have acquired a man, the angel of the Lord'. However, later on in the final text of Targum Pseudo-Jonathan (reflected by a single manuscript), this became 'And Adam knew Eve his wife, that she had conceived from Sammael, the angel (of the Lord)'.[7] It will be observed in passing that Gen. 4.1's reference to Adam's knowing Eve (in a sexual sense) has become Adam knowing about Eve. Further, it has sometimes been claimed that this understanding of Cain's literal satanic parentage is already attested in the New Testament in 1 John 3.12, where Cain is said to be 'of the Evil One'.[8] However, against this stands the fact that a spiritual or metaphorical understanding here is more likely, since just two verses earlier in v. 10 we read that 'Everyone who commits sin is a child of the devil', which can only be metaphorical, and furthermore, all the other more explicit texts referring to Cain's satanic paternity are later, from the second century CE onwards (cf. Tertullian, *On Patience* 5.5; the Gnostic *Gospel of Philip* 61.3-10; Targum Pseudo-Jonathan, Gen. 4.1; *Pirḳe de Rabbi Eliezer* 21).

Etymologies of Cain and Abel

In connecting the name Cain (*qayin*) with the verb *qnh*, 'to create', the Yahwist is offering a popular etymology of the name. This is in keeping with other etymologies of names which J offers in Genesis, which tend to be in the nature of popular word plays rather than serious scientific etymologies. The name Cain is generally believed by modern scholars to mean 'smith'; cf. Arabic *qayn*, and Aramaic *qênāyā'*, 'smith', and Tubal-Cain in Gen. 4.22, who is described as the 'forger of all instruments of bronze and iron' (Hebrew *qayin*, 'spear', in 2 Sam. 21.16 seems to be derivative from this). So Cain is, in effect, Mr Smith!

Moving on to v. 2 we read of Cain's brother Abel (*hebel*). There was a time when it was popular to connect the name's etymology with Akkadian

---

7. C.T.R. Hayward, 'Pirqe de Rabbi Eliezer and Targum Pseudo-Jonathan', *JJS* 42 (1991), pp. 215-46 (223-24).

8. E.g. J.M. Lieu, 'What Was from the Beginning: Scripture and Tradition in the Johannine Epistles', *NTS* 39 (1993), pp. 458-77 (470).

ablu, 'son'.[9] However, it would be more natural to give one's first son such a meaning rather than one's second. Elsewhere in the Old Testament the word *hebel* means 'breath', 'vapour', and there are some who assume that this is what Abel means, because his life was cut short by murder.[10] However, this hardly seems a credible name for Eve to give her son at birth. One therefore feels compelled to seek a third and more plausible possibility. The solution is probably to connect Abel with Syriac *habālā'*, which means 'swineherd' or 'camel herdsman'. The Syriac word is cognate with Arabic *'abīl*, which interestingly means not only one 'skilled in the management of camels' but also one 'skilled in the management of sheep and goats'. It will be recalled that Abel was a shepherd. Similarly, the associated Arabic verb *'abila* means 'to be or become skilled in the good management of camels, sheep and goats'. Probably, therefore, the name Abel means 'herdsman'.[11]

We may also note that, just as Cain seems to be a variant of Tubal-Cain (Gen. 4.22), so Abel is plausibly understood as a variant of Jabal, the shepherd who is Tubal-Cain's half-brother in Gen. 4.20.

The Offerings of Cain and Abel

One of the most frequently debated questions raised by the story of Cain and Abel is why the Lord should reject Cain's offering and accept Abel's.[12] It has sometimes been claimed that this reflects God's preference for shepherds over agriculturalists (e.g. H. Gunkel[13]), but this flies in the face of the fact that God specifically called Adam to be an agriculturalist (Gen. 2.15). Some scholars[14] insist that it is futile to seek a reason, sometimes claiming that God can do what he likes (cf. Exod. 33.19, 'I will be gracious

9. Cf. E. Schrader, *Die Keilinschriften und das Alte Testament* (Giessen: J. Ricker, 1st edn, 1872), pp. 8-9.

10. E.g. Westermann, *Genesis 1–11*, p. 398, ET *Genesis 1–11*, p. 292; von Rad, *Das erste Buch Mose*, p. 84, ET *Genesis*, p. 100; Wenham, *Genesis 1–15*, p. 102.

11. Cf. T.K. Cheyne, 'Abel', in *Encyclopædia Biblica* (London: A. & C. Black, one-volume edn, 1914), col. 6; T.H. Gaster, *Myth, Legend, and Custom in the Old Testament* (London: Duckworth, 1969), pp. 51, 341-42 n. 2, though Gaster (p. 341) wrongly gives the Syriac as *hablâ*.

12. For a useful survey of views over two millennia, see J.P. Lewis, 'The Offering of Abel (Gen 4:4): A History of Interpretation', *JETS* 37 (1994), pp. 481-96.

13. Gunkel, *Genesis*, p. 43, ET *Genesis*, p. 43.

14. E.g. von Rad, *Das erste Buch Mose*, pp. 84-85, ET *Genesis*, p. 101; Westermann, *Genesis 1–11*, pp. 403-404, ET *Genesis 1–11*, p. 296; Golka, 'Keine Gnade für Kain', p. 62; R.W.L. Moberly, *The Theology of the Book of Genesis* (Cambridge:

to whom I will be gracious and will show mercy on whom I will show mercy'). However, Johannes de Moor[15] has shown that elsewhere in both the Old Testament and the ancient Near East more generally sacrifices are rejected for only one of two reasons: either there is something wrong with the sacrifice or there is something wrong with the offerer. With regard to the latter, ancient writers sometimes assumed that Cain was already a bad fellow before the murder of his brother, in contrast to the righteous Abel (cf. Josephus, *Ant.* 1.2.1; Targum Neofiti, Gen. 4.8; Mt. 23.35; Heb. 11.4; 1 John 3.12; *Apostolic Constitutions* 8.12.21).

Coming to the sacrifice, the Septuagint translation implies there was something wrong with Cain's ritual, God saying, 'If you offer correctly but do not divide correctly, have you not sinned?' But this is obscure. Again, among modern scholars it has occasionally been supposed that God has a preference for blood sacrifice,[16] but there is no evidence for this elsewhere in the Hebrew Bible. In Leviticus 2, for example, meal offerings are part of the divine legislation alongside animal sacrifice. Or again, it has been suggested more recently by F.A. Spina and G.A. Herion[17] that Cain's fruit offering was unacceptable because God had previously cursed the ground in Genesis 3. Both Spina and Herion claim that the ground became uncursed again in Gen. 8.21 after the flood, where God promises never to curse the ground again. However, Gen. 8.21 is alluding specifically to the flood and there is no evidence that the difficulty in tilling the ground to which Genesis 3 refers was reversed. Furthermore, the cursing of the ground in Genesis 3 surely did not make the produce of the ground evil. Indeed, one could well argue that the difficulty in tilling the ground should have made an offering from there all the more worthy.

Cambridge University Press, 2009), pp. 93-95; Gertz, *Das erste Buch Mose*, I, pp. 160-62. Though, for one holding this view, Gertz (p. 162) unusually questions the comparison with Exod. 33.19.

15. J.C. de Moor, 'The Sacrifice which is an Abomination to the Lord', in *Loven en geloven. Opstellen van collega's en medewerkers aangeboden aan Prof. D. Nic. H. Ridderbos* (Amsterdam: Bolland, 1975), pp. 211-26.

16. E.g. Skinner, *Genesis*, pp. 105-106; B. Jacob, *Das erste Buch der Tora: Genesis* (Berlin: Schocken Verlag, 1934), p. 137.

17. F.A. Spina, 'The Ground for Cain's Rejection (Gen 4): *'ªdāmāh* in the Context of Gen 1–11', *ZAW* 104 (1992), pp. 319-32; G.A. Herion, 'Why God Rejected Cain's Offering: The Obvious Answer', in A.B. Beck *et al.* (eds.), *Fortunate the Eyes that See: Essays in Honor of David Noel Freedman in Celebration of his Seventieth Birthday* (Grand Rapids, MI: Eerdmans, 1985), pp. 52-65.

Rather, the most natural explanation for the acceptability of Abel's offering and the rejection of Cain's may be detected from close obser-vation of what the text says about their respective offerings, and this was something already noticed in antiquity (cf. Philo, *The Sacrifices of Cain and Abel* 52; Ephrem, *Commentary on Genesis* 3.2; *Gen. Rab.* 22.5; *Midrash Tanḥuma* 9). That is, that whereas Cain is said merely to have brought an offering from the fruit of the ground, Abel brought specifically the first born of his flock as well as their fat portions, i.e. the best. If the offerings were truly equivalent, Cain should have brought the first fruits, not just any fruit. One could possibly then go on to draw the further conclusion that Abel was a better person, since he offered the best to God, unlike Cain.[18]

But how did Cain and Abel know that Cain's offering had been rejected and Abel's accepted? According to Theodotion, Rashi, Ibn Ezra and Kimchi, fire came down from heaven and consumed Abel's sacrifice (cf. Lev. 9.24; 1 Kgs 18.38). However, others have supposed that some technical sign was given,[19] for example, the way the smoke rose or a sign in the liver, or that God revealed himself directly to Cain and Abel in some way,[20] or that God's blessing was manifested in the fertility of Abel's flocks but not in Cain's field.[21] But all these ideas are pure speculation; we simply do not know, as the text does not tell us.

Cain's Interactions with Yahweh following the Rejection of Cain's Offering

Following the rejection of Cain's offering we read in vv. 5-6 that 'Cain was very angry, and his countenance fell. The Lord said to Cain, "Why are you angry and why has your countenance fallen?"' In English a reference to one's countenance falling might suggest depression, and Mayer Gruber[22] has proposed that this is what the Hebrew means here.

---

18. Cf. Cassuto, *Genesis*, I, p. 205; Speiser, *Genesis*, p. 30; B.K. Waltke, 'Cain and his Offering', *WTJ* 48 (1986), pp. 363-72; Wenham, *Genesis 1–15*, p. 104; Sarna, *Genesis*, p. 32; Fischer, *Genesis 1–11*, pp. 162-63.

19. E.g. Gunkel, *Genesis*, p. 43, ET *Genesis*, p. 43.

20. Cf. Jacob, *Das erste Buch der Tora*, pp. 137-38.

21. Cf. A. Brock-Utne, Die religionsgeschichtlichen Voraussetzungen der Ḳain-Abel-Geschichte', *ZAW* 54 (1936), pp. 202-39 (210-11); Cassuto, *Genesis*, I, p. 207.

22. M. Gruber, 'The Tragedy of Cain and Abel: A Case of Depression', *JQR* 69 (1978), pp. 89-97, and in a more popular form in 'Was Cain Angry or Depressed?', *BARev* 6.6 (Nov./Dec. 1980), pp. 34-36. Similarly, Cassuto, *Genesis*, I, p. 207, and Sarna, *Genesis*, p. 33.

However, this expression occurs once elsewhere in the Hebrew Bible, in
Jer. 3.12, and there the context makes clear that the meaning is closer to
anger than depression. Jeremiah 3.12 declares, 'Return, faithless Israel,
says the Lord, I will not cause my countenance to fall upon you, for I am
merciful, says the Lord; I will not be angry for ever'. Clearly, 'I will not
cause my countenance to fall upon you' (hiphil of *npl*) means, 'I will not
look on you in anger [or displeasure]', not 'I will not cause my face to be
depressed on you'. Surely therefore, in Gen. 4.5-6 Cain's countenance or
face falling must be a synonym for being angry or displeased.[23] If we wish
to retain the facial metaphor in English, we could speak of frowning, as in
the REB's translation of Jer. 3.12.

At first v. 7 may seem very obscure, but I think it is possible to make
good sense of it. At the beginning it starts with Yahweh's words to Cain,
hᵃlō' 'im-têṭîb śᵉ'ēt, which can be rendered, 'If you do good, is there not
uplift?' *Śᵉ'ēt* is the usual infinitive construct form of *nāśā'*, which can
have a range of meanings. Most likely the verb *nāśā'* is here used in its
meaning 'lift up' by way of contrast with the verb *npl*, 'fall', just used
previously in vv. 5 and 6 with reference to Cain's countenance falling.
We should thus assume an ellipse of *pānîm*, 'face, countenance', after
śᵉ'ēt. In other words, if Cain does good, instead of wallowing in his state
of displeasure and anger, his countenance will be lifted up and he will
be in a state of cheerfulness, resulting from a clear conscience.[24] A very
comparable passage is found in Job, where Zophar similarly promises
Job that if he does good he will lift up his face and be happy: 'If you set
your heart aright, you will stretch out your hands toward him. If iniquity
is in your hand, put it far away, and let not wickedness dwell in your
tents. Surely then *you will lift up your face* without blemish; you will be
secure, and will not fear. You will forget your misery; you will remember
it as waters that have passed away. And your life will be brighter than
the noonday; its darkness will be like the morning' (Job 11.13-17). And
so it goes on.

Since *nāśā' pānîm*, 'to lift up the face', can also be used in the Old
Testament of someone showing favour to someone else, it has also been
suggested that one might render the passage as 'If you do good, will

23. So rightly M. Scarlata, *Outside of Eden: Cain in the Ancient Versions of
Genesis 4.1-16* (LHBOTS, 573; New York: T&T Clark, 2012), pp. 53-54.
24. This was supported by Ibn Ezra. It is the most popular view among modern
scholars, e.g. Driver, *The Book of Genesis*, p. 65; von Rad, *Das erste Buch Mose*,
p. 85, ET *Genesis*, p. 101; Westermann, *Genesis 1–11*, p. 407, ET *Genesis 1–11*,
p. 309; Vawter, *On Genesis*, p. 95; Gertz, *Das erste Buch Mose*, I, pp. 150, 163;
Fischer, *Genesis 1–11*, pp. 274, 288-89. Cf. JPSV, NJPSV, REB, NAB, NJB.

you not be accepted?'.[25] But I find this less appropriate, since it does not understand *nāśā' pānîm* in the direct opposite sense of *nāpal pānîm*, which would seem more natural in the context here. Also to be rejected is the view that the verb *nāśā'* here has its meaning 'forgive', hence 'If you do good, will you not be forgiven?'.[26] The following clause, to which we shall now come, seems to suggest that God is trying to prevent Cain from sinning, rather than seeking to forgive him for past sin.

In the second half of v. 7 the question is raised regarding the precise meaning and function of the word *rōbēṣ* and the problem why the words 'its desire'[27] and 'you must master it' have masculine suffixes, when the word *ḥaṭṭā't*, 'sin' is feminine. Nowhere in the Hebrew Bible is *ḥaṭṭā't* masculine, so it is inadvisable to try and get round the problem by rendering 'sin is couching at the door', as is often done, since the word for 'sin' is feminine and the word *rōbēṣ* rendered 'couching' on this understanding, is masculine.

Nor is it advisable to take the masculine suffixes as referring to Abel, as has occasionally been done, and to render 'His desire is for you but you must rule over *him*'.[28] Such a translation is unnatural, as Abel has not

25. This was supported by Theodotion, the Vulgate and Peshitta. Amongst modern scholars it is followed by F.D. Kidner, *Genesis* (TOTC; London: Tyndale, 1967), p. 75; H.G.M. Williamson, 'On Getting Carried Away with the Infinitive Construct נשא', in M. Bar-Asher, D. Rom-Shiloni, E. Tov and N. Wazana (eds.), *Shai le-Japhet: Studies in the Bible, its Exegesis and its Language* (Jerusalem: Bialik Institute, 2007), pp. 357-67* (358*-61*). Cf. RSV, NRSV, NEB, NIV.

26. This was supported by the Targums and Symmachus, and by Rashi, Rambam and Kimchi. Amongst modern scholars it is followed by Wenham, *Genesis 1–17*, pp. 104-106.

27. A.A. Macintosh has written a detailed article on 'The Meaning of Hebrew תשוקה', *JSS* 61 (2016), pp. 365-87, in which he argues that the commonly accepted rendering 'desire' is mistaken and that we should rather prefer 'concern, preoccupation, (single-minded) devotion'. He claims that the commonly accepted view lacks support in both the ancient Versions and in comparative Semitic philology (the sibilant in the commonly compared Arabic word is not the philologically correct one). However, I am not really persuaded by this alternative translation. The traditional rendering fits all three contexts well (Gen. 3.16; 4.7; Song 7.10). Moreover, the fact that postbiblical Hebrew has verbs *šûq* and *šqq* meaning 'to long for, desire' (cf. M. Jastrow, *A Dictionary of the Targumim, the Talmud Babli and Yerushalmi, and Other Midrashic Literature*, II [2 vols.; New York: Pardes, 1950 reprint], pp. 1540, 1625), together with biblical Hebrew *šôqēqâ*, 'thirsty', lit. 'desirous', 'longing' (Ps. 107.9; Isa. 29.8), suggests that the meaning 'desire' remains plausible.

28. E.g. K.A. Deurloo, 'תשוקה ›dependency‹, Gen 4,7', *ZAW* 99 (1987), pp. 405-406.

been mentioned since v. 3, three verses earlier, so his sudden return here unnamed would be totally unexpected.

It seems to make most sense if we regard *rōbēṣ* as effectively a noun, more precisely a substantival participle, and translate 'a lurker (or coucher) at the door', so that the masculine suffixes in 'its desire' and 'you must master it' will then refer back to that.[29] Moreover, we should then relate this word to the Mesopotamian demon called *rābiṣu*, which is actually attested in Akkadian texts as lurking at the door or gate.[30]

We should probably render the verse as a whole as: 'If you do good, is there not uplift? But if you do not do good, sin is a lurker (or coucher) at the door, its desire is for you, but you must rule over it.' There is some similarity here in language to Gen. 3.16b, 'Your desire shall be for your husband, and he shall rule over you'. We shall note various other parallels between the Cain and Abel story and Genesis 3 below.

Cain's Murder of Abel

Next in v. 8 Cain's anger (vv. 5-6) spills over and he kills his brother Abel. This action is preceded in the MT (including 4QGen[b]) by the words 'Cain said to Abel his brother', curiously without saying what he said! There are some scholars who defend the MT at this point, thinking it conceivable that we can understand it to mean 'Cain spoke to Abel his brother',[31] so that nothing more needs to be added. However, although there are a few instances where *wayyō'mer* appears to have this meaning (cf. Gen. 22.7; Exod. 19.25; 2 Sam. 21.2; 2 Chron. 32.24), this is extremely rare, and it is normal for *wayyō'mer* to be followed by the words spoken. In fact, there

29. Cf. Cassuto, *Genesis*, I, pp. 210-12; Speiser, *Genesis*, pp. 32-33; Gertz, *Das erste Buch Mose*, I, pp. 163-65; Fischer, *Genesis 1–11*, pp. 289-90.

30. See references cited in G.E. Closen, 'Der «Dämon Sünde» (Ein Deutungversuch des massoretischen Textes von Gen 4,7)', *Bib* 16 (1935), pp. 431-42 (438). Cf. too A.M. Kitz, 'Demons in the Hebrew Bible and the Ancient Near East', *JBL* 135 (2016), pp. 447-64. Gordon, '"Couch" or "Crouch"?', pp. 200-203, shows that 'couch' rather than 'crouch' is the basic meaning of the verb *rbṣ*, but is sceptical of the view that the Akkadian *rābiṣu* demon lies behind the reference in Gen. 4.7. However, I do not feel that Gordon satisfactorily explains the two masculine suffixes referring back to the feminine noun *ḥaṭṭā't*, 'sin', in this verse on the view that *rōbēṣ* is merely an ordinary participle 'coucher', as opposed to a participial noun related to the *rābiṣu* demon, even on his view (which I do not accept) that behind the personified (feminine) sin lies the (masculine) serpent of Gen. 3.

31. Cf. Scarlata, *Outside of Eden*, pp. 129-30; Gertz, *Das erste Buch Mose*, I, pp. 150, 166; Fischer, *Genesis 1–11*, pp. 274, 291-92.

are six other instances of *wayyō'mer* in the Cain and Abel story, in all of which we are immediately told what was said (vv. 6, 9 [×2], 10, 13, 15). There is also one example of *wattō'mer* in v. 1, which similarly recounts the words said.

Occasionally, it has been suggested that *wayyō'mer* might be rendered differently, e.g. 'Cain made a rendezvous' (Cassuto,[32] appealing to an Arabic root) or 'Cain was watching [for his brother]' (M.J. Dahood,[33] appealing to Akkadian *amāru* and Ugaritic *'mr*, 'to see'). Alternatively, conjectural emendations have been suggested, e.g. *wayyēmar*, 'and Cain was bitter' (Gunkel[34]), or *wayyitmarmar*, 'and Cain became angry' (F.W. Golka[35]). None of these, however, has gained support.

Rather, we should probably suppose that some words have fallen out of the Masoretic text after *wayyō'mer*, which are preserved in the ancient Versions. It is significant that the Samaritan version, the Septuagint and all the Targums except Onqelos presuppose the reading 'Let us go to the field' for the missing words here. It might be supposed that these Versions simply guessed the words from the context, but it is unlikely that they would have all independently come up with identical words. It is, moreover, significant that the Samaritan and Septuagint are the earliest Versions, supporting the genuineness of the reading.

But what of the Peshitta and Vulgate? The Peshitta actually renders, 'Let us go to the valley', which is similar to the above, but reflects the Syriac tradition that Paradise was located on a mountain, with Adam and Eve's life after the Fall being situated on its foothills. The Vulgate, on the other hand, translates *egrediamur foras*, 'let us go through the doors'. This relates to the door referred to just before in Gen. 4.7. It is likely that Jerome made this up so as to provide something he felt was appropriate. In his *Quaestiones Hebraicae in Genesim* Jerome made clear his rejection of the Septuagint and Samaritan rendering, 'Let us go to the field',[36] which is in keeping with his general dislike of the Septuagint.

32. Cassuto, *Genesis*, I, p. 215.

33. M.J. Dahood, 'Abraham's Reply in Genesis 20:11', *Bib* 61 (1981), pp. 90-91. Cf. V.P. Hamilton, *The Book of Genesis: Chapters 1–17*, p. 228, 'Cain was looking for Abel his brother'.

34. Gunkel, *Genesis*, p. 44, ET *Genesis*, p. 44.

35. Golka, 'Keine Gnade für Kain', p. 63.

36. See C.T.R. Hayward, *Saint Jerome's Hebrew Questions on Genesis* (Oxford: Clarendon Press, 1995), p. 34, for Jerome's comments on Gen. 4.8, and p. 122 for Hayward's comments on Jerome.

God's Interaction with Cain following the Murder of Abel

In vv. 9 and 10 we have God's inquisition of Cain, comparable to his inquisition of Adam and Eve in the garden in Gen. 3.9-13. But whereas Adam responded meekly to God's question, 'Where are you?' in Gen. 3.9, Cain gave a much more defiant reply to God's question, 'Where is Abel your brother?', answering 'I do not know; am I my brother's keeper?' The first part of Cain's answer was a blatant lie, but the second part throws back a question at God by asking 'Am I my brother's keeper?' Over the years many have assumed without question that Cain was meant to be Abel's keeper. I once even heard the former American President, Barack Obama, echo this passage by saying that we are our brother's keeper, when he was talking about social justice. Of course, in the sense that Obama meant it, we may accept this. According to Old Testament ethics we should certainly expect Cain to show compassionate concern for his brother. But the evidence suggests that being one's brother's keeper would go far beyond this. For example, Ps. 121.4 speaks of Yahweh as one who, in keeping Israel, neither slumbers nor sleeps (cf. too v. 5). Yahweh might be thought a special case, but we should note that the verb *šmr*, 'keep', is also used of the watchman of a city (e.g. Isa. 21.11; 62.6; Cant. 3.3; 5.7; Ps. 127.1), who was supposed to keep guard all the time he was on duty, of the shepherd keeping his flock, who we recall from Jesus's parable in Luke 15.3-7 was supposed to ensure that not one sheep went missing, and those guarding prisoners (Josh. 10.18; 1 Kgs 20.39), who were meant to ensure that none escaped. From all this it is difficult not to conclude that if Cain were Abel's keeper, he would be expected to keep watch over him at all times. So as the mediaeval Jewish commentator David Kimchi imagines Cain saying, 'Do I watch him every moment he is with the sheep?' However, by denying *total* responsibility for his brother Abel, Cain seeks to deny *any* responsibility for him.[37]

In v. 10 God asks Cain, 'What have you done?' This somewhat parallels Gen. 3.13, where God asks Eve, 'What is this that you have done?', though in both cases this is more of a rebuke than a request for information. God's words continue with what used to be translated, 'The voice of your brother's blood is crying to me from the ground (cf. AV, RV, the JPSV, RSV), but which more recent translations tend to render 'Listen [or Hark]! Your brother's blood is crying to me from the ground' (NEB, NAB, NIV, NRSV, NJB, NJPSV). This is because the participle 'is crying' is in the plural in Hebrew, *ṣō'ªqîm*, implying that the subject is the plural

---

37. Cf. P.A. Riemann, 'Am I My Brother's Keeper?', *Int* 24 (1970), pp. 482-91.

'blood (of your brother)', *dᵉmê 'aḥîkā*, rather than a singular voice (*qol*). *Qôl* therefore has its meaning 'Listen', as in a number of other places in the Hebrew Bible (e.g. Isa. 13.4; 52.8; Jer. 50.28).

In v. 11 God declares that Cain is cursed from the ground. From the context this most naturally means that he is cursed *away from* the (culti-vated) ground (cf. v. 14, where Cain declares, 'Behold, you have driven me this day away from the ground'). However, Cassuto[38] (following Ibn Ezra) thinks that the meaning is that the curse will come upon Cain from the ground, but this is less likely in view of the wording in v. 14. Finally, it should be noted that Targum Onqelos, *Genesis Rabbah* and Rashi maintained that it meant 'you are more cursed than the ground' (comparative *min*), but this has gained little support.

In v. 12 the Lord continues with words of judgment on Cain. First, he declares that the ground will no longer yield its produce. The word for 'produce' is literally 'strength' in the Hebrew (*kōaḥ*; similarly Job 31.39). This reminds us a bit of the curse in Gen. 3.17-19, where it is declared that men will experience hard labour when tilling the ground. But now, in Genesis 4, with regard to Cain, it is implied that the yield for Cain will be minimal. Coming now to the second half of the divine judgment enunciated in this verse, the Lord proclaims that Cain will become a 'fugitive and wanderer on the earth'. The words rendered 'fugitive and wanderer' are alliterative in Hebrew (*nā' wānād*) and usually regarded as a hendiadys (participles from the verbs *nû'a* and *nûd* respectively). Although they occur together only here in the Hebrew Bible, the two verbs underlying these participles do come together elsewhere in Isa. 24.20. I shall be discussing later whether these words have reference to the nomadic lifestyle of the Kenites or not.

In v. 13 does Cain bewail the fact that his punishment is too great to bear or that his guilt is too great to be forgiven (*gādôl ʿᵃwônî minᵉśô'*)? Both translations are possible in principle, since *'āwôn* can mean either 'punishment' or 'guilt', and the verb *nāśā'* can mean both 'to bear' and 'to forgive'. A minority (e.g. B. Jacob, U. Cassuto, H. Seebass[39]) have preferred the latter view, and *nāśā' 'āwôn* is indeed found with the sense 'to forgive guilt' (or iniquity) a number of times in the Old Testament (cf. Exod. 34.7; Num. 14.18; Hos. 14.3, ET 2; Mic. 7.18; Ps. 32.5). However, in the following verse (v. 14) it is clear that Cain is bewailing the extent of his forthcoming suffering as a wanderer on the earth, even to the point

38. Cassuto, *Genesis*, I, p. 219.

39. E.g. Jacob, *Das erste Buch der Torah*, p. 143 (in the form of a question); Cassuto, *Genesis*, I, p. 222; Seebass, *Genesis. I. Urgeschichte*, pp. 157-58.

that he might get killed. In this context, 'my punishment is greater than I can bear' makes much better sense, and for this reason is supported by almost all modern Bible translations and the majority of modern commentators (e.g. Gunkel, Skinner, von Rad, Wenham[40]). H.G.M. Williamson[41] has plausibly argued that the rarer form of the infinitive construct $n^e\acute{s}\bar{o}$' is employed here to make clear that the meaning is different from that of the more common infinitive construct form $\acute{s}^e$'ēt used earlier in the narrative in v. 7.

In v. 14 Cain continues his complaint by saying that God has driven him away from the ground, and that his being a fugitive and wanderer on the earth mans that someone may kill him. (With regard to the last idea, 'anyone who meets me may kill me', it has sometimes been suggested that Cain is a corporate figure, i.e. the tribe of Cain [Skinner] or Kenites [Moberly]).[42] But the singular verb used for 'kill' here suggests otherwise.

Next, in v. 15, following Yahweh's declaration of punishment for Cain, we see the divine grace in action alongside it. The text reads, '"Therefore, whoever kills Cain, vengeance will be taken on him sevenfold." And the Lord set a sign for Cain, lest any who came upon him should kill him.' The Masoretic text reads, 'Therefore, whoever kills Cain, etc.', but some scholars prefer to follow the Septuagint, Symmachus, Theodotion, Vulgate and Peshitta in reading 'Not so (Hebrew $l\bar{o}$' kēn), whoever kills Cain, etc.' If we accept this emendation, we would have to accept that the words following kēn would not actually be negating everything God says in v. 14, since Cain's suffering is not reversed; it is simply Cain's fear of being killed that God counters. However, what tells against this emendation and in favour of retaining the MT's lākēn, 'therefore', is the fact that $l\bar{o}$' kēn should be followed by kî, as Skinner[43] pointed out long ago.

Coming now to the substance of the verse, we note that Cain is promised sevenfold vengeance if he is slain. This later gave rise to the bizarre midrashic understanding that Cain was killed by his descendant Lamech, who was of the seventh generation from Adam!

40. E.g. Gunkel, *Genesis*, p. 45, ET *Genesis*, p. 45; Skinner, *Genesis*, p. 109; von Rad, *Das erste Buch Mose*, p. 87, ET *Genesis 1–11*, p. 103; Wenham, *Genesis 1–15*, p. 108.

41. Williamson, 'On Getting Carried Away', pp. 361*-66*.

42. Skinner, *Genesis*, p. 110; R.W.L. Moberly, 'The Mark of Cain Revealed at Last?', *HTR* 100 (2007), pp. 11-28 (16). Contrast Scarlata, *Outside of Eden*, pp. 178-79.

43. Skinner, *Genesis*, p. 110. Furthermore, as BDB, p. 487 notes, there are several other places where the LXX wrongly read lākēn as $l\bar{o}$' kēn.

The Sign of Cain

The second half of v. 15 reads, 'And the Lord set a sign for Cain in order that anyone finding him should not kill him'. This leads us to the question that has provoked endless speculation for almost two thousand years, namely the problem what exactly the sign of Cain was. Starting with Jewish interpretations, we should note that at first the subject aroused little interest: neither Philo nor Josephus discuss the precise nature of the sign. However, when we come to the Tannaitic rabbis we find a whole series of wild speculations: for Abba Jose ben Hanan (first century CE) it was a horn growing out of Cain, for rabbi Nehemiah (*c.* 150 CE) it was leprosy (thereby wrongly perceiving the sign as a punishment), whilst for Abba Arikha (175–247 CE) it was a dog, presumably to frighten away Cain's enemies (*Gen. Rab.* 22.12)! Only one of the Targums, Targum Pseudo-Jonathan, attempts an explanation: it declares the sign to be one of the letters of the tetragrammaton put on Cain's face (similarly later Rashi), while *Pirke de Rabbi Eliezer* 21 states that it was one of the letters of the Hebrew alphabet put on his arm.

Coming to Christianity, the early Church Fathers evinced little interest in the subject. However, the dominant Christian view for many centuries interpreted the sign to be Cain's trembling movement. This ultimately derived from the Septuagint, which prior to the announcement of the sign had declared that Cain would be 'groaning and trembling' (*stenōn kai tremōn*), which was its inaccurate rendering of the Hebrew *nā' wānād*, 'a fugitive and wanderer'. We find this view, for example, in the Venerable Bede (673–735), Bruno of Asti (*c.* 1045–1123), Hugo of St Victor (twelfth century), Peter Comistor (died 1179), Peter Riga (Bible translator and commentator, *c.* 1170–1209), and Pope Innocent III (1208).

However, another interpretation, found in Syriac Christianity, was that the sign consisted of dark skin, a view taken up much later in the nineteenth and twentieth centuries in a racist way in the USA, especially among Southern Baptists and Mormons. Only rarely within Christianity prior to the modern era was the sign understood as a mark on Cain's skin, a view that has become common in modern critical scholarship. However, we do find it, for example, in the Syriac *Life of Abel* (fifth century), where it is specifically a sign on Cain's forehead.[44]

We come now, therefore, to modern scholarly views. The dominant scholarly view over the last century and more has been that the sign was a mark on Cain's skin of some kind, e.g. on his forehead or possibly

44. See S.P. Brock, 'A Syriac Life of Abel', *Le Muséon* 87 (1974), pp. 467-92 (481).

on some other visible part of his body.[45] We are reminded of Ezek. 9.4, where the prophet is told to 'go through Jerusalem and put a mark upon the foreheads of the men who sigh and groan over all the abominations that are committed there'. In Cain's case we cannot know exactly what the sign was, since the text does not tell us, but it seems essential that it was a visible sign on Cain's body; otherwise it would have failed to serve its purpose in deterring anyone who met him and was on the point of killing him.

This popular view has been challenged recently by Walter Moberly,[46] who thinks that the sign was not a visible mark on his body at all, but rather was identical with God's words in v. 15, 'Whoever kills Cain, vengeance shall be taken on him sevenfold'. Moberly does not envisage these words as having been written up anywhere. Rather he thinks they constituted a popular proverbial saying that everyone would know. Against Moberly, however, it should be noted that a sign ought to be something visible. On the rare occasion when words do constitute a sign in the Old Testament (cf. Deut. 6.8), they are still something visible. Moberly is right that Gen. 4.15 does not explicitly say that Yahweh placed a sign *on* Cain, but rather set a sign *for* him, but as I noted above, if it was not actually on him it is difficult to envisage how it could serve its intended purpose of deterring would-be murderers when they encountered him.

Since the nineteenth century it has sometimes been held that the sign of Cain was a tribal mark or tattoo.[47] This relates to the notion that Cain symbolized the tribe of the Kenites, something we shall discuss shortly. As we will argue below, the evidence does indeed support the view that the story of Cain originated as an aetiology of the Kenites. However, we simply do not have enough information about the Kenites to know whether the sign of Cain originally reflected a tribal mark or tattoo.

The Conclusion of the Cain Narrative

At the conclusion of the story in v. 16 we are told that 'Cain went away from the presence of the Lord and settled in the land of Nod, east of Eden'. The name Nod means 'wandering' and is clearly related to the word 'wanderer' (*nād*) used to describe Cain's destiny in vv. 12 and 14.

45. E.g. Skinner, *Genesis*, p. 110; Speiser, *Genesis*, pp. 30-31; von Rad, *Das erste Buch Mose*, p. 87, ET *Genesis*, p. 103.
46. Cf. Moberly, 'The Mark of Cain', pp. 11-28.
47. This was most emphatically argued by B. Stade, 'Das Kainszeichen', *ZAW* 14 (1894), pp. 250-318 (299-318).

It is doubtless an imaginative creation of the Yahwist, though the fact that it is said to be east of Eden indicates that it was regarded as an actual geographical place. The Septuagint spells the name Naid, which suggests that the translator misread the middle Hebrew letter as a *yodh* instead of a *waw*.

An eccentric view has been put forward by M. Görg,[48] who sought to find an unlikely Egyptian etymology for the name Nod. He derives the word from Egyptian *t' nṯr*. 'God's land', although Hebrew *d* is not equivalent to Egyptian *ṯ*, and the absence of the final 'r' in the name Nod is left unexplained. Moreover, the Egyptians applied this name to both Phoenicia and Punt (in east Africa), neither of which is appropriate here. There is every reason to continue preferring the view that Nod is related to Hebrew *nād*, 'wanderer'.

The story of Cain and Abel thus concludes with Cain's expulsion from the presence of the Lord, providing yet another parallel to the story of Adam and Eve in Genesis 3, which similarly ends with their expulsion further east from the Garden of Eden (Gen. 3.23-24).

The Point of the Cain and Abel Story

Such then are the main exegetical and textual problems that the story of Cain and Abel raises, and my attempts to deal with them. But that still leaves broader questions to be considered. What exactly is the point of the story? In the text as it now stands, the narrative tells us of the first murder, a case of fratricide. As such, it depicts the social side of the 'Fall', the breakdown in interhuman relations, in contrast to the humanity–God aspect of the 'Fall' depicted in Genesis 3. However, some scholars have sought to discover some deeper meaning below the surface.

Some Earlier Erroneous Understandings

A number of erroneous, indeed somewhat bizarre approaches to the story of Cain and Abel, have been put forward over the years. For example, over a century ago A. Ehrenzweig[49] ended up making the original story of Cain and Abel as close to that of Romulus and Remus as he could. Genesis 4.17 speaks of Cain building a city, just as Romulus built Rome. Prior to the building of Rome Romulus had an argument with his brother

---

48. M. Görg, 'Kain und das "Land Nod"', *BN* 71 (1994), pp. 5-12.
49. A. Ehrenzweig, 'Kain und Lamech', *ZAW* 35 (1915), pp. 1-11; *idem*, 'Biblische und klassische Urgeschichte', *ZAW* 38 (1919–20), pp. 65-86.

Remus that ended with Remus getting killed. Similarly, Cain killed his brother Abel. For Ehrenzweig, Cain's murder of his brother was preceded by a disagreement. Whereas, he supposed, both Cain and Abel originally wished to build the city jointly, they consulted an oracle to decide who should rule over it, and when the oracle favoured Abel, Cain killed him. However, Ehrenzweig's thesis is clearly pure speculation, reading into it the story of Romulus and Remus, without supporting evidence. In the story as we have it, Cain's building of a city is quite separate from his killing of Abel; indeed it takes place afterwards. There is nothing to suggest a connection. And many of the features of our current story of Cain and Abel are left out of account in Ehrenzweig's reconstruction.

Somewhat later, S.H. Hooke[50] put forward another unlikely inter-pretation of the story. Hooke was the best-known representative of the so-called Myth and Ritual School in Old Testament studies. In keeping with this Hooke believed that the Cain and Abel story originated as a fertility myth. Specifically, according to Hooke, Cain's murder of Abel originated in an act of ritual human sacrifice which had the intention of promoting the fertility of the crops, while his subsequent banishment in the original myth was only a temporary measure to prevent the defilement of the community resulting from the human sacrifice. Hooke found certain parallels in the Jewish Day of Atonement (originally part of the New Year ritual) and in the Babylonian New Year festival. But in Hooke's understanding Cain was not Abel's brother in the original myth. Further, in the Genesis story the murder of Abel leads to decreased fertility rather than more, and Cain's banishment is permanent, not temporary. All these differences, which Hooke accounts for by assuming later editing of the original myth, are far too great to carry conviction, and Hooke's thesis seems excessively speculative. No one supports this view nowadays.

Cain, the Kenites and the Story's Original Setting

We come now to our concluding section. Should we see the story of Cain as an aetiology of the Kenites? Since Genesis, especially in J, is full of aetiological stories, we should not be surprised if this is the case. This idea was first put forward in the nineteenth century, popularized in particular

50. S.H. Hooke, 'Cain and Abel', *Folk-Lore* 50 (1939), pp. 58-65, reprinted in S.H. Hooke, *The Siege Perilous* (London: SCM Press, 1956), pp. 66-73. Though Hooke does not mention it, a similar theory about the Cain story presupposing human sacrifice in the context of the fertility cult was put forward previously by Brock-Utne, 'Die religionsgeschichtlichen Voraussetzungen der Ḳain-Abel-Geschichte'.

by B. Stade,[51] and it has been widely followed since, though tending to be downplayed in many recent commentaries.[52]

The reasons for seeing this story as an aetiology of the Kenites are as follows. First, the name Cain (Hebrew *qayin*) is elsewhere used as a collective singular term to denote the Kenites in both Num. 24.22 and Judg. 4.11. The first of these references comes only five verses after a reference to 'the sons of Seth (Sheth)' associated with Moab in Num. 24.17. This can hardly be a coincidence and supports an originally ethnic connection not only for Cain but also for Seth in Genesis 4. Again, the life of wandering to which Cain is destined parallels the semi-nomadic existence of the Kenites. Jael, the wife of Heber, the Kenite, for example, is said to dwell in a tent (Judg. 4.17). Some further points also support the Kenite connection. Thus, the Kenites seem to have been a kind of Midianite, since Moses' father-in-law is called both a Midianite and a Kenite (a Midianite in Exod. 3.1; 18.1 [Jethro]; Num. 10.29 [Hobab]; a Kenite in Judg. 1.16; 4.11 [Hobab]). It can hardly be a coincidence, therefore, that Cain's son in Gen. 4.17 is called Enoch (Hebrew *ḥᵃnôk*), the name of one of the Midianite clans in Gen. 25.4. Even Cain's building of a city named after Enoch, often deemed unfitting for a wandering figure or tribe, makes sense in the light of 1 Sam. 30.29, which alludes to 'the cities of the Kenites'. Other points in the list of Cain's descendants in Gen. 4.17-24 are also suggestive of a Kenite connection. Thus, amongst Cain's descendants was Jabal, the ancestor of those who live in tents (Gen. 4.20), which fits the tent-dwelling life of the Kenites already referred to above (Judg. 4.17). Again, the very name Cain means 'smith' and one of Cain's descendants was Tubal-Cain, who made all kinds of bronze and iron tools (Gen. 4.22). It is therefore interesting that an inscription in a metal mine in Sinai actually refers to 'a chief of the Kenites' (*rb bn qn*), according to M. Dijkstra.[53]

51. Stade, 'Das Kainszeichen'.

52. I have earlier defended at length the view that Gen. 4.1-16 contains an aetiology of the Kenites in my article, 'Cain and the Kenites', in G. Galil, M. Geller and A. Millard (eds.), *Homeland and Exile: Biblical; and Ancient Near Eastern Studies in Honour of Bustenay Oded* (VTSup, 130; Leiden: Brill, 2009), pp. 335-46, reprinted in Day, *From Creation to Babel*, pp. 51-60. This view has also been recently reasserted by David Carr in *The Formation of Genesis 1–11*, pp. 74-78.

53. See M. Dijkstra, 'The Statue of SR 346 and the Tribe of the Kenites', in M. Augustin and K.-D. Schunck (eds.), *"Wünschet Jerusalem Frieden": Collected Communications to the XIIth Congress of the International Organization for the Study of the Old Testament, Jerusalem 1986* (Frankfurt: P. Lang, 1988), pp. 93-103 (96-97).

However, it might be objected that, in the final form of Genesis as we now have it, the flood wipes out all humanity except for Noah and his immediate family. Noah was clearly not a descendant of Cain but of Seth, and this is attested in both the Priestly and Yahwistic genealogies (cf. Gen. 5 [P], as well as Gen. 5.29 [J fragment], which latter concludes the Sethite genealogy starting in Gen. 4.25-26). So if the story of Cain in Gen. 4.1-16 is an aetiology of the Kenites, why are they still existing many centuries later? The same objection might be made with regard to the Nephilim, who are still regarded as existing long after the flood (cf. Num. 13.33), as the gloss in Gen. 6.4 awkwardly concedes ('and also afterwards'). However, such problems are overcome if we accept, as Chapter 7 will endeavour to demonstrate, that there are good grounds for regarding the J flood narrative as a later addition to the text.

If the story of Cain constituted an aetiology of the Kenites, there is no reason why this should have been originally set in the second generation of humanity. And in fact, there are two indications in the story itself that it originally pertained to a later period when there were more humans on the earth. First, Cain fears that someone will kill him (Gen. 4.14), although the narrative has not told us of the existence of other humans on the earth at this time, apart from Adam and Eve. Secondly, just after the Cain and Abel story we read that Cain married a wife (Gen. 4.17), although we have not been told of the existence of any other women apart from Eve. Both of these problems are instantly solved if the story of Cain originally had a later setting. We must accept that, in being relocated, the story has not been fully integrated into its current context. Possibly Cain was originally in the fourth generation from Adam rather than the second, if P preserves the original genealogical order at this point in Gen. 5.9-14, where Kenan, P's equivalent to Cain, is in the fourth generation.[54] But we cannot be certain of Cain's original precise placing. However, any original placing of Cain later than Enosh, as on the view just mentioned, would solve the problem that, at the beginning of the Cain and Abel story, Eve already knows the name of Yahweh (Gen. 4.1), as does the rest of the Cain and Abel story, when according in Gen. 4.26 it was only in the days of Enosh that men started calling on the name of the Lord.[55]

---

54. Having written this, I find that my suggestion to locate Cain after Enosh, with appeal to Gen. 5, was previously proposed long ago by Stade, 'Das Kainszeichen', p. 265.

55. Accordingly, as a later addition, the story of Cain does not constitute a complete unity with the Eden narrative, contrary to what is maintained by I. German, *The Fall Reconsidered* (Eugene, OR: Wipf & Stock [Pickwick Publications], 2016). See further, my review of this book in *JSOT* 43.5 (2019), p. 165. However, the various

With regard to the question of Cain's wife, already in antiquity people were aware of the problem, and the rabbis and others solved it by assuming that Cain married his sister (whether named Awan, as in *Jub.* 4.1; Noaba in Pseudo-Philo, *Biblical Antiquities* 1.1; Lebuda, in *Testament of Adam* 3.5; *Cave of Treasures* [W] 5.20-22; or unnamed, as in Josephus, *Ant.* 1.2.1-2; Targum Pseudo-Jonathan 4.2; *Gen. Rab.* 22.7).[56] However, the biblical text does not record Cain's marriage to any such sister,[57] though in Gen. 5.4 the Priestly source later reports that Adam and Eve had other sons and daughters.

We must conclude that though the story of Cain and Abel has been brilliantly composed, it has been poorly edited for its present context. Poor editing, is of course, a well-known feature of Genesis 1–11. Contradictory creation accounts have been left standing side by side, contradictions within the flood story remain, and humans are still living for several hundred years in Genesis 11, although God had already reduced their lifespan to 120 years in Gen. 6.3. The Cain and Abel story is yet another example of poor editing.

parallels between the Cain and Eden narratives noted earlier in this chapter certainly indicate that one was modelled on the other. More likely the Cain story was modelled in part on the Eden narrative.

56. Argument over who should marry the sister even became the cause of Cain's murder of Abel in *Gen. Rab.* 22.7 and *Cave of Treasures* (W) 5.20-22 (in the latter, both Cain and Abel have a sister, but Cain's is more beautiful).

57. N. Wyatt, 'Cain's Wife', *Folklore* 97 (1986), pp. 88-95, has put forward a strange view. He claims that Cain married his mother, Eve. Eve, in turn, had previously had sex with Yahweh in the original story, later modified to read 'the man' (Adam) as in Gen. 4.1a.

Chapter 6

THE ENOCHS OF GENESIS 4 AND 5 AND THE EMERGENCE OF THE APOCALYPTIC ENOCH TRADITION

Enoch in Genesis 4 (J)

A figure called Enoch occurs in both Gen. 4.17-18 and 5.21-24, the former as a descendant of Cain in J and the latter as a descendant of Seth in P. As is well known, though appearing as different characters in the biblical text as we now have it, they are generally regarded as being parts of variant versions of what are essentially the same genealogy, a viewpoint going back – something not so well known – to Philipp K. Buttmann in 1828.[1] In J Enoch is the third name out of seven and in P the seventh name out of ten. We shall discuss the precise relationship of these two lists to each other later.

What can we say about the Enoch of Gen. 4.17-18? The text itself informs us that he was the son of Cain, that Cain built a city named after Enoch, and that Enoch was the father of Irad. There is good evidence that the story of Cain originated as an aetiology of the Kenites, a semi-nomadic people to the south of Israel.[2] This is supported both by Cain's

---

1. P. Buttmann, *Mythologus, oder gesammelte Abhandlungen über die Sagen des Alterthums* (2 vols., Berlin: Mylius, 1828–29 [1828]), I, pp. 170-72.

2. This view was first put forward by scholars such as H. Ewald, 'Erklärung der Biblischen urgeschichte. 1, 4. Die geschlechter des ersten Weltalters', *Jahrbücher der Biblischen wissenschaft* [*sic*] (1853–54), pp. 1-19, esp. pp. 5-6; Stade, 'Das Kainsze-ichen', pp. 250-318; and J. Wellhausen, *Die Composition des Hexateuchs* (Berlin: G. Reimer, 3rd edn, 1899), p. 9, but it has sometimes been ignored or even rejected in recent commentaries on Genesis. I have reargued the case in J. Day, 'Cain and the Kenites', in Galil, Geller and Millard (eds.), *Homeland and Exile*, pp. 335-46,

name and by his lifestyle. The name Cain, which appears to mean 'smith' (cf. Arabic *qayn*, 'smith' and Tubal-Cain, the first worker in bronze and iron in Gen. 4.22), is specifically used to denote the Kenites in both Num. 24.22 and Judg. 4.11. Moreover, the name of Cain's brother Seth (Hebrew Sheth) likewise has a tribal meaning in Num. 24.17,[3] only two verses before the mention of tribal Cain. Furthermore, the life to which Cain is destined in Genesis 4, one of wandering, also fits the Kenites (cf. Judg. 5.24, where Jael, the wife of Heber the Kenite, is described as a tent-dweller). The genealogy in Gen. 4.17-24 is therefore often referred to as the Kenite genealogy. One might thus expect the figure of Enoch to have some Kenite connection. That this is the case is supported by the fact that according to Gen. 25.4 and 1 Chron. 1.33 Enoch (Hanoch) was the name of a Midianite clan, since his name appears as a son of Midian. This has been obscured in our English Bibles because they here use the Hebrew spelling Hanoch rather than Enoch. Conceivably the name Enoch represents the tribal group of the Ḥanikites attested in north Arabia,[4] just as the name of his brother Ephah, also mentioned in Gen. 25.4 and 1 Chron. 1.33, is attested as a north Arabian tribal name Ḫa-a-a-ap-pa-a-a or Ḫa-ia-pa-a in Assyrian inscriptions. When we recall the close connection of the Kenites and the Midianites (Moses' father-in-law being described as a Midianite in Exod. 3.1; 18.1; Num. 10.29, and a Kenite in Judg. 1.16; 4:11), it is difficult not to connect the Enoch of Genesis 4 with the Midianite clan name in Gen. 25.4 and 1 Chron. 1.33.

reprinted in Day, *From Creation to Babel*, pp. 51-60. It might be wondered how the Kenites survived the flood. However, as I argue below at the end of Chapter 7, there are many good reasons for thinking that the flood story was a later addition to J's narrative.

3. In Num. 24.17 'all the sons of Seth [Sheth]' stands parallel to 'Moab' in Trans-jordan. Compare Shutu, a nomadic people in Transjordan mentioned in the Egyptian execration texts and elsewhere. For references in the Egyptian execration texts see K. Sethe, *Die Ächtung feindlicher Fürsten, Völker und Dinger auf altägyptischen Tongefässscherben der mittleren Reiches* (Berlin: Akademie der Wissenschaften in Kommission bei W. de Gruyter, 1926), pp. 46-47, 56 (texts e4-6, f5); Georges Posener, *Princes et pays d'Asie et de Nubie* (Brussels: Fondation égyptologique reine Elisabeth, 1940), pp. 80-90 (texts E52-53); Y. Koenig, 'Les textes d'envoûtement de Mirgissa', *REg* 41 (1990), pp. 101-25 (111; texts F4, G5). This tribal group is also attested in Akkadian under the name Suti in texts such as those from Mari; cf. J.R. Kupper, 'Sutéens et Ḫapiru', *RA* 55 (1961), pp. 197-205.

4. See E.A. Knauf, *Midian: Untersuchungen zur Geschichte Palästinas und Nordarabiens am Ende des 2. Jahrtausends v. Chr.* (Abhandlungen der deutschen Palästinavereins; Wiesbaden: O. Harrassowitz, 1988), pp. 81-84.

It is not a valid objection to Cain's having been equated with the Kenites or Midianites that his son Enoch is said to have had a city named after him (Gen. 4.17), for we know from 1 Sam. 30.29 that there were 'cities of the Kenites' in the Negeb (cf. too a Judaean town called Kain in Josh. 15.57). The Masoretic text states that 'Cain knew his wife and she conceived and bore Enoch; and he built a city and called the name of the city after the name of his son Enoch'. This clearly implies that the city was named after Enoch. However, some scholars wish to emend the text to say that Enoch either named the city after himself[5] or named it after his son, namely, Irad.[6] Neither suggestion has any textual support in Hebrew manuscripts or in any of the ancient Versions. Further, with regard to the latter suggestion, Irad has sometimes been supposed to denote the city of Eridu in Babylonia (the city of the first kings in the Sumerian King List).[7] However, not only does a Babylonian place name seem inappropriate in a Kenite genealogy, but it should be noted that it is not until the following verse (Gen. 4.18) that we learn that Enoch begat a son Irad, so an allusion to him already in v. 17 would be premature.

Enoch in Genesis 5 (P)

We have argued above that the figure of Enoch, the third from Adam and son of Cain in J's Genesis 4 account, originally derived from the name of a Midianite clan name. In the Priestly Genesis 5 a figure named Enoch also appears but now as the seventh in a list of ten antediluvian patriarchs. In view of the similarities between the names in Genesis 4 and 5 there can be no doubt that there is a relationship of some kind between the two lists,

5. Budde, *Die biblische Urgeschichte*, pp. 120-23, 527, reads *kišᵉmô ḥᵃnôk* instead of *kᵉšēm bᵉnô ḥᵃnôk*, while Westermann, *Genesis 1–11*, pp. 443-44, ET *Genesis 1–11*, 327, simply reads *kišᵉmô*.

6. W.W. Hallo, 'Antediluvian Cities', *JCS* 23 (1970), pp. 57-67 (64). In his later work H. Kvanvig, *Primeval History: Babylonian, Biblical, and Enochic: An Intertextual Reading* (JSJSup 149; Leiden: Brill, 2011), p. 418, also came round to this view. Contrast Kvanvig's earlier view in *Roots of Apocalyptic: The Mesopotamian Background of the Enoch Figure and of the Son of Man* (WMANT, 61; Neukirchen-Vluyn: Neukirchener Verlag, 1988), pp. 40-41, where he favoured the MT.

7. Hallo, 'Antediluvian Cities', p. 64; Kvanvig, *Primeval History*, p. 418. These scholars appear to have been unaware that A.H. Sayce, 'Miscellaneous Notes. 10. *Irad* and *Enoch* in Genesis', *Zeitschrift für Keilschriftforschung* 2 (1885), p. 404, had previously proposed Irad's identity with Eridu, though without seeking to emend the text.

and there can also be no doubt that Genesis 5 is later. That P's numbering system represents a later development than J's rather than the other way round, is supported by the following points. First, in addition to the traditional arguments in favour of the priority of J, which will not be rehearsed again here, Ronald S. Hendel has drawn attention to J's consistent use of the qal form *yālad* and P's uniform employment of the hiphil *hôlîd* for 'begat' in Genesis 4 and 5 respectively, and indeed throughout J and P generally.[8] This clearly supports the traditional dating of J as being earlier than P, because the hiphil form is undoubtedly the later form, as shown by the fact that it is the only form attested in biblical Hebrew texts which are clearly post-exilic or exilic. Secondly, in view of the growing importance of Enoch, it is understandable that he should have been moved to the special seventh place which he now has in Genesis 5,[9] but for him to have been moved from seventh place elsewhere is difficult to conceive.

It has sometimes been suggested that P conflated J's list of Sethite names in Gen. 4.25-26 with the Cainite list in Gen. 4.17-18, so as to produce ten patriarchs from Adam to Noah.[10] In order to have done this P would also need to have omitted the final Cainite generation in Gen. 4.20-22 and added Noah at the end instead. However, this is improbable, since the differences in several of the names in Genesis 4 and 5 (Cain/Kenan, Irad/Jared, Mehujael/Mahalalel, Methushael/Methuselah) tell against the direct dependence of Genesis 5 on Genesis 4. Also to be rejected is the proposal that J in Genesis 4 and P in Genesis 5 both drew on a common genealogy, but that J split it into separate Cainite and Sethite genealogies.[11] Against this it should be noted that in the J Sethite genealogy we read that 'he (or she) called his name X' (Gen. 4.25, 26), but this formula never occurs in the Cainite genealogy in Gen. 4.17-24, suggesting that these particular J Sethite and Cainite genealogies were never part of the same list. On the other hand this formula is found in the J genealogical note on

---

8. R.S. Hendel, '"Begetting" and "Being Born" in the Pentateuch: Notes on Historical Linguistics and Source Criticism', *VT* 50 (2000), pp. 38-46.

9. On the significance of the seventh place in genealogies, see J.M. Sasson, 'A Genealogical "Convention" in Biblical Chronography', *ZAW* 90 (1978), pp. 171-85; *idem*, 'Generation, Seventh', in *IDBSup*, pp. 354-56. In contrast, in the Cainite genealogy in Gen. 4 it is Lamech who is in seventh place, which is doubtless deliberate, since he is the highlight of the passage (Gen. 4.19-24).

10. Westermann, *Genesis 1–11*, p. 473, ET *Genesis 1–11*, p. 349 regards this as possible; D.M. Carr, *The Formation of Genesis 1–11: Biblical and Other Precursors* (Oxford: Oxford University Press, 2020), pp. 82, 110, is more confident.

11. Cf. Stade, 'Das Kainszeichen', pp. 264-67; J.M. Miller, 'The Descendants of Cain: Notes on Genesis 4', *ZAW* 88 (1974), pp. 164-73; Scullion, *Genesis*, p. 59.

the birth of Noah in Gen. 5.29, suggesting that this originally belonged in J's Sethite genealogy. So this brings us to the most likely proposal, namely that P drew on J's original full Sethite genealogy (preserved now only at the beginning in Gen. 4.25-26[12] and at the end in 5.29 with the birth of Noah[13]), but a redactor abbreviated this genealogy when P's Sethite genealogy got added, so as to avoid excessive overlap.[14] (That P could reproduce a J genealogy is shown in the postdiluvian genealogy from Arpachshad to Peleg in the table of the nations in Gen. 10.24-25 [J], which is repeated in the post-Noah genealogy in 11.10-16 [P]). We must assume that the Cainite genealogy in Gen. 4.17-24 originally came from a separate layer of J and drew on a similar but not identical genealogy when Cain rather than Seth was added as the first son of Adam and Eve.

12. The beginning of the Sethite genealogy in Gen. 4.25-26, traditionally ascribed to J, has sometimes been seen as a post-P addition intended as a bridge between the Cainite genealogy in Gen. 4 and the Sethite genealogy in Gen. 5. Cf. B.D. Eerdmans, *Die Komposition der Genesis* (Alttestamentliche Studien, I; Giessen: A. Töpelmann, 1908), pp. 80-81; M. Noth, *Überlieferungsgeschichte des Pentateuch* (Stuttgart: W. Kohlhammer, 1948), p. 12 n. 6, ET *A History of Pentateuchal Traditions* (trans. B.W. Anderson; Englewood Cliffs, NJ: Prentice-Hall, 1972), p. 12 n. 26; J. Vermeylen, 'La descendance de Caïn et le descendance d'Abel [Gen 4,17-26 + 5,28b-29]', *ZAW* 103 (1991), pp. 184-86. However, Gen. 4.25-26 has so many J characteristics that it must surely be from J, e.g. word play (on the name Seth), aetiology (Enosh and Yahweh worship), the use of the hiphil of the verb *ḥll*, 'begin' (Gen. 4.26; cf. Gen. 6.1; 9.20; 10.8; 11.6), and the verb *šît*, 'set' (Gen. 4.25; cf. Gen. 3.15)

Those who support Gen. 4.25-26 as a post-P addition appeal to Gen. 4.25's reference to Adam (like P), rather than 'the man' (as earlier in J) and to Eve's use of the divine name Elohim rather than Yahweh in this same verse. However, it is perfectly understandable that J should here refer to the first man as Adam, rather than 'the man', since by that time there were more people around and he was no longer the only man. Again, since Gen. 4.26 states that (for J) men first started calling on the name of Yahweh in the time of Enosh, it makes sense that the word Elohim should be used by humans prior to that, as with the conversations involving Eve in Gen. 3.1-5; 4.25. The story of Cain and Abel, where we find Yahweh, should be seen as later addition; see above, Chapter 5 of this volume.

13. The attribution of Gen. 5.29 to J is widely agreed and is supported by multiple arguments. Thus, it not only uses the divine name Yahweh and engages in word play on a name like J elsewhere, but also refers back to the cursing of the ground and human toil in Gen. 3.17, as well as forward to the discovery of wine in Gen. 9.20ff., both J narratives. Moreover, its use of the verb *qr'* in connection with the naming of Noah is in keeping with the verb used elsewhere in J's Sethite genealogy in Gen. 4.25-26.

14. Similarly Gunkel, *Genesis*, p. 54, ET *Genesis*, p. 54; Skinner, *Genesis*, pp. 99-100; von Rad, *Genesis*, p. 82, ET *Genesis*, p. 108.

Anyway, whatever exactly happened, Enoch in Genesis 5 now appears in seventh place and took on some attributes of one of the long-lived antediluvian figures of the Sumerian King List, Enmeduranki, who is similarly placed seventh in certain versions of the list. An important text from Ashurbanipal's seventh-century library at Nineveh, sometimes called 'Enmeduranki and the Diviners', in which Enmeduranki is instructed in the mysteries of divination by the gods Shamash and Adad in their heavenly assembly and becomes the ancestor of the guild of *bārû* diviners, reads as follows.[15]

> Shamash in Ebabbarra [appointed] Enmeduranki [king of Sippar], the beloved of Anu, Enlil [and Ea]. Shamash and Adad [brought him in] to their assembly, Shamash and Adad [honoured him], Shamash and Adad [set him] on a large throne of gold, they showed him how to observe oil on water, a mystery of Anu, [Enlil and Ea], they gave him the tablet of the gods, the liver, a secret of heaven and [underworld], they put in his hand the cedar-(rod), beloved of the great gods. Then he, in accordance with their [word (?)] brought the men of Nippur, Sippar and Babylon into his presence, and he honoured them. He set them on thrones before [him], he showed them how to observe oil on water, a mystery of Anu, Enlil and Ea, he gave them the tablet of the gods, the liver, a secret of heaven and underworld, he put in their hands the cedar-(rod), beloved of the great gods. The tablet of the gods, the liver, a mystery of heaven and underworld; how to observe oil on water, a secret of Anu, Enlil and Ea; 'that with commentary'; *Enuma Anu Enlil*; and how to make mathematical calculations. The learned savant, who guards the secrets of the great gods will bind his son whom he loves with an oath before Shamash and Adad by tablet and stylus and will instruct him. When a diviner, an expert in oil, of abiding descent, offspring of Enmeduranki, king of Sippar, who set up the pure bowl and held the cedar-(rod), a benediction priest of the king, a long-haired priest of Shamash, as fashioned by Ninḫursagga, begotten by a *nišakku*-priest of pure descent: if he is without blemish in body and limbs he may approach the presence of Shamash and Adad where liver inspection and oracle (take place).

15. W.G. Lambert, 'Enmeduranki and Related Matters', *JCS* 21 (1967), pp. 126-38 (132; pp. 132-33 of this article are devoted to this text). Elsewhere in this article (pp. 126-27, 128-31) Lambert republished another text about Enmeduranki which represents him as the ancestor of the Babylonian king Nebuchadrezzar I. The text above has been re-edited by Lambert in 'The Qualifications of Babylonian Diviners', in S.M. Maul (ed.), *Festschrift für Rykle Borger zu seinem 65. Geburtstag am 24. Mai 1994* (Cuneiform Monographs, 10; Groningen: Styx, 1998), pp. 141-58. He there translates the rest of the text following the Enmeduranki passage above, which deals with the qualifications of *bārû* diviners and the significance of various properties employed in the rites.

That the figure of Enmeduranki has influenced the depiction of Enoch, both in Genesis 5 and in subsequent postbiblical literature, is now widely accepted and goes back to Heinrich Zimmern, with later contributions from Pierre Grelot. The most thorough investigations, however, have been from James C. VanderKam and Helge Kvanvig, the latter changing some of his views in a more recent book.[16] Since these scholars are not always in agreement over all detail, one of the purposes of the subsequent sections of the present chapter will be to re-examine this subject and to evaluate how far exactly the figure of Enmeduranki has influenced the depiction of Enoch in Genesis 5 and the postbiblical literature, and how and when this came about.

Enoch as the Seventh Out of Ten Antediluvian Patriarchs
The first point is that Enoch, like Enmeduranki, is the seventh out of ten long-lived antediluvian figures in Genesis 5 climaxing with the flood hero, just as Enmeduranki (or Euedoranchos as he calls him) is in Berossus's version of the Sumerian King List.[17] There are other versions of the

16. H. Zimmern, 'Urkönige und Uroffenbarung', in E. Schrader (ed.), *Die Keilin-schriften und das Alte Testament* (Berlin: Reuther & Reichard, 3rd edn, 1903), pp. 530-43, esp. 540-41; P. Grelot, 'La légende d'Hénoch dans les Apocryphes et dans la Bible: Origine et signification [part 1]', *RSR* 46 (1958), pp. 5-26; *idem*, 'La légende d'Hénoch dans les Apocryphes et dans la Bible: Origine et signification [part 2]', *RSR* 46 (1958), pp. 181-210; J.C. VanderKam, *Enoch and the Growth of an Apocalyptic Tradition* (CBQMS, 16; Washington, DC: Catholic Biblical Association of America, 1984), pp. 8, 11-12, 18-19, 43-45, 91, 131, 188-89; *idem*, *Enoch: A Man for All Generations* (Columbia, SC: University of South Carolina Press, 1995), pp. 6-10, 13-14; Kvanvig, *Roots of Apocalyptic*, pp. 239-42, 244-46, 265-67; *idem*, *Primeval History*, pp. 255-56. In contrast, H.L. Jansen, *Die Henochgestalt: Eine vergleichende religionsgeschichtliche Untersuchung* (Det Norske Videnskaps-Akademi i Oslo, II. Hist.-Phil. Klasse, 1939, No. 1; Oslo: Jacob Dybwad, 1939), mostly ignored the parallels between Enoch and Enmeduranki. Seth Sanders has recently offered a critique of this view; for my response see the Postscript at the end of this chapter.

17. For Berossus see the English translations and introductions in S.M. Burstein (ed.), *The Babyloniaca of Berossus* (Sources and Monographs: Sources from the Ancient Near East, 1.5; Malibu, CA: Undena Publications, 1978); G.P. Verbrugghe and J.M. Wickersham, *Berossos and Manetho, Introduced and Translated: Native Traditions in Mesopotamia and Egypt* (Ann Arbor: University of Michigan Press, 1996), pp. 11-91. The Greek text of Berossus, together with a German translation of excerpts from the Armenian, may be found in P. Schnabel, *Berossos und die babyl-onisch-hellenistische Literatur* (Leipzig: B.G. Teubner, 1923), as well as F. Jacoby, *Die Fragmente der griechischen Historiker* (14 vols.; Leiden: Brill, 1923–58 [1958]), IIIC.1:364-97 (no. 680).

Sumerian King List:[18] in UCBC 9-1819 Enmeduranki is sixth out of seven or eight, in K 12054 he is sixth out of nine, in WB 444 he is seventh out of eight, in W 20030 7 he is seventh out of seven, and in WB 62 he is eighth out of ten.[19] Claus Westermann questions the dependence of Genesis 5 on the Sumerian King List on the illogical and inaccurate grounds that that earlier versions of the King List have allegedly eight kings (in fact there are variously eight, nine or ten, as just noted, and the very earliest, WB 62, has ten, like the late Berossus).[20] It should hardly surprise us that P agrees with Berossus, as both are relatively late sources. Moreover, there are, interestingly, other parallels between P and Berossus regarding the subsequent flood story. Thus, (1) both P and Berossus locate the landing of the ark in Armenia as opposed to the earlier Mt Nimush in Kurdistan mentioned in the Gilgamesh epic; (2) unlike earlier attested versions of the flood story, P and Berossus give precise dates for the start of the flood, and these are only two days different: the seventeenth day of the second month in P and the fifteenth day of the second month in Berossus (both using the spring new year); (3) unlike in earlier versions of the flood story, both P and Berossus give precise dimensions for the ark; and (4) in both P and Berossus the ark no longer has sides with identical length and breadth but is a rectangular structure in which the length is greater than the breadth.[21] Berossus was an early third-century BCE Babylonian priest

18. For the antediluvian rulers of the Sumerian king List, see T. Jacobsen, *The Sumerian King List* (Assyriological Studies, 11: University of Chicago Press, 1939), pp. 70-77; J. van Dijk, 'Die Tontafeln aus dem *rēš*-Heiligtum', in H.J. Lenzen (ed.), *XVIII vorläufiger Bericht über die von dem Deutschen Archäologischen Institut und der Deutschen Orient-Gesellschaft aus dem Mitteln der Deutschen Forschungsgemeinschaft unternommenen Ausgrabungen in Uruk-Warka* (Berlin: Gebr. Mann, 1962), pp. 43-52; J.J. Finkelstein, 'The Antediluvian Kings: A University of California Tablet', *JCS* 17 (1963), pp. 39-54 (45-46); Jean-Jacques Glassner, *Mesopotamian Chronicles* (SBLWAW; Leiden: Brill, 2004), pp. 57-59. See too the helpful chart in VanderKam, *Enoch and the Growth*, pp. 36-37, as well as Kvanvig, *Roots of Apocalyptic*, pp. 160-72, for valuable comparative material on the different versions of the Sumerian King List.

19. Hence the statement of J.J. Collins, *The Apocalyptic Imagination* (Grand Rapids, MI: Eerdmans, 3rd edn, 2016), p. 45, that 'in the *Sumerian King List* the seventh king is Enmeduranki or Enmeduranna', requires nuancing. Incidentally, Berossus's form of the name, Euedoranchos, supports reading Enmeduranki.

20. Westermann, *Genesis 1–11*, pp. 471-77, 485-86, ET *Genesis 1–11*, pp. 348-52, 358. See too G. Hasel, 'The Genealogies of Gen 5 and 11 and their Alleged Babylonian Background', *AUSS* 16 (1978), pp. 361-74.

21. I have argued all this in much greater detail in J. Day, 'The Flood and the Ten Antediluvian Figures in Berossus and in the Priestly Source in Genesis', in J.K.

and, in view of the likely sixth-century date for P, P's traditions about the flood as well as Enoch were doubtless derived from the sixth-century BCE Jewish experience of exile in Babylonia.

365 Years as Evidence of Enoch's Solar Connection

The second point of contact between Enoch in Genesis 5 and Enmeduranki is that both have a solar connection. According to Gen. 5.23 Enoch lived for a total of 365 years. Significantly, this is agreed unanimously by the Masoretic text, Septuagint and Samaritan versions, even though these sometimes differ in numerical details elsewhere in this chapter. Since the time of Heinrich Zimmern it has been common to see this as deriving from the fact that Enoch's prototype, Enmeduranki, was king of Sippar, the city of the sun god Shamash, who appointed him king, and into whose presence (alongside the god Adad) he was privileged to enter and receive instruction in divination and astronomy/astrology (see 'Enmeduranki and the Diviners' above).[22] However, this has been disputed by a minority of scholars. For example, Roland de Vaux, Walther Zimmerli and Claus Westermann prefer to see Enoch's 365-year life as symbolic of a well-rounded, full life.[23] This, however, is unlikely, since Enoch was actually by far the shortest lived of any of the ten antediluvian patriarchs of Genesis 5 (of the other nine, seven were over 900, one over 800, and one over 700 years). In any case, the idea of 365 years being symbolic of a full life is admittedly derived from the fact that 365 days is the length of a solar year, so even this explanation does not succeed in denying a

---

Aitken, K.J. Dell and B.A. Mastin (eds.), *On Stone and Scroll: A Festschrift for Graham Ivor Davies* (BZAW 420; Berlin: W. de Gruyter, 2011), pp. 211-23, reprinted in expanded form in Day, *From Creation to Babel*, pp. 61-76. I should add that G. Darshan, 'The Calendrical Framework of the Priestly Flood Story in Light of a New Akkadian Text from Ugarit (RS 94.2953)', *JAOS* 136 (2016), pp. 507-14, has drawn attention to an Akkadian text from Ugarit which, if correctly interpreted, seems to date the breaking open of a window and sending out of birds by the flood hero at the beginning of a month (new moon). Darshan compares this to Noah's sending out of a raven from the ark in the P source following the appearance of the mountains on the first day of the tenth month (Gen. 8.5, 7). But we cannot say if this text gives a date for the beginning of the flood, since earlier parts of the text are not preserved.

22. Zimmern, 'Urkönige und Uroffenbarung', p. 540; Grelot, 'La légende d'Hénoch [part 2]', p. 187; VanderKam, *Enoch and the Growth*, pp. 38, 43-44; *idem*, *Enoch: A Man*, pp. 7-8; Kvanvig, *Roots of Apocalyptic*, pp. 227-28.

23. R. de Vaux, *La Genèse* (La sainte Bible; Paris: Cerf, 1962), p. 55; W. Zimmerli, *1. Mose 1–11* (ZBK; Zurich: Zwingli, 3rd edn, 1967), p. 256; Westermann, *Genesis 1–11*, p. 485, ET *Genesis 1–11*, p. 358.

connection with the solar calendar. Further, it raises the question why this particular year-length should be chosen as the basis for fulness. Armin Schmitt,[24] however, thinks that it is possible that Enoch's relatively early disappearance was simply arranged to spare his suffering in the deluge. He further, more confidently, denies that his 365-year life has any solar connection on the grounds that P would not have been aware of the length of a solar year because the Jews used a lunar calendar. As for these two arguments, the former is quite implausible, since whether we follow the Masoretic, Septuagint or Samaritan chronology, Enoch's disappearance is represented as occurring already several hundred years before the flood. With regard to Schmitt's second argument, it is mere supposition that the Jews would not have known of the solar calendar in P's time (they certainly did later, and there was awareness of the 365-day solar year already in Egypt, Mesopotamia and Greece at the time of P). In any case, Enoch's very distinctive 365-year life span can hardly have been the result of chance, and the only plausible explanation is that it is a reflection of Enmeduranki's strong solar connection.[25]

Enoch Walked with God

A third point of comparison between Enoch and Enmeduranki is that both are said to have had intimate fellowship with God or the gods. As noted above, Enmeduranki was received into their divine assembly by Shamash and Adad, while in the case of Enoch it is stated that 'Enoch walked (*hithallēk*) with God' (Gen. 5.22, 24). This precise phrase, attributing a high degree of fellowship with God, is employed in the Old Testament elsewhere only of Noah in Gen. 6.9, where we read, 'Noah a righteous man, was blameless man in his generations. Noah walked with God.' However, Abraham is said to have walked before God (Gen. 17.1;

24. A. Schmitt, *Entrückung – Aufnahme – Himmelfahrt: Untersuchungen im Alten Testament* (FzB, 10; Stuttgart: Verlag Katholisches Bibelwerk, 1973), pp. 171-73.

25. Kvanvig, *Roots of Apocalyptic*, p. 52, claims that the length of the flood in P also presupposes knowledge of the 365-day solar year, since it lasts from the seventeenth day of the second month till the twenty-seventh day of the second month of the next year (Gen. 7.11; 8.14), which amounts to 365 days if one counts inclusively and assumes that P presupposes a lunar year of 354 days. However, Kvanvig does not discuss how he reconciles this with the fact that in P the coming of the flood waters, lasting from the seventeenth day of the second month till the seventeenth day of the seventh month, is said to amount to 150 days (Gen. 7.11, 24; 8.3-4), implying a 30-day month and presumably a 360-day year. This exceeds a 354-day lunar year, which Kvanvig's calculation of 365 days from the seventeenth day of the seventh month till the twenty-seventh day of the second month the following year implies.

24.40; 48.15) – the meaning is probably not that different – while the qal (rather than hithpael) of *hlk* in connection with walking with God is found in Mal. 2.6 and Mic. 6.8. It seems that the primary meaning of the phrase 'walk with God' is that one was a pious person having intimate fellowship with God. Moreover, the phrase 'walk with God' is repeatedly associated with righteous moral behaviour (cf. Gen. 6.9; Mic. 6.8; Mal. 2.6; similarly with 'walk before God' in Gen. 17.1). This is not something specifically attributed to Enmeduranki, though the fact that Shamash and Adad favoured Enmeduranki with their presence in the unusual way that they did might imply this.

We have above followed the usual translation, 'Enoch walked with God (*hā'ĕlōhîm*)'. James C. VanderKam, however, has conjectured that what P actually meant is that 'Enoch walked with the angels (lit. gods)', reflecting an underlying foreign polytheistic source about Enmeduranki.[26] However, though *hā'ĕlōhîm* rather than *'ĕlōhîm* is rare in P, when it does occur it is always after a preposition; in addition to Gen. 5.22, 24, note Gen. 6.9, 11; 17.18 and Exod. 2.23.[27] Moreover, apart from 'God' having the support of the ancient Versions,[28] it should be noted that the identical expression used in connection with Noah in Gen. 6.9 likewise has *hā'ĕlōhîm* instead of *'ĕlōhîm*, and moreover, the text continues using *hā'ĕlōhîm* subsequently in Gen. 6.11 to mean God. In this latter verse it is difficult to see why the meaning should be 'Now the earth was corrupt in the sight of the angels' rather than 'Now the earth was corrupt in the sight of God', especially as the next verse continues, ' *'ĕlōhîm* saw (singular) the earth, and behold it was corrupt', which has to refer specifically to God. Further, with regard to Gen. 6.9, Noah is nowhere else associated with angels, which likewise makes it more natural that God is being referred to. Similarly, therefore, with regard to Gen. 5.22, 24, the traditional rendering 'Enoch walked with God' should be retained. In addition, in support of *hā'ĕlōhîm* meaning

26. VanderKam, *Enoch and the Growth*, p. 31; *idem, Enoch: A Man*, p. 13. Cf. Skinner, *Genesis*, p. 131, who much earlier had proposed that *hā'ĕlōhîm* presupposed P's use of a polytheistic source referring to 'the gods'.

27. I am grateful to Jan Joosten for pointing this out to me. It was first noted by T. Nöldeke, *Untersuchungen zur Kritik des Alten Testaments* (Kiel: Schwers, 1869), p. 4 n. 1.

28. The Vulgate and Aquila translate literally, but the other extant versions paraphrase. All, however, render 'God' except Symmachus, who leaves *hā'ĕlōhîm* untranslated. On the LXX rendering, 'And Enoch was pleasing to God' (similarly Peshitta), see A. Schmitt, 'Die Angaben über Henoch Gen 5.21-24 in der LXX', in J. Schreiner (ed.), *Wort, Lied und Gottesspruch: Beiträge zur Septuaginta* (FzB, 1; Würzburg: Echter Verlag, 1972), pp. 161-69.

'God' when used with a preposition, we may note that Gen. 17.18 says 'And Abraham said to *hā'elōhîm*, "O that Ishmael might live in your (singular) sight"', and Exod. 2.23 states of Israel that 'their cry under bondage came up to *hā'elōhîm*', and then the next verse continues, 'And *'elōhîm* heard (singular) their groaning'. It is quite clear from all this that when P uses *hā'elōhîm* to denote 'God' it is after a preposition, and this explains Gen. 5.22, 24.

It should be noted that the phrase 'Enoch walked with *hā'elōhîm*' occurs twice, not only in Gen. 5.22 but also in v. 24. VanderKam[29] claims that whereas the former verse refers to this life, the latter alludes to Enoch's heavenly fellowship after his removal from this world. But it is surely more natural to suppose that v. 24 is simply reiterating what has been said in v. 22. If v. 24 really speaks of Enoch's post-translation existence we should expect the text to read 'he was not, for God took him. And Enoch walked with God', not 'Enoch walked with God and was not, for God took him'.

In being transformed into Enoch, the polytheistic figure of Enmeduranki was 'monotheized', as was also the case with several other characters appropriated by the Israelites from ancient Near Eastern polytheistic culture, including Noah, Balaam, Daniel and Ahiqar.

'He was Not, for God Took Him'

After being told for the second time that Enoch walked with God we are informed that 'he was not, for God took him' (Gen. 5.24). A minority view, supported by Umberto (Moshe D.) Cassuto has held that this refers to Enoch's death, an opinion anticipated in Targum Onqelos, *Genesis Rabbah* and Rashi, doubtless unsympathetic to the kind of ideas we find in the Enochic literature.[30] However, although references to people being 'no more' can refer to death (e.g. Job 7.21; 8.22; Ps. 39.14, ET 13), in the context of Genesis 5 this is extremely unlikely, since all the other nine antediluvian patriarchs are explicitly stated to have died. Something different with Enoch must therefore be intended.

Claus Westermann[31] has noted that we are not told explicitly where Enoch was taken. However, since it is mentioned in connection with his having walked with God, we may assume – as has generally been done both in antiquity and modern times – that heaven was intended, as a reward for Enoch's piety. In keeping with this, we may note that the

---

29. VanderKam, *Enoch and the Growth*, 31; *idem, Enoch: A Man*, p. 13.
30. Cassuto, *Genesis*, I, p. 285.
31. Westermann, *Genesis 1–11*, p. 486, ET *Genesis 1–11*, pp. 358-59.

same verb *lqḥ*, 'took', is also used of God's causing Elijah to ascend to heaven at the end of his earthly life in 2 Kgs 2.3, 5, 9, 10.[32] Reward for piety seems much more likely than the view of Lothar Zachmann[33] that Enoch was removed from the earth early so as to spare him contact with the sinful earth.

Granted, as is generally accepted, that Enoch was taken up into heaven at the end of his earthly life as a reward for his piety, we are faced by the situation that this does not correspond to what is known about Enmeduranki. Although Enmeduranki was taken up into the unseen world to sit with Shamash and Adad during his life, he did not ascend at the end. Rykle Borger,[34] however, believed that this problem could be dealt with by assuming that the motif of Enoch's translation was an appropriation from Enmeduranki's Apkallu (sage), Utuabzu, of whom it was stated, 'he ascended to heaven',[35] but we are not told whether this was at the end of his life or not. However, that Enoch's taking to heaven was an appropriation from Utuabzu appears less likely than the suggestion that it was borrowed from the Mesopotamian flood hero.[36] Thus, whereas we have no sure evidence that the Israelites had ever heard of such an obscure figure as the Apakallu Utuabzu, we have definite information that they knew about the Mesopotamian flood hero, much of whose story was

32. The same verb is used of the psalmists' transference to a blessed afterlife in Ps. 49.16 (ET 15) and 73.24, though here life after death rather than life without death seems to be meant. See the discussion in J. Day, 'The Development of Belief in Life after Death in Ancient Israel', in J. Barton and D.J. Reimer (eds.), *After the Exile: Essays in Honour of Rex Mason* (Macon, GA: Mercer University Press, 1996), pp. 231-57 (253-56).

Incidentally, R.B. ten Hoopen, 'Where Are You, Enoch? Why Can't I Find You? Genesis 5:21-24 Reconsidered', *JHS* 18 (2018), article 4, has argued that Enoch's location in heaven is a later idea, and that P originally conceived of Enoch as being transferred to a mythological place on earth, such as the Garden of Eden.

33. L. Zachmann, 'Beobachtungen zur Theologie in Gen 5', *ZAW* 88 (1976), pp. 272-74.

34. R. Borger, 'Die Beschwörungsserie *bît mēseri* und die Himmelfahrt Henochs', *JNES* 33 (1974), pp. 183-96, reprinted in abbreviated English translation as 'The Incantation Series *Bît Mēseri* and Enoch's Ascension to Heaven', in R.S. Hess and D.T. Tsumura (eds.), *"I Studied Inscriptions from before the Flood": Ancient Near Eastern, Literary, and Linguistic Approaches to Genesis 1–11* (Sources for Biblical and Theological Study 4; Winona Lake, IN: Eisenbrauns, 1994), pp. 234-53.

35. See Borger, 'Die Beschwörungsserie', p. 192, ET 'The Incantation Series', p. 230.

36. E.g. Grelot, 'La légende d'Hénoch', pp. 189-99; VanderKam, *Enoch and the Growth*, pp. 47-48.

appropriated in the biblical flood story. Moreover, whereas it is merely stated of Utuabzu that 'he ascended to heaven', the Mesopotamian flood hero Utanapishti specifically declares, 'They [i.e. the gods] *took* me and settled me far away, at the mouth of the river' (Gilgamesh 11.206). It will be noted that the verb 'took' (*leqû*) is cognate with the verb *lqḥ* used of Enoch, 'he was not for God *took* him'. Even closer to Gilgamesh is *Jub.* 4.23, which states, 'He [Enoch] was taken from human society, and we led him to the Garden of Eden …'

The Emergence of the Apocalyptic Enoch Tradition

A mere four verses are devoted to the figure of Enoch in Gen. 5.21-24 (plus vv. 18-20, though these are primarily about his father Jared). However, in subsequent centuries a vast literature grew up about this figure, first of all in the composite book, *1 Enoch* (the Astronomical Enoch, the Book of Watchers, the Epistle of Enoch, the Book of Dreams, and the Similitudes of Enoch), to which may be added the Book of Giants, and subsequently *2* and *3 Enoch* (cf. *Jub.* 4.16-25; Sir. 44.16; Wis. 4.10-15), just to mention the most important. How did this come about? We shall not be discussing all these works in detail here, but will consider in particular how the apocalyptic Enoch tradition arose and the extent to which this was dependent on Enmeduranki (or other Babylonian traditions), as well as on Gen. 5.21-24. The later development of the Enochic tradition will be treated more briefly.

As we shall see below, the most fundamental difference between Gen. 5.21-24 and the subsequent apocalyptic Enoch traditions is that, in the latter, Enoch is the receiver and transmitter of divine mysteries, including some of an astronomical nature, just like Enmeduranki. Similarly, Enoch also had access to the tablets of heaven, just as Enmeduranki was given the tablet of the gods, and in both provision is made for the communication of the mysteries from father to son. These facts support the supposition that the subsequent Enochic literature was also influenced by the figure of Enmeduranki, just as Enoch had been in Gen. 5.18-24. Since the Priestly source, in which this biblical passage occurs, dates from the exilic or early post-exilic period, one may speculate that the Babylonian Enmeduraki traditions were assimilated by the Jews in the sixth century BCE during the Babylonian exile, including those paralleling Enmeduranki just referred to that are not already attested in the laconic passage in Gen. 5.18-24. These Enochic traditions were preserved and continued to be developed during the post-exilic period and were taken up at Qumran, where our earliest Enoch texts have been discovered.

In the course of the process outlined above, Enmeduranki, the diviner, was transformed into Enoch, the apocalyptic seer.

Astronomical Enoch

The oldest Enochic booklet within *1 Enoch* is the Astronomical Enoch (*1 En.* 72–82), the earliest fragments of which in the Dead Sea scrolls are agreed to go back to the late third or early second century BCE. The 365 years attributed to Enoch in Gen. 5.23 indicate that Enoch already had an astronomical connection in the time of P in the sixth century BCE, derived, as we have seen, from Enmeduranki's solar connections. Józef T. Milik,[37] in fact, argued that the Astronomical Book was already known to P, and went so far as to propose that Gen. 5.23 originally read that Enoch lived on earth 364, not 365, years, in keeping with the 364-day year referred to in the Astronomical Book (*1 En.* 72.32; 74.10, 12-13; 82.4, 6). However, these views of Milik have gained no support, lacking as they do any versional or Hebrew manuscript support, and in any case it is unlikely that the Astronomical Book is as old as this.[38] The Astronomical Book's year of 364 days envisages eight months of 30 days, and four months of 31 days (months 3, 6, 9, 12). This precise calendar is not attested outside Israel, but Wayne Horowitz claims to have found evidence of a 364-day calendar in Babylonia from the seventh century BCE till the Hellenistic period, which he thinks ultimately lies behind it, though this Babylonian calendar was a 354-day lunar calendar supplemented by an additional ten days.[39] The Astronomical Enoch advocates a year of 364 rather than 365 days because it is perfectly divisible by seven, so it is schematic rather than being exactly solar. But unlike the later book of *Jubilees* it does not polemicize against the use of the lunar calendar.[40]

37. J.T. Milik, *The Books of Enoch: Aramaic Fragments of Qumrân Cave 4* (Oxford: Clarendon Press, 1976), p. 8.

38. Cf. J.C. Greenfield and M.E. Stone (eds.), 'The Books of Enoch and the Traditions of Enoch', *Numen* 26 (1979), pp. 89-103 (92-98).

39. See W. Horowitz, 'The 360 and 364 Day Year in Ancient Mesopotamia'. *JANES* 24 (1996), pp. 20-44 (40-41); *idem, Mesopotamian Cosmic Geography* (Mesopotamian Civilizations, 8; Winona Lake, IN: Eisenbrauns, 1998), p. 185; *idem,* 'The 364 Day Year in Mesopotamia, Again', *NABU* (1998), pp. 49-51 (no. 49). Horowitz's conclusions have been challenged by J. Koch, 'AO 6478, MUL.APIN und das 364 Tage Jahr', *NABU* (1996), pp. 97-99 (no. 111); *idem,* 'Ein für allemal: Das antike Mesopotamien kannte kein 364 Tage-Jahr', *NABU* (1998), pp. 112-14 (no. 121).

40. Qumran famously also employed an imperfectly solar 364-day calendar, but certain of the Dead Sea scrolls use the lunar calendar (with intercalations). In

Insofar as there is polemic, it is against omitting the four intercalary days and thus having a year of only 360 days (*1 En.* 75.1-2; 82.4-6).[41] In fact, the Astronomical Enoch also refers to the lunar calendar of 354 days in the same calm, objective way that it discusses the solar calendar, and compares them (*1 En.* 74; 78.15-16; 79.3-5). In addition to the sun and moon, the Astronomical Enoch also goes on to discuss the stars, the wind, and various geographical features of the earth. All this makes it unlikely that the contents of the Astronomical Enoch simply arose from reflection on Enoch's 365-year lifespan in Genesis 5 but supports the idea that traditions relating to Enmeduranki have exercised an influence. As stated in 'Enmeduranki and the Diviners', part of the divinatory instruction which Enmeduranki passed on is called *Enuma Anu Enlil*, which constitute the first three words of a series of important omen texts dealing with the moon, sun, meteorological phenomena, planets and fixed stars, topics almost identical to those dealt with in the Astronomical Enoch. Moreover, following the reference to *Enuma Anu Enlil* we are told that Enmeduranki passed on 'how to make mathematical calculations', the word 'mathematical calculations' (Akkadian *arû*) often being used in connection with astronomy. In fact, Matthias Albani has shown that the Astronomical Enoch book was dependent on MUL.APIN ('The Plough'), a Babylonian astronomical and astrological work closely related to *Enuma Anu Enlil*, and Henryk Drawnel has demonstrated that the Astronomical Enoch drew on *Enuma Anu Enlil* 14 itself.[42] However, in the Jewish context what had

this way Qumran stands closer to the Astronomical Enoch than it does to *Jubilees*. See J.C. VanderKam, *Calendars in the Dead Sea Scrolls: Measuring Time* (London: Routledge, 1998), esp. pp. 43-116, with notes on pp. 118-23. On the 364-day calendar, see J. Ben-Dov, 'The 364-Day Year in the Dead Sea Scrolls and Jewish Pseudepigrapha', in J.M. Steele (ed.), *Calendars and* Years. II. *Astronomy and Time in the Ancient and Medieval World* (Oxford: Oxbow Books, 2011), pp. 69-105.

41. It has been claimed that the fragmentary Aramaic text of the Astronomical Enoch (4Q208-209) might actually support a 360-day year. See M. Albani, *Astronomie und Schöpfungsglaube. Untersuchungen zum Astronomischen Henochbuch* (WMANT, 68; Neukirchen-Vluyn: Neukirchener Verlag, 1994), pp. 75-83; H.R. Jacobus, *Zodiac Calendars in the Dead Sea Scrolls and their Reception* (IJS, 14; Leiden: Brill, 2014), pp. 334-40. For the official publication of 4Q208-209 see E.J.C. Tigchelaar and Florentino García Martínez in S.J. Pfann *et al.*, *Qumran Cave 4. XXVI: Cryptic Texts and Miscellanies, Part 1* (DJD, 36; Oxford: Clarendon Press, 2000), pp. 95-103, 104-31, 132-71. Jacobus, *Zodiac Calendars*, pp. 272-74 also finds evidence of a 360-day year in the Ethiopic Enoch (*1 En.* 72.35; 74.10a, 11; 75.1-2).

42. Albani, *Astronomie und Schöpfungsglaube*, pp. 173-272; more briefly K. Koch, 'The Astral Laws as the Basis of Time, Universal History and the Eschatological Turn in the Astronomical Book and the Animal Apocalypse of 1 Enoch', in G. Boccaccini

been astrological elements were eliminated so that we now have purely astronomical references.

1 Enoch 81 is widely believed to be a later addition to the Astronomical Enoch. However, it so happens that it contains two parallels in the Enmeduranki tradition that merit attention. First, in *1 En.* 81.1-2, we have a reference to Enoch seeing the tablets of heaven. It is stated that all the deeds of humanity are written on them. Three more references to the tablets of heaven occur later in the Epistle of Enoch in *1 En.* 93.2, 103.2 and 106.19–107.1, which contain predictions or pseudo-predictions of the future, including eschatological events. The allusion in 93.2 actually refers to the predictions of the Apocalypse of Weeks (93.1-10, continued in the misplaced 91.11-17). Since Heinrich Zimmern and Pierre Grelot[43] it has been common to see these tablets of heaven as originating in the 'tablet of the gods' which Enmeduranki received from Shamash and Adad in their divine assembly and which Enmeduranki passed on to others (see above, 'Enmeduranki and the Diviners'). Unfortunately, we do not know exactly what this was but the context indicates that it was used in divination. W.G. Lambert thinks it might have been an inscribed liver model.[44]

A second parallel to Enmeduranki in *1 Enoch* 81 concerns the fact that in v. 5 Enoch is told to 'make everything known to your son Methuselah' (cf. *1 En.* 76.14; 79.1; 82.1-2), just as the text on 'Enmeduranki and the Diviners' declares that 'the learned savant, who guards the secrets of the great gods, will bind his son whom he loves with an oath before Shamash and Adad by tablet and stylus and will instruct him'.

In the Astronomical Enoch, Enoch receives all his astronomical instructions from the angel Uriel (cf. *1 En.* 72.1; 74.2; 75.3-4; 78.10; 79.2, 6; 80.1). Helge Kvanvig has conjectured that the figure of Uriel derives

and J.J. Collins (eds.), *The Early Enoch Literature* (JSJSup, 121; Leiden: Brill, 2007), pp. 119-37 (121-28); H. Drawnel, 'Moon Computation in the Aramaic Astronomical Book', *RevQ* 23 (2007), pp. 3-41. See too the discussion in J. Ben-Dov, *Head of All Years: Astronomy and Calendars at Qumran in their Ancient Context* (Studies in the Texts of the Desert of Judah, 78; Leiden: Brill, 2008), pp. 153-96; G.W.E. Nickelsburg and J.C. VanderKam, *1 Enoch. II. A Commentary on the Book of Enoch Chapters 37–82* (Hermeneia; Minneapolis, MN: Fortress Press, 2012), pp. 373-83 (esp. 377-83); J.C. VanderKam, 'Enoch's Science', in J. Ben-Dov and S. Sanders (eds.), *Ancient Jewish Sciences and the History of Knowledge in Second Temple Judaism* (New York: New York University Press, 2014), pp. 51-67 (63).

43. Zimmern, 'Urkönige und Uroffenbarung', pp. 540-41; P. Grelot, 'La légende d'Hénoch [part 1]', p. 15; VanderKam, *Enoch and the Growth*, p. 152; Kvanvig, *Roots of Apocalyptic*, pp. 239-42.

44. Lambert, 'Enmeduranki and Related Matters', p. 133.

from Adapa (also called Uanadapa and U-An; Berossus' Oannes), the first Babylonian Apkallu or sage, who revealed certain things to humanity.[45] However, this should probably be rejected, even though his short name U-An and Uriel have similar meanings, because it is not from U-An that Enmeduranki receives his heavenly instructions but rather from Shamash and Adad. One might suggest, therefore, that the figure of Uriel in *1 Enoch* 73–82 rather derives from Shamash.[46] Uriel means 'light of God' or 'My God is light', which plausibly fits an origin in the sun, and Shamash was similarly called 'light of the gods' (*nūr ilāni*). However, if so, it must be noted that Uriel, who is described as the leader of the heavenly luminaries, is now distinguished from the sun (cf. *1 En.* 75.3).

The Book of the Watchers

After the Astronomical Book, the next oldest part of *1 Enoch* is the Book of the Watchers, the earliest fragments of which from Qumran date from the first half of the second century BCE. Although *1 Enoch* 1–36 as a whole is commonly known as the Book of the Watchers, the story of the sexual intercourse between the Watchers and human women, the consequences of it and associated events, are concentrated in *1 Enoch* 6–16, and we shall discuss these chapters shortly. Subsequent to this incident a considerable part of the Book of the Watchers concerns Enoch's acquisition of cosmological knowledge as a result of his travels throughout the universe under angelic guidance (*1 En.* 17–36). There is some analogy here with the Astronomical Enoch, but two differences should be noted. First, in the Book of the Watchers the eschatological element is more marked, with repeated references to the coming punishment of the wicked angels (*1 En.* 16.1; 18.11-16; 19.1; 21.1-10; cf. 10.12-14) as well as of wicked humanity (*1 En.* 22.3-13; 27.2-4; cf. 1.2-9, which also includes salvation for the righteous). Secondly, the knowledge acquired is not so narrowly focused on astronomy, since Enoch learns the secrets of heaven, earth and the underworld more generally. At this point we are reminded that Shamash and Adad imparted to Enmeduranki 'a secret of heaven and underworld' and afterwards Enmeduranki instructed certain people in it. This terminology is suggestive of cosmological knowledge.

---

45. Kvanvig, *Roots of Apocalyptic*, pp. 237-38.

46. I thought of this myself only to discover that I had been anticipated by Albani, *Astronomie und Schöpfungsgeschichte*, pp. 300-10, who also points out various other interesting parallels between Shamash and Uriel.

The actual story of the Watchers in *1 Enoch* 6–16, however, cannot claim any background in Enmeduranki or other Babylonian traditions. There seem to be no good reasons to follow the view of Kvanvig and Amar Annus that the Watchers derive from the Apkallus.[47] As Henryk Drawnel has pointed out, the Apkallus were never represented as rebels who came down from heaven, and while the Watchers descended from heaven to earth, the Apkallus ascended from the primaeval ocean.[48] Rather, since the sons of God of Gen. 6.2, 4 lie behind the Watchers of *1 Enoch*, there seems to me no reason why they should not have an ultimately Canaanite background ('the sons of El'), like the sons of God elsewhere in the Old Testament,[49] though the story which we now have in Gen. 6.1-4 and *1 Enoch* 6–16 represents an Israelite and Jewish development.

Nevertheless, some scholars have argued in recent decades that the story in *1 Enoch* 6–16 preserves even more ancient traditions than those which we possess in Gen. 6.1-4.[50] This trend has been encouraged by the fact that the story in Gen. 6.1-4 is so laconic, suggesting that there must have been more to it than what is recounted here, combined with the fact that the Qumran manuscripts have shown the Book of the Watchers to be older than previously supposed, in addition to the tendency to date J later

47. A. Annus, 'On the Origin of the Watchers: A Comparative Study of the Antediluvian Wisdom in Mesopotamian and Jewish Tradition', *JSP* 19 (2010), pp. 277-320; Kvanvig, *Roots of Apocalyptic*, pp. 313-15.

48. H. Drawnel, review of Kvanvig, *Primeval History*, in *The Biblical Annals/ Roczike Biblijne* 2 (2012), pp. 355-61 (357-58, 361).

49. See J. Day, *Yahweh and the Gods and Goddesses of Canaan* (JSOTSup, 263; Sheffield: Sheffield Academic Press, 2000), pp. 22-24.

50. Milik, *The Books of Enoch*, pp. 30-32; M. Barker, 'Some Reflections upon the Enoch Myth', *JSOT* 15 (1980), pp. 7-29; *idem*, *The Older Testament: The Survival of Themes from the Ancient Royal Cult in Sectarian Judaism and Early Christianity* (London: SCM Press, 1987), pp. 18-19; M. Black, *The Book of Enoch or 1 Enoch: A New English Edition with Commentary and Textual Notes* (SVTP, 7; Leiden: Brill, 1985), pp. 14, 124-25; P.R. Davies, 'The Sons of Cain', in J.D. Martin and P.R. Davies (eds.), *A Word in Season: Essays in Honour of William McKane* (JSOTSup, 42; Sheffield: Sheffield Academic Press, 1986), pp. 35-56 (46-50); *idem*, 'And Enoch was not, for Genesis took him', in C. Hempel and J.M. Lieu (eds.), *Biblical Traditions in Transmission: Essays in Honour of Michael A. Knibb* (Leiden: Brill, 2006), pp. 97-107 (100-104); I. Fröhlich, 'Origins of Evil in Genesis and the Apocalyptic Traditions', in S.W. Crawford and C. Wassén (eds.), *Apocalyptic Thinking in Early Judaism: Engaging with John Collins' The Apocalyptic Imagination* (JSJSup, 182; Leiden: Brill, 2018), pp. 141-59. It should also be noted that, reversing his earlier view, Kvanvig, *Primeval History*, pp. 519-20, now thinks Gen. 6.1-4 was dependent on the Shemihazah tradition that we find in *1 Enoch*.

than earlier scholars had done. However, whilst it is surely likely that the original story contained more than is found in Gen. 6.1-4, that does not mean that it corresponds to what we find in *1 Enoch*.

There are many indications, in fact, that the story of the Watchers contained within *1 Enoch* 6–16 is rather a later elaboration of Gen. 6.1-4.[51] For example, the very fact that *1 Enoch* 1–36 is presented as a vision of Enoch (cf. *1 En.* 1.2) and that Enoch himself interacts with the Watchers (*1 En.* 12–16) implies that the Book of the Watchers already knew the Pentateuch in its final form, in which J and P were joined together, for the story of the sons of God in Gen. 6.1-4 comes from J and the note about Enoch in Gen. 5.21-24 is from P. Again, the very term 'watcher' ('*îr*) as a name for the angels appears in the Old Testament only in the late book of Daniel (Dan. 4.10, 14, 20, ET 13, 17, 23). Moreover, the fact that Gen. 6.1-4 refers to 'the sons of God', whereas *1 Enoch* alludes to these beings as 'the angels, the children of heaven' (*1 En.* 6.2), clearly implies the priority of the former. For example, the use of 'children of heaven' for 'sons of God' is readily comprehensible in the light of the later euphemistic habit of alluding to 'heaven' rather than 'God'. Again, the multitude of angelic names given in *1 En.* 6.7, in contrast to the anonymous 'sons of God' referred to in Gen. 6.2, 4, is another clear sign of the lateness of the Enoch account, for it was only with the rise of apocalyptic that angels started to receive individual names.

By expanding the text as it does, the Book of the Watchers not only filled out in an interesting way the content of the laconic Gen. 6.1-4, but by elaborating on the wickedness prevalent on the earth as a result of the Watchers' actions it also provided a more comprehensible explanation for the subsequent devastating flood (cf. *Jub.* 5.1-5; 7.21-25; Josephus, *Ant.* 1.3.1-2), which in the Genesis account is connected only loosely to what follows.

51. In this I agree with Mathias Delcor, 'Le mythe de la chute des anges et de l'origine des géants comme explication du mal dans le monde dans l'apocalyptique juive. Histoire des traditions', *RHR* 190 (1976), pp. 3-53; G.W.E. Nickelsburg, 'Apocalyptic and Myth in 1 Enoch 6–11', *JBL* 96 (1977), pp. 383-405; D. Dimant, 'Use and Interpretation of Mikra in the Apocrypha and Pseudepigrapha', in M.J. Mulder (ed.), *Mikra: Text, Translation, Reading of the Hebrew Bible in Ancient Judaism and Early Christianity* (Assen: Van Gorcum, 1988), pp. 379-419 (404-406); J.J. Collins, 'The Sons of God and the Daughters of Men', in M. Nissinen and R. Uro (eds.), *Sacred Marriages: The Divine–Human Sexual Metaphor from Sumer to Early Christianity* (Winona Lake, IN: Eisenbrauns, 2008), pp. 259-74 (264). I myself have earlier discussed this question in J. Day, 'The Sons of God and Daughters of Men and the Giants', *Hebrew Bible and Ancient Israel* 1.4 (2012), pp. 427-47 (434-36), reprinted in Day, *From Creation to Babel*, pp. 77-97 (84-85).

One may also note that a strong case can be made for supposing that the Book of the Watchers has reinterpreted Genesis 5's references to Enoch's walking with God as alluding to his walking with the angels. Whilst we have rejected above the view of VanderKam that Gen. 5.22, 24 understood *hā'elōhîm* to mean 'the angels' rather than 'God', there can be no doubt that the Book of the Watchers took it this way. Compare *1 En* 12.2, which declares of Enoch, 'And his dwelling place as well as his activities were with the Watchers and the holy ones'. Moreover, throughout his journeys in the Book of the Watchers Enoch makes repeated references to various angels who are said to be 'with me' (*1 En*. 21.5, 9; 22.3; 23.4; 27.2; 32.6; 33.3). Again, at the very opening of the book Enoch refers to the 'vision from the heavens which the angels showed me' (*1 En*. 1.2). However, the notion of cosmological knowledge imparted to Enoch in the Book of the Watchers, as also in the Astronomical Book, cannot simply derive from this reinterpretation of Gen. 5.22, 24 but implies influence from the figure of Enmeduranki, as noted above.

The Later Development of the Apocalyptic Enoch Tradition

The earliest Enoch traditions in the Astronomical Enoch and the Book of the Watchers are primarily cosmological, the former concentrating on astronomy and the latter, following the incident of the Watchers, on Enoch's journeys throughout the universe. An eschatological reference in the Astronomical Enoch is found only in *1 En*. 72.1, which alludes to 'the new creation which abides forever' that will eventually replace the current world order here being revealed to Enoch, while in the Book of the Watchers we find just a few references to the eschatological punishment of the wicked angels (*1 En*. 10.12-14; 16.1; 19.1; 21.6-10) as well as of wicked humanity (*1 En*. 22.4-13; 27.2-4).

A more dominant eschatological note comes in some later Enochic works. In both the Animal Apocalypse (85–90), part of the Book of Dreams (83–90) and the Apocalypse of Weeks (93.3-10 + 91.11-17), part of the Epistle of Enoch (91–107), dating from the second century BCE, we find pseudo-prophecies coming to a climax with a genuinely prophetic eschatological dénouement comparable to what we find in the book of Daniel. Moreover, the Epistle of Enoch as a whole (91–107) is dominated by an eschatological perspective in which right will eventually triumph over wrong. Again, in spite of some cosmological material in *1 Enoch* 41–44, 59, 60.11-22 and 69.16-25, an eschatological perspective also dominates the probably early or mid-first century BCE[52] Similitudes of

52. For this dating see in particular J.C. Greenfield and M.E. Stone, 'The Enochic Pentateuch and the Date of the Similitudes', *HTR* 70 (1977), pp. 51-65;

Enoch (*1 En.* 37–71), with their vision of the Son of Man who will judge the wicked and rule the world. In the Similitudes of Enoch the surprise comes at the end with their revelation that Enoch himself is to be this eschatological Son of Man (71.14), though this is probably redactional.[53] Herein we find a new development in the Enochic tradition in which Enoch is not simply an eschatological seer raised to heaven but a heavenly being and ruler of the highest order. This comes to a climax in *3 Enoch*, where Enoch is even called 'the lesser Yahweh' (*3 En.* 12.5; 48C.7; 48D1[90]), as well as Metatron, the precise meaning of which is disputed but clearly presents him as God's vice-gerent (cf. too Targum Ps.-Jon. 5.24, 'he was called Metatron').[54] Further evidence of the increasingly exalted status of Enoch is found in *2 Enoch*, where he is clothed with the clothes of God's glory and said to have the appearance of one of God's 'glorious ones' (*2 En.* 22.8-10) and he is carried up to the highest heaven and made to stand before God's face forever (*2 En.* 67.2). This development of the Enoch tradition takes us well beyond the role attributed to Enmeduranki, even though the latter was a king while on earth.

The amount of attention that Enoch received in some ancient circles is remarkable. One reason for this was undoubtedly that Enoch had been taken up into heaven at the end of his earthly life, thus marking him out as a special individual alongside Elijah, someone else who was taken up to heaven and became a figure of eschatological expectation (cf. Mal. 3.23-24, ET 3.5-6; Sir. 48:10; Mk 9.11-13). But another reason was surely the antiquity of the figure of Enoch as someone who pre-dated Moses,

---

Collins, *The Apocalyptic Imagination*, pp. 177-78. See too the various discussions in G. Boccaccini (ed.), *Enoch and the Messiah Son of Man: Revisiting the Book of Parables* (Grand Rapids, MI: Eerdmans, 2007), pp. 415-96, all of which date the Similitudes of Enoch to before 70 CE, either in the first century CE or the late first century BCE. It seems to me significant that the Similitudes nowhere show awareness of the destruction of the Temple in 70 CE.

53. See the discussion in J.J. Collins, 'The Heavenly Representative: The "Son of Man" in the Similitudes of Enoch', in J.J. Collins and G.W.E. Nickelsburg (eds.), *Ideal Figures in Ancient Judaism: Profiles and Paradigms* (SBLSCS, 12; Chico, CA: Scholars Press, 1980), pp. 111-33 (119-24); *idem*, *The Apocalyptic Imagination*, pp. 187-91.

54. On the etymology of Metatron, see P.S. Alexander, '3 (Hebrew Apocalypse of) Enoch', in J.H. Charlesworth (ed.), *The Old Testament Pseudepigrapha* (2 vols.; London: Darton, Longman & Todd, 1983), I, pp. 223-313 (228); *idem*, 'From Son of Adam to Second God', in M.E. Stone and T.A. Bergren (eds.), *Biblical Figures outside the Bible* (Harrisburg, PA: Trinity Press International, 1998), pp. 87-122 (107 n. 31); A.A. Orlov, *The Enoch–Metatron Tradition* (TSAJ, 107; Tübingen: Mohr Siebeck, 2005), pp. 92-96.

the giver of the law. Whereas in the modern world it is fashionable to quote the most up-to-date authority on a subject, in the ancient world there was a certain kudos in being able to cite the most ancient. One may perhaps compare the way the New Testament appeals to other things in the book of Genesis, whether the order of creation (Mk 10.5-9) or the faith of Abraham (Rom. 4; Gal. 3) as a way of 'trumping' Moses.[55] Finally, as John Collins has emphasized,[56] 'competitive historiography' was a feature of the ancient Near East; the attribution to Enoch of aspects of the achievements of Enmeduranki and the Mesopotamian flood hero thereby enabled the Jews to feed into this.[57]

Postscript

A few months after an earlier version of the above chapter was published, a book by Seth L. Sanders appeared with the title *From Adapa to Enoch*.[58] It is a very learned work displaying wide-ranging knowledge of both Assyriology and ancient Judaism, but one of its central theses I wish to question. Sanders claims that it is an error to derive the biblical and Second Temple figure of Enoch from Enmeduranki, and we should look rather to Adapa.

Adapa was the first of the seven Mesopotamian antediluvian Apkallus or wise men. Sanders notes that in Mesopotamian sources from the Old Babylonian period down to the Hellenistic era he was understood to have had various ascents into heaven (like Enoch in the postbiblical Enochic literature; in the Old Testament he only ascends at the end)[59] as well as

---

55. For evidence of the rivalry between Enoch and Moses, see Alexander, 'From Son of Adam to Second God', pp. 107-110; the non-Mosaic character of the Enoch tradition is also rightly emphasized by J.J. Collins, 'How Distinctive was Enochic Judaism?', *Meghillot* 5-6 (2007), pp. 17-34 (20-34). In contrast, the strongly Mosaic nature of the Qumran community is clear. Doubtless those at Qumran who revered the Enochic tradition did not see it as standing in conflict with the Mosaic revelation, a stance facilitated by the fact that Enoch was deemed to have lived in primaeval times, long before the Mosaic law was delivered.

56. Cf. Collins, *The Apocalyptic Imagination* (3rd edn), p. 57.

57. For a large collection of later sources about Enoch in original languages as well as translation, see J.C. Reeves and A.Y. Reed, *Enoch from Antiquity to the Middle Ages: Sources from Judaism, Christianity, and Islam*, I (Oxford: Oxford University Press, 2018).

58. S.L. Sanders, *From Adapa to Enoch: Scribal and Religious Vision in Judea and Babylon* (TSAJ, 167; Tübingen: Mohr Siebeck, 2017).

59. Cf. Sanders, *From Adapa to Enoch*, p. 228.

great importance as a revealer of wisdom to human beings.[60] He contrasts this with Enmeduranki, who was a lesser figure and the type of divination he was associated with is not attested in cuneiform sources after the sixth century BCE.[61] All this, Sanders claims, supports influence on Enoch from the figure of Adapa rather than Enmeduranki.

However, I would note that Enoch first appears in Genesis 5 in the sixth century BCE as the seventh in a list of ten long-lived antediluvian patriarchs, climaxing with the flood hero. This list is widely agreed to be ultimately indebted to the list of long-lived antediluvian kings in the Sumerian King List. Here Enmeduranki always appears as the sixth, seventh or eighth figure. In contrast, as an Apkallu, Adapa did not belong in this list. Moreover, Adapa was generally ascribed rather to the first generation of humanity.

As stated earlier, in Berossus Enmeduranki (or Euedoranchos as he calls him) is actually the seventh antediluvian king, climaxing with the tenth king, the flood hero Xisouthros, just as in Genesis 5 Enoch is the seventh antediluvian patriarch, climaxing with the tenth figure, the flood hero Noah. This is a striking parallel, all the more important in that Berossus is closer in date to the Priestly source to which we owe Genesis 5 than most of the other extant versions of the Sumerian King list. However, Sanders points out that the work of Berossus has been preserved for us by later Jewish and Christian sources, and insinuates that this might have led to the distortion of what Berossus originally wrote.[62] However, this seems an unjustified insinuation here. In general it should be noted that on many points what is preserved of Berossus has been confirmed by more ancient cuneiform sources. Coming specifically to Enmeduranki, it needs to be pointed out that nothing about him in Berossus suggests later Jewish or Christian distortion, since nothing that is said recalls what is stated about Enoch in either Genesis 5 or *1 Enoch*, apart from the fact that he was the seventh out of ten antediluvian figures. But as already stated, Enmeduranki is always the sixth, seventh or eighth figure (most often seventh) out of eight, nine or ten antediluvian kings, and moreover, no extant ancient Jewish or Christian source actually equates Enmeduranki with Enoch, or shows any particular interest in him. Furthermore, significantly the names of all ten of Berossus's antediluvian kings are paralleled in other versions of the Sumerian King List

60. Sanders, *From Adapa to Enoch*, pp. 16, 18.
61. Sanders, From *Adapa to Enoch*, p. 17.
62. Sanders, *From Adapa to Enoch*, p. 17.

and in a comparable order,[63] so any tampering with the list by later Jewish or Christian scribes would be incredible.[64]

It is rather from earlier cuneiform sources that we learn of Enmeduranki's ascension into heaven (during this life), paralleling *1 Enoch*, and of his solar connection, which would explain Enoch's 365-year life in Genesis 5. In fact, Sanders offers no explanation for Enoch's 365-year life on the basis of Adapa, whereas this can be readily explained by Enmeduranki's close association with the sun god, Shamash, who appointed him king, into whose celestial presence he entered, and whose city, Sippar, was the place from which Enmeduranki ruled. Further, in 'Enmeduranki and the Diviners' it was the sun god (with Adad) who revealed to Enmeduranki the mysteries of divination, astronomy and astrology (note the references to the astrological omens *Enuma Anu Enlil*, and 'a mystery of heaven and underworld'), paralleling the astronomical and cosmological revelations which Enoch received in the Astronomical Enoch and the Book of the Watchers.[65] Further, the heavenly tablets are associated with Enoch in *1 En.* 81.1-2; 93.2; 103.2; 106.19-107.1, just as the tablet of the gods was given to Enmeduranki. Moreover, Enoch's being told to instruct his son in *1 En.* 81.5 is comparable to Enmeduranki, who was similarly commanded to instruct his son. I know of nothing comparable with respect to Adapa, and indeed Sanders cites nothing. I argued earlier in this chapter that these traditions were all appropriated by the Jews in Babylonia during the exile in the sixth century BCE. There is therefore no problem if they are

63. See VanderKam, *Enoch and the Growth*, pp. 36-37, for a comparative chart listing the ten antediluvian kings in Berossus and in other versions of the Sumerian King List.

64. G. de Breucker, 'Berossos between Tradition and Innovation', in K. Radner and E. Robson (eds.), *The Oxford Handbook of Cuneiform Literature* (Oxford: Oxford University Press, 2011), pp. 637-57 (644), mistakenly claims that in contrast to Berossus, 'cuneiform sources list no more than nine kings'. In fact, WB 62 has ten antediluvian figures, as noted earlier. Further, De Breuker speculates that 'Jewish or Christian users very likely added a tenth name to Berossos's original list in order to create a parallel with the ten antediluvian generations and patriarchs of the Bible'. But since all ten names are paralleled in other versions of the Sumerian King List and in comparable order, one wonders how one name could possibly have been added much later by Jewish or Christian scribes, ignorant of cuneiform, and which one!

65. As noted earlier, the Astronomical Enoch actually shows dependence on *Enuma Anu Enlil* 14, as well as MUL.APIN, a work closely related to *Enuma Anu Enlil*. In addition, I would note that it is Enoch who is first said to have discovered astrology according to a fragment of a Samaritan work inaccurately attributed to Eupolemus by Eusebius, *Praeparatio evangelica* 9.17.2-9. See R. Doran, 'Pseudo-Eupolemus', in Charlesworth (ed.), *Old Testament Pseudepigrapha*, II, p. 881.

not attested in Mesopotamia during the Persian and Hellenistic periods. It is true that Enmeduranki did not ascend to heaven at the end of his life, unlike Enoch, but as noted earlier, it is plausible that this motif was appropriated from the Mesopotamian flood hero.

So in conclusion, although Enmeduranki may have been a less important figure than Adapa in Mesopotamian estimation, it does appear that it was traditions about Enmeduranki which were taken up by the Jews in Babylonia during the exile in the sixth century BCE and appropriated to Enoch.

Chapter 7

THE SOURCE ANALYSIS AND REDACTION
OF THE GENESIS FLOOD STORY

It has often been stated that the source analysis of the Flood story is a showcase for the Documentary Hypothesis. However, in recent decades a considerable number of scholars have been rejecting the Documentary Hypothesis. Some of these are conservative scholars who often have a religious motivation (whether explicit or not) for seeing the Pentateuch as a unity. But there are also a considerable number of critical scholars who question the Documentary Hypothesis. These scholars do not reject the composite nature of the Pentateuch, including the flood story, but prefer to see P as simply a supplementer or redactor of J (or non-P as they prefer to call it), not an independent source, or alternatively they envisage the traditional J (non-P) passages as a post-P supplement, not as an independent source. In this chapter I shall examine these different views and argue that the evidence still strongly supports the understanding of the flood story as being composed of two independent sources combined by a later redactor, as maintained by the Documentary Hypothesis. At the same time, I shall also argue towards the end that the Yahwistic flood story is a later addition to the narrative, though still prior to the Priestly flood story.

First I shall recount some of the strongest arguments supporting the analysis of the flood story into two sources. The arguments typically centre on the repeated presence within the narrative of duplicate passages sometimes containing discrepancies, alongside the use of two different divine names, Yahweh and Elohim.

Duplicate Passages with Overlaps and Some Discrepancies

Introductory Setting of the Scene (Gen. 6.5-8 J; 6.9-13 P)

In two introductory sections we are twice told that the earth is either wicked (Gen. 6.5) or corrupt and filled with violence (6.11, 13), that God would blot out (6.7) or destroy the earth (6.13), whilst in the midst of all this Noah found favour in the sight of God (6.8) or is described as a righteous man, blameless in his generations (6.9). Within 6.5-8 God is called Yahweh (vv. 5, 6, 7, 8), while in 6.9-13 he is called Elohim (vv. 9, 11, 12, 13), suggesting two different sources.[1]

The Announcement of the Flood and Command to Noah to Enter the Ark and Bring Animals into the Ark, and Noah's Doing So (Gen. 6.14-22 P; 7.1-5 J)

There are strong grounds for seeing the two accounts of God's announcement of the flood, the command to bring animals into the ark and the note that Noah did so, in Gen. 6.14-22 and 7.1-5, as deriving from two different sources. Not only does the former use the name Elohim (6.22; cf. 6.11, 12, 13 immediately preceding) and the latter Yahweh (7.1, 5), but both contain overlaps as well as contradictions. In both God gives a warning to Noah of a coming flood which will destroy all creatures (6.17; 7.4, the latter specifically after seven days, as in the Atrahasis epic, 3.1.37), in both God commands Noah to enter the ark (6.18; 7.1), and instructs him to bring animals with him into the ark (6.19-20; 7.2-3), and in both cases it says that Noah did all that God commanded him (6.22; 7.5). However, in the former account Noah is instructed to bring two of every animal into the ark (6.19-20) – as appears to be the case with the wild animals from the steppe in a version of the Old Babylonian Atrahasis epic recently discovered by Irving Finkel[2] – whereas in the latter account he is told to bring rather seven[3] clean and a pair of unclean

1. In Gen. 6.7aβ (J) the P-like list 'from humanity to animals, creeping things and birds of the air' is probably a later gloss (cf. P in Gen. 6.20; 7.14, 21; 9.2), as are also the earlier words 'which I created (*bārā'tî*)', as J is more prone to use the verb *'āśâ*.

2. Lines 51-52 of the new Atrahasis ark tablet. See I. Finkel, *The Ark before Noah: Decoding the Story of the Flood* (London: Hodder & Stoughton, 2014), p. 365. N. Wasserman, *The Flood: The Akkadian Sources. A New Edition, Commentary, and a Literary Discussion* (OBO, 290; Leuven: Peeters, 2020), p. 70, whilst translating 'two by two' in the Ark tablet, says that the reading is not certain. Most interestingly, on the basis of a careful re-examination of the Old Babylonian Atrahasis epic in the British Museum originally published by Lambert and Millard, Finkel claims that at the exact spot in the broken text (3.2.38) the beginning of the word for 'two' (*š[a-na]*) can be detected. See Finkel, *The Ark before Noah*, p. 189. However, Wasserman, *The Flood*, pp. 22, 44, here adopts a quite different reconstruction on the basis of Gilgamesh 11.86.

3. Grammarians generally agree that *šib'â šib'â* (Gen. 7.2, 3) strictly means 'in sevens', just as *š^{e}nayim š^{e}nayim* means 'in twos'. See GKC 134*q*. However, most Bible translations and commentators inconsistently render the former expression as 'seven pairs', even though they translate the latter as 'a pair'. If the former really

animals (7.2-3).[4] Noah cannot literally have done both. We may plausibly suppose that the odd number of seven clean animals was because after the flood Noah offered of every clean animal (including birds) in sacrifice to the Lord (Gen. 8.20). On the other hand, there is no sacrifice in P until the time of Moses in Leviticus (Lev. 7.1-7), so two of every animal was sufficient for this source.

It is noticeable, however, that what we are given from J has no command to build the ark with constructional details such as we find in P (Gen. 6.14-16). P was particularly keen on numbers and details, which is why I find J. Van Seters' view[5] that 6.14-16 rather derives from J unconvincing.[6] We may nevertheless assume that J originally did say something about the building of the ark, even if it was less detailed than P, whose account was followed by the redactor. Later in 8.6 J does refer back to

means 'seven pairs' then the latter ought to mean 'two pairs', but nobody translates it that way. Indeed, the fact is that the former means 'in sevens' and the latter 'in twos'. Those who get it right include Skinner, *Genesis*, p. 152, Seebass, *Genesis*. I. *Urgeschichte*, p. 201, and Gertz, *Das erste Buch Mose*, I, p. 219, and the JB and NIV. What has misled scholars is the presence of the words 'a male (lit. "man") and its mate', suggesting to some that there were seven of each of these. However, the expression is simply J's equivalent of P's 'male and female', and we similarly read of 'two and two … male and female' or the like in Gen. 6.9, 7.15-16 (P) and 7.8 (R), without anyone supposing it means two of every male and two of every female.

4. Gen. 7.3a further speaks of the birds of the air, male and female, going into the ark by sevens. This is most probably a later gloss, since it curiously fails to distinguish between clean and unclean birds in a J context, and oddly combines J's number seven with P's terminology of male and female. The Samaritan and Peshitta translations both attempt to correct this by adding 'clean' to the 'birds of the air', while the LXX goes even further by referring to the clean birds going in by sevens and the unclean birds in twos. However, it is probable that the original Hebrew text already included the birds in its reference to animals in v. 2. Cf. Ps. 36.7, ET 6, *'ādām ûbᵉhēmâ*, 'humans and beasts'.

5. See Van Seters, *Prologue to History*, pp. 162-63.

6. Further, the style used in connection with the building of the ark in Gen. 6.16 closely parallels P's style in connection with the building of the table of shewbread in the tabernacle in Exod. 25.29. Cf. *qānîm taʿᵃśeh 'et-hattēbâ*, 'you shall make the ark of reeds' (Gen. 6.16), with *zāhāb ṭāhôr taʿᵃśeh 'ōtām*, 'you shall make them of pure gold' (Exod. 25.29), reading *qānîm*, 'reeds', for *qinnîm*, 'rooms' (lit. 'nests'), in Gen. 6.14. See J. Day, 'Rooms or Reeds in Noah's Ark (Gen. 6.14)?', in *From Creation to Babel*, pp. 113-22 (119-20), reprinted as 'Rooms or Reeds in Noah's Ark? קנים in Genesis 6.14', in C. Gottlieb, C. Cohen and M. Gruber (eds.), *Visions of Life in Biblical Times in Honor of Meir Lubetski – A Tribute to his Scholarship, Teaching and Research* (HBM, 76; Sheffield: Sheffield Phoenix Press, 2015), pp. 47-57 (53-54).

the building of a window in the ark by Noah, so presumably this was something mentioned in his original account. Genesis 8.13b (J) also refers to Noah's removing the cover of the ark, something else not included in P's account of the building of the ark in Genesis 6

The Entering of Noah and his Family into the Ark (Gen. 7.7 J; 7.13 P)

Another doublet is that we are twice told that Noah and his family entered the ark (Gen. 7.7, 13). In a truly unified account once would have been enough. Moreover, we have further confirmatory evidence that the two verses derive from different sources, since in 7.7 the entry into the ark takes place seven days before the flood waters appear (cf. 7.4, 10), whereas in 7.13 it is stated that Noah and his family entered the ark 'on the very same day', clearly referring to the day the flood started (7.11; cf. v. 12).[7]

The Flood Begins (Gen. 7.10 J; 7.11P)

Again, we are twice told that the flood began. In Gen. 7.10 the flood waters came upon the earth after seven days, something we associate with J (cf. 7.4), whereas in 7.11 we are given very precise dates for the beginning of the flood after the manner of P, and Noah is hundreds of years old, as in P's genealogy in 5.32: 'In the six-hundredth year of Noah's life, in the second month, on the seventeenth day of the month all the fountains of the great deep burst forth, and the windows of heaven were opened'. It will be noticed that, whereas v. 10 speaks merely of rain, v. 11 refers not only to the rain (the opening of the windows of heaven) but also to the upsurge of the deep.

The Source of the Flood Waters (Gen. 7.4, 12; 8.2b J; 7.11, 8.2a P)

As previously noted, we sometimes read that the flood is simply caused by the rain, while in other places we are told that it was a combination

---

7. Gen. 7.8-9 appear to be the work of the redactor who combined the two sources. Thus, v. 8 speaks of clean and unclean animals like J, but unlike J appears to treat them together with regard to the number going into the ark (as v. 9 makes explicit). Further, though using P language ('two and two' and Elohim for 'God'), v. 9 speaks of the animals going into the ark, which P explicitly spells out in vv. 14-15, so P has no need to mention it twice. For a recent defence of this redactional view see B. Levinson, 'A Post-Priestly Harmonization in the Flood Narrative', in F. Giuntoli and K. Schmid (eds.), *The Post-Priestly Pentateuch* (Tübingen: Mohr Siebeck, 2015), pp. 113-23.

of the opening of the fountains of the deep and the windows of heaven. Interestingly, when we read simply of rain coming this is in the context of the flood lasting for forty days (Gen. 7.4, 12), but when we read of the opening and closing of the fountains of the deep and the windows of heaven it is in the context of the flood lasting 150 days, beginning on the seventeenth day of the second month and ending on the seventeenth day of the seventh month (7.11; 8.2-4). So there can be no doubt that these differences are again signs of different sources.[8]

The Length of the Flood (Gen. 7.4, 17 J; 7.24; 8.3b P and Implicit in 7.11 with 8.4)

As just alluded to, we are also given two different accounts of the length of the flood. In Gen. 7.4 it is stated that it will rain for forty days and forty nights, and this comes in a Yahwistic context, as seen above (7.1, 5). The same length is given in 7.17 (8.6 doubtless also originally referred to it, but these 40 days have now been given a later context). However, elsewhere the flood waters are said to have come for 150 days: this is stated both in terms of the explicit number 150 days (7.24; 8.2) and also in terms of the rain having started on the seventeenth day of the second month and ending on the seventeenth day of the seventh month (7.11; 8.4). This liking for precise dates is characteristic of P.

The Waters Increase (Gen. 7.17 J; 7.18-20 P)

Further, we are twice told in successive verses that the waters increased. Genesis 7.17 (using the verb *rbh* for 'increase') mentions this in connection with the waters continuing for forty days, something we associate with J (cf. above 7.4), while 7.18-20 gives more detailed information (v. 18 using the verb *gbr* for 'increase'), telling us that the mountains were covered to a depth of fifteen cubits (7.20). We will recall that it was P who likewise gave the precise dimensions of the ark in cubits (6.15), as well as referring to a cubit in 6.16.

---

8.   J.A. Berman, *Inconsistency in the Torah: Ancient Literary Convention and the Limits of Source Criticism* (Oxford: Oxford University Press, 2017), pp. 243-44, fails to grasp the point. He argues that the flood could have involved both rain and the upsurge of the deep, and these two need not necessitate different sources. But that is not in dispute. The point is that we sometimes read of the opening of the windows of heaven (rain) and the upsurge of the deep, and sometimes simply of the rain, and these are associated with different lengths of the flood.

Everything on the Earth Dies (Gen. 7.21 P; 7.22 J)

Yet again, we are twice told that, as a result of the flood, everything on the earth died (Gen. 7.21, 22). Each verse uses distinctive vocabulary for dying, v. 21 the verb *gāwaʻ*, often rendered 'expired' (cf. P's use of this same verb in 6.17), and v. 22 the more common verb for 'die', *mût*. Also supporting v. 21's derivation from P is the occurrence of the phrase 'all flesh' (cf. 6.12-13, 19; 9.11, 15-17) and the somewhat lengthy list of animals entering the ark.

The Flood Waters Cease (Gen. 8.2a P; 8.2b J)

Once more, we are twice told that the flood waters ceased. We can be sure that these are from separate sources, since v. 2a says 'the fountains of the deep and the windows of heaven were closed', while v. 2b declares that 'the rain from the heavens was restrained', using the terminology of P and J respectively (see above). The language is needlessly repetitive, since the cessation of rain from heaven is already mentioned in the first half of the verse's statement that 'the windows of heaven were closed'. If it was simply one author, why repeat the reference to the rain of heaven but not to the waters from the deep?

The Sending out of Birds from the Ark (Gen. 8.6, 8-12 J; 8.7 P)

A well-known part of the flood story, often compared with the Babylonian account attested in Gilgamesh (11.148-56), and probably also originally in Atrahasis (the text is broken at this point), concerns the sending out of birds from the ark in order to determine whether the waters of the flood had subsided. Although there is no divine name to guide us here, the story as a whole has the vividness of touch that we generally associate with J, and the reference to the 'forty days' in Gen. 8.6 also betokens J (though in the current context referring to a subsequent period of forty days, not the original forty days of the flood as J originally intended). However, many scholars rightly see that, though this is generally true, v. 7 (the sending out of the raven) is more plausibly attributed to another source. The reason for this is that the explanation of why birds are sent out from the ark is not given at the beginning, with the sending out of the raven, where we would expect it,[9] but only with the sending out of the second

---

9. The LXX, however, does add the words 'to see whether the water had abated' in connection with the sending out of the raven in Gen. 8.7, and this is followed by Josephus, *Ant.* 1.3.5. However, Origen put these words under an obelus (but not the entire verse as Codex M has it) in order to indicate that they were not in the MT.

bird, the first dove, in v. 8. This is odd if we have here a unified account, but explicable if two different sources have been not quite elegantly spliced together. A number of scholars simply see it as a later supplement to J,[10] but such an addition seems pointless. As with other discrepancies in the flood story, it is more naturally seen as P.[11] This is consistent with v. 7's use of the infinitive absolute, something which P has employed just before (cf. Gen. 8.3, 5).

Some of the ancient Versions held that the raven kept going to and fro without returning to the ark until the flood was over.[12] But this is the opposite of what would be expected. Since literally the raven is said to keep 'going out and returning', it is more natural to suppose that it kept leaving the ark and returning there, for as long as there was no other place to rest.[13] This would be consistent with what happened to the dove subsequently (vv. 8-12), which kept coming back till the earth was dry. Accordingly, we may suppose that the raven and dove were two alternative means of ascertaining whether and when the earth was dry. To use both would have been superfluous, which further supports the view that the references to these derive from separate sources.

---

10. Cf. Dillmann, *Genesis*, p. 147, ET *Genesis*, I, p. 284; Westermann, *Genesis 1–11*, p. 597, ET *Genesis 1–11*, p. 445; Gertz, *Das erste Buch Mose*, I, p. 268.

11. Cf. Friedrich Delitzsch, *Wo lag das Paradies?* (Leipzig: J.C. Hinrichs, 1881), pp. 157-58; von Rad, *Das erste Buch Mose*, pp. 94, 96, ET *Genesis*, pp. 122, 125; A. Schüle, *Der Prolog der hebräischen Bibel. Der literar- und theologiegeschichtliche Diskurs der Urgeschichte (Gen 1–11)* (ATANT, 86; Zurich: Theologischer Verlag, 2006), pp. 251, 266, though for Schüle P in Gen. 8.7 is the *Grundschrift* and Gen. 8.8-12 is a post-P supplement. D. Marcus, 'The Mission of the Raven (Gen. 8:7)', *JANES* 29 (2002), pp. 71-80 (71 n. 3) claims that H. Holzinger, J. Wellhausen, H. Gunkel and J. Morgenstern also attributed Gen. 8.7 to P, but none of the references he cites for these scholars specifically mentions P.

12. Cf. LXX Gen. 8.7, 'after it had gone out it did not return until the water was dried up from the earth'. Similarly the main Vulgate tradition and Peshitta. However, it has been argued that the Peshitta was emended in the light of the LXX. So M.P. Weitzman, *The Syriac Version of the Old Testament: An Introduction* (Cambridge: Cambridge University Press, 1999), p. 144.

13. So J. Göttsberger, 'וְשׁוֹב יָצוֹא in Gn 8,7', *BZ* 6 (1908), pp. 13-16; O. Keel, *Vögel als Boten: Studien zu Ps 68,12-14; Gen 8,6-12; Koh 10,20 und dem Aussenden von Botenvögeln in Ägypten* (OBO, 14: Freiburg: Universitätsverlag, and Göttingen: Vandenhoeck & Ruprecht, 1967), pp. 79-91 (86-87); N.M. Sarna, *Genesis* (JPS Torah Commentary; Philadelphia: JPS, 1989), p. 57. Cf. Targum Neofiti and Fragment Targum.

The Drying of the Face of the Ground/Earth (Gen. 8.13b P; 8.14b J)

Again, Gen. 8.13b states that 'the face of the ground was dry (*ḥrb*)', while v. 14b says that 'the earth was dry (*ybš*)'. This seems needlessly repetitive if it was the same author. The former is generally attributed to J and the latter to P, the latter cohering with evidence for attributing Gen. 8.7 to P noted above, which similarly uses *ybš*.

God's Promise Never to Flood the Earth Again (Gen. 8.21-22 J; 9.8-17 P)

At the end of the flood story we have two quite different versions of God's promise never to flood the earth again. Again, their contents strongly support the view that they derive from two different sources. The first, brief account in Gen. 8.21-22 uses the name Yahweh, has typical J anthropomorphism in its reference to Yahweh's smelling the sacrifice, and reads like a sudden immediate response on Yahweh's part to Noah's offering of sacrifice. The second much longer account in 9.8-17, unlike 8.21-22, not only uses the name Elohim for God but also additionally associates the promise with a divine covenant with Noah. Moreover, far from being a sudden response on God's part, this divine covenant is already anticipated in Gen. 6.18, where even before the flood waters had started appearing God declares his intention to make a covenant with Noah.

It will be observed that the P version is somewhat more complete than the J version. P appears to have provided the framework into which large parts of J were inserted. Missing from the J version in our text is an account of the building of the ark (though Gen. 8.6 refers back to it, as we have seen), and an account of the exit from the ark.

A reasonable source analysis would be as follows: J Gen. 6.5-8; 7.1-5, 7, 10, 12, 16b, 17b, 22-23; 8.2b-3a, 6, 8-12, 13b, 20-22; P Gen. 6.9-22; 7.6, 11, 13-16a, 17a, 18-21, 24; 8.1-2a, 3b-5, 7, 13a, 14-19; 9.1-17; R (Redactor) Gen. 6.7aβ; 7.3a, 8-9 (on the R verses see above nn. 1, 4, 7). From this it will be noted that in the flood account larger blocks of J and P tend to alternate towards the beginning (6.5-8 J; 6.9-22 P; 7.1-5 J) and end of the story (8.8-12 J; 8.14-19 P; 8.20-22 J; 9.1-17 P), while the middle part of the story in much of ch. 7 and beginning of ch. 8 is much more mixed up with shorter extracts from J and P frequently spliced together.

Recent Attempts to Disprove or Shed Doubt on the Source Analysis of the Flood Story

Over thirty years ago John Emerton provided an extremely thorough and meticulous demolition of attempts up to the time of his articles

(1987/1988) to defend the unity of the flood narrative.[14] However, since then, a few scholars have continued to attempt to defend the unity of the flood narrative. Arguments that have been employed in support of this include the following.

Arguments from Chiasm and Pattern

One point that has repeatedly been emphasized by defenders of the unity of the flood story in recent decades is its allegedly impressive chiastic structure, which embraces all of it, whether J or P. John Emerton already offered a thorough and meticulous refutation of this in 1987,[15] but the chiastic structure has been continually put forward up to the present day by scholars variously ignorant or at least ignoring, being dismissive of or downplaying Emerton's article.

Wenham's chiastic structure is as follows, and it has been subsequently reasserted by Kikawada and Quinn, Rendsburg, Berman (in modified form), Georg Fischer, as well as Wenham himself.[16]

14. J.A. Emerton, 'An Examination of Some Attempts to Defend the Unity of the Flood Narrative in Genesis', Part I, *VT* 37 (1987), pp. 401-20; Part II, *VT* 38 (1988), pp. 1-21.

15. Emerton, 'An Examination … Part II', pp. 6-11.

16. G.J. Wenham, 'The Coherence of the Flood Narrative', *VT* 28 (1978), pp. 336-48; *idem*, 'Method in Pentateuchal Criticism', *VT* 41 (1991), pp. 84-109; I.M. Kikawada and A. Quinn, *Before Abraham Was: The Unity of Genesis 1–11* (Nashville, TN: Abingdon Press, 1985; reprinted San Francisco, CA: Ignatius Press, 1989), p. 104; Berman, *Inconsistency in the Torah*, pp. 260-63, with a modified version of Wenham's palistrophe (p. 261); similarly, *idem*, 'Critiquing Source Criticism: The Story of the Flood', in *Ani Maamin: Biblical Criticism, Historical Truth, and the Thirteen Principles of Faith* (Jerusalem: Maggid, 2020), pp. 109-27 (121-22, with chart on p. 122). G.A. Rendsburg, *The Redaction of Genesis* (Winona Lake, IN: Eisenbrauns, 1986), p. 13 n. 13, accepts Wenham's chiastic structuring of the flood story, whilst accepting that it interweaves two accounts. Contrast Rendsburg's later work, 'The Biblical Flood Story in the Light of the Gilgameš Flood Account', in J. Azize and N. Weeks (eds.), *Gilgameš and the World of Assyria: Proceedings of the Conference Held at Mandelbaum House, The University of Sydney, 21-23 July 2004* (Ancient Near Eastern Studies, Supplement 21; Leuven: Peeters, 2007), pp. 115-27, where his central argument is that the Genesis story is not made up of two sources, basing his argument on the parallels with Gilgamesh; Fischer, *Genesis 1–11*, pp. 400-401.

A   Noah (6.10a)
B   Shem, Ham and Japheth (6.10b)
C   Ark to be built (6.14-16)
D   Flood announced (6.17)
E   Covenant with Noah (6.18-20)
F   Food in the ark (6.21)
G   Command to enter ark (7.1-3)
H   7 days waiting for flood (7.4-5)
I   7 days waiting for flood (7.7-10)
J   Entry to ark (7.11-15)
K   Yahweh shuts Noah in (7.16b)
L   40 days flood (7.17a)
M   Waters increase (7.17b-18)
N   Mountains covered (7.19-20)
O   150 days water prevailed (7.[21-]24)
P   GOD REMEMBERS NOAH (8.1)
O'   150 days waters abate (8.3)
N'   Mountain tops visible (8.4-5)
M'   Waters abate (8.5)
L'   40 days (end of) (8.6a)
K'   Noah opens window of ark (8.6b)
J'   Raven and dove leave ark (8.7-9)
I'   7 days waiting for waters to subside (8.10-11)
H'   7 days waiting for waters to subside (8.12-13)
G'   Command to leave ark (8.15-17 [22])
F'   Food outside ark (9.1-4)
E'   Covenant with all flesh (9.8-10)
D'   No flood in future (9.11-17)
C'   Ark (9.18a)
B'   Shem, Ham and Japheh (9.18b)
A'   Noah (9.19)

As Emerton's careful analysis has shown (see n. 15), there are
numerous problems with Wenham's proposed chiastic structure. I can
only summarize his many points here. First, the choice of items included
in the chiasm is sometimes arbitrary. For example, some references to
Noah, the ark, forty days, and Shem, Ham and Japheth in the story are
deemed relevant to the palistrophe, while others are ignored. Again, for a
writer allegedly having such a strong sense of symmetry, it is surprising
that the parallels vary between about half a verse and seven verses in
length. Next, we should note that several important events are omitted
from the palistrophe: for example, the exit from the ark (Gen. 8.18-19) is
not included, even though the entry is (7.11-15), the latter being paired

instead by Wenham with the sending out of the raven and dove (8.7-9), which is less appropriate. Nor are such important events as the death of every living creature (7.21-23), Noah's sacrifice following the flood (8.20-22) or the opening and closing of the springs (7.11; 8.2) included. Though it might have proved difficult finding pairs for the first two, the last mentioned would have made a really excellent pair. On the other hand, the pairing of Gen. 7.16b with Gen. 8.8b is not very appropriate, since in the former it is God who closed the door of the ark on Noah, whereas in the latter it is the window which is opened, and by Noah himself. Finally, the seven days referred to in H and I in Wenham's table allude to the same period (7.4-5, 7-10), whereas the two parallel seven days in I' and H' (8.10-11, 12-13) constitute different, successive periods. Further, a couple of points not mentioned by Emerton are that 6.11-13 play no role in the palistrophe and that the covenant with all flesh, singled out as 9.8-10, is not confined to these verses but occurs within 9.8-17 as a whole. Overall, Wenham's construction seems rather contrived. In any case, some parallelism between the two halves of the flood account is naturally to be expected, as in turn people and animals enter the ark, the waters gradually rise, the waters gradually fall, and people and animals finally exit the ark.

Joshua Berman[17] has produced a modified version of Wenham's palistrophe, eliminating references to highly used terms like 'Noah' and 'ark' which Emerton had criticized, while retaining much of the rest of Wenham's palistrophe. I will not print it all out here, but it has to be said that Berman's palistrophe proves nothing, since only two of his parallels transcend the two sources, and even they are open to criticism. On his palistrophe chart he claims that there are actually five parallels transcending the sources, but strange to say he mistakenly attributes Gen. 9.8-10, 9.15 and 9.17 to non-P, when all critical scholars agree they are from P. Of the two alleged parallels genuinely transcending sources, one is inappropriate in terms of content: Berman makes 7.8 (which is probably R, not P as he claims; see above n. 7) with its entering of the birds into the ark parallel with 8.10b-12, where simply one dove leaves the ark. The appropriate parallel would rather have been Gen. 8.19, where the birds generally exit the ark. The other parallel transcending sources is Gen. 7.1-5 (non-P) and 8.15-19 (P), which Berman refers to respectively as 'Command to enter the ark + fulfilment' and 'Command to leave the ark + fulfilment'. However, whereas the latter part of Gen. 8.15-19 (viz. vv. 18-19) explicitly states that Noah and his family exited the ark, the

17. Berman, *Inconsistency in the Torah*, pp. 260-63 (chart on p. 261).

actual entering into the ark occurs in Gen. 7.7-9 and 7.13-16, not in Gen. 7.1-5; v. 5 is simply implicit, stating that 'Noah did all that the Lord had commanded'.

A much more modest but more realistic chiastic structure for the flood narrative has been proposed by B.W. Anderson.[18] But unlike the above scholars, he fully accepts the composite nature of the narrative, whilst seeing the final form as a redactional unity.

A Transitional introduction (6.9-10)
B Violence in God's creation (6.11-12)
C   First divine speech: resolution to destroy (6.13-22)
D   Second divine address: command to enter the ark (7.1-10)
E   Beginning of the flood (7.11-16)
F   The rising flood waters (7.17-24)
G   GOD'S REMEMBRANCE OF NOAH
F'   The receding flood waters (8.1-5)
E'   The drying of the earth (8.6-14)
D'   Third divine address: command to leave the ark (8.15-19)
C'   God's resolution to preserve order (8.20-22)
B' Fourth divine address: covenant blessing and peace (9.1-17)
A' Transitional conclusion (9.18-19)

It seems to me that in broad terms this does correspond to the structure of the flood story. However, in order to improve it I would start the flood story at Gen. 6.5, where it actually begins. More significantly, I would conflate items A and B and A' and B' respectively. In the process, the transitional section parallels would be abolished, and we would be left with just four parallels preceding and succeeding Gen. 8.1: the resolution to bring the flood//the declaration that there will be no more flood, the command to enter the ark//the command to exit the ark, the beginning of the flood//the drying of the earth, and the rising of the flood waters//the receding of the flood waters. However, not only does this greatly slimmed down chiastic structure not provide an argument for the unity of the flood story, but this structure might possibly have been entirely unconscious, since the items correspond to the general sequence that one would expect in a flood narrative, which would naturally to some extent have a symmetrical structure as the flood successively rose and declined.

A different kind of parallel has been alleged by Joshua Berman[19] in favour of the flood story being a unity, though his argument pertains to

---

18. B.W. Anderson, 'From Analysis to Synthesis: The Interpretation of Genesis 1–11', *JBL* 97 (1978), pp. 23-39 (chart on p. 38).

19. Berman, *Inconsistency in the Torah*, pp. 255-60 (chart on p. 259).

only part of the story. This consists not of a chiasm but of what he sees
as sequential parallels between certain items in the creation narrative in
Genesis 1 and part of the flood story in Gen. 8.1–9.3. Berman's point
is that the alleged parallels in 8.1–9.3 sometimes transcend traditional
source divisions and include both so-called J and P material, therefore
supporting the unity of the narrative.

Day 1

Gen. 1.2 ורוח אלהים מרחפת	Gen. 8.1 ויעבר אלהים רוח

Day 2

Gen. 1.6-8 Separation of waters of the higher and lower firmaments	Gen. 8.2 Blocking of the deep and the flood-gates of the sky

Day 3a

Gen. 1.9-10 Appearance of dry land ותראה היבשה	Gen. 8.5 Appearance of mountain peaks נראו ראשי ההרים

Day 3b

Gen. 1.11-13 Creation of vegetation	Gen. 8.11 Dove returns with olive branch

Day 4

Gen. 1.14-19 Creation of sun and moon to distinguish day and night	Gen. 8.11 Dove returns 'at evening time'

Day 5

Gen. 1.20-22 Creation of birds	Gen. 8.12 Dove leaves the ark and takes its place in the new order

Day 6a

Gen. 1.24-27 Creation of animals and man [*sic*]	Gen. 8.15-19 Noah and animals disembark the ark

Day 6b

Gen. 1.28-29 Command to be fruitful and multiply + sustenance, לכם יהיה לאכלה	Gen. 9.1-3 Command to be fruitful and multiply + sustenance, לכם יהיה לאכלה

However, this is uncompelling. The only real parallels are the first and
last ones, and both of these pertain to the Priestly source in each case, so
are irrelevant to the question of the overall unity of the flood story. The
final parallel, regarding the command to be fruitful and multiply, has long
been recognized, since Gen. 9.1ff. clearly represents a new beginning for
the world after the flood, paralleling the original creation in Genesis 1.
The first parallel also probably has something in it, since the flood may
be seen as a reassertion of the power of the primaeval waters, and God's

making the wind blow over the waters at the climax of the flood parallels God's wind blowing to and fro over the waters in Gen. 1.2 (even though the original function of the wind is not explicitly expressed in the latter passage). On the other hand, the two halves of parallel 2 are not exactly equivalent, since in Genesis 1 the waters are separated by a firmament, whereas in Genesis 8 the firmament is already there and the rain and upsurging of the deep are simply stopped by divine fiat. As for parallel 3, 8.5 refers merely to the tops of mountains appearing, whereas in 1.9-10 it is the dry land that appears, i.e. the earth as a whole minus seas and rivers.

Berman's other alleged parallels are even weaker. Thus, although he alleges parallels in Genesis 1 to three dove references in Genesis 8, on inspection we find that these pertain to only two of the doves and also the first and second dove references are in the wrong chronological order vis-à-vis Genesis 1. Further, the third dove is said to parallel the creation of birds in Genesis 1, whereas if the latter were to parallel anything, one would expect it to correspond to the first bird in Genesis 8, namely the raven. It should also be observed that, whereas animals are created before humans in 1.24-27, in 8.15-19 Noah and the other humans are mentioned before the animals prior to their exit from the ark. Finally, it is important to note that many things in 8.1–9.3 have no parallel at all in Genesis 1, and that Berman's parallels – mostly weak as they are – pertain to about only half of the verses in merely one section of the flood narrative.

Argument from Mesopotamian Parallels

One particular argument had already been put forward by Gordon Wenham[20] and was replied to by Emerton,[21] but since then it has been repeated by both Gary Rendsburg and Joshua Berman,[22] so I will deal briefly with it again here. All these scholars find it odd that it should be the final form of the flood narrative which we have, not the alleged individual underlying sources J and P, that have the fullest range of parallels with the Mesopotamian flood tradition, and in the same order, and they feel this supports the narrative's unity. But it is actually not at all odd. If both J and P were each basing themselves on more or less the same underlying Mesopotamian story, as would appear, and if each had a more or less complete version, as also seems likely, the redactor sometimes choosing one in preference to the other, and sometimes citing both, it is only logical

20. Wenham, 'The Coherence of the Flood Narrative', pp. 345-47.

21. Emerton, 'An Examination, Part II', pp. 14-15.

22. Rendsburg, 'The Biblical Flood Story'; Berman, *Inconsistency in the Torah*, pp. 251-55.

that it should be the final version which has the fullest range of parallels (and in the same order). I have previously given reasons for believing that the common source both J and P knew was a version of the Atrahasis epic, not the Gilgamesh epic (in P's case with some later traditions also attested in Berossus). It is Atrahasis which also underlies the more well-known flood account in tablet 11 of the Gilgamesh epic.[23]

Arguments Regarding the Use of Different Divine Names

Isaac M. Kikawada and Arthur Quinn and later Joshua Berman[24] both make the point that the use of different divine names for the same god is well attested in ancient Near Eastern literature, so need not imply different sources. However, this is not a satisfactory explanation of the alternating divine names in the flood story, since these different divine names sometimes go hand in hand with other discrepancies in the text. The clearest examples in the flood story are at the very beginning and end. Thus, in both Gen. 6.9-22 and 7.1-5 God announces the flood, commands Noah to enter the ark and bring in animals, and in each case it is reported that he did so. However, the former calls God Elohim and two of every animal are to enter the ark, whereas the latter uses the name Yahweh and commands that seven of clean animals and two of unclean enter the ark. Then at the end we have two passages in which God promises never to flood the earth again, one (Gen. 8.20-22) using the name Yahweh in which the promise seems a spur of the moment response to Noah's sacrifices, and the latter (Gen. 9.8-17) using the name Elohim, where the promise is bound up with a covenant promised already in Gen. 6.18.

Arguments about the Nature of Repetition

Kikawada and Quinn and Wenham[25] further argue that repetitions in the flood story, as elsewhere in Genesis 1–11, can be explained as attempts to create emphasis. But since almost everything in the flood narrative

23. For the sources' common dependence on Atrahasis, see J. Day, 'The Genesis Flood Narrative in Relation to Ancient Near Eastern Flood Accounts', in K.J. Dell and P.M. Joyce (eds.), *Biblical Interpretation and Method: Essays in Honour of Professor John Barton* (Oxford: Oxford University Press, 2013), pp. 74-88, reprinted in Day, *From Creation to Babel*, pp. 98-112. For parallels between P and Berossus, see Day, 'The Flood and the Ten Antediluvian Figures in Berossus and in the Priestly Source in Genesis', reprinted in expanded form in Day, *From Creation to Babel*, pp. 61-76.

24. Kikawada and Quinn, *Before Abraham Was*, pp. 90-92; Berman, *Inconsistency in the Torah*, p. 265.

25. Kikawada and Quinn, *Before Abraham Was*, p. 92; Wenham, 'Method in Pentateuchal Criticism', pp. 99-101.

gets repeated, this would be ridiculous. Moreover, like the preceding argument, this is subject to the damning criticism that the repetitions are sometimes accompanied by various discrepancies, as is well illustrated by our analysis of the flood story earlier. The same point counts against R.N. Whybray's claim[26] that the repetitions were intended to give a sense of solemnity and awesomeness to the flood narrative.

The Work of the Redactor

Redactor Allegedly Integrating Everything

David Clines,[27] in raising a number of queries about the documentary analysis of the flood story, argues that scholars need to take more seriously the role of the redactor, who integrated such sources as there were into the unity that we now have. However, on close inspection I find it difficult to maintain that the redactor has actually succeeded in integrating the sources properly.

Thus, if we take the chronology, there are two areas where discrepancies are still visible. First, on the one hand, Gen. 7.4 (following J) clearly states that the rain will come down for just forty days and nights. On the other hand, in Gen. 8.3 (following P), where we read that both 'the fountains of the deep and the windows of heaven were closed', the context clearly indicates that this was actually after a full 150 days had passed (cf. Gen. 7.24; 8.4). So it is not satisfactory to say that the redactor saw the forty days as simply part of a larger period of 150 days, as reconcilers customarily do, since both periods of time are stated to refer to the overall length of the rain coming down.

Again, secondly with regard to chronology, if the flood story is truly integrated Gen. 8.8-12 should indicate a period of 61 days from the first day of the tenth month, when the tops of mountains other than Ararat appeared (Gen. 8.5) till the time when the dove was sent out for a third time and never returned, indicating that the waters had subsided from the earth (8.12; cf. v. 8). These 61 days consist of forty days till the raven was sent out (8.6), followed by three periods of seven days in which the dove was repeatedly sent out (twice explicitly in 8.10, 12, the former's reference to 'another seven days' implying also an additional previous period of seven days in v. 8). Now this brings us to the first day of the

26. R.N. Whybray, *The Making of the Pentateuch: A Methodological Study* (JSOTSup, 53; Sheffield: JSOT Press, 1987), p. 83.

27. D.J.A. Clines, 'Putting Source Criticism in its Place: The Flood Story as a Test Case', in Dell and Joyce (eds.), *Biblical Interpretation and Method*, pp. 3-14 (9-12).

twelfth month, when the earth should be dry. If the account was properly integrated one would therefore expect a reference to the drying up of the earth by the first day of the twelfth month, but we do not find that. Instead 8.12 states that the face of the ground was drying on the first day of the first month. This could explain why the Septuagint speaks of the mountains having appeared on the first day of the eleventh rather than tenth month (8.5), thereby accommodating the 61 days by the first day of the first month,[28] rather than leaving an awkward month unaccounted for between the first day of the twelfth and the first day of the first month. Even so, it was still not till the twenty-seventh day of the second month that the earth was completely dry (8.14) so that Noah and everyone else in the ark, both humans and beasts, could be let out (8.15ff.).

Again, with regard to the number of animals going into the ark, P speaks of two of every animal and J of seven of clean animals and two of unclean animals. Both these statements have been left in the text and are clearly contradictory. Those trying to reconcile the figures tend to claim that the former is speaking in general terms while the latter is being more specific. Clines[29] similarly takes this as the redactor's understanding. But this is clearly not credible. The one statement does not amplify the other but contradicts it.

Other contradictions mentioned earlier have also still been retained by the redactor. For example, the careful reader will be at a loss to know whether the flood started seven days before Noah entered the ark (Gen. 7.7) or on the very same day (7.13).

P as Source or Redactor/Supplementer?

Traditionally P has been seen as a source, but in recent years a number of scholars have understood it rather as the redactor or supplementer of J (or non-P), including F.M. Cross, R. Rendtorff, B.W. Anderson, E. Blum and J. Van Seters.[30] However, this is unconvincing. For example, this

---

28. Van Seters, *Prologue to History*, p. 164, curiously states that Gen. 8 itself allows for the 61 days to be incorporated within the precise dates given. But he misunderstands Skinner, *Genesis*, pp. 167-68, at this point, who was clearly speaking of the LXX. See Van Seters, *Prologue to History*, p. 172 n. 16.

29. Clines, 'Putting Source Criticism in its Place', p. 10.

30. See F.M. Cross, 'The Priestly Work', in *Canaanite Myth and Hebrew Epic* (Cambridge, MA: Harvard University Press, 1973), pp. 293-325; R. Rendtorff, *Das überlieferungsgeschichtliche Problem des Pentateuch* (BZAW, 147; Berlin: W. de Gruyter, 1977), ET *The Problem of the Process of Transmission in the Pentateuch* (trans. J.J. Scullion; JSOTSup, 89; Sheffield: JSOT Press, 1990); Anderson, 'From

view is forced to conclude that in the flood story the alleged P redactor left in J's references to clean and unclean animals and to Noah's sacrifice after the flood, when he had deliberately chosen not to include these very things in his own account, because they conflicted with his own theology that sacrifice and the distinction between clean and unclean animals only began later with Moses (Lev. 1–7; 11). Again, one is also forced to conclude that the alleged P redactor introduced further contradictions into the flood account he was editing by including such details as the length of the flood, the number of animals entering the ark, and the timing of the entry into the ark with respect to the flood, which all disagreed with the source he was editing. If P had truly edited J's account one would expect the two accounts to be better integrated. So it is more natural to envisage an independent redactor as having combined two separate accounts, J and P. Although we might deem it odd for a redactor to combine two somewhat contradictory accounts, it would be far odder for a Priestly redactor to introduce his own contradictions into the account he was editing, rather than revising it. Another important point is that it is difficult to envisage P as merely a redactor of J, when both J and P have pretty full accounts of the flood, which is much more suggestive of two independent accounts that a redactor has subsequently combined. So much of what is regarded as supplementation by P is needless repetition, in addition to contradictions noted earlier.

The motivation of those scholars who see P as a redactor rather than an originally separate source is the absence in P of certain events in Genesis and Exodus which were important in J, most importantly the covenant making on Mt Sinai. But as others have pointed out, it is a mistake to presume that everything in J should also be found in P. And in the case of covenant making, the evidence of Genesis 9 and 17 shows that it was P's policy to write his own covenant-making accounts (those with Noah and Abraham), so why not also with Moses? It is therefore more natural to suppose, as argued by W. Zimmerli and widely accepted since, that for P the legislation on Mt Sinai was seen as an extension of the Abrahamic covenant.[31]

Analysis to Synthesis', pp. 30-31; E. Blum, *Studien zur Komposition des Pentateuch* (BZAW, 189; Berlin: W. de Gruyter, 1990), pp. 280-85; Van Seters, *Prologue to History*, pp. 160-73.

31. See W. Zimmerli, 'Sinaibund und Abrahambund. Ein Beitrag zum Verständnis der Priesterschrift', *TZ* 16 (1960), pp. 268-80, reprinted in Zimmerli (ed.), *Gottes Offenbarung. Gesammelte Aufsätze zum Alten Testament* (TBü; Munich: Chr. Kaiser Verlag, 2nd edn, 1969), pp. 205-16. On P as an independent source, not a redactor, see

B.T. Arnold's Theory of an H Redaction of the Flood Story

Bill T. Arnold[32] has argued that the redactor of the flood story was H (the author of the so-called Holiness Code in Lev. 17–26). But his view is highly speculative, and on his reconstruction so much of what is generally attributed to P is ascribed to H, so that the role of H greatly exceeds what we normally understand by a redactor (Gen. 6.11-22; 7.8-10, 13-24;[33] 8.15-17; 9.1-17), and P becomes little more than the author of various numerical details and associated material (Gen. 7.6-7, 11; 8.1-2a, 3b-5, 13-14, 18-19 – in addition to 5.28, 30-32; 9.28-29, though these are not actually part of the flood narrative). Also a 150-day flood is found in both P (Gen. 7.11; 8.3b, 4) and H (Gen. 7.24) in Arnold's reconstruction. So if H essentially agreed with P over the length of the flood it is surprising that he kept the length of the flood given by J of forty days. Arnold's recon-struction also presupposes that H is later than P, which though currently popular, is not universally accepted, as he himself notes.[34]

J as Source or Redactor/Supplementer?

Traditionally J has also been regarded as a source (prior to P), which was subsequently combined with P by a redactor. However, in recent years quite a number of scholars have preferred to see J (non-P) as a redactor/ supplementer of P rather than an originally independent source conflated with P by a separate redactor.[35] However, some of the same objections to P

K. Koch, 'P – Kein Redaktor! Erinnerung an zwei Eckdaten der Quellenschei-dung', *VT* 37 (1987), pp. 446-67; J.A. Emerton, 'The Priestly Writer in Genesis', *JTS* NS 39 (1988), pp. 381-400 (392-98); E.W. Nicholson, *The Pentateuch in the Twentieth Century: The Legacy of Julius Wellhausen* (Oxford: Clarendon Press, 1998), pp. 197-213.

32. B.T. Arnold, 'The Holiness Redaction of the Flood Narrative (Genesis 6:9–9:29)', in B.T. Arnold, N.L. Erickson and J.H. Walton (eds.), *Windows to the Ancient World of the Hebrew Bible: Essays in Honor of Samuel Greengus* (Winona Lake, IN: Eisenbrauns, 2014), pp. 13-40.

33. Arnold, 'The Holiness Redaction', p. 25, also refers to Gen. 8.1-5 as H using J and P fragments, but he includes 8.1-2a, 3b-5 in his reconstruction of P on p. 40.

34. Arnold, 'The Holiness Redaction', p. 3, with n. 3b.

35. Cf. J.-L. Ska, 'El relato del Diluvio un relato sacerdotal y algunos fragment redaccionales posteriores', *EstBíb* 52 (1994), pp. 37-62, ET 'The Story of the Flood: A Priestly Writer and Some Editorial Fragments', in *idem, The Exegesis of the Pentateuch: Exegetical Studies and Basic Questions* (FAT, 66; Tübingen: Mohr Siebeck, 2009), pp. 1-22; J. Blenkinsopp, *The Pentateuch: An Introduction to the First Five Books of the Bible* (London: SCM Press, 1992), pp. 54-67, esp. pp. 77-78; D. Petersen, 'The Formation of the Pentateuch', in D. Petersen, J.L. Mays and K.H.

as a redactor of J noted above apply also to J being a redactor of P. Thus, if J redacted P he will have introduced into the account he was editing contradictions on various matters, including the number of animals entering the ark, the length of the flood, and the time between Noah's entering the ark and the start of the flood. Further, the pretty full nature of J's flood account and its sheer length, together with its numerous overlaps with and repetitions of points in P, is much more suggestive of J as an independent source rather than a mere supplementer of P.

The J/Non-P Flood Story as a Later Addition to J's Original Primaeval History

A number of earlier scholars such as J. Wellhausen, K. Budde and H. Gunkel[36] argued that J's version of the flood story was a later addition to the narrative, and this view has been taken up by a number of more recent scholars, including Reinhard Kratz, Konrad Schmid, I. Dershowitz and David Carr.[37] These scholars do not all agree exactly among themselves

---

Richards (eds.), *Old Testament Interpretation: Past, Present, and Future. Essays in Honor of Gene M. Tucker* (Nashville, TN: Abingdon Press, 1995), pp. 31-45 (41-43); T. Krüger, 'Das menschliche Herz und die Weisung Gottes: Elemente einer Diskussion über Möglichkeiten und Grenzen der Tora-Rezeption im Alten Testament', in R.G. Kratz and T. Krüger (eds.), *Rezeption und Auslegung im Alten Testament und in seinem Umfeld. Ein Symposion aus Anlass des 60. Geburtstags von Odil Hannes Steck* (Fribourg and Göttingen: Universitätsverlag and Vandenhoeck & Ruprecht, 1997), pp. 65-92 (74-78); E. Bosshard-Nepustil, *Vor uns die Sintflut: Studien zu Text, Kontexten und Rezeption der Fluterzählung Genesis 6–9* (BWANT, 9.5; Stuttgart: Kohlhammer, 2005), pp. 49-77; Schüle, *Der Prolog der hebräischen Bibel*, pp. 258-60; M. Arneth, *Durch Adams Fall ist ganz verderbt: Studien zur Entstehung der alttestamentlichen Urgeschichte* (FRLANT, 217; Göttingen: Vandenhoeck & Ruprecht, 2007), pp. 171-98; K. Schmid, *The Old Testament: A Literary History* (ET, trans. L.M. Maloney; Minneapolis, MN: Fortress Press, 2012), pp. 155-59. G.J. Wenham, 'The Priority of P', *VT* 49 (1999), pp. 240-58, curiously accepts the existence of a P source, which he thinks was redacted by J, even though he is sceptical of the source division of the flood story, as seen above, and oddly also thinks Gen. 1 may be from J.

36. Wellhausen, *Die Composition des Hexateuchs*, pp. 10-12; Budde, *Die biblische Urgeschichte*, esp. pp. 309-311, 321-22, 325-26; Gunkel, *Genesis*, pp. 1-3, 25-26, 53-54, ET *Genesis*, pp. 2-4, 25-27, 54-55, 79.

37. R. Kratz, *Die Komposition der erzählenden Bucher des Alten Testaments: Grundwissen der Bibelkritik* (UTB, 2137; Göttingen: Vandenhoeck & Ruprecht, 2000), pp. 252-63, ET *The Composition of the Narrative Books of the Old Testament* (trans. J. Bowden; London: T&T Clark, 2005), pp. 251-59; Schmid, *The Old*

what was in the original non-P Primaeval History or when exactly the non-P flood story was added, but they all agree that the flood story was originally lacking. Although at first sight it might appear surprising that such an important narrative would be lacking, we cannot automatically assume that it was there from the first in the non-Priestly account simply because it was present in P. In fact, a whole series of factors make probable its original absence.

First, it has long been noticed as distinctly odd that J currently has the story of the sons of God and daughters of men in Gen. 6.1-4 as the immediate prelude to the flood narrative, since it centres not on human sin but rather on that of the heavenly sons of God.[38] Moreover, in Gen. 6.4, where we read, 'The Nephilim were on the earth in those days and also afterward ...', the words 'and also afterward' look distinctly like a later gloss, pointing out that the Nephilim were still around later in the post-flood world too (cf. Num. 13.33). All this sits naturally with the assumption that the flood story did not originally follow on here. Further, the flood story presupposes that Noah and his family were the only humans to survive the flood, although the Nephilim were a kind of human as is presupposed by Gen. 6.4, which calls them 'men of renown'. For the same reasons some scholars have rather preferred to see Gen. 6.1-4 as a later addition,[39] but its theme of the transcendence of divine–human boundaries fits very well with Gen. 3.22-24 and 11.1-9, and it also

---

Testament: A Literary History, pp. 173-77; D.M. Carr, *The Formation of Genesis 1–11*, pp. 159-77, thus changing his view from what he had earlier expressed in *Reading the Fractures of Genesis: Historical and Literary Approaches* (Louisville, KY: Westminster/John Knox, 1996), pp. 241-45. The position of I. Dershowitz, 'Man of the Land: Unearthing the Original Noah', *ZAW* 128 (2016), pp. 357-73, is unusual, since he posits that originally there was a universal famine, not flood, which ended in Gen. 8.20-22.

38. It was because of the poor fit between Gen. 6.1-4 and what follows that *1 En.* 6–9 greatly magnified the dire consequences of the angelic marriages for humanity so as to justify the coming of the flood in *1 En.* 10. Thus, we are told that it was due to angelic influence that all kinds of weapons were introduced to humanity, and that *inter alia* bloodshed, impiety, fornication, corruption, astrology and spell-casting became widespread.

39. E.g. J. Rogerson, *Genesis 1–11* (OTG; Sheffield, JSOT Press, 1991), p. 69. Some more recent scholars see Gen. 6.1-4 as post-P, e.g. M. Witte, *Die biblische Urgeschichte. Redaktions- und theologiegeschichtliche Beobachtungen zu Genesis 1,1–11,26* (BZAW, 265; Berlin: W. de Gruyter, 1998), pp. 65-74, 293-97; W. Bührer, 'Göttersöhne und Menschentöchter. Gen 6,1-4 als innerbiblische Schriftauslegung', *ZAW* 123 (2011), pp. 395-515; also, with reserve, Gertz, *Das erste Buch Mose*, I, pp. 205-206.

displays characteristic J grammar and vocabulary (passive qal *yullad* and hiphil of *ḥālal*, 'to begin', both in Gen. 6.1).[40]

Secondly, in Gen. 5.29 we have in the midst of the P genealogy a fragment of J's pre-flood Sethite genealogy, where Lamech says of his son Noah, 'Out of the ground this one shall bring us relief from our work and from the toil of our hands'. With a typical J word play on Noah's name, this verse looks forward to Noah's discovery of wine in Gen. 9.20-27. It is somewhat surprising, if the quite lengthy non-P flood story was recounted soon afterwards, that Gen. 5.29 chose to highlight Noah's discovery of wine rather than his much more dramatically important and imminent act in saving a remnant of humanity and animals from a universal flood. However, if we omit the flood, the story in Gen. 9.20-27 follows on soon afterwards, and what is said in Gen. 5.29 sounds more appropriate.

Thirdly, Gen. 4.20-22 recount various culture heroes who were the first to undertake different professions. Thus, when it is declared that Jubal 'was the father of those who dwell in tents and have cattle' (4.20) and 'Jabal was the father of all those who play the lyre and harp' (4.21), this sounds as if they are the father of all in those professions, not simply those confined to the antediluvian period. This is distinctly odd if all this knowledge and experience was soon to be destroyed by a universal flood. This suggests that the author of 4.20-22 was unfamiliar with the flood story, as has often been noted by earlier scholars.

Fourthly, in the story in Gen. 9.20-27 about Noah's drunkenness and three sons, Shem, Ham and Japheth, the three sons are unmarried and living in Noah's tent. However, in the preceding flood story all three sons are married. This clearly does not cohere with the flood story having immediately preceded 9.20-27. However, all the references to Noah's sons' wives in the flood story are from P, not J. Nevertheless, the story in 9.20-27 focuses on Shem, Ham and Japheth, but it was clearly originally Shem, Canaan and Japheth (cf. 9.25),[41] and Noah's prophecies about his sons all centre on Palestine. Since the preceding flood story ended with Noah in Armenia (Urartu) – assuming J had the same notion as P (8.4),

40. For other objections to seeing Gen. 6.1-4 as post-P, see D.M. Carr, 'Looking at Historical Bckground, Redaction and Possible Bad Writing in Gen 6,1-4: A Synchronic and Diachronic Analysis', *BN* 181 (2019), pp. 7-24.

41. Cf. J. Day, 'Noah's Drunkenness, the Curse of Canaan, Ham's Crime, and the Blessing of Shem and Japheth (Genesis 9.18-27)', in D. Baer and R.P. Gordon (eds.), *Leshon Limmudim: Essays on the Language and Literature of the Hebrew Bible in Honour of Andrew Macintosh* (LHBOTS, 593; London: Bloomsbury T&T Clark, 2014), pp. 31-44 (34-35), republished in expanded form in Day, *From Creation to Babel*, pp. 137-53 (140-41).

as seems likely from the similarly located ark landing on Mt Nimush (northern Kurdistan) in the Gilgamesh epic (11.142-46) – it is somewhat surprising to find Noah apparently in distant Palestine so soon afterwards.

Fifthly, if as I have previously argued,[42] the story of Cain originated as an aetiology of the Kenites, and as we know that the Kenites were still in existence at the time of the writer, it is thereby presupposed that the Kenites were not wiped out by a flood. This again coheres with J's flood story being a later addition.

All the above problems would be solved at a stroke if there was originally no J flood story in the narrative and it was added at a later stage. But there are good grounds for still seeing it as a pre-Priestly insertion, as David Carr has convincingly argued,[43] rather than envisaging it as a post-P supplement, as a number of other recent scholars have done. Amongst many other reasons, as we have noted above, the sheer length of the Yahwistic flood story and the existence of so many overlaps and contradictions with the Priestly flood narrative, tell against its being a mere supplement to P. Finally, a small but telling point is that the Yahwistic flood narrative employs the word *'ānōkî* for 'I', not *'ᵃnî* (Gen. 7.4), just as J does elsewhere in Genesis 1–11 (cf. 3.10; 4.9), although *'ᵃnî* was overwhelmingly the norm in post-Priestly biblical Hebrew (as in P itself).[44]

42. See Day, 'Cain and the Kenites', in Galil, Geller and Millard (eds.), *Homeland and Exile* pp. 335-46, reprinted in Day, *From Creation to Babel*, pp. 51-60.

43. Carr, *The Formation of Genesis 1–11*, pp. 141-77.

44. See the chart in Hendel and Joosten, *How Old Is the Hebrew Bible?*, p. 18.

Chapter 8

THE COVENANT WITH NOAH
AND THE NOACHIC COMMANDMENTS

The Covenant with Noah

Introduction

The covenant with Noah is the least studied of all the covenants between God and human beings in the Old Testament (except the little-known covenant with Phinehas). But this is hardly surprising, since the amount of space devoted to it is small: the enactment of the event itself is described in Gen. 9.8-17, it is anticipated in Gen. 6.18, and referred back to in Isa. 54.9-10, and also, as we shall see, implicitly in Isa. 24.5.

The covenant with Noah in Genesis derives from the Priestly source, and in it God declares that he will never destroy the earth again with a flood. The sign of this covenant is the rainbow, which functions as a reminder to God of his promise. It is important to note that for P the commandments of God given to Noah in Gen. 9.1-7 are not part of this covenant. The word 'covenant' occurs seven times in 9.8-17 but not once within vv. 1-7. With his love for repetition it would not have been difficult for P to have added a reference or two to the covenant in vv. 1-7, if God's commandments there were really intended as a part of it. But the covenant with Noah in vv. 8-17 is purely promissory. This point is sometimes overlooked. However, as we shall see later, for some Jews the covenant with Noah did come to include the commandments of God to Noah in vv. 1-7, and this (mis)understanding seems to have begun fairly early.

It is noteworthy that God's covenant with Noah encompasses not only all his descendants but also all animals, including every sort of creature that came out of the ark (see vv. 10, 12, 15, 16, 17). It is, therefore, truly a cosmic covenant. In this regard it is unique among the divine covenants in the Old Testament.[1]

---

1. Robert Murray wrote a whole book entitled *The Cosmic Covenant* (HM; London: Sheed & Ward, 1992). Whilst displaying admirable environmental concern, Murray's

Before we study P's Noachic covenant in more detail, it should be noted that Gen. 9.8-17 is P's equivalent to J's conclusion to the flood story in Gen. 8.21-22, where Yahweh likewise promises not to destroy the earth again as he had with Noah's flood. Yahweh's promise is in the wake of his smelling the pleasing savour of Noah's sacrifice (Gen. 8.20-21), so rather on the spur of the moment. This contrasts with P, for whom there is no sacrifice till the time of Moses (Lev. 1–7). The other important difference is that in P God's promise is bound up with his covenant with Noah, already anticipated in Gen. 6.18, but in J's version there is no mention of covenant.

Structure

One thing that immediately strikes the reader is the highly repetitive nature of Gen. 9.8-17. Thus, the covenant (Gen. 9.9, 11), its sign (9.12, 17) and rainbow (9.13, 14) are each announced twice. This has led some scholars, including G. von Rad,[2] to posit two different recensions that have been combined here (A: 9.11a, 13, 16, 17; B: 9.9, 10, 11b, 12, 14, 15). However, this is unnecessary, since repetition is one of the character-istics of the P source (cf. 1.27; 2.2-3; 7.14-16; 9.5; 23.17-20; 49.29-32). Moreover, there is no sign of any contradictions within these verses, contrary to what we often find in passages that combine different sources. Rather, the repetition here is better understood as an attempt to give emphasis to what is said, thus highlighting the importance of the covenant with Noah for P.

As S. McEvenue[3] has noted, in Gen. 9.8-17 P has made deliberate use of numerical patterns. Thus, the following expressions all occur precisely three times: *wayyō'mer 'elōhîm*, 'God said' (vv. 8, 12aα, 17a), *'ôt beʳît*, 'sign of the covenant' (vv. 12a, 13b, 17b), *qešet be'ānān*, 'bow in the clouds' (vv. 13a, 14b, 16a), various forms of *hāqîm beʳît*, 'establish covenant' (vv. 9a, 11a, 17b), and the promise that the *mabbûl*, 'flood', will not return (vv. 11aδ, 11b, 15b). Again, both various forms of *zkr beʳît*, 'remember the covenant' (vv. 15a, 16b), as well as *'ôlām*, 'eternity'

attempt to find what he calls 'the Cosmic covenant' throughout the Old Testament, apart from what we explicitly have in Gen. 9.8-17 (cf. Gen. 6.18; Isa. 24.5; 54.9-10) consti-tutes an artificial and dubious construct.

2. G. von Rad, *Die Priesterschrift im Hexateuch, literarisch untersucht und theol-ogisch gewertet* (BWANT, 65; Stuttgart: Kohlhammer, 1934), pp. 1-11; *idem, Das erste Buch Mose*, p. 110, ET *Genesis*, pp. 129-30.

3. S. McEvenue, *The Narrative Style of the Priestly Author* (AnBib, 50; Rome: Biblical Institute Press, 1971), p. 72.

(vv. 12b, 16b), occur twice. One could also add that the word *bᵉrît*, 'covenant' occurs seven times (something not noted by McEvenue), itself a particularly symbolic number.

Some scholars[4] have seen a chiastic structure within the passage as follows:

> 9-11   'establish the covenant'
>   12a   'sign of the covenant'
>   12b   a covenant 'for eternal generations'
>   13-16   'my bow'
>   16   'eternal covenant'
>   17a   'sign of the covenant'
> 17b   'establish the covenant'

At first this may seem superficially attractive. However, objections can be made. For example, a whole three verses (vv. 9-11) are set over against a mere two words (v. 17b) in the first parallel, which is highly discrepant. Again, in the third parallel, the wording is not exact: whereas in the second half (v. 16) it speaks of an 'eternal covenant', the first half (v. 12b) has 'for eternal generations' (plural) and the word 'covenant' cannot properly be included, since this word was already part of the second parallel in v. 12a, 'sign of the covenant'.

What is clear, however, is that this passage consists of three divine speeches, each beginning with the words 'And God said'. The first speech (vv. 8-11) sets out the terms of the covenant, which is intended for Noah and his descendants, as well as for all animals, namely the divine promise never to destroy the earth again with a flood. The second speech (vv. 12-16) focuses on the rainbow, which functions as the sign of the covenant to remind God of his promise. The third speech (v. 17) is much briefer and simply recapitulates the second speech.

God's 'Establishment' rather than 'Cutting' of the Noachic Covenant

It is a peculiarity of the Priestly source that God is said to make covenants not by cutting them (*kārat*, the usual expression) but rather by establishing them (*hēqîm*). This is the case not only with the covenant with Noah (Gen. 6.18; 9.9, 11, 17), but also with the other P covenant with Abraham (Gen.

---

4. E.g. Wenham, *Genesis 1–15*, p. 194. Though note that Wenham renders 'maintain' rather than 'establish' here, on which see below.

17.7, 19, 21; Exod. 6.4). Why should this be? Some will doubtless feel that this is a mere minor stylistic variation with no particular significance. But one would expect there to be some reason for P to depart from the customary terminology. Others have claimed that it serves to emphasize the unilateral nature of these covenants.[5] However, against this it may be noted that Yahweh's unilateral grace is actually less emphasized in P's Genesis 17 version of the Abrahamic covenant, which likewise has *hēqîm*, than in the earlier Genesis 15 version of the Abrahamic covenant, which uses *kārat*. Thus, Genesis 17 requires circumcision as a condition of the covenant if one is not to be cut off, whereas in Genesis 15 the covenant is a pure act of grace with no conditions. Again, it has been claimed by a few scholars[6] that these passages refer to God's 'maintaining' the covenant rather than 'establishing' it. However, the fact that in the same context P also speaks of God's 'giving' (*ntn*) of these covenants (Gen. 9.12; 17.2; cf. Num. 25.12-13, God's covenant with Phinehas) as an alternative expression, clearly supports the idea that something new is taking place, namely the establishment and not merely subsequent maintenance of the covenant. It would also be strange if we only read of the maintaining of God's covenant with Noah and never of its actual establishment

Rather, it is probable that the verb *hēqîm* was preferred because the usual verb *kārat* had sacrificial overtones.[7] Now it was important for P to avoid sacrificial overtones in covenant making, since his two major covenants, with Noah and Abraham, were made in the era before sacrifice took place. For P sacrifice did not start till the time of Moses (Lev. 7.1-7). That the verb *kārat* had sacrificial overtones occasioned by the cutting up of an animal in sacrifice is shown by the fact that these two come together in Gen. 15.9-10, 17-18; Jer. 34.18-19. In addition, it may be noted that there are various related Greek expressions, such as *horkia temnein*, 'to cut oaths', which are found as early as Homer, who recounts several instances of cutting up an animal in sacrifice in connection with

---

5. E.g. Eichrodt, *Theologie des Alten Testaments*, I, p. 23, ET *Theology of the Old Testament*, I, p. 56; J. Barr, 'Reflections on the Covenant with Noah', in A.D.H. Mayes and R.B. Salters (eds.), *Covenant as Context: Essays in Honour of E.W. Nicholson* (Oxford: Oxford University Press, 2003), pp. 11-22 (12), reprinted in Barton (ed.), *Bible and Interpretation*, II, pp. 188-96 (188).

6. E.g. P. de Boer, 'Quelques remarques sur l'arc dans la nuée: Gen. 9:8-17', in C. Brekelmans (ed.), *Questions disputées d'Ancien Testament: Méthode et Théologie* (BETL, 33; Leuven: Leuven University Press, 1974), pp. 105-14; Wenham, *Genesis 1–15*, p. 175.

7. See J. Day, 'Why Does God "Establish" Rather than "Cut" Covenants in the Priestly Source?', in Mayes and Salters (eds.), *Covenant as Context*, pp. 91-109, reprinted in Day, *From Creation to Babel*, pp. 123-36.

the swearing of an oath (cf. Homer, *Iliad* 3.103-107, 271-301; 4.153-59; 19.252-68).

The Symbolism of the Rainbow

In the second part of God's speech in vv. 12-16 he emphasizes the role of the rainbow as a sign of the covenant, guaranteeing his promise never to destroy the earth again with a flood. Interestingly, God represents the rainbow as a reminder to himself (though of course, in reality, it serves too to give humanity a reminder).

How exactly are we to envisage the role of the rainbow? Based on the fact that the word for a rainbow in Hebrew is the same as that for a war bow used to fire arrows (*qešet*), many scholars in recent times have argued that in setting the rainbow in the heavens in Genesis 9 God is hanging up his war bow which had previously been used in unleashing the flood, thereby symbolizing peace. Although generally attributed to J. Wellhausen, this often-repeated view was already known to the Jewish mediaeval rabbi Nachmanides (Ramban), and has been widely followed in modern times.[8]

In support of this view, it has sometimes been pointed out that following Marduk's defeat of the sea monster Tiamat in *Enuma elish*, his bow was hung up in the heavens. This is referred to in *Enuma elish* 6.86-94:

> Anu lifted it up in the divine assembly,
> He kissed the bow, saying: 'It is my daughter!'
> Thus he called the names of the bow:
> 'Long stick' was the first; the second was, 'May it hit the mark'.
> With the third name, 'Bow star', he made it to shine in the sky,
> He fixed its heavenly position along with its divine brothers.
> After Anu had fixed the destiny of the bow,
> He set down a royal throne, a lofty one even for a god,
> Anu set it there in the assembly of the gods.[9]

---

8. Nachmanides on Gen. 9.12 in M. Carasik (ed.), *Miqraot Gedolot: The Commentators' Bible* (Philadelphia: JPS, 2018), p. 89; Wellhausen, *Prolegomena zur Geschichte Israels*, p. 328 n. 1, ET *Prolegomena to the History of Israel*, p. 311 n. 1; Gunkel, *Genesis*, pp. 150-51, ET *Genesis*, pp. 150-51; U.(M.D.) Cassuto, *A Commentary on the Book of Genesis*. II. *From Noah to Abraham* (Jerusalem: Magnes Press, 1964) p. 136; W. Brueggemann, *Genesis*, p. 84; U. Rüterswörden, 'Der Bogen in Genesis 9. Militärhistorische und traditionsgeschichtliche Erwägungen zu einem biblischen Symbol', *UF* 20 (1988), pp. 247-63 (259); Seebass, *Genesis*. I. *Urgeschichte*, p. 227; Fischer, *Genesis 1–11*, p. 504; Gertz, *Das erste Buch Mose*, I, p. 285.

9. Translation by Lambert, *Babylonian Creation Myths*, p. 115.

It will be noted, however, that Marduk's bow is not here transformed into a rainbow (something visible by day) but rather into a star (something visible by night). But even apart from this difference, there are good grounds for rejecting the popular view that the rainbow in Genesis 9 was God's war bow.[10] First, it is surely significant that the imagery of the divine warrior is nowhere to be found in the story of the flood, or indeed anywhere else in Genesis 1–11 (contrast God's shooting of arrows in Ps. 18.13, ET 14 // 2 Sam. 22.14, ET 15; Hab. 3.9). Though God is responsible for the flood, its rising and decline are depicted in a purely naturalistic way in Genesis. Secondly, the rainbow is simply an arc and lacks anything corresponding to the string of a bow. In the light of these serious problems, we can also reject an alternative view that the rainbow in Genesis 9 was a drawn war bow,[11] indicating the deity's willingness to fight his enemies in battle.

Rather than having been God's war bow, it is more natural to assume that the rainbow in Genesis 9 is simply that, a rainbow. That makes sense, since rainbows are sometimes seen after a rain storm, and Noah's flood was a gigantic rain storm. Whilst accepting this, L.A. Turner[12] also believes that the rainbow was intended as a pictorial representation of the dome-shaped firmament, which holds back the cosmic waters of the flood (*mabbûl*). However, there is nothing in the text of Genesis 9 to suggest this. Turner[13] claims support in Ezekiel 1, where he says the firmament and rainbow are linked. But there is no obvious connection between them (except their common arc shape): the firmament is described as being below God's throne (Ezek. 1.26), whereas what resembles a rainbow is the brightness around God (Ezek. 1.28), which is higher up. Ezekiel 1.28 compares a rainbow to Yahweh's glory, not with the firmament.

The Anticipation of Noah's Covenant in Genesis 6.18

In Gen. 6.18, part of the Priestly narrative's introduction to the flood story, we have the very first reference to covenant in the Bible. Having

---

10. Those who reject the war bow view include Jacob, *Genesis*, p. 256; Westermann, *Genesis 1–11*, p. 634, ET *Genesis 1–11*, p. 473; Wenham, *Genesis 1–15*, p. 196.

11. De Boer, 'Quelques remarques', p. 111; E. Zenger, *Gottes Bogen in den Wolken. Untersuchungen zu Komposition und Theologie der priesterschriftlichen Urgeschichte* (Stuttgart: Katholisches Bibelwerk, 1983), pp. 128-29.

12. L.A. Turner, 'The Rainbow as the Sign of the Covenant in Genesis ix 11-13', *VT* 43 (1993), pp. 119-24. P.J. Harland, *The Value of Human Life: A Study of the Story of the Flood (Genesis 6–9)* (VTSup, 64; Leiden: Brill, 1996), p. 138, is also sympathetic to this view.

13. See Turner, 'The Rainbow as the Sign of the Covenant', p. 122.

just described the imminent coming of the flood that will destroy the inhabitants of the earth, God declares to Noah, 'But I will establish my covenant with you; and you shall come into the ark, you, your sons, your wife, and your sons' wives with you'. God's words at this point may at first sight seem rather surprising, since they appear to anticipate what will happen only after the flood is over, the enactment of the Noachic covenant described in Gen. 9.8-17. For this reason, some scholars have made other proposals. Some, such as Hermann Gunkel,[14] have held that the reference must rather be to a different covenant with Noah from that described in Genesis 9, one that God was about to establish in Genesis 6. But this seems unlikely. There is no evidence of any other covenant with Noah than the one described in Genesis 9, and as J. Skinner[15] has noted, this would be 'contrary to the usage of P, to whom the $b^e r\hat{\imath}t$ is always a solemn and permanent embodiment of the divine will, and never a mere occasional provision'. Others, like U.(M.D.) Cassuto,[16] have held that what we have here is a re-enactment of the covenant with Adam in Gen. 1.26-30, although there is no evidence to support this, and Genesis does not speak of a covenant with Adam.[17] Again, the mediaeval rabbis Ibn Ezra and Nachmanides, as well as P. de Boer and Gordon Wenham[18] have proposed that God is speaking of a pre-existing covenant with Noah, and that God is rather saying 'I will maintain my covenant with you ...' But as we have already seen, since *ntn $b^e r\hat{\imath}t$*, lit. 'give a covenant', is an alternative expression to *hēqîm $b^e r\hat{\imath}t$* in Gen. 9.12 (and 17.2), the latter expression must refer to the establishing rather than maintaining of a covenant. Moreover, it would be odd to read of God's maintaining a covenant of whose existence not a word has previously been said. Genesis 6.18 has been well explained long ago by A. Dillmann,[19] who wrote: 'But in this universal destruction God has already in view His new relationship with Noah and his posterity (9:9ff.). Noah is to enter into the ark hopefully and have confidence in this.'

---

14. Gunkel, *Genesis*, p. 143, ET *Genesis*, p. 145.

15. Skinner, *Genesis*, pp. 162-63.

16. Cassuto, *Genesis*, II, p. 68.

17. On the idea of an alleged Adamic covenant, see Day, 'Why Does God "Establish" Rather than "Cut" Covenants?', pp. 102-103, reprinted in Day, *From Creation to Babel*, pp. 133-34.

18. Ibn Ezra and Nachmanides on Gen. 6.18 in Carasik (ed.), *Miqraot Gedolot*, p. 70, who refer it to God's promise that Noah would survive the flood; De Boer, 'Quelques remarques', pp. 105-14; Wenham, *Genesis 1–15*, p. 175.

19. Dillmann, *Die Genesis*, p. 141, ET *Genesis*, p. 273.

The Reference Back to the Covenant with Noah in Isaiah 54.9-10

The one explicit reference back to the covenant with Noah is in Isa. 54.9-10. The exilic prophet there declares: 'For this is like the days of Noah to me: as I swore that the waters of Noah should no more go over the earth, so I have sworn that I will not be angry with you and will not rebuke you. For the mountains may depart and the hills be removed, but my steadfast love shall not depart from you, and my covenant of peace shall not be removed, says the Lord, who has compassion on you.' But is this referring back to J's version of the divine promise in Gen. 8.21-22 or to P's version in Gen. 9.8-17? Probability is on the side of the latter, since v. 10 actually uses the term 'covenant' and explicitly mentions the waters, both like P but unlike J.

Mesopotamian Background of the Covenant with Noah

It is well known to Old Testament scholars that the Genesis flood story represents a transformation of the Mesopotamian flood myth. Best known is tablet 11 of the Gilgamesh epic, but I have argued elsewhere that it is the version in the Atrahasis epic that has been taken up in Genesis.[20] Less well known are the points of contact between the post-flood events in Genesis 9 and the Atrahasis epic. Thus, it is the case that, just as after the flood in Gen. 9.8-17, God promises never to bring a flood again, so in a Neo-Babylonian fragment of the Atrahasis epic the god Ea declares that there will not be another flood:[21]

> Henceforth let no flood be brought about,
> But let the people live forever.

Significantly this is not found in the Gilgamesh epic. Further, this time in both Atrahasis (3.6.2-4) and Gilgamesh (11.164-67), immediately following the reference to the gods smelling the sweet savour of the flood hero's sacrifice, which underlies Gen. 8.20-21, we read that the Mother goddess looked upon a lapis lazuli fly necklace so as to remind her forever of the flood, an event which she heartily disapproved of. In a similar way in Genesis 9 God looks on the rainbow to remind him forever never to bring another flood. Though these are not identical, it is noteworthy that

20. Day, 'The Genesis Flood Narrative'.

21. See W.G. Lambert, in I. Spar and W.G. Lambert (eds.), *Cuneiform Texts in the Metropolitan Museum of Art*. II. *Literary and Scholastic Texts of the First Millennium B.C.* (Metropolitan Museum of Art, New York: Brepols, 2005), p. 199, reverse, col. 5, lines 13-14; George, *The Babylonian Gilgamesh Epic*, I, p. 527.

they occur in identical places in the flood narrative, and one can easily envisage how, with the monotheization of the story, one got transformed into the other.[22] A necklace is, of course, arc-shaped, but we have no evidence that a necklace could actually symbolize a rainbow.

The Noachic Commandments

God's Commands to Noah in Genesis 9.1-7

Occasionally scholars have incorporated the whole of Gen. 9.1-17 under the heading of 'God's covenant with Noah' or suchlike,[23] but as we have noted earlier, this designation only applies to vv. 8-17. In addition to the divine blessing, Gen. 9.1-7 consists rather of various commands of God to Noah in the aftermath of the flood, and the covenant in vv. 8-17 remains forever in force whether the commandments in vv. 1-7 are obeyed or not.

The period after the flood constitutes the beginning of a new age for humanity when everything starts afresh. Hence in Gen. 9.1 God reiterates the command originally given to the first humans in Gen. 1.28 to be fruitful and multiply and fill the earth. It is attractive to see here a polemic against the Atrahasis epic (3.6.45-7.11, text only partly preserved), which at this very point, immediately after the flood, put various restrictions on human procreation in the post-flood period. It will be recalled that it was human overpopulation, leading to people becoming noisy and disturbing the sleep of the chief god Enlil, that led to the flood in the Atrahasis epic. Anyway, in Atrahasis the regulations divinely imposed after the flood by Enki (Ea) are as follows in the fully preserved part of the text (3.7.1-8):

---

22. For the necklace comparison see A.D. Kilmer, 'The Symbolism of the Flies in the Mesopotamian Flood Myth and Some Further Implications', in F. Rochberg-Halton (ed.), *Language, Literature, and History: Philological and Historical Studies Presented to Erica Reiner* (AOS Series, 67; New Haven, CT: American Oriental Society, 1987), pp. 175-80; Kvanvig, *Primeval History*, p. 232. However, they actually think the necklace symbolized the rainbow.

23. Among the commentators doing this are: Jacob, *Genesis*, p. 241; Hamilton, *The Book of Genesis: Chapters 1–17*, p. 311; J. McKeown, *Genesis* (Two Horizons OT Commentary; Grand Rapids, MI: Eerdmans, 2008), p. 63; T. Longman III and S. McKnight, *Genesis* (Story of God Commentary; Grand Rapids, MI: Zondervan, 2016), p. 120; A. Steinman, *Genesis* (TOTC; IVP: Downers Grove, IL, 2019), p. 104. Possibly some of these scholars are using language loosely (though it is still careless), as their detailed discussions make no attempt justify the application of the term 'Covenant' to Gen. 9.1-7. However, my former colleague, Jan Joosten, told me he is definitely of the view that the Noachic covenant applies to the whole of Gen. 9.1-17.

> In addition let there be a third category among the peoples,
> (Let there be) among the peoples women who bear and women who do not bear.
> Let there be among the peoples the *Pašittu*-demon
> To snatch the baby from the lap of her who bore it.
> Establish *Ugbabtu*-women, *Entu*-women, and *Igiṣītu*-women,
> And let them be taboo and so stop childbirth.[24]

Interestingly these restrictions on future births do not feature at all at the end of the Gilgamesh version of the flood story, thus providing yet further evidence that it was not this but rather the Atrahasis epic which lies behind the biblical flood story.

The importance of humans being fruitful and multiplying for P is emphasized by the fact that that the command is given at the end as well as at the beginning of God's speech in this section (vv. 1, 7). Herein lies continuity with Gen. 1.28. But from now on humans are permitted to eat meat,[25] in contrast to the pre-flood era described in Gen. 1.29, when humans are represented as vegetarians. In consequence animals will henceforth fear humans (Gen. 9.2). However, while God henceforth gives humans permission to eat meat, it is crucial that they do not eat the blood (Gen. 9.4). This is in keeping with Priestly theology elsewhere in the Old Testament, which emphasizes that the blood is the seat of life (cf. Lev. 7.26-27; 17.10-14; also Deut. 12.16, 23). However, while humans may now eat meat, God insists that human life is sacrosanct, since human beings are made in the image of God, so murder is strictly forbidden (Gen. 9.5-6).

The Coming Together of the Noachic Commandments and the Covenant with Noah

Another reference to the Noachic covenant appears to come in Isa. 24.5, where we read that 'The earth lies polluted under its inhabitants; for they have transgressed the laws, violated the statutes, broken the eternal covenant'. That this alludes to the Noachic covenant[26] is crucially supported

---

24. Translation from Lambert and Millard, *Atra-ḥasīs*, p. 103.

25. Interestingly, Hesiod spoke of four world ages, and for him likewise the period of meat eating followed after an age of vegetarian diet: for him, meat eating started in the Bronze age, following vegetarianism during the Golden and Silver ages (cf. Hesiod, *Works and Days* 117-18, 146-47). However, I doubt the proposal of Gnuse, *Misunderstood Stories*, p. 219, that P actually knew Hesiod.

26. So O. Kaiser, *Der Prophet Jesaja, Kapitel 13–39* (ATD, 18; Göttingen: Vandenhoeck & Ruprecht, 1973), pp. 148-49, ET *Isaiah 13–39* (trans. R.A. Wilson; OTL; London: SCM Press, 1974), p. 183; A. Schoors, *Jesaja* (De Boeken van het

by the fact that the covenant here is universal (cf. *tēbēl*, 'world', Isa. 24.4), unlike the Mosaic[27] or Abrahamic covenants. It further coheres with the allusion to it as an 'eternal covenant' (*bᵉrît 'ôlām*; cf. Gen. 9.16). Other covenants were regarded as eternal too, including the Mosaic covenant, though the precise phrase 'eternal covenant' is never directly used of the latter. Isaiah 24, however, appears to have transformed Genesis 9's unconditional covenant into a conditional one, by taking the commands to Noah in Gen. 9.1-7 as part of the covenant, as apparently also the case in some later Jewish works, as we shall see shortly. Isaiah 24.5 speaks of the earth as polluted. If this alludes to bloodshed, something attributed to the inhabitants of the earth in Isa. 26.21 (cf. the pollution and bloodshed connection in Num. 35.33), we could well have a reference back to Gen. 9.6, where shedding of human blood is condemned. In keeping with the idea that Isa. 24.5 has conditionalized the Noachic covenant is the fact that a few verses later, in Isa. 24.18, we actually read of judgment taking the form of a flood: 'For the windows of heaven are opened, and the foundations of the earth tremble', echoing the language of the flood story in Gen. 7.11 (cf. 8.2).

That some Jews did come to see the commands of God to Noah in Gen. 9.1-7 as part of the Noachic covenant is explicitly shown in ch. 6 of the book of *Jubilees* (second century BCE).[28] This is most clear in *Jub.*

Oude Testament; Roermond: J.J. Romen, 1972), pp. 145-46; B.S. Childs, *Isaiah* (OTL; Louisville, KY: Westminster John Knox Press, 2001), p. 179; J. Blenkinsopp, *Isaiah 1–39* (AB, 19; New York: Doubleday, 2000), pp. 351-52. J.T. Hibbard, *Intertextuality in Isaiah 24–27: The Reuse and Evocation of Earlier Texts and Traditions* (FAT, 2. Reihe 16; Tübingen: Mohr Siebeck, 2006), pp. 64-68, sees the primary reference in Isa. 24.5 as being to the Noachic covenant. However, in a later article, 'Isaiah 24–27 and Trito-Isaiah: Some Connections', in J.T. Hibbard and H.C.P. Kim (eds.), *Formation and Intertextuality in Isaiah 24–27* (Atlanta, GA: SBL, 2013), pp. 183-199 (194-99) has modified his view and now emphasizes the diversity of covenants he believes are included here.

27. R.E. Clements, *Isaiah 1–39* (NCB; Grand Rapids, MI: Eerdmans; London: Marshall, Morgan & Scott, 1980), pp. 201-202, thinks we may have here a universalization of the Mosaic covenant. Similarly, with much more discussion, D.C. Polaski, 'Reflections on the Mosaic Covenant: The Eternal Covenant (Isaiah 24.5) and Intertextuality', *JSOT* 77 (1998), pp. 55-73. D.G. Johnson, *From Chaos to Restoration: An Integrative Reading of Isaiah 24–27* (JSOTSup, 61; Sheffield: Sheffield Academic Press, 1988), pp. 27-29, also sees the Mosaic covenant here, but believes that the judgment in Isa. 24 only pertains to Israel. But *tēbēl*, 'world', as the subject of the judgment in Isa. 24.4 proves that *hā'āreṣ* refers to the earth, not merely the land.

28. As correctly pointed out by Barr, 'Reflections on the Covenant with Noah', p. 20-21, reprinted in Barton (ed.), *Bible and Interpretation*, II, p. 195.

6.11-14. Verse 11 speaks of the making of the Noachic covenant, and as part of this vv. 12-14 immediately afterwards mention that it is prescribed that forever blood should not be eaten. It is also significant that earlier in the chapter God's commands to Noah to be fruitful and multiply, avoiding murder and the eating of blood (taken up from Gen. 9.1-7), occur in a passage that both begins and ends with a reference to God's making of the covenant with Noah (*Jub.* 6.4, 10). This covenant is to be renewed every year at the feast of Weeks (*Jub.* 6.17). After this it is stated that, following Noah's death, his sons became corrupt and ate blood till the days of Abraham, and it is clearly implied that this constituted a breaking of the covenant. Verses 20-22 then reiterate the need to keep the feast of Weeks.

Pseudo-Philo (probably first century CE) also appears to conflate the covenant with Noah and God's commandments to Noah. Chapter 3, vv. 11-12 read:

> And the Lord spoke again to Noah and to his sons, saying, 'Behold I will establish my covenant with you and your seed after you, and no more will I destroy the earth by the water of a flood. And everything that moves and lives will be food for you. But meat with its lifeblood you may not eat. For whoever will shed the blood of a man, his own blood will be shed, because man was made after the image of God. But you, increase and multiply and fill the earth, like a school of fish multiplying in the waves.' And God said, 'This is the covenant that I have established between me and you. And it will happen that when I cover the heaven with clouds, my bow will appear in the cloud: and it will be a memorial of the covenant between me and you and all those inhabiting the earth.'[29]

It will be noticed that God's allowing meat eating but forbidding consumption of the blood, as well as the commands to abstain from bloodshed and fill the earth, are all listed in between references to the Noachic covenant at the beginning and the end.

Josephus, *Ant.* 1.3.7-8, curiously, never uses the word 'covenant' in connection with God and Noah. After Noah's offering of sacrifice and entreating God not to punish the world in such a way again, God grants his request, promising never again to bring a worldwide flood. But God emphasizes the necessity of not committing murder, and although humans may now eat of all beasts, they must not consume the blood. Finally, mention is made of the rainbow as a sign that God has foresworn his anger. Yet again, it will be noted that the commands not to murder or eat blood are squeezed in between references to God promising not to flood

---

29. Translation by D.J. Harrington, 'Pseudo-Philo', in Charlesworth (ed.), *Old Testament Pseudepigrapha*, II, p. 297-377 (307).

the earth again and a reference to the rainbow, suggesting that the two parts of Gen. 9.1-17 are being brought together.

The Later Development of the Noachic Commandments

Finally, the concept of seven Noachic commandments developed in rabbinic Judaism as a basic minimum of the divine law that should be adhered to by the gentiles. We have, of course, God's commands to Noah in Gen. 9.1-7, which include the avoidance of murder and eating blood, and these were taken up into the later Noachic commandments (the former explicitly, and the second implicitly by the law against eating a limb torn from a living animal). However, the rabbinic Noachic commandments far transcend them.

Louis Finkelstein[30] argued that the Noachic laws went back to the Maccabaean period. He saw them as originating as a result of the fact that some gentile nations were subject to the rule of Hasmonaean monarchs such as John Hyrcanus. He further thought that the Noachic commandments were reflected in the book of *Jubilees*. However, this view is to be rejected, as David Novak[31] has shown. Thus, the Idumaeans and Ituraeans were forced to convert to Judaism by John Hyrcanus, which is contrary to the tolerant spirit implied by the Noachic laws. Moreover, the Sadducees were dominant at this period, for whom only the written Torah was authoritative, in which the Noachic commandments are not fully found.

Moreover, the notion that the beginnings of the concept of Noachic commandments for gentiles are present in *Jubilees* is unconvincing. Sometimes the beginning of this process has been found in *Jub.* 7.20. This declares:

> And in the twenty-eighth jubilee Noah began to command his grandsons with ordinances and commandments and all of the judgments which he knew. And he bore witness to his sons so that they might do justice and cover the shame of their flesh and bless the one who created them and honor father and mother, and each one love his neighbour and preserve themselves from fornication and pollution and from all injustice.[32]

---

30. L. Finkelstein, 'Some Examples of Maccabean Halaka', *JBL* 49 (1930), pp. 20-42, reprinted in L. Finkelstein, *Pharisaism in the Making: Selected Essays* (New York: Ktav, 1972), pp. 222-44.

31. David Novak, *The Image of the Non-Jew in Judaism: An Historical and Constructive Study of the Noahide Laws* (Toronto Studies in Theology, 14; New York: Edwin Mellen Press, 1983), pp. 11-14.

32. Translation by O.S. Wintermute, 'Jubilees', in Charlesworth (ed.), *Old Testament Pseudepigrapha*, II, pp. 35-142 (69-70).

Subsequent to this, in exhorting his sons for the future, Noah pays particular attention to not eating the blood and causing human bloodshed, thereby taking up the theme of Gen. 9.4-6.

However, with the exception of fornication, the six commands listed previously are quite different from those later known in the rabbis as the seven Noachic commandments. Moreover, the commands in *Jub.* 7.20. should not be seen as intended specifically for gentiles. An important point of *Jubilees* was to show that the Torah was already observed prior to Moses, and this included Noachic times.[33]

The earliest complete version of the seven Noachic laws is to be found in Tosefta *Avodah Zarah* 8.4:

> Concerning seven requirements were the sons of Noah admonished: setting up of courts of justice, idolatry, blasphemy, fornication, bloodshed, theft, and a limb torn from a living animal.

As already mentioned, the law against murder is already explicitly one of the Noachic commandments in Gen. 9.5-6, and the law against eating an animal's torn limb may be seen to be implicit in Gen. 9.4's law against eating meat containing blood. As for the law about the institution of law courts, this too can be seen to have arisen from reflection on Gen. 9.5-6, namely its insistence on retribution for murder, since it was important that this took place in a proper legal setting rather than through unbridled personal revenge. This is made clear by Targum Pseudo-Jonathan on Gen. 9.6, which reads, 'Whoever sheds the blood of man in the presence of witnesses, the judges shall condemn him to death; but whoever sheds (it) without witnesses, the Lord of the world will take revenge on him on the day of the great judgment ...'[34] Again, since big differences between the Jewish and pagan world were Jewish insistence on monotheism and strict sexual morality, it is easy to understand how the laws on idolatry, blasphemy and fornication got added. Then finally, the addition of the law rejecting theft is understandable as the inclusion of an important ethical principle. It will be noted that five of the Noachic commandments resemble laws in the Decalogue. This is not surprising, since both were seeking to lay down basic ethical and religious precepts, one for gentiles and one for Israel.

33. Ch. Albeck, *Das Buch der Jubiläen und die Halacha* (Berlin: Hochschule für die Wissenschaft des Judentums, 1930), p. 34.

34. Translation from Maher, *Targum Pseudo-Jonathan: Genesis*, p. 45.

These seven Noachic laws should be seen as going back to the early part of the second century CE, since they are alluded to by Rabbi Meir (fl. 130–160 CE).[35] A similar list appears in *b. Sanh.* 56a, except blasphemy is there listed before idolatry instead of after it. Up to the third century there was a certain fluidity in the Noachic commandments, with individual rabbis making variations,[36] while 'Ulla (*c.* 280) even extended the number to thirty (*b. Hull.* 92a-b). Nevertheless, the standard seven eventually set in.

However, there have been some scholars[37] who have seen the Noachic commandments as already implied in the New Testament in Acts 15.20, 29; 21.25, where the council of Jerusalem set out the minimal legal requirements for gentiles: 'to abstain from the pollutions of idols and from unchastity and from what is strangled and from blood'. In Acts 15.29 and 21.25 the four laws are cited in a different order: 'that you [they] should abstain from what has been sacrificed to idols and from blood and from what is strangled and from unchastity'. However, although there are more or less three in common, the Noachic laws were seven, not four in number, and do not appear to have arisen till the second century CE. Moreover, the Noachic laws are primarily ethical, whereas the laws in Acts are mostly ritual. A better case can be made that these laws in Acts are dependent on Leviticus 17–18.[38] First, the four laws are all present and come in exactly the same order in Leviticus 17–18 as in Acts 15.29 and 21.25. (For what has been sacrificed to idols, cf. Lev. 17.5-9 [esp. v. 7], for not eating blood, cf. Lev. 17.10-14, for not eating what is strangled, cf. Lev. 17.15-16, and for avoiding unchastity, cf. Lev. 18.6-20[23].) Secondly, in Leviticus 17–18 the laws in question are specifically said to be incumbent upon the resident alien, not just Jews (cf. Lev. 17.8,

35. M. Bockmuehl, 'The Noachide Commandments and the New Testament Ethics: With Special Reference to Acts 15 and Pauline Halaka', *RB* 102 (1995), pp. 72-101 (89).

36. For these variations, see J.P. Lewis, *A Study of the Interpretation of Noah and the Flood in Jewish and Christian Literature* (Leiden: Brill, 1978), p. 186.

37. E.g. H.-J. Schoeps, *Theologie und Geschichte des Judenchristentums* (Tübingen: J.C.B. Mohr [Paul Siebeck], 1949), pp. 259-60.

38. So rightly G. Strecker, 'Noachische Gebote', in *RGG*³, IV (Tübingen: J.C.B. Mohr [Paul Siebeck], 1960), cols. 1500-1501 (1501); E. Haenchen, *Die Apostelgeschichte* (Göttingen: Vandenhoeck & Ruprecht, 14th edn, 1965), p. 411, ET, *The Acts of the Apostles: A Commentary* (trans. B. Noble, G. Shinn, H. Anderson and R. McL. Wilson; Oxford: Blackwell, 1971), p. 469; J.A. Fitzmyer, *The Acts of the Apostles* (AB, 31; New York: Doubleday, 1998), pp. 557-58.

10, 12-13, 15; 18.26), so it makes sense that Acts should take up these
Leviticus 17–18 laws for gentiles. Thirdly, Acts 15.21 implies that the
basis is Moses, i.e. the Pentateuchal laws. No mention is made of Noah,
and in any case, most of what became known as the Noachic laws are not
actually found in Genesis 9. It seems that the purpose of these laws in
Acts was to facilitate fellowship between gentile and Jewish Christians
(especially table fellowship).

The idea grew up among some rabbis that six of the seven laws arose
already in the time of Adam, and only the law about the torn limb of an
animal actually originated with Noah. By fanciful eisegesis the six supposedly Adamic laws were read out of Gen. 2.16, 'The Lord commanded the
man …' (*Gen. Rab.* 16.6; cf. 24.5; *Deut. Rab.* 1.16; *b. Sanh.* 56b).[39]

The classic formulation of the Noachic laws appears later in Maimonides.
He declared (*Mishneh Torah, Book 14, Judges: Laws of Kings* 9.1):

> Six items were commanded to Adam concerning idolatry, blasphemy,
> bloodshed, illicit sexuality, theft, and law courts … God added to Noah the
> law of not eating from the flesh of a live animal.

This ordering of the Noachic laws here follows that given earlier by Rabbi
Isaac (*bSanh.* 56b). Putting the law against idolatry first must have been
a way of emphasizing the theological foundation of the laws. He held
that those who observed these laws were 'considered one of the "pious
among the gentiles" and will be assured of a portion in the world to come'.
However, it was necessary for gentiles to affirm the divine origin of these
laws (*Laws of Kings* 8.11).

Later still during the Enlightenment there were those like Hugo Grotius
(*De Jure Belli ac pacis* I.1.16; II.5.13) who saw the Noachic laws as an
expression of natural law. Even in modern times the Noachic laws have
had influence. It is in particular the Chabad-Lubavitcher Jews who have
striven to promote them throughout the world, sometimes with success.
On March 20th, 1991 the US Congress passed H.J. Res. 104, subsequently
signed into law by President George H.W. Bush and became Public Law
102-14, which declared that the 'Seven Noahide Laws' are the ethical
values of a civilized society and are the basis on which the American
nation was founded.

---

39. For a summary of these fanciful arguments, see Lewis, *A Study of the Interpretation of Noah and the Flood*, p. 187.

Chapter 9

THE TABLE OF THE NATIONS IN GENESIS 10

Introduction

For many people the table of the nations in Genesis 10 might at first sight look like a boring list of names. It is, in fact, the least studied part of Genesis 1–11. But this chapter is, actually, the best evidence we have of the ancient Israelites' knowledge of the geography of the world. As we shall see, it shows awareness of the world as far west as southern Spain (Tarshish), as far east as Elam (south-west Persia – modern Iran), as far south as East Africa (Seba) and Yemen (Sheba), and as far north as Ukraine (Ashkenaz, i.e. the Scythians). The only comparable passage (apart from the derivative 1 Chron. 1.5-23) is Ezekiel 27, which is limited to listing Tyre's trading partners throughout the world, though it does also give informative details about what the various nations traded.

Genesis 10 contains a list of the names of the nations (and some cities) of the world, represented as the descendants of Noah's three sons, Shem, Ham and Japheth. Although this ancestry is, of course, mythical, the place names themselves are certainly historical, often being mentioned elsewhere in the Hebrew Bible and extra-biblical documents, and reflecting geographical locations of the known world in the time of the authors of Genesis 10. It is hardly a coincidence that it consists of precisely 70 place names (if we exclude the distinct narrative section on Nimrod in vv. 8-12, which is likely a later addition), since we know that the Jews envisaged there being 70 nations on the earth (cf. *1 En.* 89.59; 90.22, 245; Targum Pseudo-Jonathan, Deut. 32.8).[1] The number 70

---

1. Although these passages, which speak of 70 angels of the nations, are late, underlying them is the much older concept of the 70 gods of the nations. This is implied in Deut. 32.8, which speaks of the Most High dividing up the nations according to the number of the sons of God (reading *bᵉnê ᵉlōhîm* for MT *bᵉnê yiśrā'ēl*

symbolized totality (cf. Gen. 46.27; Exod. 1.5; Deut. 10.22; Judg. 8.30; 2 Kgs 10.1). The 70 nations seem to be comprised of 14 descendants of Japheth, 30 descendants of Ham, and 26 descendants of Shem.

Careful analysis of this chapter shows that the list is composite. Some of the names are introduced by the words 'the descendants [lit. sons] of A' (vv. 1-7, 20, 22-23, 31-32), while others are introduced by the words 'A became the father of B' (vv. 8-19, 24, 26-30) or on a couple of occasions, 'to A was born B' (vv. 21, 25). That these respective formulae are indicative of two different sources is supported by the fact that three names, Havilah, Sheba and Assyria, are listed twice, both under the former formula in vv. 7 and 22, and also under the latter formula in vv. 29, 28 and 11 (though v. 11 is part of the additional Nimrod section). It is similarly probable that Lud (Lydia) in v. 22 and the plural form Ludim in v. 13 represent the same people, each of them again being introduced by a different formula. We must therefore conclude that the redactor has not done his work as efficiently as possible, something manifest elsewhere in Genesis. Anyway, as noted above, vv. 1-7, 20, 22-23, 31-32 are attributable to one source and vv. 8-19, 21, 24-30 to the other. The Documentary Hypothesis identifies these as P and J respectively. In the case of P, this is supported by the occurrence of the world *tôl\u1e17dōt*, 'generations' (vv. 1, 32) and by the use of repetitive formulae (vv. 5, 20, 31). In the case of J this is supported by the use of the qal rather than the hiphil of *yld* to denote 'was the father of' (vv. 8, 13, 15, 24, 26), as well as the use of the passive qal *yullad*, 'was born' (vv. 21, 25). However, in spite of the composite nature of the chapter, a redactor has ensured that 70 nations are included overall.

There is no single principle of organization in the table, though as we shall see below, it is primarily geographical. But B. Oded[2] has attempted an original interpretation according to which the Shemites were nomadic nations, the Hamites sedentary nations, and the Japhethites seafaring peoples. However, in each case there are problems. Under Shem are included Arpachshad (Chaldaea), Assyria, Elam and Lud (Lydia), which were not nomadic; the Hamites include certain Arab tribes in v. 7, which were distinctly non-sedentary; and many of the Japhethites were in

---

with the support of 4QDeut[j] *b\u1e17nê 'elôhîm* and LXX). The notion of the sons of God derives from the Canaanite sons of El, and we know from the Ugaritic texts that these were 70 in number; cf. *KTU³* 1.4.VI.46, 'the seventy sons of Athirat', El's consort.

2. B. Oded, 'The Table of the Nations (Genesis 10) – A Socio-Cultural Approach', *ZAW* 98 (1986), pp. 14-31. This is viewed favourably by Arnold, *Genesis*, p. 116.

landlocked Anatolia and hence not seafaring. Oded attempts to get round these problems by claiming that the original table was later edited by those who did not understand its construction. But this simply makes the whole theory totally speculative and without firm evidence.

Theological Significance

What theological significance does Genesis 10 have? Well, first of all, it clearly implies the unity of the human race. All nations, whether friends or enemies, are blood relatives, descendants of Noah (and through him of the first man, Adam). As Acts 17.26 was later to put it, 'From one man he made all the nations to inhabit the whole earth'.

In addition, Genesis 10 represents the fulfilment of God's command given to Noah in Gen. 9.1 (P), 'Be fruitful and multiply, *and fill the earth*' (cf. Gen. 9.19). For P, the spread of humanity throughout the world, thereby forming different nations, must have been perceived as a gradual process following the flood. For P the table of the nations thus follows on naturally after Genesis 9. For J, by contrast, the spread of the nations was rather the consequence of God's scattering of human beings following the Tower of Babel incident (Gen. 11.8-9). The table of the nations in Genesis 10 looks somewhat premature in the light of the subsequent Babel story. Possibly the redactor of the final form of Genesis envisaged the Tower of Babel story as a flash back. However, already Josephus detected a problem and placed his paraphrase of Genesis 10 (*Ant.* 1.6.1-4) after the Babel incident (*Ant.* 1.4.3). It would indeed seem logical that J's passage referring to Nimrod's rule over Babylon in Gen. 10.10 originally occurred after Babylon had received its name in Gen. 11.9, and indeed that all the other nations and places mentioned in J passages in Genesis 10 were originally placed after the scattering of the people had taken place in Gen. 11.7-8.[3]

Some may be surprised that the author failed to mention his own nation, Israel, in this list. However, as we shall see later, Shem's son Eber is to be understood as the eponymous ancestor of the Hebrews (vv. 21, 24-25), and explicit mention of Israel, alongside other nations such as the Ammonites, Moabites, Edomites and certain northern Arabs, occurs later on in Genesis after their emergence (Gen. 19.30-38; 25.1-4, 12-16, 30; 34.7; 36.1-43; 49.7).

---

3. Cf. Seebass, *Genesis. I. Urgeschichte*, p. 266; Wellhausen, *Die Composition des Hexateuchs*, p. 12, also thinks this is possible.

The Threefold Division of the Nations

Although Genesis 10 is actually a table of the nations (including some cities), in form it presents itself as a genealogy of Noah's three sons, Shem, Ham and Japheth. However, they are treated in reverse order: Japheth, Ham and Shem. The reason for this will be considered later. It was, in fact, common in antiquity (cf. the ancient Greeks) to divide the nations of the world up into three groups: Europe, Africa and Asia. It so happens that Shem does consist exclusively of Asian nations: the ancestors of the Hebrews (indicated by Eber), the Aramaeans, Chaldaeans and Elamites, as well as many tribal groups in Arabia. Also, Japheth, though not strictly equivalent to Europe (not much of which was really known to the Israelites then), clearly denotes nations to the north and west of Israel, including as it does primarily various people in Anatolia and its vicinity, who were ethnically Indo-European, but also a few Mediterranean nations. Finally, as for Ham, it does indeed include all the African peoples mentioned in this chapter: Egypt, Put (Libya), Kush (Nubia) and Seba (part of East Africa). However, Ham also, curiously, encompasses Canaanites of various kinds, who belong more naturally under Shem in terms of their language, geography and ethnicity. In addition, there is a significant section about Nimrod (vv. 8-12), who although presented as a son of Kush (Nubia), clearly inhabits Mesopotamia (Babylonia and Assyria). There are also, finally, other names that seem out of place here (Sheba in Arabia, Seba in east Africa, Caphtorim [Cretans], Lud [Lydia]). We shall attempt to deal with these problems later.

The Sons of Japheth (vv. 1-5)

The first part of the table of the nations gives a list of the sons of Japheth (vv. 1-5). The names are entirely from P, but J must have had a list of Japhethites too, since he knew the names of all three of Noah's sons (9.20-27), and for J the Philistines appear to be among the descendants of Japheth in 9.27 (in contrast to the later gloss in 10.14).[4] As already noted, the Japhethites are all Indo-European nations, either in Anatolia or its vicinity or in the Mediterranean. It seems likely that the name Japheth is to be connected with the name of the Titan Iapetos, who was the ancestor of the Hellenic races in Greek mythology through his grandson, Deucalion, the Greek flood hero.[5] Similarly, Japheth was the

---

4. See Day, *From Creation to Babel*, pp. 143-47.

5. Deucalion's son Hellen was the father of three sons, Dorus (ancestor of the Dorians), Aeolus (ancestor of the Aeolians) and Xulus (ancestor of the Achaeans

ancestor of the Greeks (Ionians) and related people, and the son of the Hebrew flood hero, Noah.[6] In addition, it may be noted that Iapetos's wife, Klymene, received the name of Asia, betokening her connection with Anatolia.

Verse 3 lists the seven sons of Japheth. The first-born is called Gomer. It is generally agreed that Gomer denotes the Cimmerians[7] (Greek *Kimmerioi*, Akkadian *Gimirrāya*, their land *Gamir*, etc.[8]). They originated north of the Caucasus and the Black Sea (cf. Homer, *Odyssey* 11.14, where they are said to dwell beyond Oceanus) but moved southwards towards the end of the eighth century BCE after being pushed away by the Scythians, reaching Anatolia in the seventh century (cf. Herodotus, *Histories* 4.11-12). Ezekiel 38.6 includes Gomer in the army of Gog, alongside Beth-Togarmah, Togarmah being a son of Gomer in Gen. 10.3. Their name is still preserved in the Armenian name for Cappadocia, Gamir. It has also sometimes been thought to lie behind the name Crimea,

---

and Ionians). See M.L. West, *The Hesiodic Catalogue of Women* (Oxford: Clarendon Press, 1985), pp. 50-53. G. Darshan, 'The Biblical Account of the Post-Diluvian Generation (Gen. 9:20–10:32) in the Light of Greek Genealogical Literature', *VT* 63 (2013), pp. 515-35 (521-22, 530-34), and *After the Flood: Stories of Origins in the Hebrew Bible and Eastern Mediterranean* (Biblical Encyclopaedia, 35; Jerusalem: Bialik Institute, 2018 [Hebrew]), pp. 57-77, sees a connection here with Gen. 10, which he attributes to a common Levantine background. It is to be noted, however, that the three sons are actually Deucalion's grandsons, in contrast to Noah's own three sons, and that Deucalion is here only the ancestor of various Greek peoples, whereas Noah in Gen. 10 is the ancestor of all known nations. However, Darshan does also cite another Greek parallel, a tradition of Argos, in which the various known nations are all descendants of one man, but in this case the man is the Argive first man Phoroneus, not the flood hero Deucalion. See West, *The Hesiodic Catalogue of Women*, pp. 76-91, 144-54.

6. M.L. West, *The East Face of Helicon: West Asiatic Elements in Early Poetry and Myth* (Oxford: Clarendon Press, 1997), pp. 289-90, whilst admitting the similarity in the names, holds that it is difficult to see any significant point of contact between Japheth and Iapetos to justify a connection, but I believe the points I have listed above do make it plausible. At the other extreme, B. Louden, 'Iapetos and Japheth: Hesiod's *Theogony*, *Iliad* 15.187-93, and Genesis 9–10', *Illinois Classical Studies* 38 (2013), pp. 1-12, reprinted in B. Louden, *Greek Myth and the Bible* (London: Routledge, 2019), pp. 37-56, finds all kinds of fanciful connections between the two figures.

7. For a useful survey of what is known of the Cimmerians, see E. Yamauchi, *Foes from the Northern Frontier* (Eugene, OR: Wipf & Stock, 1982), pp. 49-61.

8. Cf. S. Parpola, *Neo-Assyrian Toponyms* (AOAT, 6; Neukirchen-Vluyn: Neukirchener Verlag, 1970), pp. 132-34.

but that is highly questionable,[9] and the view that it provides the origin of Cymru, the Welsh name for Wales,[10] is now also rejected.

Next comes Magog. Unlike almost all the other descendants of Japheth, the name Magog is not attested outside the Bible in any ancient sources. But it is mentioned in Ezek. 38.2 as the seat of 'Gog, of the land of Magog, the chief prince of Meshech and Tubal' (cf. Ezek. 39.1, 6), who is to lead his hordes against Israel and will subsequently be defeated by Yahweh. It is generally thought that the name Gog derives from that of Gyges (Akkadian Gugu), king of Lydia from *c.* 680–652 BCE. It may be that the name Magog derives from Akkadian *māt Gūgi*, 'land of Gog'. Much later in Rev. 20.8 Magog became the name of a leader alongside Gog, rather than the name of a country.

Next Madai. This name clearly denotes the Medes (Persian Māda, Akkadian Madaya), who lived east of the Zagros mountains and south of the Caspian Sea in the north-west of Iran, with their capital at Ecbatana (modern Hamadan). After the Judaean exile they were often associated with the Persians in Jewish thought (e.g. Dan. 5.28; Est. 1.19).

After this comes Yawan. Everyone agrees that this denotes Ionia and thus refers to certain Greeks (cf. Ezek. 27.13; Isa. 66.19). After the time of Alexander the Great the Jews came to use this name for the Greeks generally (e.g. Dan. 8.21; 10.20; 11.2), including mainland Greece. In view of the likely date of Genesis 10, Yawan here must be restricted to Ionia in western Anatolia.

Next we have Tubal and Meshech. Since these two places usually occur together in the Old Testament (except Ps. 120.5, where Meshech appears alone), we shall treat them together here. Their identity is well known: they appear as Tabali and Mushki in Akkadian sources and as the Tibarēnoi and Moschoi in Herodotus, *Histories* 3.94.2; 7.78. Both were powerful military states in Anatolia, Meshech in Phrygia and Tubal further east, north of Cilicia. The Akkadian and Herodotean spellings

---

9. The name Crimea for the peninsula is not attested till the fourteenth century, and it is agreed to derive from the name of the town now known as Staryi Krym, called Qirim from the thirteenth century. Since the Crimea was under Turco-Mongol control from 1239 to 1441 it is attractive to suppose that this name derives from Turco-Tatar *qyrym*, 'fortress'. Although recollection of the ancient Cimmerians was retained in Graeco-Roman times in the name of what is now called the Kerch strait (Greek *Kimmerios Bosporos*, Latin *Cimmerianus Bosporos*), and in a town on the southern shore of the Kerch peninsula (Greek *Kimmerikon*, Latin *Cimmericum*), there is a long time gap between then and the thirteenth century, so that a Turco-Tatar derivation seems more natural for the name Crimea.

10. Cf. Speiser, *Genesis*, p. 66.

suggest that the first vowel of Meschech should actually be an 'o' or 'u', and this is further supported by the Septuagint's rendering Mosoch and the Samaritan spelling Mushak. The famous king Midas, of whom legend told that everything he touched turned to gold (Ovid, *Metamorphoses* 11.135-235), was an actual king (late eighth century BCE), known to the Assyrians as Mita king of the Mushki (Meshech).

The identity of the last son of Japheth, Tiras, is more uncertain. The context suggests it was somewhere in Anatolia or its vicinity. The view that it refers to Thrace, an opinion common in antiquity (e.g. Josephus, *Ant.* 1.6.1), has long been abandoned, since the name (Greek *Thrakē*) is not particularly close, and the 's' in *Thrakes* (Thracians) is simply the Greek nominative plural ending. Over the last hundred years and more scholars have generally equated Tiras with the Tyrsenoi, the Greek name for the Etruscans, who according to Herodotus, *Histories* 1.94 originated in Lydia (western Asia Minor). However, modern biblical scholars are often unaware that the consensus of modern Etruscanologists is that Herodotus was mistaken and that the Etruscans did not come from Asia Minor but rather originated within Italy from the earlier Vilanovan civilization.[11] Since from the context a reference to Italy is unlikely in Gen. 10.2, it seems as if we have to seek some other location for Tiras, one that was within Asia Minor. Possibly it could be Troy or the area around Troy (the Troad, Greek *Troas*), which is now known to have been called Taruisa in Hittite.[12] However, certainty is not possible.

Following the listing of the immediate sons of Japheth, Gen. 10.3 goes on to enumerate the three sons of Japheth's firstborn, Gomer. First comes Ashkenaz, who it is generally accepted denotes the Scythians.[13] These were an Indo-European people originating from southern Siberia, who came to dwell north of the Black Sea, where they displaced the Cimmerians (with whom they were associated in Assyrian records), before settling around Lake Urmia. Hence their association with Gomer (Cimmerians) is appropriate. The name Ashkenaz is related to the Assyrian term for the Scythians, Ashkuza or Ashguza. Indeed, it has sometimes been proposed that Ashkenaz (*'ašk^enaz*) should be emended to Ashkuz (*'aškûz*) to bring it

11. E.g. M. Grant, *The Etruscans* (London: Weidenfeld & Nicolson, 1980), pp. 71-81.

12. Cf. T. Bryce, *The Kingdom of the Hittites* (Oxford: Oxford University Press, 2005), pp. 359-61.

13. On the Scythians see the marvellous British Museum exhibition book, St J. Simpson and S. Pankova (eds.), *Scythians: Warriors of Ancient Siberia* (London: Thames & Hudson and the British Museum, 2017); also Yamauchi, *Foes from the Northern Frontier*, pp. 63-129.

into line with the Akkadian spelling. However, since the Hebrew spelling is Ashkenaz not only here (and in the dependent 1 Chron. 1.6) but also in Jer. 51.27, the Masoretic spelling should probably be retained. Much later during the Middle Ages Ashkenazim became a term for central and Eastern European Jews, and it is still used today for Jews of such ancestry. Doubtless this usage arose because in the Babylonian Talmud, *b. Yoma* 10a rendered Gomer as Germanya (Germany).

By contrast, the next name, Riphath is obscure. The context (between Ashkenaz and Togarmah) suggests eastern Anatolia. Some (e.g. Lipiński, Hendel) support reading Diphath with 1 Chron. 1.6,[14] though the Samaritan and Septuagint support the Masoretic text in reading Riphath.

The last son of Gomer is Togarmah. This name is also attested in the derivative 1 Chron. 1.6 and in the form Beth-Togarmah in Ezek. 27.14; 38.6. In the latter reference it is listed after Gomer as constituting a part of Gog's army and is described as being in the remotest part of the north. It is widely accepted that Togarmah is to be equated with a city and district called Tegarama or Tagarama in Hittite texts and Til-Garimmu in Assyrian records, which was near the Upper Euphrates north of Carchemish. Both philologically and geographically this fits biblical Togarmah very well. Today it is called Gürün (classical Gauraena). This seems more likely than Lipiński's emendation of *twgrmh* to *twgdmh*, the name of a Cimmerian chief who conquered much of Anatolia in 652–636 BCE, until he was defeated at the Cilician Gates.[15]

Genesis 10.4 next lists the four sons of Japheth's son Yawan (Greece). First comes Elishah. It is now widely agreed that this is the Hebrew form of Alashiya, an old name for Cyprus or part of it, in Akkadian, Hittite and Ugaritic texts. This coheres with the abundance of copper in Alashiya attested by the El-Amarna letters (cf. letters 33-36, 40, esp. 35) and Papyrus Anastasi IV, copper being something Cyprus was famous for (hence the name Cyprus). This identification has finally been proved by petrographic analysis of the clay of both the El-Amarna and Ugaritic texts sent from Alashiya.[16] We know that the ancient name was still used in the first millennium BCE, since a fourth-century BCE Cypriot inscription

14. E. Lipiński, 'Les Japhétites selon Gen 10,1-4 et 1 Chr 1,5-7', *ZAH* 3 (1990), pp. 40-53 (pp. 49-50); R.S. Hendel, *The Text of Genesis 1–11: Textual Studies and Critical Edition* (New York: Oxford University Press, 1998), p. 142.

15. See Lipiński, 'Les Japhétites', p. 50.

16. Y. Goren, S. Buminovitz, I. Finkelstein and N. Na'aman, 'The Location of Alashiya: New Evidence from Petrographic Investigation of Alashiyan Tablets from El-Amarna and Ugarit', *AJA* 107 (1993), pp. 233-55.

from Tamassos refers to Apollo Alasiotas.[17] Elishah is also mentioned in Ezek. 27.7 alongside Kittim in v. 6, another name for part of Cyprus (on which see below). Cyprus had a mixed population, part Phoenician and part non-Phoenician (Eteo-Cypriot and Greek), and Elishah probably refers to the latter part in Ezekiel and Gen. 10.4, since the name Kittim is suggestive of the Phoenicians.[18]

Next comes Tarshish. The Old Testament notes Tarshish as a source of valuable metals, especially silver, but also iron, tin and lead (Ezek. 27.12; Jer. 10.9). There are clear indications that Tarshish was a distant place in the west reached by sea (cf. Ps. 72.10; Isa. 66.19; Jon. 1.12; 4.2), an impression highlighted by the fact that ships that went to distant places like Ophir (probably in southern Arabia) are called 'ships of Tarshish' (cf. 1 Kgs 10.22; 22.49, ET 48; Isa. 2.16; 23.1, 14; 60.9; Ezek. 27.25; Ps. 48.8, ET 7). The dominant modern view has been that Tarshish is Tartessus in southern Spain, the furthest west that the ancient world knew about, and where, according to classical sources, the Phoenicians procured the very same metals that the Old Testament associates with Tarshish.[19] But recently some scholars[20] have preferred to equate Tarshish with Tarsus in southern Anatolia, whose adjacent Taurus mountains were also a source for the metals alluded to above. However, in Akkadian Tarshish is Tarsisi and Tarsus is Tarzi, and all the indications are that Tarsus was insufficiently far west. For example, an inscription of Esarhaddon implies that Tarshish (Tarsisi) was further away from Assyria than Cyprus and Ionia were[21]

---

17. For this inscription, written in the Cypriot syllabary, see P.M. Steele, *A Linguistic History of Ancient Cyprus: The Non-Greek Languages and their Relations with Greek, c. 1600–300* (Cambridge: Cambridge University Press, 2013), p. 204.

18. Cf. J.C. Greenfield, 'Elishah', *IDB*, II, p. 92.

19. For a detailed defence of the traditional view that Tarshish is Tartessus, see J. Day, 'Where was Tarshish?', in I. Provan and M.J. Boda (eds.), *Let us Go up to Zion: Essays in Honour of H.G.M. Williamson on the Occasion of his Sixty-Fifth Birthday* (VTSup, 153; Brill: Leiden, 2012), pp. 359-69; reworked as 'Where was Tarshish (Genesis 10.4)?', in Day, *From Creation to Babel*, pp. 154-65.

20. Note especially A. van der Kooij, *The Oracle of Tyre: The Septuagint of Isaiah XXIII as Version and Vision* (VTSup, 71; Leiden: Brill, 1998), pp. 40-47; A. Lemaire, 'Tarshish-*Tarsisi*: problème de topographie historique biblique et assyrienne', in G. Galil and M. Weinfeld (eds.), *Studies in Historical Geography and Biblical Historiography Presented to Zecharia Kallai* (VTSup, 81; Leiden: Brill, 2000), pp. 44-62.

21. Esarhaddon declares, 'All the kings from amidst the sea – from Cyprus, Ionia, as far as Tarsisi – bowed to my feet and I received heavy tribute from them.' Cf. R. Borger, *Die Inschriften Asarhaddons, Königs von Assyrien* (AfO, 9; Graz: Im Selbstverlage des Herausgabers, 1956), p. 86.

(which was not true of Tarsus); further, Ps. 72.10's parallelism of Tarshish with Sheba and Seba implies it was one of the most distant known places from Israel. Again, Ezek. 27.12-23 broadly lists places from west to east, and Tarshish comes first. Further, if Jonah were really heading for Tarsus when he set out from Joppa (Jon. 1.3), he would actually have been travelling nearer Nineveh, the place he was trying to avoid, rather than away from it. That Gen. 10.4 should list Tarshish as a son of Greece (Yawan, Ionia) is no problem, since between the mid-seventh century and the time of P, Tartessus had come under Greek influence, as archaeology attests[22] (cf. Herodotus, *Histories* 1.63; 4.152). Contrast the earlier Isaiah 23, where Tarshish is still clearly aligned with Tyre.

Next comes Kittim, generally agreed to denote Cyprus or a part of it (cf. Num. 24.24; Isa. 23.1, 12; Jer. 2.10; Ezek. 27.6). The name derives from Kition, a town in south-eastern Cyprus near Larnaca (*Kty* in Phoenician), originally founded by the Phoenicians. However, subsequently Kittim was employed by the Jews as a name for Macedonia (1 Macc. 1.1; 8.5) and later still of the Romans (Dan. 11.30; Qumran). Doubtless these meanings arose by way of interpretation of Num. 24.24, which refers to 'ships of Kittim' coming to attack the Near East. We pointed out above that Cyprus appears to be represented already by the name Elishah (Alashiya) earlier in Gen. 10.4. The two names are mentioned in close conjunction in Ezek. 27.6-7. As noted above, if the two names represent different parts of the population, Kittim more naturally represents the Phoenician part. After all, the name Kittim derives, as previously mentioned, from the town of Kition founded by the Phoenicians.

Finally, Rodanim. Although the Masoretic text reads Dodanim, the Septuagint and Samaritan versions both support Rodanim, as does the parallel text in 1 Chron. 1.7. This is generally accepted to denote the island of Rhodes (off the south-west coast of Asia Minor). There were Greek settlements there, cohering with its being a son of Yawan (Greece), and the Rhodians are already mentioned by Homer in *Iliad* 2.654f. Other suggested meanings of the name are improbable.[23]

In v. 5 we read, 'From these the coastland peoples spread'. These words only make proper sense with reference to the maritime peoples listed in v. 4. Wayne Horowitz,[24] however, interprets them as speaking of all the Japhethites in vv. 2-5, even though this was not historically correct.

22. See Y.B. Tsirkin, 'The Greeks and Tartessos', *Oikumene* 5 (1986), pp. 163-71.

23. For some earlier suggestions, see Skinner, *Genesis*, p. 199.

24. W. Horowitz, 'The Isles of the Nations: Genesis x and Babylonian Geography', in J.A. Emerton (ed.), *Studies in the Pentateuch* (VTSup, 41; Leiden: Brill, 1990), pp. 35-43.

However, in support of the usual view we may note that it is probable that the words 'These are the sons of Japheth' have fallen out, prior to the concluding words of v. 5, 'in their lands, each with their languages, by their families in their nations', referring to the Japhethites as a whole, as with the comparable concluding words regarding the Hamites and Shemites in vv. 20 and 31.[25] In that way, it becomes easier to relate the words 'From these the coastal peoples spread' simply to the appropriate nations in v. 4.

The Sons of Ham (vv. 6-20)

The first son of Ham listed is Kush (v. 6). Although the traditional translation of this name has been Ethiopia, this is not appropriate in the modern sense of that name (i.e. Abyssinia), though it is for the classical sense. Kush denoted the area south of Aswan, whose people were dark skinned (cf. Jer. 13.23). It is the area more accurately described today as Nubia, that is, northern Sudan and the far south of Egypt.

Next comes Egypt. The identity of Egypt is, of course, uncontroversial. The problem lies in its name. Mișrayim at first looks like a dual form, and it has been popular for scholars to suppose that this refers to the union of Upper and Lower Egypt. But the problem with this is that in the earliest references, in Akkadian, the name appears in the singular (Akkadian Mușur[u], Mușur, Mișir, Amarna Mișrî). Furthermore, in Isa. 11.1 the name Mișrayim seems to refer to Lower Egypt alone, while there is no reason to think that the few instances of the clearly singular form Mașôr (Isa. 19.6; 37.25 = 2 Kgs 19.24; Mic. 7.12) refer to anything but the whole country. Mașôr appears to be just a more poetic form of the name.

After Egypt we find mention of Put. This has sometimes been equated with the land of Punt in east Africa, to which Egyptian expeditions sometimes ventured (most famously under Queen Hatshepsut), a land now more often equated with parts of Eritrea, Ethiopia and southern Sudan rather than Somalia, which was often preferred in the past.[26] However, against Put being Punt stands the fact that Punt has an 'n', unlike Put, and ends in 't', whereas Put has a 'ṭ'. Put is now generally equated with Libya, or rather a part of it. This is supported by the Septuagint and Vulgate (cf. Jer. 26.9 = MT 46.9; Ezek. 27.10; 30.5; 38.5), and coheres with Nah. 3.9, where Put is mentioned alongside the Libyans and Cush as an ally

---

25. So most commentators.

26. See R. Herzog, *Punt* (Abhandlungen des deutschen archaeologischen Instituts Kairo, Ägyptologische Reihe, 6; Glückstadt: J.J. Augustin, 1968); K.A. Kitchen, 'Punt and How to Get There', *Or* NS 40 (1971), pp. 184-207.

of Egypt in the seventh century BCE. This does not seem appropriate for distant Punt at that time.

Why is Canaan included under the sons of Ham? It has sometimes been supposed that this is a recollection of the fact that the Egyptians exercised dominion over Canaan for much of the Eighteenth to Twentieth Dynasties in the Late Bronze Age (c. 1550–1150 BCE).[27] However, there is no recollection of this anywhere else in the Old Testament (e.g. in Joshua or Judges), and it is therefore unlikely to be the case here. Alternatively, it has been conjectured that the descendants of Ham were a natural depository for Israel's enemies.[28] But the southern Arabian tribes included under Ham in P are not regarded as enemies elsewhere in the Old Testament, and in J are even included under Shem (Gen. 10.26-30). Nevertheless, the failure to include Canaan under Shem, with whom it naturally belongs ethnically, linguistically and geographically, certainly reflects Israel's sense of alienation from the Canaanites, and it is arguable that the Hamites consist of those peoples from whom the Israelites came to feel remote, either geographically (the southern Arabians) or in terms of kinship (Egypt, [Nimrod's Mesopotamia – a later addition to Gen. 10]), and in the case of Canaan to the point of active hostility. Hence Canaan, originally one of the three sons of Noah in earlier tradition alongside Shem and Japheth (cf. Gen. 9.25), became incorporated under Ham with its African nations, including Egypt (the latter explicitly stated to be in the land of Ham in Pss. 78.51; 105.23, 27; 106.22).

Next come the sons of Kush in Gen. 10.7. The first of the sons of Kush is Seba. The evidence points to its having been in east Africa rather than Arabia. In both Isa. 43.3 and 45.14 it is mentioned after Cush (Nubia), which in turn follows Egypt. Further, according to Isa. 45.14 the people of Seba were 'men of stature', just like the people of Kush mentioned in Isa. 18.2, 7. On the other hand, if the modern inhabitants of southern Arabia are anything to go by, the people there were not notably tall. Biblical Seba surely corresponds to the Saba mentioned by Strabo (*Geography* 16.4.8, 10; cf. Ptolemy, *Geography* 4.7.7f.) on the African side of the Red Sea (south of Suakin in southern Sudan). Its mention alongside Sheba in Ps. 72.10 (parallel to Tarshish) indicates that it was one of the most far flung parts of the world from the Israelite point of view.

27. E.g. D.B. Redford, *Egypt, Canaan, and Israel in Ancient Times* (Princeton, NJ: Princeton University Press, 1992), p. 405; Longman III and McKnight, *Genesis*, pp. 145-46.

28. Cf. J. Vermeylen, 'La «table des nations» (Gn 10): Yaphet figure-t-il l'Empire perse?', *Transeuphratène* 5 (1992), pp. 113-32 (127).

The second son of Kush is Havilah (possibly cf. *ḥôl*, 'sand'), a name which also occurs later in v. 29 as a son of Joktan among the descendants of Shem. Verse 7 is from P, whereas v. 29 is from the earlier J source. Both refer to the same place, which appears to be in southern Arabia, possibly to be equated with Ḥawlan north of Yemen. According to Gen. 2.11-12 it was noted for gold, bdellium and onyx.

The third son of Kush is Sabtah. There is no reason to follow the suggestion of M.C. Astour[29] that Sabtah reflects a misunderstanding of the name of the Twenty-Fifth Dynasty Kushite pharaoh Shabako; Sabtah lacks the 'k' of Shabako and has a 't' which the latter lacks. Sabtah's placing between Havilah and Raamah further suggests a location in Arabia, and most likely this is the southern Arabian city of Sabatah or Sabotah, the capital of Hadramaut (between modern Yemen and Oman). This could therefore be equivalent to J's Hazarmaweth (Hadramaut) in v. 26. In classical sources the name is spelled Sabata, Sabatha or Sabota, and Pliny tells us that it was a centre of the frankincense trade (Pliny, *Natural History* 12.32.63).

Next comes Raamah. Raamah is generally accepted to be in Arabia, as it is the father of Dedan and Sheba, and it is also mentioned alongside Sheba in Ezek. 37.22. It is usually equated with south Arabian *rgmtm* (probably vocalized Ragmatum – often referred to by scholars as Ragmah), which is mentioned in Minaean and Sabaean inscriptions, the earliest reference being in an inscription *c.* 500 BCE. If the *'ayin* in the name Ra'amah reflects an original *ghayin*, this identification is plausible.

Following Raamah we have Sabteca. From the context we should again expect this place most likely to be in Arabia. There are various possibilities, but none is certain. What, however, is unlikely is that the name derives from that of the Twenty-Fifth Dynasty pharaoh Shabatako, a view point forward by M.C. Astour[30] and adopted by several subsequent scholars. That a Kushite pharaoh's name should be misunderstood as a place name seems unlikely. Although we cannot be sure of its precise identity, an Arabian location seems more likely.

The end of Gen. 10.7 lists the two sons of Raamah: Sheba and Dedan. However, in J, unlike P, Sheba was a son of Joktan (see below, v. 28). The evidence supports Sheba's equation with Saba in south-west Arabia (modern Yemen). Compare Jer. 6.20 and Joel 4.8 (ET 3.8), where it is called 'a distant land' and 'far off', and Ps. 72.10, where it symbolizes the furthest known part of the world. Though distant, Israel

---

29. M.C. Astour, 'Sabtah and Sabteca: Ethiopian Pharaoh Names in Genesis 10', *JBL* 84 (1965), pp. 422-25.

30. Astour, *loc. cit.*

was familiar with it because of its important incense trade. However, there appear also to have been Sabaean colonies in north Arabia, since Tiglath-pileser III records conquering the Sabaeans, and all the other places he lists were in northern Arabia,[31] and Saba was over a thousand kilometres to the south. In addition, the fact that Job in the land of Uz (Edom) was attacked by Sabaeans in Job 1.15 similarly suggests invaders from northern rather than southern Arabia.[32] The people of Ethiopia still believe that Sheba is in their country but this is based on a later misunderstanding embedded in their national epic, the Kebra Nagast.[33] However, Josephus already referred to the Queen of Sheba as the Queen of Egypt and Ethiopia (*Ant.* 8.6.5) or Queen of Ethiopia (*Ant.* 8.6.6), and he states that Saba (which he says was later named Meroe) was the capital of Ethiopia (*Ant.* 2.10.2). So this misunderstanding goes back at least to the late first century CE.

Dedan, by contrast, was in north Arabia. Various Old Testament references indicate it was not so far from Edom (Jer. 49.9; Ezek. 25.13), but it was only with the discovery of Arabian inscriptions that its precise location at El-Ula was established,[34] a city in north-west Arabia (the Hejaz area), south-west of Tema. This is much further north than most of the other Arabian place names in Genesis 10.

Nimrod (vv. 8-12)[35]

Within the table of nations vv. 8-12 constitute a distinct section about the figure of Nimrod. It reads like an addition, since it is a short narrative

31. H. Tadmor, *The Inscriptions of Tiglath-pileser III King of Assyria* (Jerusalem: Israel Academy of Sciences and Humanities, 1994), pp. 142-43, Summary inscription 4, line 27.

32. Cf. J.A. Montgomery, *Arabia and the Bible* (Philadelphia, PA: University of Pennsylvania Press, 1934), pp. 59-61, 180; I. Eph'al, *The Ancient Arabs: Nomads on the Borders of the Fertile Crescent, 9th–5th Century B.C.* (Jerusalem: Magnes Press, 1982), pp. 88-89, 227-29.

33. For Kebra Nagast, see the translation by E.A.W. Budge, *The Queen of Sheba and her Only Son Menyelek (I)* (London: Oxford University Press [Humphrey Milford], 2nd edn, 1932). For a critique of the Ethiopian tradition, see J. Day, 'Whatever Happened to the Ark of the Covenant?', in *idem, Temple and Worship in Biblical Israel* (LHBOTS, 422; London: T&T Clark, 2005), pp. 250-70 (252-53).

34. See W.F. Albright, 'Dedan', in *Geschichte und Altes Testament* (FS A. Alt; Beiträge zur historischen Theologie, 16; Tübingen: J.C.B. Mohr [Paul Siebeck], 1955), pp. 1-12 (esp. p. 1).

35. For much more detailed consideration of the Nimrod passage, including bibliography, see the next chapter.

about a king rather than simply a list of names, though some places are included. The name Nimrod occurs in the Old Testament only once elsewhere, in Mic. 5.5 (ET 6), where it stands parallel with Assyria. But Nimrod's kingdom is here said to start in Babylonia and subsequently extends to Assyria.

Who Was Nimrod?

There is no consensus on the origin of Nimrod. Over the years a whole series of Mesopotamian kings have been proposed, which I have documented in full in the following chapter. None of these have much to be said for them. Over the past 60 years some have supposed the king to be the Assyrian ruler Tukulti-Ninurta I (*c.* 1243–1207 BCE). The last part of the name might correspond to Nimrod, but if so, the first part of the name must have dropped off, something elsewhere unattested. Further, Tukulti-Ninurta I was an Assyrian king who conquered Babylonia, whereas Nimrod arose in Babylonia and conquered Assyria. In recent years some scholars have argued that Nimrod is simply the personification of the Mesopotamian kingship ideology rather than any particular individual, but these scholars fail to offer a plausible explanation of the name Nimrod.

The most plausible view is that the name Nimrod derives from that of Ninurta, the Mesopotamian god of hunting and war. He was a source of inspiration for Neo-Assyrian kings who liked to boast of their prowess in hunting. This could therefore explain why Nimrod is a mighty hunter. Not only is the name Nimrod plausibly derived from Ninurta, but there is actually one place in the Old Testament where the god Ninurta appears to be called Nimrod. The Masoretic text of 2 Kgs 19.37 refers to Sennacherib having been assassinated in the temple of the god Nisroch, a name totally unknown from cuneiform records. However, one of the chief gods was Ninurta. Graphically, it is very plausible that נסרך (Nisroch) could be a corruption from נמרד (Nimrod).

Nimrod is called 'a mighty hunter before the Lord', a description that sounds rather complimentary. This makes unlikely the rabbinic view that the name Nimrod means 'let us/we shall rebel', any more than the later Jewish understanding which took the text to mean that he was 'a mighty hunter *against* the Lord'.

Kush as the Father of Nimrod

One problem about Nimrod is why he is depicted as a son of Kush (Nubia), when his kingdom was in Mesopotamia. One popular view is that Kush, the father of Nimrod, denotes the Kassites, a Mesopotamian people. Though not impossible, it has to be accepted that the redactor equated

Nimrod's father with the Kush of v. 6, which clearly denotes Nubia. But even if this was a misunderstanding by the redactor, it is still not clear why specifically the Kassites should be Nimrod's father (a people nowhere else mentioned in the Old Testament, incidentally). Moreover, the same J source a few chapters earlier in the Garden of Eden narrative clearly implies that the great Mesopotamian rivers, the Tigris and Euphrates, shared a common source with the Gihon river (Nile), which flows round the whole land of Kush. Furthermore, the Greek writer Pausanias (*Description of Greece* 2.5.3) reported a view that the Euphrates and the Nile were equivalent.

Nimrod's Cities (vv. 10-11)

Verses 10-11 list the Mesopotamian cities which Nimrod founded. Several of these are straightforward (Babylon, Erech [Uruk], Accad, Nineveh and Calah), even if the precise location of Accad is uncertain. For various reasons it is clear that Nimrod, not Ashur (Assyria), is the subject of v. 11, and Calneh should be revocalized *kullānāh*, 'all of them' (with support from the Samaritan Aramaic Targum), since the only place called Calneh that we know of was in Syria (Amos 6.2), far from southern Mesopotamia. Rehoboth-ir and Resen are still uncertain.

It appears that Calah, which Nimrod built, is called 'the great city'. This term most naturally applies to the last city mentioned before it, Calah. This is significant, since Calah (later called Nimrud, from Nimrod) was the capital of Assyria between *c.* 879 and 706 BCE. This appears to give an indication of the date of the J source (*c.* 790 plus or minus 85–90 years). If the source dates from later than this, Nineveh should have been called 'the great city', as in the book of Jonah (Jon. 3.2).

Further Hamites

Genesis 10.13-14 state that Egypt was the father of a number of peoples. The first one, Ludim, most likely means 'Lydians'. This is odd, because the Lydians were a people in western Anatolia, quite unrelated to the Egyptians ethnically or geographically. However, we do find Lydians mentioned as mercenaries or supporters of Egypt in both Jer. 46.9 and Ezek. 30.5, so this is the most likely explanation of their inclusion here. At first sight it might seem more likely that we should emend Ludim to Lubim, 'Lybians' here. But not only is that without textual support in any of the Versions, but also Ludim is the harder reading, and probably therefore to be preferred. One could more easily imagine Ludim being corrupted to Lubim than the reverse.

Next come Anamim. This probably reflects the name of the *A-na-mi*, a people of Cyrene referred to in an Akkadian text from the time of Sargon II.[36] Consistent with that, Lehabim appears to be a variant spelling of Lubim, 'Libyans'. Since the next but one name, Pathrusim, certainly denotes the people of Upper Egypt (Pathros), the Naphtuhim probably refers to the people of Lower Egypt. Just as Pathros (Egyptian *p'-t'-rsy*) means 'the South land' and was the regular term for Upper Egypt, so in Egyptian *p'-t'-ḥmw* was the regular term for 'Lower Egypt' and meant 'the North land'. Most probably, therefore, with A. Erman,[37] we should understand Hebrew Naphtuhim as a corruption of Patmuhim, 'the people of Lower Egypt', a Hebrew form of the word for the inhabitants of that region. Although the need to emend Naphtuhim to Patmuhim here means there is some element of doubt, this is the most plausible view, both words have *pth*, amongst their root letters, and the alternative proposals are definitely less likely. Thus, W. Spiegelberg[38] also thought that Naphtuhim meant 'the people of Lower Egypt', but on the erroneous assumption that the (for him) underlying Delta place name Natho meant 'the Delta marshes' (Egyptian *N'-idhw*), when actually it means 'those belonging to the Mansion [of Rameses III]' (Egyptian *N'y-t'ḥwt*).[39] Finally, E. Lipiński and D.B. Redford[40] interpret Naphtuhim as meaning 'the people of No-Ptaḥ [City of Ptaḥ]', i.e. Memphis, but this is an imaginary name that nowhere existed in Egyptian, and in any case, 'Memphites' seems geographically too restrictive a location alongside 'the people of Upper Egypt' here in Genesis. Further, by analogy with the name No-Amon for Thebes (Nah. 3.8; cf. Jer. 46.25), we should expect an 'o' vowel and an aleph in the Hebrew after the 'n', if this view were correct.

It is very probable that the words 'whence came the Philistines' (v. 14) were originally a marginal gloss that was intended to go with Caphtorim (since elsewhere the Philistines are regularly associated with Caphtor; cf. Amos 9.7; Jer. 47.4), but which when it got into the text became

36. Cf. W.F. Albright, 'A Colony of Cretan Mercenaries on the Coast of the Negeb', *JPOS* 1 (1920–21), pp. 187-94 (191-92).

37. A. Erman, 'נפתחים', *ZAW* 10 (1890), pp. 118-19.

38. W. Spiegelberg, 'נפתחים (Gen. X, 13)', *OLZ* 9 (1906), cols. 276-79.

39. See Redford, *Egypt, Canaan, and Israel in Ancient Times*, p. 406, with n. 58, citing A.H. Gardiner, *Ancient Egyptian Onomastica*, II (3 vols.; Oxford: Oxford University Press, 1947), pp. 146ff., and W. Helck, *Die altäyptische Gaue* (Wiesbaden: L. Reichert, 1974), p. 178.

40. E. Lipiński, 'Les Chamites selon Gen 10,6-20 et 1 Chr 1,8-16', *ZAH* 5 (1992), pp. 135-62 (151-52); Redford, *Egypt, Canaan, and Israel in Ancient Times*, pp. 406-407.

mistakenly attached to 'Casluhim'. The Casluhim are a complete mystery, though various suggestions have been made.[41] The Caphtorim refer to the people of Caphtor, that is, Crete.

Verses 15-20 list the sons of Canaan and give details of the boundaries of Canaan. Canaan is said to be the father of Sidon, his first born, and Heth, followed by the Jebusites, the Amorites, the Girgashites, the Hivites, the Arkites, the Sinites, the Arvadites, the Zemarites and the Hamathites. It will be noted that apart from Sidon and Heth, the names of all the other sons of Canaan are listed in the plural, suggesting peoples rather than eponymous individual ancestors. Almost certainly these plural names were a later addition, expanding the list of Canaanite names. Further, it will be observed that the names fall into two groups. Some of the names denote peoples whom the Israelites subdued as part of their settlement in the Promised Land (Heth = Hittites, Jebusites, Amorites, Girgashites, Hivites), whilst others denote inhabitants of Phoenicia, peoples who maintained their independence from the Israelites (Sidon, the Arkites, Sinites, Arvadites, Zemarites and Hamathites). The terms Heth (Hittites) and Amorites could, however, also be used to denote certain peoples further north who remained independent of Israel.

The Phoenician peoples are broadly but not perfectly arranged in order from south to north. The exact location of the Sinites is uncertain, though various places in the north of Lebanon have been proposed. As for the others, Sidon, the Arkites (from Arqa in north Lebanon, Akkadian Irqata), Arvadites (from the island of Arvad, now off the coast of Syria), and the Hamathites (from Hamath in Syria, the only inland site) are all in correct geographical order going from south to north. The Zemarites, however, from the city called Ṣumur in the Amarna letters, just inside modern Syria, should come before, rather than after, the Arvadites in terms of geographical position.

The geographical extent of the Canaanites in vv. 19-20 is somewhat obscure. Most likely, the unknown *lāša'*, which ought to denote the north-east border of Canaan, should be read as Laish, the old name of Dan (Judg. 18.29).

---

41. G. Rendsburg, 'Gen 10:13-14: An Authentic Hebrew Tradition Concerning the Origin of the Philistines', *JNSL* 13 (1987), pp. 89-96, has argued that Casluhim refers to Lower Egypt, and appeals to Sir Arthur Evans' claim that the Cretans had an Egyptian background to justify his view that the Philistines came from Casluhim, as in the MT of this verse. Alternatively, he suggests there might be an allusion to the Philistines coming from Lower Egypt following their defeat by Rameses III. However, the notion that Casluhim refers to Lower Egypt has no linguistic support.

The Sons of Shem (vv. 21-31)

The third section of the table of the nations is devoted to the descendants of Shem. Incidentally, it is from the name Shem that we get the word Semitic, which is first attested being used as an ethnic term in 1771 and as a term applied to languages in 1781.[42] The sons of Shem are introduced twice (vv. 21, 22), the first verse being from J and the second from P. But why are Shem's descendants listed last, when he was apparently the oldest of the three brothers (cf. v. 21, 'the elder brother of Japheth') and the fact that they are characteristically listed as Shem, Ham and Japheth? The answer becomes apparent immediately after his mention in v. 21, for we are told there that Shem was 'the father of all the children of Eber'. Neither of the other two brothers, Japheth and Ham, has anyone highlighted in their introductions like this, and we can only conclude that there was something special about the sons of Eber. Eber must be the ancestor of the Hebrews, Eber (*'ēber*) being a back formation from *'ibrî*, 'Hebrew'. Thus, the writer clearly wished to put the ancestor of the Hebrews at the climax. However, Israel is not explicitly mentioned in Genesis 10, any more than the Moabites, Ammonites, Edomites and many northern Arabs are, since these are regarded as descendants of Abraham who emerged later on in Genesis (cf. 34.7; 36.31; 49.7 for Israel; 19.30-38 for the Moabites and Ammonites; 25.30 and 36.1-43 for the Edomites; and 25.1-4, 12-16 for certain mostly northern Arabs). However, 11.14-16 does clearly include Eber in the Priestly genealogy from Shem to Abraham.

Over the years there has been much debate about whether there is any connection between the Hebrews and the Ḫabiru/Ḫapiru attested in Akkadian (Sumerian SA.GAZ), referred to as the 'Apiru in Egyptian and as *'prm* in Ugaritic. It is now generally agreed that the 'Apiru or

---

42. See the detailed study of M.F.J. Baasten, 'A Note on the History of "Semitic"', in M.F.J. Baasten and W.T. van Peursen (eds.), *Hamlet on a Hill: Semitic and Greek Studies Presented to Professor T. Muraoka on the Occasion of his Sixty-Fifth Birthday* (Leuven: Peeters and Leuven Oriental Department, 2003), pp. 57-72. From meticulous research he demonstrates that the assertion sometimes made that the term 'Semitic languages' goes back to the famous polymath G.W. Leibniz in 1710 is mistaken. J.G. Eichhorn's own claim to have invented the term is also erroneous, even though his influence did contribute to its widespread use, which was almost universal by about 1800. Rather, it was A.L. Schlözer who first employed the expression 'Semitic languages' in 1781, though he had spoken of 'the language of the Semites' already in 1771, the same year as J.C. Gatterer similarly used the term 'Semitic' in an ethnic sense.

Ḥabiru/Ḫapiru denote a despised social class (mostly with Semitic but some with Hurrian names) and is not an ethnic term, unlike Hebrews.[43] In the Amarna letters the word essentially seems to denote outlaws or rebels.[44] So the two terms cannot simply be equated. Furthermore, it has to be noted that the vocalization of 'Apiru and Ḥabiru/Ḫapiru is quite different from *'ibrî*. Moreover, the evidence of both Ugaritic and Egyptian, which clearly distinguish 'p' and 'b', unlike Akkadian, strongly suggests that the first consonant is 'p', not 'b', hence Ḫapiru, thus further distancing it from the word for Hebrew.

Eber is said to be the father of Peleg and Joktan. The location of Peleg is uncertain but is possibly Phaliga, a town at the junction of the Khabur and Euphrates rivers. Joktan is interestingly the ancestor of various tribes in Arabia. Verses 26-29 list as many as thirteen sons of Joktan.[45] Islamic tradition identifies Joktan (Hebrew *yoqṭān*) with Qaḥṭān, the eponymous ancestor of the southern Arabian tribes, though the names are philologically incompatible; a tribe called Qaḥṭān is already attested in pre-Islamic times.[46] In Gen. 25.3 the name Joktan also appears in the biform Jokshan (*yoqšān*) as the father of the Arabian tribes Dedan and Sheba. Although some of the Joktanite tribes are difficult to identify with certainty (Almodad, Jerah, Hadoram, Uzal, Diklah, Obal, Abimael and Jobab), those that can be identified are certainly in southern Arabia: Sheleph, Hazarmaweth, Sheba and Havilah, and apparently Ophir. We have already dealt with Sheba and Havilah above, as they were also listed from P in Gen. 10.7. As for Sheleph, there is a Yemenite tribe called Salif or Sulaf, as well as a district in Yemen called Silf. Also, as noted earlier, Hazarmaweth is Hadramaut in southern Arabia, an area between Yemen and Oman.

43. See J. Bottéro, *Le problème des Ḥabiru* (Paris: Société asiatique, 1954); M. Greenberg, *The Ḥab/piru* (New Haven, CN: American Oriental Society, 1955); R. Borger, 'Das Problem der 'apīru („Habiru")', *ZDPV* 74 (1958), pp. 121-32; O. Loretz, *Ḥabiru-Hebräer: eine sozio-linguistische Studie über die Herkunft des Gentiliziums 'ibrî vom Appelativum ḫabiru* (BZAW, 160; Berlin: W. de Gruyter, 1984); A.F. Rainey, Review of Loretz, *Ḥabiru-Hebräer, JAOS* 101 (1987), pp. 541-43; *idem*, *The El-Amarna Correspondence*, I (2 vols.; Leiden: Brill, 2015), pp. 31-35.

44. See E.F. Campbell, 'The Amarna Letters and the Amarna Period', in E.F. Campbell and D.N. Freedman (eds.), *The Biblical Archaeologist Reader*, III (Anchor Books; Garden City, NY: Doubleday, 1970), pp. 54-75 (66-68).

45. Possibly originally twelve. The LXX, in fact, omits Obal from the list in v. 28.

46. See A. Fischer [A.K. Irvine], 'Ḳaḥṭān, *The Encyclopaedia of Islam*, IV (Leiden: Brill, 2nd edn, 1978), pp. 447-49.

Ophir was noted especially for its gold (1 Kgs 9.28; 10.11; 22.48; 1 Chron 29.4; 2 Chron. 8.18; 9.10; 29.4; Isa. 13.12; Ps. 45.10, ET 9; Job 22.24; 28.16). Occasionally Ophir was regarded in the past as an imaginary land like Eldorado, but this was disproved by the discovery of an eighth-century BCE ostracon from Tel Qasile referring to 'gold of Ophir to Beth-Horon, 30 shekels'.[47] Again, Ophir was sometimes located in wildly far-off places like India[48] and southern Africa,[49] but it was almost certainly in southern Arabia, since it is listed between Sheba and Havilah in Gen. 10.29, and all the other known Joktanites are in southern Arabia. In keeping with this, Hiram king of Tyre's bringing precious objects from Ophir in 1 Kgs 10.11-12 actually interrupts the narrative of the Queen of Sheba's visit to Solomon in 1 Kgs 10.1-13. The main alternative view held by some modern scholars is that Ophir was in east Africa, perhaps in or near Punt,[50] because of the similarity between the objects brought from there by the Egyptian Queen Hatshepsut to those brought back to Solomon in 1 Kgs 10.22. The ivory there mentioned is particularly suggestive of Africa. However, 1 Kgs 10.22 does not actually mention the objects as coming from Ophir, but even if they did, Ophir might have acted as an *entrepôt* for products from the other side of the Red Sea. The only objects explicitly stated as coming from Ophir in 1 Kings are gold (1 Kgs 9.28; 10.11), almug wood and precious stones (1 Kgs 10.11).

The fact that not only the Hebrews but also the Arabs are descendants of Eber in J bespeaks a remarkable sense of ethnic kinship between the Hebrews and the Arabs here. Contrast P, where certain Arabian entities, again including Sheba and Havilah (Gen. 10.7), are ascribed to the sons of Ham, suggesting a more distant sense of relationship at P's later date.

47. See B. Maisler (Mazar), 'Two Hebrew Ostraca from Tell Qasîle', *JNES* 10 (1951), pp. 265-67.

48. First proposed by Josephus, *Ant.* 1.6.4, alongside other Joktanite tribes, as well as *Ant.* 8.6.4 (cf. 7.7.1). Compare even earlier, the LXX spelling of Ophir as Sophera and Souphir in 1 Kgs 9.28 and 10.11 (= 2 Chron. 8.18; 9.10) respectively, as well as Souphir in Isa. 13.12 and 1 Chron. 29.4, which encouraged its equation with Suppara in India, north of Bombay. Also Jerome's Vulgate renders Ophir as India in Job 28.16.

49. This view is found, for example, in John Milton's *Paradise Lost* 11.400, which locates it at Sofala in Mozambique. This reflects the spelling of Ophir with S in some LXX references (see the preceding footnote).

50. Cf. G. Van Beek, 'Ophir', *IDB*, III, pp. 605-6; W.F. Albright, *Archaeology and the Religion of Israel* (Garden City, NY: Doubleday, 5th edn, 1969), p. 130; G. Ryckmans, 'Ophir', in *Supplément au dictionnaire de la Bible*, VI (1959), cols. 744-51.

Another remarkable thing about this list is the impressive knowledge which J displays of the south Arabian tribes. This is surely attributable to the fact that Israel had extensive trading contacts with southern Arabia, including incense,[51] spices and gold. The relative predominance of southern Arabian tribes in Genesis 10 is doubtless accounted for by the fact that the more northerly Arabian tribes are listed later on in Genesis as sons of Keturah and Ishmael in Gen. 25.1-4, 12-16.

Coming back to Shem, we read in v. 22 that his sons included Eber, Ashur, Arpachshad, Lud and Aram. First Elam. The mention of Elam is interesting for several reasons. First, it is the most eastern nation mentioned in the whole of Genesis 10, indicating the extent of the writer's knowledge in that direction. Secondly, it is noteworthy that it is Elam, not India, which is the furthest eastern place mentioned, although India was known to the second-century BCE author of the book of Esther (1.1). This suggests that Genesis 10 is not that late. Thirdly, it is interesting that the name employed is Elam, not Persia. Elam is in the south-west of modern Iran, and probably if this list had dated from after 539 BCE, and certainly after 500 BCE, when the Persian empire was in full swing, we would expect Persia to be mentioned (cf. already Ezek. 27.10). J.C. Gertz thinks Persia is included under Media (Gen. 10.2),[52] but this is unlikely, as the Persians conquered Media. Fourthly, it is somewhat surprising that Elam is the first of the sons of Shem listed, although it is not actually a Semitic nation. Its inclusion here must be for geographical reasons: it is to the east of the other nations listed in v. 22.

Next among the sons of Shem is Ashur, that is 'Assyria'. Throughout the Old Testament Ashur always denotes the country, not the city of Ashur,[53] and is always found in the singular. The plural Ashurim is only used of an Arab tribe (Gen. 25.3). We also need to note that Assyria had already been mentioned before in the section about Nimrod (v. 11), though that comes from J, not P, and the Nimrod section is probably a later addition, originally having been located subsequent to the tower of Babel story.

---

51. On the south Arabian incense trade see G. Van Beek, 'Frankincense and Myrrh in Ancient South Arabia', *JAOS* 78 (1958), pp. 141-52; N. Groom, *Frankincense and Myrrh: A Study of the Arabian Incense Trade* (London: Longman, 1981).

52. Gertz, *Das erste Buch Mose*, I, p. 305.

53. It is sometimes supposed that Ashur in Gen. 2.14 is the city, rather than the country of Assyria, since otherwise the description of its location is inaccurate. However, the other comparable places mentioned here (Kush, Havilah) certainly denote countries, which supports the notion that it is the country of Assyria that is in mind here, as with all the other many instances of Ashur in the Old Testament.

In contrast, the third name, Arpachshad, has been subject to some controversy. This is mentioned by both P (v. 22) and J (v. 24), as well as in the P post-diluvian genealogy in Gen. 11.12-13.[54] No country is known by this precise name. It has sometimes been supposed that Arpachshad is Arrapḫa in northern Mesopotamia,[55] but Akkadian *ḫ* is not equivalent to Hebrew *kaph*, and the ending in *shad* is unaccounted for by this understanding. There is no reason to think that Arpachshad is a designation for Israel, as von Rad curiously proposed.[56] Most likely Arpachshad refers to Chaldaea (i.e. Babylonia), as *Jubilees* (*Jub.* 9.4) and Josephus (*Ant.* 1.6.4) already perceived. Its position after Assyria is in keeping with this, and if this is not it then we curiously have no reference to the Chaldaeans in this part of the table (though note Babylon in J with regard to Nimrod, part of a later insertion in Gen. 10.10). *Kšd* at the end of Arpachshad is suggestive of the name *Kaśdîm*, 'Chaldaeans', which would originally have been spelled *Kašdu* with *shin* in Akkadian.[57] There is also a Kesed (*keśed*) in Gen. 22.22, seemingly the ancestor of the Chaldaeans. It is possible that Arpachshad is a deliberately distorted form of the name for Chaldaea because of the country's negative image.[58] One may compare the so-called

54. Arphaxad (the LXX spelling of Arpachshad) also appears in the book of Judith as the name of an alleged king of Media (Jdt. 1.1), supposedly defeated by Nebuchadnezzar (Jdt. 1.13-16), inaccurately described as king of the Assyrians in Nineveh (Jdt. 1.1; cf. 1.7, 11, 16). This Median king is fictitious. The writer must have derived the name from Gen. 10.22, 24. It coheres with this that Jdt. 1–2 also mention Assyria (Jdt. 1.1, 11, etc.), Elam (Jdt. 1.6) and Lud (Jdt. 2.23), referred to alongside Arpachshad in Gen. 10.22, as well as Japheth (Jdt. 2.25) and Put (Jdt. 2.23) mentioned in Gen. 10.1, 2, 5, and 6 respectively. For more on Arphaxad, see A.D. Roitman, 'The Mystery of Arphaxad (Jdt. 1): A New Proposal', *Henoch* 19 (1995), pp. 301-10.

55. This is equivalent to Arrhapachitis in northern Assyria, referred to by Ptolemy, *Geography* 6.1.2; cf. 6.1.6, which mentions a city called Arrhapa.

56. Von Rad, *Das erste Buch Mose*, pp. 120-21, ET *Genesis*, p. 141. Von Rad sounds quite confident here, but only a couple of pages earlier (*Das erste Buch Mose*, p. 119, ET *Genesis*, p. 139) he had suggested that Arpachshad might possibly be Arrapḫa or Chaldaea!

57. The Akkadian spelling *Kaldu* (reflected in the Greek *Chaldaioi* and our 'Chaldaeans') came later, following the tendency for a sibilant letter before a dental to become *l*.

58. Seebass, *Genesis. I. Urgeschichte*, p. 263, and Gertz, *Das erste Buch Mose*, I, p. 323, are sympathetic to such a view. Earlier, G. Hölscher, *Drei Erdkarten. Ein Beitrag zur Erdkenntnis des hebräischen Altertums* (Sitzungsberichte der Heidelberger Akademie der Wissenschaften, Phil.-hist. Klasse, 1944/48; Heidelberg: Carl Winter, 1949), p. 47, had ingeniously proposed that *'rpkšd* is a deliberate distortion of *'rṣ kśd*, 'land of Chaldaea', *ṣ* being replaced by the preceding letter in the Hebrew

atbash spellings of Chaldaea as Leb qamay (*lēb qāmāy*) in Jer. 51.1 and of Babylon as Sheshak (*šēšak*) in Jer. 25.26 and 51.41.

Aram at the end of the list is uncontroversial, denoting Syria. I see no reason to follow J. Simons[59] in thinking that the term is here restricted to Aram-Naharaim.

But the inclusion of Lud here is a mystery, since if it denotes Lydia, as seems likely, it alludes neither to a Semitic nation nor to a country which is geographically appropriate here. Lydia was in western Asia Minor, so more appropriately listed under Japheth, but is here listed by P under Shem. In contrast, J lists Ludim under Ham as a son of Egypt (v. 13), but we have earlier suggested a likely reason for this.

The first of the sons of Aram is called Uz (Gen. 10.23). This name is best known as the land from which Job came (Job 1.1). Scholars have debated whether Uz was in Edom/north Arabia or in Syria. Most of the evidence supports Edom.[60] Thus, in Gen. 36.28 Uz is a descendant of Esau (Edom) and in Lam. 4.21 Edom is said to dwell in the land of Uz. Moreover, Job's 'comforter' Eliphaz the Temanite (Job 2.11, etc.) clearly comes from Teman (a region of Edom) and Bildad the Shuhite (Job 2.11, etc.) surely came from Shuach, mentioned in Gen. 25.2 alongside Midian and other north Arabian locations, not so far from Edom. Further, Elihu the Buzite (Job 32.2, 6) must come from Buz (Jer. 25.23; mentioned alongside Uz in Gen. 22.21), equivalent to Bâzu (in north Arabia), which is referred to in Esarhaddon's inscriptions.[61] The fact that Uz is a son of Aram does not tell against all this evidence, since we know that the Nabataeans spoke a dialect of Aramaic, even though they lived in southern Edom and northern Arabia. This general location is also supported by the addition in the Septuagint at the end of Job 42, which states that Job lived 'in the land of Ausis, on the borders of Idumaea and Arabia'.

The other three sons of Aram are unfortunately more obscure. Hul is uncertain; Lipiński[62] suggests it might allude to the Huleh region of Syria,

---

alphabet, *p*, just as in the book of Daniel the name Abed-Nego (Dan. 1.7, etc.) is a distortion of Abed-Nebo, 'Servant of Nebo', *g* being the letter after *b* in the Hebrew alphabet. Nebo (Nabu) was a prominent Babylonian god.

59. J. Simons, 'The "Table of Nations" (Gen. X): Its General Structure and Meaning', in P. de Boer (ed.), OTS 10 (Leiden: E.J. Brill, 1954), pp, 155-84 (174)

60. For a detailed defence of Edom, see J. Day, 'How Could Job Be an Edomite?', in W.A.M. Beuken, *The Book of Job* (Leuven: Leuven University Press and Peeters, 1994), pp. 392-99.

61. See Eph'al, *The Ancient Arabs*, pp. 130-37.

62. E. Lipiński, 'Les Sémites selon Gen 10,21-30 et 1 Chr 1,17-23', *ZAH* 6 (1992), pp. 193-215 (201).

south-east of Hama. Gether is also uncertain; Lipiński[63] conjectures that it might be a recent spelling of Geshur, known as a territory in Aram in 2 Sam. 15.18: Old Aramaic *shin* became a *taw* in the seventh/sixth century BCE and later, which fits the traditional date of P. However, it is a bit odd that the Bible should preserve both spellings, seeing that the Deuteronomistic history and P are probably not so distant in date. Finally, Mash is also uncertain. The suggestion of the Mashu mountains of the Gilgamesh epic (9.37-39) is too far east, as they were the mountains of the sunrise. Mount Masius (Strabo, *Geography* 11.14.21), north of Nisibis (modern Tur Abdin), separating Armenia from Mesopotamia, would be geographically more appropriate. But although certainty is not possible, the most plausible suggestion is perhaps to read Massa (Hebrew *maśśā'*), as supported by the Samaritan Pentateuch, which reads Masha, the same as the name of the son of Ishmael in Gen. 25.14. Massa was in northern Arabia, and Massaite wisdom appears to be preserved in Proverbs 30 and 31.1-9 (cf. Prov. 30.1; 31.1).

63. Lipiński, 'Les Sémites', pp. 201-202.

Chapter 10

IN SEARCH OF NIMROD:
PROBLEMS IN THE INTERPRETATION
OF GENESIS 10.8-12

Introduction

In the midst of the of the table of the nations in Genesis 10 we find a
somewhat intrusive narrative section about a king and mighty man called
Nimrod (Gen. 10.8-12). This passage may be rendered as follows:

> Kush became the father of Nimrod; he was the first on earth to become
> a mighty warrior. He was a mighty hunter before the Lord; therefore it is
> said, 'Like Nimrod a mighty hunter before the Lord'. The beginning of his
> kingdom was Babylon, Erech and Akkad, all of them[1] in the land of Shinar.
> From that land he went into Assyria, and built Nineveh, Rehoboth-ir, Calah,
> and Resen between Nineveh and Calah, which is the great city.

This short passage has given rise to a large number of problems of interpretation concerning which there is no consensus, so it is these questions
which I shall seek to tackle in this chapter.

Over the years many different suggestions have been made regarding
the identity of the figure who lies behind Nimrod in Gen. 10.8-12. These
include the following.

Views Now Totally Abandoned

Nazimaruttash

Over a century ago it was proposed by scholars such as P. Haupt, A.H.
Sayce and T.K. Cheyne[2] that behind Nimrod lay the Kassite king of

---

1. For this widely accepted emendation, see the discussion below.
2. P. Haupt, 'The Language of Nimrod, the Kashite', *Andover Review* 2 (1884),
pp. 88-98 (94); A.H. Sayce, *Patriarchal Palestine* (London: SPCK, 1895), p. 269;

Babylon, Nazimaruttash (*c.* 1307–1282 BCE), the former name being held to be an abbreviation of the latter. The fact that Nazimaruttash was a Kassite was thought to explain Nimrod's being the son of Kush. However, this ruler was actually defeated by the Assyrian king Adadnirari I, which rather conflicts with the picture of an all-conquering king Nimrod who became a symbol of Assyria (Mic. 5.5, ET 6). Also he was not associated with hunting. (The first Mesopotamian ruler to boast of his prowess in hunting was the Assyrian king Tiglath-pileser I, *c.* 1115–1097 BCE.) It would also be surprising if the Hebrews were aware of this little-known king centuries later. This view no longer has any support.

Lugalbanda

A century ago it was also occasionally suggested that Nimrod derives from a Sumerian post-diluvian king of Uruk (Erech) named Lugalbanda.[3] E.G.H. Kraeling claimed that the name Lugalbanda could also be read LUGAL-MARAD-DA, and that EN-MARAD-DA, 'lord of Marad', could be a synonym of this, which could have given rise to the name Nimrod. However, this king is not associated with hunting, unlike Nimrod, and since he was a king of Uruk in Babylonia, it is unlikely that he would have become a symbol of Assyria in Mic. 5.5 (ET 6). This view no longer has any following.

Amenhotep III

Another view without any following nowadays is the idea that Nimrod is a reflection of the Egyptian Eighteenth Dynasty pharaoh Amenhotep III (*c.* 1390–1353 BCE). This was proposed by the distinguished German Egyptologist Kurt Sethe,[4] who noted that his prenomen, Neb-ma(at)-re, appears as Nimmuria or Mimmuria in the el-Amarna letters, which he felt lay behind the name Nimrod. Moreover, this king was noted for his hunting prowess and he boasted that his empire extended from Nubia to the Euphrates (the former allegedly explaining his being a son of Kush).

T.K. Cheyne, 'Nimrod', in *Encyclopædia Biblica* (London: A. & C. Black, one-volume edn, 1914), cols. 3417-19 (3418). Sayce thereby reversed his earlier view that Nimrod was Marduk (see below, n. 6).

3. See, e.g., E.G.H. Kraeling, 'The Origin and Real Name of Nimrod', *AJSL* 38 (1922), pp. 214-20.

4. K. Sethe, 'Heroes and Hero-Gods (Egyptian)', in J. Hastings, J.A. Selbie and L.H. Gray (eds.), *Encyclopædia of Religion and Ethics*, VI (13 vols.; Edinburgh: T. & T. Clark, 1913), pp. 647-52 (650a); von Rad, *Das erste Buch Mose*, p. 122, ET *Genesis*, p. 146, found this view attractive.

However, the problem with this view is that Nimrod's activity was firmly centred on Mesopotamia, whereas Amenhotep III was an Egyptian king, who in spite of his empire, did not actually rule over Babylonia or Assyria. The 'd' at the end of Nimrod is also not easy to explain on this view.

Nmrt

The great German ancient historian Eduard Meyer[5] believed that behind Nimrod lay the figure of a Libyan hunter called Nmrt. He noted that Nmrt appears frequently as a personal name among princes and army commanders of the Twenty-second Egyptian Dynasty (early first millennium BCE), a dynasty that was of Libyan origin, and that this name is un-Egyptian. Seeing this as the same name as Nimrod, Meyer postulated that a Libyan hunter called Nmrt must lie behind the biblical character. He conceded that this figure did not originally belong within the Mesopotamian context of Genesis 10, but it is precisely this that highlights the weakness of his viewpoint. How did a Libyan prince or army commander come to be seen as a Mesopotamian king in Genesis 10?

Views Now Only Rarely Held

Marduk

The view that Nimrod reflected the Babylonian god Marduk was first put forward by A.H. Sayce and J. Grivel.[6] Later it was reargued by E. Lipiński, who suggested that the name Nimrod was a deliberate corruption (a *tiqqun sopherim*) of the name of the god Marduk, with the addition of an 'n' at the beginning and the elimination of the 'k' at the end.[7] This, however, seems fanciful. The Old Testament elsewhere was content to write the name of the god Marduk (Merodach) in Jer. 50.2, as well as in the proper names Merodach-baladan (2 Kgs 20.12// Isa. 39.1) and Evil-Merodach (2 Kgs 25.27//Jer. 52.31). In addition, in

5. E. Meyer, 'Miszellen. 2. Nimrod', *ZAW* 8 (1888), pp. 47-49; cf. *idem, Die Israeliten und ihre Nachbarstämme* (Halle: Niemeyer, 1906), pp. 448-49. This view was followed by A. Jirku, 'Nimrod', *OLZ* 20 (1917), cols. 169-72.

6. A.H. Sayce, 'On Nimrod and the Assyrian Inscriptions', *TSBA* 2 (1873), pp. 243-49; J. Grivel, 'Nemrod et les écritures cunéiformes', *TSBA* 3 (1874), pp. 136-44. Both Sayce and Grivel wrongly assumed that 'the land of Nimrod' in Mic. 5.5 (ET 6) referred to Babylonia, whereas the poetic parallelism with 'the land of Assyria' in the previous line and the reference to the Assyrians in the following line make clear that Nimrod is rather a symbol for Assyria.

7. E. Lipiński, 'Nimrod et Aššur', *RB* 73 (1966), pp. 77-93.

Mic. 5.5 (ET 6) Nimrod is employed specifically as a symbol of Assyria, which is out of keeping with the fact that Marduk was the supreme god of Assyria's rival power, Babylon.

Hammurapi

So far as I am aware the view that Nimrod was a reflection of the great Babylonian king Hammurapi (*c.* 1792–1750 BCE) has been proposed by only one scholar, J.H. Walton.[8] He recently suggested that Nimrod is a Hebraized version of EN.MARDU, '[chief] man of the Amorites', which he speculates might have been an epithet of Hammurapi. However, this is entirely conjectural, since we have no evidence that Hammurapi was ever called by this epithet (though the epithet LUGAL.MARDU, 'King of the Amorites', is occasionally attested). Moreover, Hammurapi was not particularly associated with hunting. This view appears to have gained no further support.

Views with a Certain Measure of Support

Gilgamesh

One hundred years ago the most common view amongst scholars was that the biblical figure of Nimrod derived from the famous Mesopotamian hero Gilgamesh. In the early days of Assyriology this understanding was first put forward by George Smith (who called Gilgamesh Izdubar) and followed by E. Schrader, and was viewed favourably by S.R. Driver, H. Gunkel and J. Skinner, and it was more recently revived by W.H. Gispen, M. Witte and R.E. Gmirkin, while H. Seebass sees Nimrod as indebted to both Gilgamesh and probably Tukulti-Ninurta I.[9] Gilgamesh was certainly

---

8. J.H. Walton, *Genesis: The NIV Application Commentary* (Grand Rapids, MI: Zondervan, 2001), pp. 370-71.

9. G. Smith, 'The Chaldean Account of the Deluge', *TSBA* 2 (1873), pp. 213-34 (215-16); *idem, The Chaldean Account of Genesis* (London: Sampson Low, Marston, Searle & Rivington, 1876), pp. 174-76; E. Schrader (ed.), *Die Keilinschriften und das Alte Testament* (Berlin: Reuther & Reichard, 3rd edn, 1903), p. 581; Driver, *Genesis*, p. 123; Gunkel, *Genesis*, p. 89, ET *Genesis*, p. 90; Skinner, *Genesis*, p. 209; W.H. Gispen, 'Who Was Nimrod?', in J.H. Skilton, M.C. Fisher and L.W. Sloar (eds.), *The Law and the Prophets: Old Testament Studies Presented in Honor of Oswald Thompson Allis* (Nutley, NJ: Presbyterian and Reformed Publication Company, 1974), pp. 207-14; Witte, *Die biblische Urgeschichte*, pp. 109-10 n. 120; R.E. Gmirkin, *Berossus and Genesis, Manetho and Exodus: Hellenistic Histories and the Date of the Pentateuch* (LHBOTS, 433; New York/London: T&T Clark, 2006),

a king and mighty hero early on in the post-diluvian era, who according to myth fought with the Bull of Heaven, as well as with lions and leopards, but it is impossible to understand how he would have acquired the name Nimrod[10] or how he would have become a symbol for Assyria (Mic. 5.5, ET 6) when he was king of Uruk (Erech) in Babylonia. So this view has only a limited following nowadays.

Naram-Sin/Sargon I

Long ago C. van Gelderen and N.D. van Leeuwen[11] argued that Nimrod derived from the early Mesopotamian king Naram-Sin (*c.* 2254–2219 BCE), while much more recently Y. Levin[12] has argued that Nimrod is a conflation of Naram-Sin and his grandfather and third predecessor, Sargon of Akkad (*c.* 2334–2279 BCE). The name of Kush, Nimrod's father, is further claimed to derive from the city of Kish in Mesopotamia, where Sargon had started his career as king. Levin's view has also been followed recently by I. Knohl and B.T. Arnold.[13] These scholars claim that the name Nimrod derives, in fact, from that of Naram-Sin. However, the names are not so close: both vowels are different, we have to assume a metathesis of 'r' and 'm', the addition of a 'd' in Nimrod, and the omission of Sin from the ancient king's name. All this rather stretches credulity. Recently, it has been claimed that Nimrod derives from Sargon I alone,[14] though it is inexplicable why he would be called Nimrod. Further, it should be noted that neither Sargon nor Naram-Sin had any particular

pp. 118-19; Seebass, *Genesis*, I, p. 259. Gmirkin's thesis is based on the assumption that Genesis used Berossus, which involves an impossibly late date for Genesis; see Day, *From Creation to Babel*, pp. 74-76.

10. The name Gilgamesh was, after all, still recalled in the third century BCE as the name of a giant at Qumran; cf. 4QGiants[b] (4Q530) 2.2 and 4QGiants[c] (4Q531), fragment 2.12.

11. C. van Gelderen, 'Who Was Nimrod?', *The Expositor* (8th series) (1914), pp. 274-82; N.D. van Leeuwen, 'Wie waren Kus en Nimrod?', *Gereformeerd Theologisch Tijdschrift* 21 (1921), pp. 18-31.

12. Y. Levin, 'Nimrod the Mighty, King of Kish, King of Sumer and Akkad', *VT* 52 (2002), pp. 350-66.

13. I. Knohl, 'Nimrod, Son of Cush, King of Mesopotamia, and the Dates of P and J', in C. Cohen *et al.* (eds.), *Birkat Shalom: Studies in the Bible, Ancient Near Eastern Literature, and Postbiblical Judaism Presented to Shalom M. Paul on the Occasion of his Seventieth Birthday*, I (2 vols.; Winona Lake, IN: Eisenbrauns, 2008), pp. 45-52 (49); Arnold, *Genesis*, p. 116.

14. D. Petrovich, 'Identifying Nimrod of Genesis 10 with Sargon of Akkad by Exegetical and Archaeological Means', *JETS* 56 (2013), pp. 273-306.

connection with hunting, something which is emphasized in connection with Nimrod. The attraction of this viewpoint for certain conservative scholars is that it enables them to presume a kernel of historicity behind the figure of Nimrod, Sargon/Naram-Sin having been early rulers in the so-called post-flood era who ruled over an empire which had extended from Babylonia to Assyria, as with Nimrod. But these views are unlikely for the reasons stipulated above.

Tukulti-Ninurta I

In 1958 E.A. Speiser originated a new explanation according to which Nimrod was a reflection of Tukulti-Ninurta I (*c.* 1243–1207 BCE), the first Assyrian king to conquer Babylon, a view regarded as probable by R. de Vaux, and possible by J. Van Seters.[15] It was supposed that Nimrod's father Kush was a reflection of the Kassites, who ruled Babylonia for much of the second millennium (*c.* 1595–1157 BCE). However, if Tukulti-Ninurta I lies behind Nimrod, one would have to assume that the first part of the name, Tukulti, dropped out, but this is otherwise unattested. There is also the problem that Tukulti-Ninurta I was an Assyrian king who conquered Babylonia, whereas Nimrod arose in Babylonia and conquered Assyria. Moreover, Speiser is forced to concede that we have no documentation associating Tukulti-Ninurta I with hunting, although this is well known in connection with the god Ninurta (see below), whose name appears as part of that of the king.[16]

15. E.A. Speiser, 'In Search of Nimrod', in M. Avi-Yonah, H.Z. Hirschberg, Y. Yadin and H. Tadmor (eds.), *Eretz Israel* 5 (Benjamin Mazar volume; Jerusalem: Israel Exploration Society, 1958), pp. 32*-36*, reprinted in J.J. Finkelstein and M. Greenberg (eds.), *Oriental and Biblical Studies: Collected Writings of E.A. Speiser* (Philadelphia: University of Pennsylvania Press, 1967), pp. 31-52, and further reprinted in Hess and Tsumura (eds.), *"I Studied Inscriptions from before the Flood"*, pp. 270-77; R. de Vaux, *La Genèse* (La Sainte Bible; Paris: Cerf, 2nd edn, 1962), p. 69; Van Seters, *Prologue to History*, p. 186 n. 17.

16. Speiser further argues that Tukulti-Ninurta I also underlies the figure of Ninus, known from various classical sources, especially Diodorus Siculus (*Universal History* 2.1-28). However, of Diodorus's three main themes relating to Ninus – his foundation of Nineveh, his queen Semiramis, and his conquest of almost all known Asia (as well as Egypt) – the first two are completely untrue of Tukulti-Ninurta I and the third would be a gross exaggeration if relating to him. The name of King Ninus, never attested in cuneiform inscriptions, is a back projection from that of the city of Nineveh (Akkadian Ninua), eponymous founders of cities being common in Greek tradition, but Nineveh was actually founded many centuries before Tukulti-Ninurta I. The name Semiramis derives from that of queen Sammu-ramat, but she was the wife

Views with Increasing Support

A Personification of the Mesopotamian Kingship Ideology
Unlike all the previous views, in recent years a number of scholars, such as W. Bührer, J.C. Gertz and G. Fischer,[17] have proposed that we should stop looking for a single individual figure lying behind Nimrod and see him rather as a primaeval ruler representing the general royal ideology of ancient Mesopotamia. Somewhat similarly but not exactly, J. Blenkinsopp[18] prefers to see Nimrod as a composite figure combining several Mesopotamian conquerors from Sumerian to Persian times, though without being able to specify precisely which ones. The depiction of Nimrod in Genesis 10 is, of course, a literary construct, but does that mean we should not envisage a particular figure as lying at the root of it, as represented by the name? Why the name Nimrod?

None of these scholars suggests an original Mesopotamian name but all find it significant that in Hebrew Nimrod means 'we shall rebel' or 'let us rebel', from the Hebrew root *mrd*, 'to rebel'.[19] But if so, should

---

of Shamshi-Adad V (*c.* 824–811 BCE), hundreds of years after Tukulti-Ninurta I. As for Ninus's supposed conquest of Egypt and most of known Asia, it is true that Tukulti-Ninurta I was a conquering king, but his conquests did not go anything like that far. Tukulti-Ninurta I conquered Babylonia, including Babylon, and although Ninus is similarly said to have conquered Babylonia, Babylon allegedly did not yet exist. Tukulti-Ninurta I is alleged to have maintained control of Armenia, whereas Ninus is said actually to have conquered Urartu (Armenia). Tukulti-Ninurta I did invade Arabia, like Ninus, and conquered the Hittite-controlled parts of Asia Minor, but did not rule the whole of Asia Minor as is recounted of Ninus. Again, while Tukulti-Ninurta I did conquer some areas immediately to the east of Mesopotamia, his rule did not extend as far as Bactria (Afghanistan), such as is claimed of Ninus. Nor did Tukulti-Ninurta I conquer Egypt. So even with regard to Ninus's conquests, it is far from certain that they reflect those of Tukulti-Ninurta I. Equally conjecturally, A.R. Millard, 'Ninos', in D.O. Edzard (ed.), *Reallexikon der Assyriologie*, IX (Berlin: de Gruyter, 1998–2001), pp. 479-80, thinks they may rather be shadowy reflections of the conquests of Sargon of Akkad, while with more argumentation, H. Lewy, 'Nitokris-Naqî'a', *JNES* 11 (1952), pp. 264-86 (264-70), saw echoes of Sennacherib and Shamshi-Adad V, and F.W. König, *Die Persika des Ktesias von Knidus* (AfO, Beiheft 18; Graz: E. Weidner, 1972), pp. 34-37, of Sargon II.

17. W. Bührer, 'Nimrod coram Domino – Nimrod coram Israhel [*sic*]: Inhalt und Tendenz der Nimrod-Notiz Gen 10,8-12', *BN* 173 (2017), pp. 3-22; Gertz, *Das erste Buch Mose*, I, p. 316; Fischer, *Genesis 1–11*, p. 563.

18. J. Blenkinsopp, *Creation, Un-Creation, Re-Creation: A Discursive Commentary on Genesis 1–11* (London: T&T Clark, 2011), pp. 161-62.

19. Bührer, 'Nimrod coram Domino', pp. 15-16; Blenkinsopp, *Creation, Un-Creation, Re-Creation*, pp. 162-63; Gertz, *loc. cit*; Fischer, *loc cit*.

we see him as a rebel against God?[20] This was indeed a popular view in rabbinic Judaism (cf. *b. Pes.* 94b; Pseudo-Jonathan and Palestinian Targums to Gen. 10.9). However, this is unlikely. Whereas in later Jewish tradition Nimrod was seen in negative terms, and the words of Gen. 10.9, 'He was a mighty hunter before the Lord', were understood to mean 'He was a mighty hunter against the Lord', this is an obvious distortion of the original meaning. Again, Nimrod was later presumed to have taken the lead in building the hubristic tower of Babel; this is already attested in Philo, *Quaestiones in Genesim* 2.81-82 and Josephus, *Ant.* 1.4.3, and taken up subsequently in the Talmud and Christian tradition, and is reflected in the Arabic name for the ziggurat at Borsippa, Birs Nimrud, long but mistakenly regarded as the site of the tower of Babel. However, there is nothing of this in the biblical text itself. In fact, the way Nimrod is spoken of in Gen. 10.9, 'He was a mighty hunter before the Lord; that is why it is said, "Like Nimrod, a mighty hunter before the Lord"', sounds rather positive. (We may compare 2 Kgs 5.1, where Naaman 'was a great man before his master', i.e. in the estimation of his master.) Such words do not cohere well with seeing Nimrod as a rebel against God. Bührer[21] recognizes this, and suggests that the name rather denotes Nimrod as a political rebel, something not always regarded negatively in the Old Testament. But the fact that Nimrod is a dominant king makes it difficult to see who he would be politically rebelling against. In the light of all

---

20. So explicitly, Gertz, *loc. cit.*; and seemingly Blenkinsopp, *loc. cit.*; Fischer, *loc. cit.*

21. Bührer, *loc. cit.* It should be noted that, though Bührer does not think Nimrod is depicted negatively in Gen. 10.9, he does (pp. 16-19) somewhat contradictorily hold that the overall context implies this, viz. his association with Babel (cf. Gen. 11.1-9) and inclusion under Ham, whose descendants included a number of Israel's enemies. However, the Nimrod passage surely belonged originally in the J source subsequent to Babel receiving its naming in Gen. 11.9, and therefore Nimrod was not involved in what brought about its judgment there. Further, not all the sons of Ham are viewed negatively, e.g., the southern Arabians and Dedan in Gen. 10.7 (P), the southern Arabians even being included under the sons of Shem in J (Gen. 10.26-29), as indeed are the Assyrians and Babylonians in P (Gen. 10.22). If the Nimrod passage dates from before the time that the Assyrians (and Babylonians) became really aggressive, before 745 BCE, as the description of Calah as 'the great city' in Gen. 10.12 makes possible (see below), Nimrod and Mesopotamia's inclusion under Ham may be more due to a sense of their geographical distance (like the southern Arabians) than to active hostility. By the way, Bührer also thinks Gen. 10.9's description of Nimrod as a mighty hunter is a later addition to the Nimrod passage, since it depicts him as a hunter rather than a king. But the propensity of Assyrian kings for hunting (cf. the Nimrud [Calah] reliefs in the British Museum) makes this quite unnecessary.

this, I do not believe that the name Nimrod was originally understood in Genesis to mean 'we shall rebel' or 'let us rebel'. Rather, this was a later, postbiblical interpretation.

Ninurta

We come now to the most likely explanation of the origin of the figure of Nimrod, namely in the Mesopotamian war and hunter god Ninurta, though reconceptualized in Genesis 10 as a Mesopotamian king.[22] This was first proposed by certain Assyriologists in the first half of the twentieth century such as P. Jensen and A. Deimel,[23] but Old Testament scholars rarely registered it till the second half of the twentieth century. Significantly, it has been favoured more recently by top cuneiform scholars such as W. von Soden and W.G. Lambert, as well as in the thorough surveys of the subject undertaken by K. van der Toorn and C. Uehlinger, as well as others.[24]

22. For a good overall survey of the cult and mythology of Ninurta, see A. Annus, *The God Ninurta in the Theology and Royal Ideology of Ancient Mesopotamia* (State Archives of Assyria Studies, 14; Helsinki: The Neo-Assyrian Text Project, 2002).

23. P. Jensen, *Das Gilgamesch-Epos in der Weltliteratur*, I (Strasbourg: J. Trübner, 1906), p. 87 n. 1; A. Deimel, 'Nimrod', *Or* 26 (1927), pp. 76-80.

24. W. von Soden, 'Nimrod', in H. von Campenhausen, K. Galling and W. Werbeck (eds.), *RGG*[3], IV (Tübingen: J.C.B. Mohr [Paul Siebeck], 1960), cols. 1496-97 (1497); Lambert, 'A New Look at the Babylonian Background of Genesis', p. 298 n. 40, reprinted in expanded format in 1994, p. 108 n. 40; *idem*, 'Assyrien und Israel', in G. Krause and G. Müller (eds.), *Theologische Realenzyklopädie*, IV (Berlin: W. de Gruyter, 1979), pp. 265-77 (272); K. van der Toorn in K. van der Toorn and P.W. van der Horst, 'Nimrod before and after the Bible', *HTR* 83 (1990), pp. 1-29 (1-16); C. Uehlinger, 'Nimrod', in K. van der Toorn, B. Becking and P.W. van der Horst (eds.), *Dictionary of Deities and Demons in the Bible* (Leiden: Brill, 2nd edn, 1999), pp. 627-30; T. Fenton, 'Nimrod's Cities: An Item from the Rolling Corpus', in K.J. Dell, G. Davies and Y.V. Koh (eds.), *Genesis, Isaiah and Psalms: A Festschrift to Honour Professor John Emerton on his Eightieth Birthday* (VTSup, 135; Leiden: Brill, 2010), pp. 23-31 (23). R.S. Hendel, 'Nimrod', in B.M. Metzger and M.D. Coogan (eds.), *The Oxford Guide to People and Places of the Bible* (New York: Oxford University Press, 2001), p. 218; *idem*, 'Genesis 1–11 and its Mesopotamian Problem', in E.S. Gruen (ed.), *Cultural Borrowings and Ethnic Applications in Antiquity* (Oriens et Occidens, 8; Stuttgart: Franz Steiner Verlag, 2005), pp. 23-36 (30-31), also equated Nimrod with Ninurta, but in his latest work sees rather a combination of Ninurta and Tukulti-Ninurta I (R.S. Hendel, *Genesis 1–11* [AYB, IA; New Haven: Yale University Press, forthcoming]); similarly, S. Dalley, 'The Influence of Mesopotamia upon Israel and the Bible', in Dalley (ed.), *The Legacy of Mesopotamia* (Oxford: Oxford University Press, 1998), pp. 57-83 (66-67). However, as noted above, Tukulti-Ninurta I's rule moved from Assyria to Babylonia, not Babylonia to Assyria as was the case with Nimrod. A. van der Kooij, 'The City of Babel and

Philologically, this view provides the most plausible explanation for the name Nimrod (*nnrt – nmrt – nmrd*). In addition to the appropriateness of the name, it should be noted that Ninurta was regarded as the patron of hunting, having overcome such creatures as the monstrous demon Azag (Akkadian Asakku), the giant bird Anzu, and various other mythical animals such as a seven-headed serpent and a six-headed boar. As a consequence, the Neo-Assyrian kings, who liked to boast of their prowess in hunting, claimed Ninurta as the source of their inspiration. This fits very well the description of Nimrod as 'a mighty hunter before the Lord' (Gen. 10.9). Ninurta was thereby domesticated for an Israelite audience. Also, just as Ninurta was regarded as a *qurrādu*, a hero or warrior, so Nimrod was described as a *gibbôr*. Ninurta was divine, not human, but we can compare Nimrod with the Nephilim in Gen. 6.4. Although there called 'men of renown' and *gibbōrîm*, the Nephilim were in origin semi-divine beings, the offspring of the sons of God and daughters of men.[25] So the transformation of the god Ninurta into the *gibbôr* Nimrod is quite credible. Further, Ninurta was, like Nimrod, a king, having been granted dominion over the gods and the world as a result of his victory over Anzu. Again, although he is never spoken of as founding cities, unlike Nimrod, he was nevertheless regarded as the founder of Mesopotamian civilization, and one of the cities mentioned in Genesis 10, Calah, was actually the chief centre of the Assyrian cult of Ninurta.[26]

Assyrian Imperialism: Genesis 11:1-9 Interpreted in the Light of Mesopotamian Sources', in A. Lemaire (ed.), *Congress Volume: Leiden, 2004* (VTSup, 109; Leiden: Brill, 2006), pp. 1-17 (12), also sees the name Nimrod as deriving from Ninurta but functioning as a symbolic name of Mesopotamian kings generally here.

25. However, in my view in Gen. 6.4 the Nephilim are no longer presented as such offspring, already being on the earth when the divine or angelic marriages took place. See J. Day, 'The Sons of God and Daughters of Men and the Giants: Disputed Points in the Interpretation of Genesis 6:1-4', *HBAI* 4.1 (2012), pp. 427-47 (432-34), reprinted in Day, *From Creation to Babel*, pp. 77-97 (81-83).

26. Another scholar who has connected Nimrod with Ninurta is Hendel, 'Nimrod', p. 218; *idem*, 'Genesis 1–11 in its Mesopotamian Problem', pp. 30-31, who has argued that the name Nimrod should be seen as a polemical distortion by J of the name Ninurta involving the root *mrd*, 'to rebel'. But whereas the rabbis saw this name as reflecting Nimrod's participation in rebellion against God, Hendel proposes that the name was intended by J as a rebuke of Mesopotamian imperialism, the expression 'let us rebel' being aimed at Nimrod himself, though he was unaware of its significance. However, this seems unlikely, since as already noted, the reference to Nimrod sounds rather positive, and further, Nimrod cannot adequately symbolize Mesopotamian imperialism, as his rule does not extend beyond Mesopotamia. I am grateful to Ron Hendel for e-mail correspondence clarifying his view.

Although Nimrod in Gen. 10.8-12 is presented as a primaeval hero, not a god, there is evidence that the Israelites were aware of Nimrod as an Assyrian divine name. 2 Kings 19.37 mentions Sennacherib as having been assassinated in the temple of his god Nisroch. Nisroch (*nisrōk*) is totally unknown in cuneiform records as the name of a Mesopotamian deity but is plausibly explained as a corruption from Nimrod (*nimrōd*) with reference to Ninurta, the most prominent Assyrian deity after Asshur. In the square Hebrew script מ (m) could easily have become corrupted to ס (s) and ד (d) to ך (k).[27] This is much more likely than other suggestions that have been made: the view that Nisroch is a corruption of the name of the light and fire god Nusku,[28] a much less significant deity than Ninurta, or that the name represents Ashur[29] or Marduk,[30] neither of which is graphically close to Nisroch, Marduk also being rather the supreme Babylonian deity.

Some Other Questions Concerning Nimrod

The Problem of Kush as the Father of Nimrod

It has long been felt a problem by many scholars that Nimrod is described as the son of Kush (Gen. 10.8, J), since Nimrod's activities were clearly centred on Mesopotamia, whereas elsewhere in the Old Testament Kush is the name for Nubia, the area immediately south of Egypt in the Sudan (traditionally called Ethiopia, but further north than the modern country of that name). It certainly cannot be denied that this is its current meaning in Genesis 10, since Kush's brothers in 10.6 (P) include Egypt and Put (Libya; not Punt!) and his sons include Seba in East Africa (10.7, P). However, because of the seeming oddity of the Mesopotamian Nimrod being the son of the Nubian Kush, it has sometimes been supposed that underlying Nimrod's father Kush there must rather have been the Kassites, or less often Kish.[31] Those favouring the Kassite view have sometimes appealed to Gen. 2.10-14, where the river of Eden, which

27. See, e.g., von Soden, 'Nimrod', col. 1497; Uehlinger, 'Nimrod', p. 628.

28. See, e.g., J. Gray, *I & II Kings: A Commentary* (OTL; London: SCM Press, 1977), p. 694.

29. See, e.g., D.J. Wiseman, *1 and 2 Kings: An Introduction and Commentary* (TOTC, 9; Leicester: IVP, 1993), p. 285. Wiseman appealed to the LXX variant readings Esdrach and Asrach (for the latter of which Wiseman miswrote Asorach).

30. See, e.g., J.A. Montgomery and H.S. Gehman, *A Critical and Exegetical Commentary on the Books of Kings* (ICC; Edinburgh: T. & T. Clark, 1951), p. 500.

31. See above under Nazimaruttash and Tukulti-Ninurta I (Kassites) and under Naram-Sin/Sargon (Kish).

divides into the Mesopotamian rivers Tigris and Euphrates as well as the Pishon, also divides into the river Gihon, which encompasses all the land of Kush. However, there can be little doubt that the Gihon is the Nile, as in LXX Jer. 2.18; Ecclus 24.27 [Greek]; Genesis Apocryphon; Josephus, *Ant.* 1.1.3, and Kush is Nubia, as elsewhere. Accordingly, rather than providing evidence for a Kush in the immediate vicinity of Mesopotamia, Gen. 2.10-14 might rather provide evidence of geographical confusion according to which it was supposed that the Nubian Kush was related in some way to Mesopotamia (cf. Pausanias, *Description of Greece* 2.5.3, who reports the story that the rivers Euphrates and Nile were connected). If so, it might not be so outlandish that Kush should be described as the father of Nimrod in Genesis 10. Even so, it is difficult to see why Kush specifically should be chosen as Nimrod's father. But it should be borne in mind that Genesis 10 similarly represents Egypt as the father of the Cretans (Caphtorim, v. 14) and Shem as the father of Lydia (Lud, v. 22), both of which are also unfathomable, whether on geographical, ethnic or linguistic grounds. Accordingly, it may be that we should not be overly concerned if Nubia (Kush) is depicted as the father of the Mesopotamian Nimrod.

However, the view that Kush refers to the Kassites is not impossible for the source underlying Gen. 10.8 (J), even though, as previously stated, it must denote Nubia in our present text. Though normally spelled *kaššu* in Akkadian, 'Kassite' is spelled *kuššu* in the Akkadian of Nuzi, while the Greek spelling has the related 'o' in the form of the noun *Kossaioi* (cf. Polybius, *Histories* 5.44.7; Strabo, *Geography* 11.13.6; Diodorus Siculus, *Universal History* 17.3.4-6; Arrian, *Anabasis* 7.15.1-3), so it is not inconceivable that it might have become confused with the Nubian Kush. Nevertheless, it is still surprising if Kassites were regarded as the father of Nimrod, deriving as he does, in our view, from the god Ninurta, though it should be noted that Nimrod's kingdom starts from Babylon, which was ruled by the Kassites for much of the second millennium BCE.

B. Oded,[32] however, thinks that Kush, and thereby Nimrod, was included under Ham because in the original text underlying Genesis 10 Ham encompassed settled populations and Shem nomadic tribes. However, since this is not always the case in the current text of Genesis 10 (e.g. various Arabian tribes are included under Ham in Gen. 10.7, and Elam and Assyria are included under Shem in Gen. 10.22), Oded's reconstructed original text is entirely hypothetical.

32. Oded, 'The Table of Nations (Genesis 10)'.

Recently I. Knohl[33] has suggested that Nimrod and Mesopotamia are included under Ham because this is where the traditional enemies of Israel are listed, including Egypt, Canaan and the Philistines. However, while at first this might appear an attractive view, it should be noted that some of the descendants of Ham are not particularly Israel's enemies (e.g. the various Arabian tribes in v. 7), Egypt was far from always being an enemy of Israel but sometimes served as an ally against the Mesopotamian powers (Isa. 30.15; 31.1-3; Jer. 37.5, 7; cf. Deut. 23.6, ET 7), while Nimrod appears to be portrayed somewhat positively, so it is not obvious that Assyria and Babylonia are treated hostilely at this point. If the Nimrod passage dates from before 745 BCE, the time Assyria started becoming really aggressive throughout the Near East (which is quite possible in view of the reference to Calah as the capital; see below), this becomes credible. Further, it is widely accepted that the reference to the Philistines arose as a later marginal gloss, since in the Masoretic text it is wrongly attached to the Casluhim rather than the following Caphtorim (Gen. 10.14).

Nimrod and Assyria in Micah 5.4-5 (ET 5-6)

Outside Genesis 10, apart from 1 Chron. 1.10, where Nimrod appears briefly as part of a genealogy, the name Nimrod occurs once more in the Old Testament as part of the passage in Mic. 5.4-5 (ET 5-6). This reads:

> 'If Assyria comes into our land and treads on our soil,[34] we shall raise against it seven shepherds and eight princes of men. They shall rule the land of Assyria with the sword, and the land of Nimrod with the drawn sword. They shall rescue us from Assyria if it comes into our land and if it treads within our border.'

Nimrod clearly stands parallel with Assyria, so must be another term to denote that country, not Babylonia, as has already been noted.[35] This is fully comprehensible if the name Nimrod derives from that of Ninurta. Chapter 5 is part of the book of Micah which is commonly denied to the eighth-century prophet Micah, whose work is generally held to be restricted to chs. 1–3. It is indeed unlikely to derive from the original prophet Micah, since this passage envisages victory for Judah over the

---

33. Knohl, 'Nimrod Son of Kush', pp. 48-49.
34. Reading with LXX b^e *'admātēnû*, 'on our soil', instead of b^e *'arm^{e}nōtênû*, 'in our palaces', the former providing better parallelism with b^e *'arṣēnû*, 'in our land'.
35. See n. 6 above.

Assyrians, should they invade, whereas in Mic. 3.12 the fall of Zion is expected. Nevertheless, it is natural to suppose that 'Assyria' was originally meant literally rather than being a code name for an imperial power, as some have supposed.[36] Thus, it has sometimes been held that Assyria (and hence Nimrod) was a code name for the Seleucid empire in the second century BCE, but this is impossibly late, since Ecclus 49.10 already attests the Book of the Twelve, of which Micah is a part, in the early second century BCE, prior to the Maccabean crisis when hostility to the Seleucids is most likely to have been manifest. Again, another view has been that Assyria is a code name for Persia, as it is indeed in Ezra 6.22.[37] However, against this being the case in Micah 5 it should be noted that the passage is hostile to 'Assyria', but within the Old Testament elsewhere there is never a harsh word uttered against the Persians (unlike the Assyrians), except implicitly in the late Dan. 7.6. This is in marked contrast to the ancient Greeks, for whom the Persians were rather the archetypal enemy. Nevertheless, while in origin the passage was a pre-exilic reference to Assyria, it is possible that in its final post-exilic redaction it acquired a secondary meaning.[38]

Nimrod's Cities

Genesis 10.10-11 goes on to list Nimrod's cities. C. Westermann[39] thought these verses are a secondary expansion of the tradition, but this is unnecessary, as J. Van Seters[40] has rightly argued.

Calneh or 'All of Them'? If we follow the Masoretic text, the beginning of Nimrod's kingdom was 'Babylon, Erech, Akkad and Calneh in the land of Shinar'. The first three were important cities in Babylonia, but Calneh is completely unknown there. The only place named Calneh that we know of was in Syria (Amos 6.2; spelled Calno in Isa. 10.9), which is inappropriate here, as this is far away from southern Mesopotamia.

36. So rightly B. Renaud, *La formation du livre de Michée. Tradition et actualization* (Etudes bibliques; Paris: J. Gabalda, 1977), pp. 252-54.

37. Cf. W. McKane, *The Book of Micah: Introduction and Commentary* (Edinburgh: T. & T. Clark, 1998), p. 163, who declares that Assyria could have been used for the Persians or the Seleucids.

38. Cf. H.G.M. Williamson, 'Micah', in J. Barton and J. Muddiman (eds.), *The Oxford Bible Commentary* (Oxford: Oxford University Press, 2001), pp. 595-99 (598), who has suggested 'the world powers in general'.

39. Westermann, *Genesis 1–11*, p. 687, ET *Genesis 1–11*, p. 514.

40. Van Seters, *Prologue to Genesis*, p. 178.

The proposal that we should emend the name to Kullaba[41] does not seem particularly compelling, as this place name does not appear to have been sufficiently well known in the Levant. Since W.F. Albright[42] first suggested it, it has been common to emend the vocalization from *kalnēh* to *kullānāh*, 'all of them' (cf. Gen. 42.36; 1 Kgs 7.37; Prov. 31.29), so that we may read that Nimrod's kingdom was 'Babylon, Erech and Akkad, all of them in the land of Shinar'. This brilliant solution has been widely accepted and finds support in the Samaritan Aramaic Targum, as J.A. Thompson has noted.[43]

Nimrod or Ashur as the Subject of Verses 11-12? There is a disagreement among scholars regarding v. 11 as to whether we should translate 'From that land he [Nimrod] went into Assyria, and built Nineveh, Rehoboth-ir, Calah, and Resen between Nineveh and Calah, which is the great city' (cf. RV, RSV, NRSV, NAB, NEB, REB, NIV) or 'From that land Ashur went out and built Nineveh ...' (cf. AV, NJPSV, JB, NJB). Although grammatically the latter might at first seem more natural, as Ashur lacks the *he locale* here, this is not that significant, since there are other cases where *he locale* is lacking on a place name where there is a directional meaning (e.g. Gen. 35.1, 3; 43.15; Exod. 4.19; Hos. 7.11, the last example actually with 'Assyria'). Moreover, a very strong case can be made for the former rendering. First, Gen. 10.10's reference to *rē'šît mamlaktô* in connection with Nimrod most naturally means 'the beginning of his kingdom', making it plausible to suppose that the text continues by telling us about the rest of Nimrod's kingdom, which is the case if Nimrod is the subject of vv. 11-12 but not otherwise. Secondly, in Mic. 5.5 (ET 6) Nimrod is a symbol of Assyria, which is explicable if Nimrod is represented as the founder of the various Assyrian cities mentioned in vv. 11 and 12, but not on the alternative translation in which Nimrod has nothing to do with them. Thirdly, those who render 'From that land Ashur went out and built

---

41. See, e.g., Delitzsch, *Wo lag das Paradies?*, p. 225; P. Jensen, Review of J.F. McCurdy, *History, Prophecy and the Monuments*, I (New York and London: Macmillan, 1894), in *TLZ* 20 (1895), cols. 508-10 (510).

42. W.F. Albright, 'The End of Calneh in Shinar', *JNES* 3 (1944), pp. 254-55.

43. J.A. Thompson, 'Samaritan Evidence for "All of Them in the Land of Shinar" (Gen 10:10)', *JBL* 90 (1971), pp. 90-102. A.S. Yahuda, 'Calneh in Shinar', *JBL* 65 (1946), pp. 325-27, however, rejected Albright's view but had nothing to put in its place except to propose that Calneh is a hitherto unknown Mesopotamian place name. However, that such a place name should still be unattested in cuneiform records, if it really existed, seems improbable.

Nineveh ...' tend to think in terms of Ashur the city, but elsewhere in the Old Testament Ashur never denotes the city but always the country of Assyria.

Rehoboth-ir. Rehoboth-ir is represented in Gen. 10.11 as the name of an Assyrian city founded by Nimrod (it is preceded by *wᵉ'et*, like the other city names in vv. 11-12), but no city with this name is attested anywhere in cuneiform literature and is unlikely ever to be so. Rather, the name means 'squares of [the] city' (cf. Lam. 2.12, where the identical expression is used of Jerusalem). Some scholars suppose that this term originally denoted part of a city, probably Nineveh, which has just been referred to. It has been noted that in Akkadian the equivalent phrase *rebīt āli*, 'squares of [the] city', is attested, and *rebīt Ninua*, 'the squares of Nineveh', is used of Nineveh.[44] So we could suppose that what originally was a part of the city of Nineveh eventually became misunderstood as the name of a distinct city.[45] However, it seems a bit odd for the squares of the city to be singled out in this particular context and J.M. Sasson[46] has suggested that a more likely meaning is 'the broadest city', literally 'broad of city', with reference to Nineveh, emending *rᵉḥōbōt 'îr* to *raḥᵃbat 'îr*, an epithet which would then parallel Calah as 'the great city' later in the verse (see below). It would then be this epithet which later got misunderstood and revocalized as the name of a separate city. However, certainty is not possible in this matter.

Resen. The city of Resen, which Nimrod is also alleged to have built (Gen. 10.12), has similarly posed problems for scholars, since no city with this name existed in the position indicated between Nineveh and Calah. However, in recent years there has been a tendency among some scholars to understand Resen as referring to Dur-Sharrukin (modern Khorsabad), Sargon II's new but short-lived capital, but various divergent ways have been proposed to attain this. Thus, on the one hand, it had long been noted that the only place name in the area that remotely resembles Resen was

44. This view is sometimes followed in the modern scholarly literature; see, e.g., P. Machinist, 'Nimrod', in *ABD*, IV, pp. 1116-17 (1117). It was first proposed by Friedrich Delitzsch, *Wo lag das Paradies?*, pp. 261-62.

45. The ingenious view of G. Dossin, 'Le site de Reḥoboth-'ir et de Resen', *Le Muséon* 47 (1934), pp. 107-21 (112-16), that Rehoboth-ir is a cryptogram for Ashur has gained no support.

46. J.M. Sasson, 'Reḥōvōt 'îr', *RB* 90 (1983), pp. 94-96; followed by van der Toorn in van der Toorn and van der Horst, 'Nimrod before and after the Bible', p. 5.

that of the village of Resh-eni (meaning 'head of the source'),[47] though it was not actually situated between Nineveh and Calah, as Gen. 10.12 says of Resen, but rather probably a good 20 kilometres north-east of Nineveh.[48] It would be surprising if the name of such an insignificant village, which is attested in an inscription of Sennacherib alongside a number of other little-known villages,[49] was known to the Israelites. However, V.A. Hurowitz[50] has recently proposed that this place name was used in Gen. 10.12 as a substitute for Dur-Sharrukin in order to avoid anachronism. Y. Levin and T. Fenton,[51] on the other hand, have proposed that Resen is rather a textual corruption from the name Dur-Sharrukin, *Drsrgn* in Hebrew, which somehow ended up as *Rsn* (Resen). However, such a radical emendation of the Masoretic text makes one feel cautious about accepting its likelihood. Again, K. van der Toorn notes the Septuagint spelling (Dasem) and thinks it not impossible that this could be a corruption from Dur-Sharrukin, but he admits this is hardly more than a strained guess, and feels it is best to confess our ignorance regarding Resen.[52] Moreover, Dur-Sharrukin does not actually lie between Nineveh and Calah as is stated of Resen, and furthermore, it was capital of Assyria for such a brief period under Sargon II that one wonders whether many in Judah would have registered the fact.[53] Furthermore, the very name Dur-Sharrukin, 'Fort Sargon', betokens its foundation by Sargon, so it would be highly odd for its foundation to be attributed to Nimrod.

It seems best to conclude that no place name underlies the name Resen and it is unlikely that any unknown place name corresponds to it either. As in the case of Rehoboth-ir, it seems most likely that some other expression pertaining to a place got misunderstood as a place name in our Masoretic

47. Lambert, 'Assyrien und Israel', p. 272.

48. S. Parpola, *Neo-Assyrian Toponyms* (AOAT, 6; Neukirchen-Vluyn: Neukirchener Verlag, 1970), p. 293.

49. D.D. Luckenbill, *Annals of Sennacherib* (University of Chicago Oriental Institute Publications, 2; Chicago, IL: University of Chicago Press, 1924), p. 79, line 9.

50. V.A. Hurowitz, 'In Search of Resen (Genesis 10:12): Dur-Šarrukīn?', in Cohen *et al.* (eds.), *Birkat Shalom*, pp. 511-24; followed by Knohl, 'Nimrod, Son of Cush', pp. 49-50.

51. Levin, 'Nimrod the Mighty', p. 365; Fenton, 'Nimrod' Cities', pp. 27-28, 31.

52. Van der Toorn in van der Toorn and van der Horst, 'Nimrod', p. 14.

53. It should be mentioned that Dossin, 'Le site de Reḥoboth-'ir et de Resen', pp. 109-11, 116-18, saw Resen as another cryptogram for Ashur, comparable to Rehoboth-ir noted above. But this view has gained no support and it is not clear why, on Dossin's view, Ashur should be listed twice.

text. Sometimes Resen is connected with Akkadian *risnu* and therefore believed to denote an irrigation canal.[54] It so happens that there actually was an irrigation canal in the area of Calah, the Patti-hegalli, built by Ashurnaṣirpal II in the early ninth century (and restored by Esarhaddon in the seventh century). This might be what is referred to here, later to be misunderstood as a place name.[55] However, we cannot be certain.

Calah as the Great City and the Date of J. Which of the cities listed in v. 12 constitutes 'the great city'? Occasionally, it has been proposed that the term refers to all four Assyrian cities listed in this verse.[56] But that seems most implausible, since the two we know of (Calah and Nineveh) were 30 kilometres apart. Some scholars believe that the term 'the great city' must refer to Nineveh, because Nineveh receives that epithet in the book of Jonah (Jon. 1.2; 3.2; 4.11; cf. 3.3, 'a great city to God'); it was the capital from the time of Sennacherib down to 612 BCE. However, the words 'the great city' do not immediately follow Nineveh in Gen. 10.12, which we should expect if this were correct, so those taking this view presume some alteration of the original text,[57] for which there is no evidence. Moreover, there is every reason to believe that Genesis 10 (in both its J and P aspects) is older than the book of Jonah, so there is no reason why we should judge what Genesis 10 says by the book of Jonah. Grammatically possible is the view that 'the great city' refers to Resen, but as we have already seen above, what this name denotes is obscure, so it is unlikely that it would be dubbed 'the great city'. Most likely, 'the great city' refers to Calah, which is mentioned immediately preceding this epithet.[58] That it should be

54. See, e.g., Lipiński, 'Nimrod et Aššur', pp. 85-86; Machinist, 'Nimrod', p. 1117.

55. Cf. Machinist, 'Nimrod', p. 1117. Machinist also mentions a huge canal system built around Nineveh by Sennacherib.

56. See, e.g., Franz Delitzsch, *Neuer Commentar über die Genesis* (Leipzig: Dörffling & Franke, 5th edn, 1887), p. 16, ET *A New Commentary on Genesis* (trans. S. Taylor; 2 vols.; Edinburgh: T. & T. Clark, 1888–89).

Delitzsch, *Neuer Commentar über die Genesis*, p. 216, ET *A New Commentary on Genesis*, p. 327.

57. Some, e.g., Gunkel, *Genesis*, p. 80, ET *Genesis*, p. 90, and Skinner, *Genesis*, p. 212, suggest 'the great city' is a misplaced gloss on Nineveh, while others, e.g., Westermann, *Genesis 1–11*, p. 691, ET *Genesis 1–11*, p. 518, and C. Levin, *Der Jahwist* (FRLANT, 157; Göttingen: Vandenhoeck & Ruprecht, 1993), p. 125, hold that all the city names between 'Nineveh' and 'the great city' are a later addition.

58. See, e.g., Seebass, *Genesis. I. Urgeschichte*, p. 90; Hendel, *Genesis 1–11* (AYB Commentary, forthcoming).

called 'the great city' is entirely plausible when we consider that it was the capital of Assyria from the time of Ashurnaṣirpal II (*c.* 879 BCE) down to the reign of Sargon II, when Dur-Sharrukin was briefly made the capital (*c.* 706–705 BCE), after which Sennacherib made Nineveh the capital, which it remained until the end of the Assyrian empire in 612 BCE. It is also interesting to note in the context of its having been built by Nimrod (a figure, originating as we have argued in Ninurta), that Calah (still today called Nimrud) was the most important centre of the cult of Ninurta in Assyria.

If 'the great city' refers to Calah, as seems probable, this gives us a clue to the date of J, since as just stated, it was the capital of Assyria from *c.* 879 till 706 BCE. A date of *c.* 790 +/- 85-90 years for J is thereby indicated. This is similar to the date suggested by H. Seebass and R.S. Hendel.[59] I would incline to narrowing down the date further by noting that Gen. 27.40 seems to refer to Judah's loss of Edom in *c.* 850 BCE (cf. 2 Kgs 8.20), while the prophet Hosea appears to know of J traditions *c.* 730 BCE in Hosea 12. This again gives a date for J of *c.* 790 BCE, but this time +/- 60 years.

59. Seebass, *Genesis. I. Urgeschichte*, p. 34, dates J to the beginning of the eighth century BCE; R.S. Hendel, 'Historical Context', in Evans, Lohr and Petersen (eds.), *The Book of Genesis*, pp. 51-82 (80), argues for the ninth to eighth century BCE.

Chapter 11

FROM ABRAHAM OF UR TO ABRAHAM
IN THE FIERY FURNACE

Abraham of Ur

The Biblical References

There are just a few places in the Old Testament where the patriarch Abraham and his family are said to have come from Ur of the Chaldaeans (sometimes known as Ur of the Chaldees). In Gen. 11.28 we read that Haran (brother of Abram) 'died before his father Terah in the land of his birth, in Ur of the Chaldaeans'. Three verses later (Gen. 11.31), we read that 'Terah took Abram his son and Lot the son of Haran, his grandson, and Sarai his daughter-in-law, his son Abram's wife, and they went forth together from Ur of the Chaldaeans to go into the land of Canaan; but when they came to Haran they settled there'. Later, in Gen. 15.7, God declares to Abram, 'I am the Lord who brought you from Ur of the Chaldaeans, to give you this land to possess'. Finally, in Neh. 9.7, we read, 'You are the Lord, the God who did choose Abram and bring him forth out of Ur of the Chaldaeans and gave him the name Abraham'.

Urfa and Uruk

Prior to the mid-nineteenth century it was common to associate Ur of the Chaldaeans with Urfa in south-east Turkey, just north of the modern border with Syria. In fact, this is the site that Islamic tradition equates with Abraham's home of Ur. The Cave of Abraham (or Ibraham as he is known) is shown there, where he was allegedly born, and the chief mosque there is called the Mosque of Abraham, and in its grounds is the pool of Abraham, which is reputed to be the place where Nimrod threw Abraham into the fire. But Allah turned the flames into water and the burning logs into fish. Many fish are still found in this pool. Known as

Urfa, or Şanliurfa in Turkish, the place was called Orhai in Syriac, but the Greeks knew it as Edessa, the name given to it by Seleucus I Nicator when he founded it in 304 BCE. But the name Orhai is not attested before 150 CE; the name is totally unknown in earlier cuneiform sources. However, there is evidence from Syriac that the place was also called *'dm'*, and this seems to correspond to the town known in cuneiform sources as Adme.[1] It is therefore most unlikely that this site is identical with the biblical Ur. In any case, it is not in the area of the Chaldaeans (see below).

However, another view found in the Talmud and some mediaeval Arabic sources identified Ur of the Chaldaeans with Warka (Erech), now known to be the site of the ancient Sumerian and later Babylonian city of Uruk. But it is now absolutely clear that Uruk and Ur were quite different places. Uruk is the city known as Erech in the Old Testament (Gen. 10.10; LXX Orech, the Orchoē of the Greeks), not Ur.

Ur of the Chaldaeans in Southern Mesopotamia

Already in antiquity we know that there were some who located Ur in Babylonia. Thus, Pseudo-Eupolemus, quoted by Alexander Polyhistor, is cited by Eusebius, *Praeparatio evangelica* 9.17 as stating that 'Abraham was born in the tenth generation in the Babylonian city Camarina, although others state that the city was named Ourie'.[2] (Rightly or wrongly,[3] this name has sometimes been connected with Arabic *qamar*, 'moon', in the light of Ur's strong association with the Babylonian moon god Sin, earlier Sumerian Nanna.) Again, Josephus in *Ant.* 1.7.2, without explicitly mentioning Ur, cites Nicolaus of Damascus as stating that Abraham 'came with an army out of the land above Babylon, called the land of the Chaldaeans'. Somewhat later, in the ninth/tenth century, the Arabic writer Al-Ṭabarī located Ur very accurately between al-Kūfah and al-Baṣrah, as we shall see later in the second half of this chapter.

However, it was only from the mid-nineteenth century onwards that it has become common for scholars to equate biblical Ur with the site of Ur (Akkadian Uru, Sumerian Urim) in southern Babylonia near Naṣiriyah, located at Tell el-Muqayyar, lit., 'the Pitched Mound', or 'the Mound of the Pitch', after the material from which many of the ruined buildings

---

1. See A. Harrak, 'The Ancient Name of Edessa', *JNES* 5 (1992), pp. 209-14.

2. Translation by Doran, 'Pseudo-Eupolemus', p. 880.

3. Cf. T.G. Pinches, *The Old Testament in the Light of the Historical Records and Legends of Assyria and Babylonia* (London: SPCK, 3rd edn, 1908), p. 197; P. Schnabel, *Berossos und die babylonisch-hellenistische Literatur* (Leipzig: B.G. Teubner, 1923), p. 69.

were constructed. Following J.E. Taylor's 1854 excavations at Tell el-Muqayyar and the discovery of four cylinder seals of Nabonidus there, which named the city as Ur, Sir Henry Rawlinson in 1856 became the first person to equate it with the biblical Ur.[4] Subsequently the most important excavations at Ur were undertaken by Leonard, later Sir Leonard Woolley, from 1922 to 1934, who also accepted this identification. In fact, he went out of his way to emphasize the connection of Ur with the biblical Abraham so as to drum up support for his excavations. These excavations revealed particularly spectacular finds from the Sumerian period, now in the British Museum and the Penn Museum, Philadelphia. However, the city experienced a revival in the Neo-Babylonian period in the sixth century BCE, when Nebuchadrezzar practically rebuilt the city and Nabonidus rebuilt the ziggurat which had originally been constructed by Ur-Nammu of the Third Dynasty of Ur (*c.* 2100 BCE).[5]

The strongest argument for biblical Ur being in Babylonia is the addition of the words 'of the Chaldaeans', for elsewhere in the Old Testament Chaldaea clearly denotes Babylonia, i.e. southern Mesopotamia. References to the Chaldaeans are particularly frequent in the period from the time of Nebuchadrezzar till Cyrus (cf. 2 Kgs 25.4, 5, 10, 13, 24, 25; Isa. 13.19; 43.14; 47.1, 5; 48.14, 20; Jer. 37.5, 8, 9, 10, 11, 13; 39.5, 8; 40.8, 10; 41.3, 18; 43.3; 50.1, 8, 25, 35, 45; 51.4, 54; Ezek. 1.3; Hab. 1.6), just to cite some of the allusions. In the light of this abundant evidence 'Ur of the Chaldaeans' can only refer to the well-known Babylonian city of Ur. Incidentally, the Hebrew word *Kaśdîm*, 'Chaldaeans', is generally held to reflect an original postulated Akkadian **Kaśdu*,[6] with the English

---

4. H.C. Rawlinson, Comments made on a lecture by William K. Loftus, 'Notes on a Journey from Baghdad to Basrah with Descriptions of Original Chaldaean Remains' (Feb. 25th, 1856), in *Proceedings of the Royal Geographical Society of London* (1857), pp. 45-49 (47); *idem*, 'Biblical Geography', *The Athenæum* 1799 (April, 1862), pp. 529-31 (531). Earlier Rawlinson, 'On the Inscriptions of Assyria and Babylonia', *JRAS* 12 (1850), pp. 401-83 (481), had equated Abraham's Ur with Warka.

5. See P.R.S. Moorey's excellent updating of Sir Leonard Woolley, *Ur 'of the Chaldees'* (London: Herbert Press, 1982). This was a thorough revision of Woolley's *Excavations at Ur: A Record of Twelve Years' Work* (London: Ernest Benn, 1955), which in turn was a revision of his *Ur of the Chaldees* (London: Penguin Books, 2nd edn, 1950), first published by Ernest Benn in 1929. Cf. his book *Abraham: Recent Discoveries and Hebrew Origins* (London: Faber & Faber, 1936), pp. 57-63. For Woolley's ten official Ur excavations volumes, see the list in Woolley, *Ur 'of the Chaldees'* (revised by Moorey), p. 266.

6. Cf. BDB, p. 505; KB, p. 458, *HALAT*, II, p. 477, *HALOT*, II, p. 502.

form 'Chaldaeans', deriving from Greek *Chaldaioi* and Latin *Chaldaei*, going back to the later attested Akkadian form of the name, *Kaldu*. It is a well-known curiosity of Akkadian for a sibilant letter before a dental to change to an *l*, and so *šd* would become *ld*. However, the form *Kašdu* is not actually attested in Akkadian.[7] How can we explain this? It is probable that the Hebrew *Kaśdîm* reflects the original sibilant as heard early on by the Hebrews, probably from direct contact with the Chaldaeans, who originally spoke an Aramaic dialect.[8] In contrast, our preserved Akkadian sources all reflect the transformed form of the name, *Kaldu*.

Cyrus Gordon's Thesis of a Northern Ur

It was a common view till the nineteenth century that Abraham's Ur was in northern Mesopotamia. But in modern times a majority of scholars have accepted the view that Abraham's Ur was in Babylonia. However, a minority continue to prefer to locate it further north and east. In particular, Cyrus Gordon[9] was the scholar who undertook the most thorough defence of a northern Ur and against the identity of Abraham's Ur with the famous Ur (Tell el-Muqayyar) in southern Babylonia, though his arguments have been further developed by Victor Hamilton and Gary Rendsburg, and expounded in more popular form by Hershel Shanks, amongst others.[10] Over against this, the most thorough defence of the traditional view up to now has been undertaken by H.W.F. Saggs, and in much briefer form by Alan Millard.[11]

First, one of Gordon's arguments is that the southern Babylonian Ur is never referred to as Ur of the Chaldaeans in cuneiform documents. But this is a very weak argument. In fact, the designation 'Ur of the

---

7. Cf. D.O. Edzard. 'Kaldu', in Edzard *et al.* (eds.), *Reallexikon der Assyriologie*, V (Berlin: W. de Gruyter, 1976–80), pp. 291-97 (296).

8. Cf. A.F. Rainey, 'Chaldea, Chaldeans', in *Encyclopaedia Judaica*, V (Jerusalem: Keter, 1971), cols. 330-31 (330).

9. C.H. Gordon, 'Abraham and the Merchants of Ura', *JNES* 17 (1958), pp. 28-31; *idem*, 'Abraham of Ur', in D.W. Thomas and W.D. McHardy (eds.), *Hebrew and Semitic Studies Presented to G.R. Driver* (Oxford: Clarendon Press, 1963, pp. 77-84; *idem*, 'Where is Abraham's Ur?', *BARev* 3.2 (June, 1977), pp. 20-21.

10. Hamilton, *The Book of Genesis: Chapters 1–17*, pp. 363-65; Gary Rendsburg, 'Ur Kasdim: Where is Abraham's Birthplace?', in *The Torah.com* (online, 2019); H. Shanks, 'Is the Pope Going to the Wrong Place?', *BARev* 25.1 (Jan./Feb. 2000), pp. 16-19, 66-67.

11. H.W.F. Saggs, 'Ur of the Chaldees: A Problem of Identification', *Iraq* 22 (1960), pp. 200-209; A.R. Millard, 'Where Was Abraham's Ur? The Case for the Babylonian City', *BARev* 27.3 (May/June, 2001), pp. 52-53, 57.

Chaldaeans' absolutely requires a location in Babylonia, since that is where the Chaldaeans were when the biblical text was written. It is not impossible that the epithet 'of the Chaldaeans' may have been added as a way of distinguishing it from other Urs, such as those referred to in documents from Ebla, Nuzi, Alalakh and Ugarit. However, those attested in the first three were probably mere villages, and we cannot be sure that they even existed in the time of P. Thus, the Ebla tablets (*c.* 2500–2250 BCE) attest unimportant places with names like Ura and Uru nearby.[12] Tablets from Alalakh[13] from *c.* 1600 BCE know a place Urê at the western edge of the Fertile Crescent, while other texts from Alalakh *c.* 1450 BCE refer to a village called Ura and another place called Urê.[14] Tablets from Nuzi *c.* 1400 BCE mention a Great Uri and a Small Uri in the neighbourhood of Nuzi.[15] It should be noted that none of these places is referred to as 'Ur of the Chaldaeans' either; indeed, they were not located where the Chaldaeans dwelt. Gordon's attempt to find evidence for Chaldaeans in northern Mesopotamia is decidedly weak, as we shall see shortly. Clearly the term 'Ur of the Chaldaeans' was a particular Hebrew designation in Genesis 11 (and elsewhere in the Bible) in order to clarify for Israelite readers where it was situated, whether it was consciously aimed at distinguishing it from other Urs or not.

Moreover, Gordon's own preferred location for biblical Ur, namely the site of Ura, a city mentioned in an Akkadian text from Ugarit as under the rule of the Hittites,[16] is actually known from texts from Hattusha and Ugarit to have been a port on the coast of Cilicia (southern Turkey), possibly modern Gilindere.[17] This was some considerable distance from Haran,

12. M. Bonechi, *I nomi geographici dei testi di Ebla* (Répertoire géographique des textes cunéiformes, 12.1; Wiesbaden: Ludwig Reichert, 1993), pp. 309-12, attest Ura, Ura'u, Uram, Uri'um, Urru; A. Archi *et al.*, *I nomi di luogi di testi di Ebla* (Rome: Missione archeologica Italiana in Siria, 1995), pp, 44, 456-57, 463-65, attest Ura, Ura'u, Uri, Uru.

13. D.J. Wiseman, *The Alalakh Tablets* (London: British Institute of Archeology at Ankara, 1953), 56.8.

14. Wiseman, *The Alalakh Tablets*, 105.1 (Urê); 162.4, 16 (Urri), 142.13 and 154.10 (Uri).

15. J. Fincke, *Die Orte- und Gewässernamen der Nuzi-Texte* (Répertoire géographique des textes cunéiformes, 10; Wiesbden: Ludwig Reichert, 1993), p. 332.

16. See J. Nougayrol, *Le Palais royal d'Ugarit*, IV (Paris: Imprimerie Nationale, 1956), pp. 103-105.

17. R.H. Beal, 'The Location of Cilician Ura', *AnSt* 42 (1995), pp. 65-73 (66 n. 6). Cf. already W.F. Albright, 'Abraham the Hebrew', *BASOR* 163 (1961), pp. 36-54 (44 n. 42, Seleucia on the Cilician coast); A.F. Rainey, 'Business Agents at Ugarit', *IEJ* 13 (1963), pp. 313-21 (319, with nn. 63 and 64, on the Cilician coast).

so does not really fit Gordon's concept of a northern Mesopotamian Ur. Moreover, Cilicia does not cohere with the biblical understanding of Chaldaea. However, Gordon also kept open the possibility that biblical Ur was at Urfa, the site hallowed in Islamic tradition referred to above, an option actually preferred by Rendsburg,[18] but we have already dismissed this view earlier on both historico-linguistic and geographical grounds.

Secondly, Gordon attempts to show that there is evidence for Chaldaeans in northern Mesopotamia. He alludes to Ḥaldi in Armenia, but Ḥaldi or Khaldi was the name of a Urartian god, not the name of a people. And Urartu is not the same as northern Mesopotamia but equivalent to Armenia. Gordon further seeks to argue for Chaldaeans in northern Mesopotamia on the basis of three passages in Xenophon which locate certain Chaldaeans near Armenia (*Anabasis* 4.3.4, 5.5.17; *Cyropaedia* 3.1.34). However, even if there were some Chaldaeans living there *c.* 400 BCE, this is not what the Old Testament means by Chaldaea. Further, as Saggs points out,[19] these northern Chaldaeans were probably descendants of colonists planted there in the Neo-Babylonian period. Nabonidus, for example, attached great importance to the control of Haran and Neriglissar undertook campaigns in Cilicia.

Thirdly, Gordon points to Gen. 22.22, where Chesed (the supposed ancestor of the Chaldaeans) is listed after Aram (Syria) mentioned in v. 21. However, the Chaldaeans in Babylonia were in fact of Aramaean origin. Moreover, the position of Chesed in Gen. 22.22 does not militate against Chaldaea's presence in its usual place in Babylonia, since Arpachshad in Gen. 10.22, which surely denotes Chaldaea (coming as it does after Elam and Assyria – and otherwise Chaldaea/Babylonia is not mentioned here) is alluded to just two names before Aram in that verse (see further above, Chapter 9). Saggs argued unconvincingly against Gordon's view on the grounds that Aram in Gen. 22.21 cannot denote Syrian Aram, because Aram is there the son of Nahor and Milcah, whereas Syrian Aram in Gen. 10.22 is the son of Shem. But this is no problem at all: Gen. 22.21-22 is a genealogy from the J source, whereas Gen. 10.22 comes from P. Moreover, Uz appears both as a son of Aram in Gen. 10.23 and as a son of Nahor and Milcah in Gen. 22.21. As with Aram, there is no reason at all to postulate two different places called Uz, each related to different places called Aram. These are simply genealogical variants.

18. See Gordon, 'Abraham of Ur', p. 83; Rendsburg, *loc. cit.*
19. Saggs, 'Ur of the Chaldees', p. 206 n. 39.

Fourthly, another unconvincing argument for a north Mesopotamian Chaldaea is found by Gordon in Isaiah 23. Gordon appeals to the reference to 'Chaldaea' in v. 13, which he claims cannot here be in Babylonia, because what precedes and follows points to a northern location. But this is a strange comment, since Isaiah 23 is clearly an oracle directed against Tyre (far from northern Mesopotamia) and is speaking of the judgment that comes upon it. As R.E. Clements observes,[20] the words of Isa. 23.13, 'Behold the land of the Chaldaeans! This is the people; it was not Assyria', are most naturally to be understood as reapplying an older oracle about Tyre and Assyria to one concerning Tyre and Chaldaea. The originally late eighth or more likely seventh century (Esarhaddon) conquest of Tyre has been reapplied to the Chaldaeans, relating to Nebuchadrezzar's siege of Tyre in 585–573 BCE (cf. Ezek. 26–28). There is thus no support for a northern Chaldaea here.

Fifthly, an important part of Gordon's case is that elsewhere in the Old Testament patriarchal origins are located in northern Mesopotamia. For example, Gordon points to Gen. 24.4, 7, where Abraham refers to the area of Haran and Paddan-Aram (cf. v. 10) as the land of his birth (*môladtî*). Saggs attempts to counter Gordon's argument by arguing that *môledet* may have the meaning 'kindred' rather than 'birth' here. Both meanings are possible. However, Saggs fails to note that these verses are all from the J source, and the same is true of Gen. 12.1ff., which also suggests Abraham's origin in the Haran area, whereas the reference in Gen. 11.31 to Abraham coming from 'Ur of the Chaldaeans' is generally agreed to derive from P. There is nothing in the J passages to suggest that the patriarchs originally migrated from elsewhere. It is very likely that J and P reflect two different viewpoints as to the original home of the patriarchs, one in northern Mesopotamia and the other at Ur in Babylonia. Incidentally, the reference to 'Ur of the Chaldaeans' in Gen. 11.28 is probably the work of the redactor who joined J and P.[21]

Furthermore, it should be noted that several of Abraham's ancestors have names which seem to reflect place names in northern Mesopotamia. Thus, the name of his father, Terah (Gen. 11.26), reflects that of the town Til Turaḫi (variant Til ša Turaḫi) in the Baliḫ valley, west of the Baliḫ

20. Clements, *Isaiah 1–39*, p. 194.

21. See J.A. Emerton, 'The Source Analysis of Genesis xi 27-32', *VT* 42 (1992), pp. 37-46, for convincing, detailed arguments for affirming the general view that Gen. 11.27, 31-32 derive from P and 11.28-30 from J, with the exception of 'Ur of the Chaldaeans' in Gen. 11.28 being a later redactional addition.

river, the name of his grandfather, Nahor (Gen. 11.24), echoes that of the town Naḫur, *c.* 100 miles east of Haran in the Ḫabur river valley, often mentioned in second millennium texts, and the name of his grandfather, Serug (Gen. 11.23), reflects the name of the town Sarugi, mentioned in ninth-century Neo-Assyrian texts, west of Haran in the Baliḫ valley. (Admittedly, the ancestor Arpachshad, son of Shem, probably denotes Chaldaea, but that is much further back in the genealogy.) Interestingly, this genealogy comes from the Priestly source, which we have already noted clearly represents Abraham as originating from Chaldaea. We can only conclude that the allusion to Ur was added quite late in the Priestly tradition, and that earlier Priestly tradition, reflected in the genealogy, had agreed with J in locating Abraham's origins in northern Mesopotamia. But this does not at all mean that P in its final form shared this view.

Moreover, Gordon argues that a journey from the Babylonian Ur to Canaan via Haran would have been a roundabout route to take. This is true if Terah was consciously striving to reach Canaan from the time he left Ur. But the text we have depicts him as staying quite a while at Haran before setting off again for Canaan, and a journey from Ur to Haran is credible, since both were centres of the cult of the moon god Sin. However, what is depicted is in all probability not historical. The earlier J source consistently depicts the area around Haran as the original home of the patriarchs, and the counterclaim of Ur is a later addition of P in the sixth century BCE. The depiction of Haran as a stopping point on the way from Ur to Canaan (Gen. 11.31) was an attempt by P to combine the two traditions, and it is this which creates the impression of a roundabout journey.

Again, Gordon claims that, if Abraham's Ur was the Babylonian site, Abraham would not have had to cross the Euphrates, since it was on the western side of the river. He makes this point in connection with Josh. 24.2-3, where the dwelling place of Terah, the father of Abraham, is said to have been 'beyond the Euphrates' and 'beyond the River'. However, it should be noted, first, that Joshua does not explicitly mention Ur; the passage may have been thinking of Haran, where J placed patriarchal origins. Secondly, Sir Leonard Woolley states that there is evidence that in antiquity the Euphrates actually ran west of Ur, unlike nowadays.[22]

___

22. See Woolley, *Ur of the Chaldees*, pp. 206-207, repeated in Woolley, *Ur 'of the Chaldees'* (revised by Moorey), p. 263. What precisely this evidence is Woolley makes clear in *Abraham*, p. 63, where he states: 'air photographs clearly shew the old river-bed running from al 'Ubaid past the foot of the western wall of Ur towards the ancient city of Eridu in the south ... in ancient times the city did indeed lie "beyond the river".'

Gordon also notes that Jacob had to cross the Euphrates when fleeing from Laban in Gen. 31.21, but this is irrelevant, since there is no reference to Abraham or Ur here.

Finally, we may note another weak argument that has been put forward, this time by Rendsburg.[23] He appeals to the famous passage in Deut. 26.5, 'A wandering Aramaean was my father ...' He claims this refers to Abraham, but most scholars think it actually refers to Jacob, since the passage continues with a reference to his going down to Egypt as the prelude to oppression and the exodus (vv. 5-8). But whoever it refers to, it is irrelevant to the location of Ur, since the author was doubtless dependent on the J tradition locating patriarchal origins in Aram-Naharaim rather than the later Priestly placing of their ultimate origin in Ur of the Chaldaeans.

Why Ur?

It is apparent that P in the sixth century BCE has changed the original homeland of Abraham from the northern Mesopotamian land around Haran to the city of Ur in southern Mesopotamia.[24] Ur was prominent in the mid-sixth century BCE, since Nebuchadrezzar and Nabonidus respectively rebuilt the city and its ziggurat. Further, Ur, like Haran, was associated with the cult of the moon god Sin, to whom Nabonidus was devoted at the expense of the leading Babylonian god Marduk.[25] But why would P associate Abraham with Ur, so distant from the original location? I would suggest that it is most likely because the Jews at this time were in exile in Babylonia. Ezekiel, for example, was in exile in Tel Abib by the river Chebar (cf. Ezek. 3.15), near Nippur, just as we know Jews were among the clients of the Murashu bank at Nippur over a century later.

23.   Rendsburg, *loc. cit.*

24.   J.M. Miller, 'Ur of the Chaldeans and Interdisciplinary Research', in T.J. Sandoval and C. Mandolfo (eds.), *Relating to the Text: Interdisciplinary and Form-Critical Insights on the Bible* (JSOTSup 384; London: T&T Clark [Continuum], 2003), pp. 307-20 (319), similarly agrees that early storytellers located Abraham's origins in northern Mesopotamia but during the Neo-Babylonian period he was relocated to southern Babylonia. However, Miller implausibly supposes that the most likely original northern Mesopotamian location was in Urfa. As we have seen above, Urfa was only called Orhai from about 150 CE, and there is no evidence that it bore a name resembling Ur in earlier periods.

25.   Cf. J. Van Seters, *Abraham in History and Tradition* (New Haven, CT: Yale University Press, 1975), pp. 24-26, 38, 121, who righty sensed a connection between the prominence of Ur and Haran in the time of Nabonidus and P's Abrahamic tradition. But unlike Van Seters, I reject the assignation of J too to the exilic period.

Again, more recent discoveries have highlighted the presence of Jews in the exilic period at Al-Yahudu,[26] which was south-east of Nippur. Since the Jews in reclaiming the Promised Land were thereby following in the footsteps of Abraham, to whom originally the land had been promised, it made sense that Abraham too should have come from Babylonia.

Abraham in the Fiery Furnace

The southern Babylonian city of Ur was at an end about 300 BCE.[27] It is therefore not surprising that the Greek Septuagint translation of Genesis, dating from the third century BCE, was clearly unaware that Ur was a city. In all three Septuagint Genesis allusions (Gen. 11.28, 31; 15.7), as well as the second-century BCE Septuagint reference in Neh. 9.7, it translates 'Ur of the Chaldaeans' as 'the land (*chōra*) of the Chaldaeans'. Similarly Acts 7.4 in the New Testament, echoing the Septuagint, states that Abraham 'departed from the land (*gē*) of the Chaldaeans'.

However, the beginnings of the tradition of a fiery furnace are first found in the second-century BCE book of *Jubilees*, but here there is not yet a reference to Abraham escaping it but rather to his brother Haran being burnt in it:

> In the sixtieth year of the life of Abram, i.e. the fourth week, in its fourth year, Abram arose in the night and burned the house of idols. And he burned everything in the house. And there was no man who knew. And they rose up in the night, and they wanted to save their gods from the midst of the fire. And Haran rushed to save them, and the fire flared up over him. And he was burned in the fire and died in Ur of the Chaldaeans before Terah, his father. And they buried him in Ur of the Chaldees. (*Jub.* 12.12-14)[28]

The reference to Haran being burnt in the fiery furnace is clearly a midrashic development based on Gen. 11.28, where we read, 'Haran died before his father Terah in the land of his birth, in Ur of the Chaldaeans'. However, curiously in *Jubilees* 'fire' has not totally replaced the place name Ur, but both are mentioned together. Further, in contrast to later references to Haran in the fiery furnace, it is not explicitly stated whether Haran's death in the fire is to be seen as an accident or a divine punishment.

---

26. See L.E. Pearce and C. Wunsch, *Documents of Judean Exiles and West Semites in Babylonia in the Collection of David Sofer* (Cornell University Studies in Assyriology and Sumerology, 28; Bethesda, MD: CDL Press, 2014).

27. See Woolley, *Ur 'of the Chaldees'* (revised by Moorey), p. 263.

28. Translation follows Wintermute, 'Jubilees', in Charlesworth (ed.), *Old Testament Pseudepigrapha*, II (1985), p. 80.

It is somewhat later, in Pseudo-Philo's *Biblical Antiquities* (probably first century CE), that we find the first reference to Abraham himself being in the fire. Curiously the incident is bound up with Abraham's unwillingness to participate in the building of the tower of Babel, so clearly the setting is in Babylonia. However, Abraham's opponent is not Nimrod (as in later tradition, both Jewish and Islamic), but rather Joktan (a person mentioned in Gen. 10.25 and 1 Chron. 1.19 as the son of Eber). Note that, unlike in *Jubilees*, there is no mention of Ur here at all, and it has been completely replaced by mention of the fire. We read:

> And they took him [i.e. Abram] and built a furnace and lit it. And they threw bricks burned with fire into the furnace. And then the leader Joktan with great emotion took Abram and threw him along with the bricks into the fiery furnace. But God caused a great earthquake, and the fire gushing out of the furnace leaped forth in flames and sparks of flame. And it burned all those standing around in sight of the furnace. And all those who were burned in that day were 83,500. But there was not the least injury to Abram from the burning of the fire. And Abram came up out of the furnace, and the fiery furnace collapsed. And Abram was saved and went away to the eleven men who were hidden in the mountains, and he reported to them everything that had happened to him. (*Ps.-Philo* 6.16-18)[29]

Targums

We turn now to the Targums. Whereas the Babylonian Targum Onqelos (third century CE) simply renders the Hebrew literally ('Ur'), the Palestinian Targums Neofiti and Pseudo-Jonathan (approximately fourth century CE) make reference to the story of Abraham in the fiery furnace. Thus, Targum Neofiti, having stated that 'Haran died during the lifetime of Terah his father in the land of his birth, in the furnace of fire of the Chaldaeans', its rendering of Gen. 11.31 declares that 'Terah took Abraham his son and Lot, his grandson, and Sarai his daughter-in-law, his son Abram's wife, and went forth with them from the furnace of the fire of the Chaldaeans ...' Finally, in Targum Neofiti's rendering of Gen 15.7 God declares to Abraham, 'I am the Lord who brought you out of the furnace of fire of the Chaldaeans to give you this land to inherit it'.[30]

However, it is in Targum Pseudo-Jonathan that we first encounter the notion that it was Nimrod who placed Abraham in the fiery furnace. There is a big insertion about this in Gen. 11.28, which reads:

---

29. Translation follows Harrington, 'Pseudo-Philo', in Charlesworth (ed.), *Old Testament Pseudepigrapha*, II, p. 312.

30. Translations follow McNamara, *Targum Neofiti 1: Genesis*, pp. 85, 86, 95.

It came to pass, when Nimrod cast Abram into the furnace of fire because he would not worship his idol, the fire had no power to burn him. Then Haran was undecided, and he said: 'If Nimrod triumphs, I will be on his side; but if Abram triumphs, I will be on his side'. And when all the people who were there saw that the fire had no power over Abram, they said to themselves: "Is not Haran the brother of Abram full of divination and sorcery? It is he who uttered charms over the fire so that it would not burn his brother.' Immediately fire fell from the heavens on high and consumed him; and Haran died in the sight of Terah his father, being burned in the land of his birth in the furnace of fire which the Chaldaeans had made for Abram his brother.[31]

Similarly, with respect to Gen. 11.31 Targum Pseudo-Jonathan states that Terah, Abram, Lot and Sarai 'went forth together from the fire of the Chaldaeans ...',[32] and in Gen. 15.7 God says to Abraham, 'I am the Lord who brought you out of the fiery furnace of the Chaldaeans ...'[33]

Other Jewish Works

The story of Nimrod and Abraham in the fiery furnace was developed further in *Genesis Rabbah* 38.13. *Genesis Rabbah* was probably compiled in the fourth and fifth centuries CE, but with some later additions.

AND HARAN DIED IN THE PRESENCE OF HIS FATHER TERAH (Gen. 11.28). R. Ḥiyya said: Terah was a manufacturer of idols. He once went away somewhere and left Abraham to sell them in his place. A man came and wished to buy one. 'How old are you?' Abraham asked him. 'Fifty years', was the reply. 'Woe to such a man' he exclaimed, 'you are fifty years old and would worship a day-old object!' At this he became ashamed and departed. On another occasion a woman came with a plateful of flour and requested him, 'Take this and offer it to them'. So he took a stick, broke them, and put the stick in the hand of the largest. When his father returned he demanded, 'What have you done to them?' 'I cannot conceal it from you', he rejoined, 'A woman came with a plateful of fine meal and requested me to offer it to them. One claimed, "I must eat first", while another claimed, "I must eat first". Thereupon the largest arose, took the stick, and broke them.' 'Why do you make sport of me', he cried out; 'have they then any knowledge!' 'Should not your ears listen to what your mouth is saying', he retorted. Thereupon he seized him and delivered him

---

31. Translation from Maher, *Targum Pseudo-Jonathan: Genesis*, p. 51.
32. Translation from Maher, *Targum Pseudo-Jonathan: Genesis*, p. 51.
33. Translation from Maher, *Targum Pseudo-Jonathan: Genesis*, p. 60.

to Nimrod. 'Let us worship the fire!' he [Nimrod] proposed. 'Let us rather worship water, which extinguishes the fire', replied he. 'Then let us worship water!' 'Let us rather worship the clouds which bear the water'. 'Then let us worship the clouds.' 'Then let us worship the wind!' 'Let us rather worship human beings, who withstand the wind.' You are just bandying words', he exclaimed; 'we will worship nought but the fire. Behold, I will cast you into it, and let your God whom you adore come and save you from it.' Now Haran was standing there undecided. If Abram is victorious, [thought he], I will say that I am of Abram's belief, while if Nimrod is victorious I will say that I am on Nimrod's side. When Abram descended into the fiery furnace and was saved, he [Nimrod] asked him, 'Of whose belief are you?' 'Of Abram's', he replied. Thereupon he seized and cast him into the fire; his inwards were scorched and he died in his father's presence. Hence it is written, AND HARAN DIED IN THE PRESENCE OF ('AL PENE) HIS FATHER TERAH.

Gen. Rab. 38.13[34]

New elements in the story here, not previously attested, include the representation of Nimrod as a fire worshipper, and the occurrence of a theological debate between Abraham and Nimrod about the worship of fire and other natural forces.

The incident of Abraham in the fiery furnace is also alluded to elsewhere, in *Gen. Rab.* 44.13. In contrast to most Jewish accounts that regard God himself as delivering Abraham, we read here of the view of Rabbi Eliezer ben Jacob that 'Michael descended and rescued Abraham from the fiery furnace'.[35] Interestingly, this passage goes on to note that Michael also delivered Hananiah, Mishael and Ananiah (i.e. the three friends in the fiery furnace in Daniel 3, otherwise known as Shadrach, Meshach and Abed-nego). In contrast to this view, in the Babylonian Talmud, *Pesaḥim* 118a records that the angel Gabriel wanted to deliver Abraham from Nimrod's fiery furnace, but God insisted on doing this himself.[36]

Other Jewish works also make reference to the incident of Abraham in the fiery furnace. For example, in the Babylonian Talmud, *'Erubin* 53a implies that Nimrod and Amraphel (the king of Babylon [Shinar] in Gen. 14) were two names of the same king. In that connection, Rab

34. Translation is taken from H. Freedman, *Midrash Rabbah: Genesis* (London: Soncino Press, 1939), pp. 310-11.

35. Translation from Freedman, *Midrash Rabbah: Genesis*, p. 369.

36. See I. Epstein (ed.), *The Babylonian Talmud*. VI. *Seder Mo'ed, Pesahim* (London: Soncino Press, 1938), pp. 608-609.

(Rabbi Arikha) is reported as claiming that Nimrod was called Amraphel 'Because he ordered our father Abraham to be cast into the fiery furnace' – Amraphel, it is fancifully implied, derives from *'mr*, 'he said', and *pl*, 'cast' (from *npl*, 'to cast').[37]

Later, perhaps in the early ninth century CE, *Pirḳe de Rabbi Eliezer*[38] also makes reference twice to the incident. In ch. 26 God's deliverance of Abraham from the fiery furnace is cited as the second of ten trials that Abraham had to undergo. Then, in ch. 52 Abraham's deliverance from the fiery furnace is recorded as the first time anyone was delivered by God in this way. This is cited as one of seven wonders of old.

Amongst the mediaeval Jewish commentators, Rashi and Nachmanides refer to the story of Abraham in the fire. Rashi writes:

> Terah complained to Nimrod that Abram had chopped up his idols, and Abram was thrown into a fiery furnace. Haran said to himself, 'If Abram wins, I will be on his side, but if Nimrod wins, I will be on his side'. When Abram emerged safely, they said to Haran, 'Which side are you on?' Haran said, 'I am on Abram's side'. They tossed him into the furnace, and he was burnt alive. That is the meaning of 'Ur' of the Chaldaeans – the Chaldaeans' furnace, though Menahem takes 'Ur' to mean 'valley'.[39]

We have clear echoes here of *Gen. Rab.* 38.13 in Haran's hedging his bets on whether to support Abraham or Nimrod, and subsequently losing his life in the fire after claiming he supported Abraham. There are also some parallels with Targum Pseudo-Jonathan, but *Genesis Rabbah* stands closer.

Nachmanides refers more briefly to the incident. He states

> Our Sages, of course, understood 'Ur' not as a place name, but as a common noun: fire, as in 'Ah, I am warm! I can feel the heat! (Isa. 44.16). Terah, of course, did not 'go forth' from the fiery furnace, but Abraham is the main actor there. And I suppose the place may have been named after the miracle, as were Taberah, Massah, Kibroth-hattaavah, and the like.[40]

37. See Epstein (ed.), *The Babylonian Talmud.* V. *Seder Moʿed, ʿErubin* (London: Soncino Press, 1938), p. 368.

38. See Gerald Friedlander, *Pirḳe de Rabbi Eliezer* (London: Kegan Paul, Trench, Trübner, 1916), pp. 188, 420.

39. Translation (Rashi on Gen. 11.28) is from Carasik (ed.), *Miqraot Gedolot*, pp. 105-106.

40. Translation of Nachmanides is from Carasik (ed.), *Miqraot Gedolot*, p. 106.

Even later in Jewish sources the story of Abraham in the fiery furnace is found in *Yalḳut Shimoni*, par. 77, *Yashar Noah* 27a, and *Zohar* 77b. It should also be noted that the incident is depicted in Hebrew manuscripts.[41]

James Kugel[42] claims that a variant of the fiery furnace story is to be found in the *Apocalypse of Abraham* (8.1-6), a work probably dating from the end of the first century CE. The text reads as follows:

> And it came to pass as I was thinking things like these with regard to my father Terah in the court of my house, the voice of the Mighty One came down from the heavens in a stream of fire, saying and calling, 'Abraham, Abraham!' And I said, 'Here I am'. And he said, 'You are searching for the God of gods, the Creator, in the understanding of your heart. I am he. Go out from Terah, your father, and go out of the house.' And I went out. And it came to pass, as I went out – I was not yet outside the entrance of the court – that the sound of a great thunder came and burned him and his house and everything in his house, down to the ground, forty cubits.[43]

However, in this story the fire comes down directly from God in heaven in the form of a thunderbolt rather than being the result of a man-made furnace, and Abraham is saved because he heeded God's warning to leave Terah's house, members of which are to be punished for their sins. Moreover, the story makes no mention of 'the fire of the Chaldaeans' or even of Chaldaea. Indeed, it is implied that the incident took place not there but in Haran, since Terah (as well as his household) died from the fire, and it is clearly stated in Gen. 11.32 that Terah died in Haran, where he had settled after leaving Ur. In the light of all these points, it does not appear likely that this particular story is a midrashic development from Genesis 11's references to Abraham going up from Ur of the Chaldaeans.

Christian Interpretations

From the late fourth century onwards we find Christian awareness of the Jewish story of Abraham in the fiery furnace. Jerome in his *Quaestiones Hebraicae in Genesim* on Gen. 11.28 (written *c.* 389–391) rejects the

41. See J. Gutmann, '"Abraham in the Fire of the Chaldaeans": A Jewish Legend in Jewish, Christian and Islamic Art', *Frühmittelalterliche Studien* 7 (1978), pp. 342-52 (345-47).

42. James Kugel, *Traditions of the Bible: A Guide to the Bible As It Was at the Start of the Common Era* (Cambridge MA: Harvard University Press, 1998), pp. 252-53.

43. Translation follows R. Rubinkiewicz, 'Apocalypse of Abraham', in Charlesworth (ed.), *Old Testament Pseudepigrapha*, I, pp. 681-705 (693).

Septuagint rendering '*in the land of the Chaldaeans*', maintaining that the Hebrew has '*in ur Chesdim*, that is in the fire of the Chaldaeans'. Jerome continues:

> Moreover, the Hebrews, taking the opportunity afforded by this verse, hand on a story of this sort to the effect that Abraham was put into the fire because he refused to worship fire, which the Chaldaeans honour; and that he escaped through God's help, and fled from the fire of idolatry. What is written [in the Septuagint] in the following verses, that Thara with his offspring 'went out from the land of the Chaldaeans' stands in place of what is contained in the Hebrew, *from the fire of the Chaldaeans*. And they maintain that this refers to what is said in this verse: *Aran died before the face of Thara his father in the land of his birth in the fire of the Chaldaeans*; that is, because, he refused to worship fire he was consumed by fire. Then afterwards the Lord spoke to Abraham: *I am the One who led you out of the fire of the Chaldaeans*.[44]

These last words, referring to Gen. 15.7, are repeated in Jerome's commentary on that latter verse. As Robert Hayward notes, 'Jerome accepts the truth of it; see his comments below on 12:4; *In Isa.* 18.65:8; *In Osee* 3.14:5-9; *In Zech.* 2.9:13; and his Vg translation of Neh. (2 Esdras) 9.7'. One should add that Abraham's refusing to worship the fire, which Jerome mentions, has echoes of *Gen. Rab.* 38.13.

In book 16, ch. 15 of his *City of God* (a work completed by 420), Augustine refers in passing to 'Abraham when he departed out of Haran from the time of his deliverance from the fire of the Chaldaeans'.[45] Much later, in the twelfth century, Peter Comestor in his *Historia Scholastica* notes that the Jews take Ur (Hur) to mean 'fire', whence they tell the story that Abraham and Haran (Aram) were unwilling to worship the fire, but Haran died and Abraham was delivered.[46]

It should also be noted that Syrian Christians devoted January 25th to commemorating Abraham's deliverance from the fire of the Chaldaeans.[47] Further, the incident was depicted in Christian manuscripts.[48]

---

44. Translation is from C.T.R. Hayward, *Saint Jerome's Hebrew Questions on Genesis* (Oxford: Oxford University Press, 1995), p. 43 (except I have substituted 'land of the Chaldaeans' for 'territory of the Chaldaeans' when referring to the LXX, for consistency with our LXX translation earlier).

45. Translation by R.W. Dyson, *Augustine, The City of God against the Pagans* (Cambridge: Cambridge University Press, 1998), p. 722.

46. See J.P. Migne, *PL* 198, col. 1091.

47. Cf. B. Beer, *Das Leben Abrahams nach Auffassung der jüdischen Sage* (Leipzig: O. Leiner, 1859), p. 113.

48. Gutmann, '"Abraham in the Fire of the Chaldaeans"', pp. 347-48.

Islam

Interestingly, the legend about Abraham in the fiery furnace, which is first attested among the Jews in the first century CE (with a precursor in the second century BCE), and became known to the Christians by the end of the fourth century, is attested in Islam from the seventh century onwards. It is well known that Muhammad took up various Jewish[49] (and Christian) sources known to him in Arabia on the basis of oral tradition, and the story of Abraham in the fiery furnace is one of these, found no fewer than three times in the Quran.

The fullest account is to be found in Surah 21 ('The Prophets'), lines 51-70. We read there that Abraham opposed the images which his father and the people were worshipping and got into an argument with the people about this. This ended with Abraham's breaking all the images in pieces, except that of their supreme god, in the hope that they might return to him. Outraged by this and Abraham's further arguments, Abraham was placed in the fire but God delivered him. The passage reads as follows:

> We bestowed guidance on Abraham, for We knew him well. He said to his father and to his people: 'What are these images to which you are so devoted?'
>
> They replied: 'They are the gods our fathers worshipped'.
>
> He said: 'Then you and your fathers are in the grossest error'.
>
> 'Is it the truth that you are preaching', they asked, 'or is this but a jest?'
>
> 'Indeed', he answered, 'your Lord is the Lord of the heavens and the earth. It was He that made them: to this I bear witness. By the Lord, I will overthrow your idols, as soon as you have turned your backs.'
>
> He broke them all in pieces, except their supreme god, so that they might return to Him.'
>
> 'Who has done this to our deities?' asked some. 'He must surely be a wicked man.'
>
> Others replied: 'We have heard a youth called Abraham speak of them'.
>
> 'They said: Then bring him here in sight of all the people, that they may act as witnesses.'
>
> 'Abraham', they said, 'was it you who did this to our deities?'
>
> 'No', he replied, 'It was their chief who smote them. Ask *them*, if they can speak.'
>
> Thereupon they turned their thoughts upon themselves and said to each other: 'Surely you are the ones who have done wrong'.
>
> Confounded as they were, they said to Abraham: 'You know they cannot speak'.

49. E.g. A. Geiger, *Was hat Mohammed aus dem Judenthume aufgenommen?* (Leipzig: M.W. Kaufmann, 1902).

He answered: 'Would you then worship that, instead of God, which can neither help nor harm you? Shame on you and on your idols! Have you no sense?'

They cried: 'Burn him and avenge your gods, if you must punish him!'

'Fire', We said, 'be cool to Abraham and keep him safe'.

They sought to lay a snare for him, but they themselves were ruined. We delivered him ...[50]

There is a striking series of parallels between this passage and that given in *Gen. Rab.* 38.13 cited above, suggesting strongly that the Quran is dependent on *Genesis Rabbah*, though Muhammad doubtless learnt of the story through oral tradition. First, in both accounts Abraham's father is an idol worshipper. Secondly, when his father was not around, Abraham smashed the idols except the chief one. Thirdly, when challenged, Abraham claimed that it was the chief idol which had smashed the others. Fourthly, Abraham was delivered up to be burnt. Fifthly, God delivered him from the fire. However, there are also a few differences, for example there is no explicit mention of Nimrod by name in the Quran, though this does occur in later Islamic literature – see below – and there is no dialogue between him and Abraham about specifically worshipping the fire.

Interestingly, God's words in the above Quranic passage, '"Fire", We said, "be cool to Abraham and keep him safe"' (Surah 21.69) are also somewhat similarly attested in a later work of the Jewish rabbi and kabbalist, Elijah HaKohen (died 1729), *Shevet Musar*, which is dependent on it.[51]

Surah 37 ('The Ranks') similarly recounts that Abraham condemned his father and his people for worshipping false deities, and likewise destroyed their idols.

The people came running to the scene. 'Would you worship that which you have carved with your hands', he said, 'when it was God who created you and all that you have made?'

They replied: 'Build up a pyre and cast him into the blazing flames'. Thus did they scheme against him but we abused them all.[52]

The final reference in the Quran to this incident comes in Surah 29 ('The Spider') but it is less detailed. However, again in the context of Abraham's rejection of idolatry we read:

50. Translation is from N.J. Dawood, *The Koran* (Penguin Classics; London: Penguin Books, 1990), pp. 230-31.

51. See M. Grünbaum, *Neue Beiträge zur semitischen Sagenkunde* (Leiden: Brill, 1893), p. 129.

52. Translation from Dawood, *The Koran*, p. 315.

His people's only reply was: 'Kill him!' or 'Burn him!'

But from the fire God delivered him. Surely in this there are signs for true believers.[53]

Within Islamic literature the story of Abraham in the fiery furnace is recounted in more detail later in al-Ṭabarī's *History*. This is far too long to recite here,[54] so I shall summarize the main points. We read that Abraham's father Āzar (= Terah) fled with his family from a town called Ur between al-Kufāh and al-Baṣrah. Abraham's father was a maker of idols, but Abraham discouraged people from buying them. Abraham brought food to the idols but they did not eat, and he also reproached them for not speaking. He further engaged in argument about God with the people, as well as with the king, Nimrod. Citing the Quran we read that Nimrod and his people joined against Abraham, saying, 'Burn him and stand by your gods, if you will be doing'[55] (cf. Quran, Surah 21.68). Further citing the Quran, we read that when they cast Abraham into the fire God declared, 'O fire! Be coolness and peace for Abraham', and the fire did as God ordered (Quran, Surah 21.69-70). Al-Ṭabarī also tells us that another person, a man-like angel, called the angel of shade (= protection), was seen in the fiery furnace. This was seen by the king, Nimrod, who asked Abraham if he could come out of the furnace, and he did. Further, Nimrod offered sacrifice to Abraham's God.

There are several interesting features about this story. First, it is striking that it still knows the name of the city of Ur and locates it accurately in between al-Kufāh and al-Baṣrah in southern Mesopotamia. Secondly, this is the first time in Islamic accounts that we learn that it was Nimrod who put Abraham in the fiery furnace. And thirdly, it is interesting that Abraham is accompanied in the furnace by a particular angel. This echoes some Jewish accounts in which the angel Michael or Gabriel is in the fiery furnace, and must ultimately reflect the story of Shadrach, Meshach and Abed-nego in the fiery furnace in Daniel 3, in which Nebuchadrezzar sees an angel with them in the fire (v. 25; cf. v. 28). Similarly, somewhat comparable to the story in al-Ṭabarī, we read in Dan. 3.26, 28 that Nebuchadrezzar called them out of the fiery furnace and blessed their God.

Finally, it should be noted that the incident is depicted in Islamic art.[56]

53. Translation is from Dawood, *The Koran*, p. 280.

54. See William M. Brinner (trans.), *The History of al-Ṭabarī*. II. *Prophets and Patriarchs* (Albany, NY: State University of New York Press, 1987), pp. 50-61.

55. That is, 'if you want to act'.

56. Gutmann, 'Abraham in the Fire of the Chaldaeans', pp. 349-51.

BIBLIOGRAPHY

Abou-Assaf, A., P. Bordreuil and A.R. Millard, *La statue de Tell Fekherye et son inscription assyro-araméenne* (Etudes assyriologiques, 7; Paris: Editions Recherche sur les civilisations, 1982).

Agrippa von Nettesheim, H.C., *De nobilitate et praecellentia foeminei sexus* (Geneva: Droz, 1529, reprinted 1990), ET *Female Pre-eminence: Or the Dignity and Excellency of that Sex, above the Male* (London: Million, 1670).

Albani, M., *Astronomie und Schöpfungsglaube. Untersuchungen zum Astronomischen Henochbuch* (WMANT, 68; Neukirchen-Vluyn: Neukirchener Verlag, 1994).

Albeck, Ch., *Das Buch der Jubiläen und die Halacha* (Berlin: Hochschule für die Wissenschaft des Judentums, 1930).

Albertz, R., '"Ihr werdet sein wie Gott". Gen 3, 1-7 auf dem Hintergrund des alttestamentlichen und des sumerisch-babylonischen Menschenbildes', *WO* 24 (1993), pp. 89-111.

Albright, W.F., 'Abraham the Hebrew', *BASOR* 163 (1961), pp. 36-54.

Albright, W.F., *Archaeology and the Religion of Israel* (Garden City, NY: Doubleday, 5th edn, 1969).

Albright, W.F., 'A Colony of Cretan Mercenaries on the Coast of the Negeb', *JPOS* 1 (1920–21), pp. 187-94.

Albright, W.F., 'Dedan', in *Geschichte und Altes Testament* (A. Alt Festschrift; Beiträge zur historischen Theologie, 16; Tübingen: J.C.B. Mohr [Paul Siebeck], 1955), pp. 1-12.

Albright, W.F., 'The End of Calneh in Shinar', *JNES* 3 (1944), pp. 254-55.

Alexander, P.S., '3 (Hebrew Apocalypse of) Enoch', in J.H. Charlesworth (ed.), *The Old Testament Pseudepigrapha*, I (2 vols.; London: Darton, Longman & Todd, 1983), pp. 223-313.

Alexander, P.S., 'From Son of Adam to Second God', in M.E. Stone and T.A. Bergren (eds.), *Biblical Figures outside the Bible* (Harrisburg, PA: Trinity Press International, 1998), pp. 87-122.

Alonso-Schökel, L., 'Motivos sapienciales y de allianza en Gn 2–3', *Bib* 43 (1962), pp. 295-316.

Amos, C., *The Book of Genesis* (Epworth Commentaries; Werrington: Epworth Press, 2004).

Anderson, B.W., 'Human Dominion over Nature', in M. Ward (ed.), *Biblical Studies in Contemporary Thought* (Burlington, VT: Trinity College Bible Institute, 1975), pp. 27-45.

Anderson, B.W., 'From Analysis to Synthesis: The Interpretation of Genesis 1–11', *JBL* 97 (1978), pp. 23-39.

Angerstorfer, A., 'Ebenbild eines Gottes in babylonischen und assyrischen Keilschrifttexten', *BN* 88 (1997), pp. 47-58.

Annus, A., *The God Ninurta in the Theology and Royal Ideology of Ancient Mesopotamia* (State Archives of Assyria Studies, 14; Helsinki: The Neo-Assyrian Text Project, 2002).

Annus, A., 'On the Origin of the Watchers: A Comparative Study of the Antediluvian Wisdom in Mesopotamian and Jewish Tradition', *JSP* 19 (2010), pp. 277-320.

Archi, A. *et al.*, *I nomi di luogi di testi di Ebla* (Rome: Missione archeologica Italiana in Siria, 1995).

Arneth, M., *Durch Adams Fall ist ganz verderbt: Studien zur Entstehung der alttestamentlichen Urgeschichte* (FRLANT, 217; Göttingen: Vandenhoeck & Ruprecht, 2007).

Arnold, B.T., *Genesis* (NCBC; Cambridge: Cambridge University Press. 2009).

Arnold, B.T., 'The Holiness Redaction of the Flood Narrative (Genesis 6:9–9:29', in B.T. Arnold, N.L. Erickson and J.H. Walton (eds.), *Windows to the Ancient World of the Hebrew Bible: Essays in Honor of Samuel Greengus* (Winona Lake, IN: Eisenbrauns, 2014), pp. 13-40.

Astour, M.C., 'Sabtah and Sabteca: Ethiopian Pharaoh Names in Genesis 10', *JBL* 84 (1965), pp. 422-25.

Baasten, M.F.J., 'A Note on the History of "Semitic"', in M.F.J. Baasten and W.T. van Peursen (eds.), *Hamlet on a Hill: Semitic and Greek Studies Presented to Professor T. Muraoka on the Occasion of his Sixty-Fifth Birthday* (Leuven: Peeters and Leuven Oriental Department, 2003), pp. 57-72.

Baden, J.S., '"His Tent": Pitched at the Intersection of Orthography and Source Criticism', in J. Lam, E. Reymond and H.H. Hardy (eds.), *Dennis Pardee Festschrift* (forthcoming).

Barker, M., *The Older Testament: The Survival of Themes from the Ancient Royal Cult in Sectarian Judaism and Early Christianity* (London: SCM Press, 1987).

Barker, M., 'Some Reflections upon the Enoch Myth', *JSOT* 15 (1980), pp. 7-29.

Barr, J., *Biblical Faith and Natural Theology* (Oxford: Clarendon Press, 1993).

Barr, J., *The Garden of Eden and the Hope of Immortality* (London: SCM Press, 1992).

Barr, J., 'The Image of God in the Book of Genesis: A Study in Terminology', *BJRL* 51 (1968–69), pp. 11-26, reprinted in J. Barton (ed.), *Bible and Interpretation: The Collected Essays of James Barr*. II. *Biblical Studies* (3 vols.; Oxford: Oxford University Press, 2013), pp. 66-77.

Barr, J., 'Man and Nature – The Ecological Controversy and the Old Testament', *BJRL* 55 (1972), pp. 9-32, reprinted in J. Barton (ed.), *Bible and Interpretation: The Collected Essays of James Barr*. II. *Biblical Studies* (3 vols.; Oxford: Oxford University Press, 2013), pp. 344-60.

Barr, J., 'Reflections on the Covenant with Noah', in A.D.H. Mayes and R.B. Salters (eds.), *Covenant as Context: Essays in Honour of E.W. Nicholson* (Oxford: Oxford University Press, 2003), pp. 11-22, reprinted in J. Barton (ed.), *Bible and Interpretation: The Collected Essays of James Barr*. II. *Biblical Studies* (3 vols.; Oxford: Oxford University Press, 2013), pp. 188-96.

Barr, J., '"Thou art the Cherub": Ezekiel 28.14 and the Post-Ezekiel Understanding of Genesis 2–3', in E.C. Ulrich *et al.* (eds.), *Priests, Prophets and Scribes: Essays on the Formation and Heritage of Second Temple Judaism in Honour of Joseph Blenkinsopp* (JSOTSup, 140; Sheffield: JSOT Press, 1992), pp. 213-22, reprinted in J. Barton (ed.), *Bible and Interpretation: The Collected Essays of James Barr*. II. *Biblical Studies* (3 vols.; Oxford: Oxford University Press, 2013), pp. 220-28.

Barr, J., 'Was Everything that God Created Really Good? A Question in the First Verse of the Bible', in T. Linafelt and T.K. Beal (eds.), *God in the Fray: A Tribute to Walter Brueggemann* (Minneapolis, MN: Fortress Press, 1998), pp. 55-65, reprinted in J. Barton (ed.), *Bible and Interpretation: The Collected Essays of James Barr*. II. *Biblical Studies* (3 vols.; Oxford: Oxford University Press, 2013), pp. 178-87.

Barth, K., *Kirchliche Dogmatik* 3.1 (Zollikon: Evangelischer Verlag, 1945), ET *Church Dogmatics* 3.1 (trans. G.W. Bromiley; Edinburgh: T. & T. Clark, 1958).

Bauks, M., *Die Welt am Anfang. Zur Verständnis von Vorwelt und Weltentstehung in Gen 1 und in der altorientalischen Literatur* (WMANT, 74; Neukirchen-Vluyn: Neukirchener Verlag, 1977).

Bauks, M., 'Sacred Trees in the Garden of Eden and their Ancient Near Eastern Precursors', *JAJ* 3 (2012), pp. 267-301.

Beal, R.H., 'The Location of Cilician Ura', *AnSt* 42 (1995), pp. 65-73.

Bechtel, L.M., 'Genesis 2.4b–3.24: A Myth about Human Maturation', *JSOT* 67 (1995), pp. 3-26.

Becker, J., *Messiaserwartung im Alten Testament* (SBS, 83; Stuttgart: Katholisches Bibelwerk, 1977), p. 29, ET *Messianic Expectation in the Old Testament* (trans. D.E. Green; Edinburgh: T. & T. Clark, 1980).

Becking, B., and M.C.A. Korpel, 'To Create, to Separate or to Construct: An Alternative for a Recent Proposal as to the Interpretation of ברא in Genesis 1.1–2.4a', *JHS* 10 (2010), article 3.

Beer, B., *Das Leben Abrahams nach Auffassung der jüdischen Sage* (Leipzig: O. Leiner, 1859).

Ben-Dov, J., 'The 364-Day Year in the Dead Sea Scrolls and Jewish Pseudepigrapha', in J.M. Steele (ed.), *Calendars and Years. II. Astronomy and Time in the Ancient and Medieval World* (Oxford: Oxbow Books, 2011), pp. 69-105.

Ben-Dov, J., *Head of All Years: Astronomy and Calendars at Qumran in their Ancient Context* (STDJ, 78; Leiden: Brill, 2008).

Berkouwer, C.G., *Man: The Image of God* (Grand Rapids, MI: Eerdmans, 1962).

Berman, J.A., 'Critiquing Source Criticism: The Story of the Flood', in *Ani Maamin: Biblical Criticism, Historical Truth, and the Thirteen Principles of Faith* (Jerusalem: Maggid, 2020), pp. 109-27.

Berman, J.A., *Inconsistency in the Torah: Ancient Literary Convention and the Limits of Source Criticism* (Oxford: Oxford University Press, 2017).

Bernard, R., *L'image de Dieu d'après saint Athanasius* (Paris: Aubier, 1952).

Bird, P., '"Male and Female He Created Them": Gen 1:27b in the Context of the Priestly Account of Creation', *HTR* 74 (1981), pp. 129-59, reprinted in P. Bird, *Missing Persons and Mistaken Identities: Women and Gender in Ancient Israel* (Minneapolis, MN: Fortress Press, 1997), pp. 123-54.

Black, M., *The Book of Enoch or 1 Enoch: A New English Edition with Commentary and Textual Notes* (SVTP, 7; Leiden: Brill, 1985).

Blenkinsopp, J., *Creation, Un-Creation, Re-Creation: A Discursive Commentary on Genesis 1–11* (London: T&T Clark, 2011).

Blenkinsopp, J., 'Gilgamesh and Adam: Wisdom through Experience in *Gilgamesh* and in the Biblical Story of the Man, the Woman, and the Snake', in *Treasures Old and New: Essays in the Theology of the Pentateuch* (Grand Rapids, MI: Eerdmans, 2004).

Blenkinsopp, J., *Isaiah 1–39* (AB, 19; New York: Doubleday, 2000).

Blenkinsopp, J., *The Pentateuch: An Introduction to the First Five Books of the Bible* (London: SCM Press, 1992).

Blum, E., *Studien zur Komposition des Pentateuch* (BZAW, 189; Berlin: W. de Gruyter, 1990).

Boccaccini, G. (ed.), *Enoch and the Messiah Son of Man: Revisiting the Book of Parables* (Grand Rapids, MI: Eerdmans, 2007).

Bockmuehl, M., '*Creatio ex Nihilo* in Palestinian Judaism and Early Christianity', *SJT* 65 (2012), pp. 253-70.

Bockmuehl, M., 'The Noachide Commandments and the New Testament Ethics: With Special Reference to Acts 15 and Pauline Halaka', *RB* 102 (1995), pp. 72-101.

Boer, P. de, 'Quelques remarques sur l'arc dans la nuée: Gen. 9:8-17', in C. Brekelmans (ed.), *Questions disputées d'Ancien Testament: Méthode et Théologie* (BETL, 33; Leuven: Leuven University Press, 1974), pp. 105-14.

Bokovoky, D.E., 'Did Eve Acquire, Create, or Procreate with Yahweh? A Grammatical and Contextual Reassessment of קנה in Genesis 4:1', *VT* 63 (2013), pp. 19-35.

Bonechi, M., *I nomi geographici dei testi di Ebla* (Répertoire géographique des textes cunéiformes, 12.1; Wiesbaden: L. Reichert, 1993).

Bonhoeffer, D., *Schöpfung und Fall* (Dietrich Bonhoeffer Werke, 3; Munich: Chr. Kaiser, [1933] 1989), ET *Creation and Fall: A Theological Exposition of Genesis 1–3* (Dietrich Bonhoeffer Works, 3; Minneapolis, MN: Fortress Press, 1988).

Borger, R., 'Das Problem der 'apīru („Habiru")', *ZDPV* 74 (1958), pp. 121-32.

Borger, R., 'Die Beschwörungsserie *bît mēseri* und die Himmelfahrt Henochs', *JNES* 33 (1974), pp. 183-96, reprinted in abbreviated English translation as 'The Incantation Series *Bît Mēseri* and Enoch's Ascension to Heaven', in Richard S. Hess and David T. Tsumura (eds.), *"I Studied Inscriptions from before the Flood": Ancient Near Eastern, Literary, and Linguistic Approaches to Genesis 1–11* (Sources for Biblical and Theological Study, 4; Winona Lake, IN: Eisenbrauns, 1994), pp. 234-53.

Borger, R., *Die Inschriften Asarhaddons, Königs von Assyrien* (AfO, 9; Graz: Im Selbstverlage des Herausgabers, 1956).

Bosshard-Nepustil, E., *Vor uns die Sintflut: Studien zu Text, Kontexten und Rezeption der Fluterzählung Genesis 6–9* (BWANT, 9.5; Stuttgart: Kohlhammer, 2005).

Bottéro, J., *Le problème des Ḫabiru* (Paris: Société asiatique, 1954).

Brandon, S.G.F., *Creation Legends of the Ancient Near East* (London: Hodder & Stoughton, 1963).

Breucker, G. de, 'Berossos between Tradition and Innovation', in K. Radner and E. Robson (eds.), *The Oxford Handbook of Cuneiform Literature* (Oxford: Oxford University Press, 2011), pp. 637-57.

Brinner, W.M. (trans.), *The History of al-Ṭabarī. II. Prophets and Patriarchs* (Albany, NY: State University of New York Press, 1987).

Brock, S.P., 'A Syriac Life of Abel', *Le Muséon* 87 (1974), pp. 467-92.

Brock-Utne, A., 'Die religionsgeschichtlichen Voraussetzungen der Ḳain-Abel-Geschichte', *ZAW* 54 (1936), pp. 202-39.

Brueggemann, W., *Genesis* (Interpretation; Atlanta, GA: John Knox Press, 1982).

Brunner, E., *Der Mensch im Widerspruch* (Berlin: Furche-Verlag, 1937), ET *Man in Revolt* (London: Lutterworth Press, 1939).

Bryce, T., *The Kingdom of the Hittites* (Oxford: Oxford University Press, 2005).

Budde, K., *Die biblische Urgeschichte (Gen. 1–12,5)* (Giessen: J. Ricker, 1883).

Budge, E.A.W., *The Queen of Sheba and her Only Son Menyelek (I)* (London: Oxford University Press [Humphrey Milford], 2nd edn, 1932).

Bührer, W., *Am Anfang... Untersuchungen zur Textgenese und zur relativ-chronologischen Einordnung von Gen 1–3* (FRLANT, 256; Göttingen: Vandenhoeck & Ruprecht, 2014).

Bührer, W., 'Göttersöhne und Menschentöchter. Gen 6,1-4 als innerbiblische Schriftauslegung', *ZAW* 123 (2011), pp. 395-515.

Bührer, W., 'Nimrod coram Domino – Nimrod coram Israhel [*sic*]: Inhalt und Tendenz der Nimrod-Notiz Gen 10,8-12', *BN* 173 (2017), pp. 3-22.

Bührer, W., 'The Relative Dating of *Gen 2–3', *VT* 65 (2015), pp. 365-76.

Burstein, S.M. (ed.), *The* Babyloniaca *of Berossus* (Sources and Monographs: Sources from the Ancient Near East, 1.5; Malibu, CA: Undena Publications, 1978).

Buttmann, P., *Mythologus, oder gesammelte Abhandlungen über die Sagen des Alterthums* (2 vols., Berlin: Mylius, 1828–29).

Byron, J., *Cain and Abel in Text and Tradition: Jewish and Christian Interpretations of the First Sibling Rivalry* (Themes in Biblical Narrative: Jewish and Christian Traditions, 14; Leiden: Brill, 2011).

Cairns, D., *The Image of God in Man* (London: Collins, rev. edn, 1973).

Calvin, J., *Commentaries on the First Book of Moses*, I (trans. J. King; Edinburgh: Calvin Translation Society, 1847).

Campbell, E.F., 'The Amarna Letters and the Amarna Period', in E.F. Campbell and D.N. Freedman (eds.), *The Biblical Archaeologist Reader*, III (Anchor Books; Garden City, NY: Doubleday, 1970), pp. 54-75.

Carasik, M. (ed.), *Miqraot Gedolot: The Commentators' Bible* (Philadelphia, PA: JPS, 2018).

Carr, D.M., *The Formation of Genesis 1–11: Biblical and Other Precursors* (New York: Oxford University Press, 2020).

Carr, D.M., 'The Politics of Textual Subversion: A Diachronic Perspective on the Garden of Eden Story', *JBL* 112 (1993), pp. 577-95.

Carr, D.M., *Reading the Fractures of Genesis: Historical and Literary Approaches* (Louisville, KY: Westminster/John Knox, 1996).

Cassuto, U.(M.D.), *A Commentary on the Book of Genesis*. I. *From Adam to Noah* (ET, trans. I. Abrahams; Jerusalem: Magnes Press, 1961).

Cassuto, U.(M.D.), *A Commentary on the Book of Genesis*. II. *From Noah to Abraham* (Jerusalem: Magnes Press, 1964).

Chambers, N.J., 'Genesis 1.1 as the First Act of Creation', *JSOT* 43 (2019), pp. 385-94.

Chambers, N.J., *Reconsidering Creatio ex Nihilo in Genesis 1* (Journal of Theological Interpretation Supplement, 19; University Park: Pennsylvania State University Press [Eisenbrauns], 2020).

Charlesworth, J.H., *The Good and Evil Serpent* (AYB Reference Library; New Haven, CT: Yale University Press, 2010).

Cheyne, T.K., 'Abel', in *Encyclopædia Biblica* (London: A. & C. Black, one-volume edn, 1914), col. 6.

Cheyne, T.K., 'Nimrod', in *Encyclopædia Biblica* (London: A. & C. Black, 1914), cols. 3417-19.

Childs, B.S., *Isaiah* (OTL; Louisville, KY: Westminster John Knox Press, 2001).

Childs, B.S., *Myth and Reality in the Old Testament* (SBT, 17; London: SCM Press, 1960).

Clark, W.A.M., 'A Legal Background to the Yahwist's Use of "Good and Evil" in Genesis 2–3', *JBL* 88 (1969), pp. 266-78.

Clements, R.E., *Isaiah 1–39* (NCB; Grand Rapids, MI: Eerdmans; London: Marshall, Morgan & Scott, 1980).

Clines, D.J.A., 'The Image of God in Man', *TynBul* 19, pp. 53-103, reprinted as 'Humanity as the Image of God', in *On the Way to the Postmodern: Old Testament Essays 1967–1998*, II (2 vols.; JSOTSup, 293, Sheffield: Sheffield Academic Press, 1998), pp. 447-97.

Clines, D.J.A., 'Putting Source Criticism in its Place: The Flood Story as a Test Case', in K.J. Dell and P.M. Joyce (eds.), *Biblical Interpretation and Method: Essays in Honour of John Barton* (Oxford: Oxford University Press, 2013), pp. 3-14.

Closen, G.E., 'Der «Dämon Sünde» (Ein Deutungversuch des massoretischen Textes von Gen 4,7)', *Bib* 16 (1935), pp. 431-42.

Collins, J.J., *The Apocalyptic Imagination* (Grand Rapids, MI: Eerdmans, 3rd edn., 2016).

Collins, J.J., 'The Heavenly Representative: The "Son of Man" in the Similitudes of Enoch', in J.J. Collins and G.W.E. Nickelsburg (eds.), *Ideal Figures in Ancient Judaism: Profiles and Paradigms* (SBLSCS, 12; Chico, CA: Scholars Press, 1980), pp. 111-33.

Collins, J.J., 'How Distinctive was Enochic Judaism?', *Meghillot* 5-6 (2007), pp. 17-34.

Collins, J.J., 'The Sons of God and the Daughters of Men', in M. Nissinen and R. Uro (eds.), *Sacred Marriages: The Divine–Human Sexual Metaphor from Sumer to Early Christianity* (Winona Lake, IN: Eisenbrauns, 2008), pp. 259-74.

Coppens, J., *La connaissance du bien et du mal et la péché du Paradis* (Gembloux: J. Duculot, 1948).

Cross, F.M., *Canaanite Myth and Hebrew Epic* (Cambridge, MA: Harvard University Press, 1973).

Crouch, C.L., 'Genesis 1:26-7 as a Statement of Humanity's Divine Parentage', *JTS* NS 61 (2010), pp. 1-15.

Dahood, M.J., 'Abraham's Reply in Genesis 20:11', *Bib* 61 (1981), pp. 90-91.

Dalley, S., 'The Influence of Mesopotamia upon Israel and the Bible', in S. Dalley (ed.), *The Legacy of Mesopotamia* (Oxford: Oxford University Press, 1998), pp. 57-83.

Darshan, G., *After the Flood: Stories of Origins in the Hebrew Bible and Eastern Mediterranean* (Biblical Encyclopaedia, 35; Jerusalem: Bialik Institute, 2018 [Hebrew]).

Darshan, G., 'The Biblical Account of the Post-Diluvian Generation (Gen. 9:20–10:32) in the Light of Greek Genealogical Literature', *VT* 63 (2013), pp. 515-35.

Darshan, G., 'The Calendrical Framework of the Priestly Flood Story in Light of a New Akkadian Text from Ugarit (RS 94.2953)', *JAOS* 136 (2016), pp. 507-14.

Darshan, G., '*Ruaḥ 'Elohim* in Genesis 1:2 in Light of Phoenician Cosmogonies: A Tradition's History', *JNSL* 45.2 (2019), pp. 51-78.

Davidson, R., *Genesis 1–11* (CBC; Cambridge: Cambridge University Press, 1973).

Dawood, N.J., *The Koran* (Penguin Classics; London: Penguin Books, 1990).

Davies, P.R., 'And Enoch was not, for Genesis took him', in C. Hempel and J.M. Lieu (eds.), *Biblical Traditions in Transmission: Essays in Honour of Michael A. Knibb* (Leiden: Brill, 2006), pp. 97-107.

Davies, P.R., 'The Sons of Cain', in J.D. Martin and P.R. Davies (eds.), *A Word in Season: Essays in Honour of William McKane* (JSOTSup, 42; Sheffield: Sheffield Academic Press, 1986), pp. 35-56.

Day, J., 'Cain and the Kenites', in G. Galil, M. Geller and A.R. Millard (eds.), *Homeland and Exile: Biblical and Ancient Near Eastern Studies in Honour of Bustenay Oded* (VTSup 130; Leiden: Brill, 2009), pp. 335-46, reprinted in J. Day (ed.), *From Creation to Babel: Studies in Genesis 1–11* (LHBOTS, 592; London: Bloomsbury T&T Clark, 2013), pp. 51-60.

Day, J., 'The Daniel of Ugarit and Ezekiel and the Hero of the Book of Daniel', *VT* 30 (1980), pp. 174-84.

Day, J., 'The Development of Belief in Life after Death in Ancient Israel', in J. Barton and D.J. Reimer (eds.), *After the Exile: Essays in Honour of Rex Mason* (Macon, GA: Mercer University Press, 1996), pp. 231-57.

Day, J., 'The Flood and the Ten Antediluvian Figures in Berossus and in the Priestly Source in Genesis', in J.K. Aitken, K.J. Dell and B.A. Mastin (eds.), *On Stone and Scroll: A Festschrift for Graham Ivor Davies* (BZAW 420; Berlin: W. de Gruyter, 2011), pp. 211-23, reprinted in expanded form in J. Day (ed.), *From Creation to Babel: Studies in Genesis 1–11* (LHBOTS, 592; London: Bloomsbury T&T Clark, 2013), pp. 61-76.

Day, J., 'Foreign Semitic Influence on the Wisdom of Israel and its Appropriation in the Book of Proverbs', in J. Day, R.P. Gordon and H.G.M. Williamson (eds.), *Wisdom in Ancient Israel: Essays in Honour of J.A. Emerton* (Cambridge: Cambridge University Press, 1995), pp. 55-70.

Day, J., *From Creation to Babel: Studies in Genesis 1–11* (LHBOTS, 592; London: Bloomsbury T&T Clark, 2013).

Day, J., 'The Genesis Flood Narrative in Relation to Ancient Near Eastern Flood Accounts', in K.J. Dell and P.M. Joyce (eds.), *Biblical Interpretation and Method: Essays in Honour of Professor John Barton* (Oxford: Oxford University Press, 2013), pp. 74-88, reprinted in J. Day, *From Creation to Babel: Studies in Genesis 1–11* (LHBOTS, 592; London: Bloomsbury T&T Clark, 2013), pp. 98-112.

Day, J., *God's Conflict with the Dragon and the Sea: Echoes of a Canaanite Myth in the Old Testament* (Cambridge: Cambridge University Press. 1985).

Day, J., 'How Could Job Be an Edomite?', in W.A.M. Beuken, *The Book of Job* (Leuven: Leuven University Press and Peeters, 1994), pp. 392-99.

Day, J., *Molech: A God of Human Sacrifice in the Old Testament* (UCOP, 41; Cambridge: Cambridge University Press, 1989).

Day, J., 'Noah's Drunkenness, the Curse of Canaan, Ham's Crime, and the Blessing of Shem and Japheth (Genesis 9.18-27)', in D. Baer and R.P. Gordon (eds.), *Leshon Limmudim: Essays on the Language and Literature of the Hebrew Bible in Honour of Andrew Macintosh* (LHBOTS, 593; London: Bloomsbury T&T Clark, 2014), pp. 31-44, republished in expanded form in J. Day, *From Creation to Babel: Studies in Genesis 1–11* (LHBOTS, 592; London: Bloomsbury T&T Clark, 2013), pp. 137-53.

Day, J., *The Recovery of the Ancient Hebrew Language: The Lexicographical Writings of D. Winton Thomas* (HBM, 20; Sheffield: Sheffield Phoenix Press, 2013).

Day, J., Review of I. German, *The Fall Reconsidered*, in *JSOT* 43.5 (2019), p. 165.

Day, J., 'Rooms or Reeds in Noah's Ark (Gen. 6.14)?', in *From Creation to Babel: Studies in Genesis 1–11* (LHBOTS, 592; London: Bloomsbury T&T Clark, 2013), pp. 113-22, reprinted as 'Rooms or Reeds in Noah's Ark? קנים in Genesis 6.14', in C. Gottlieb, C. Cohen and M. Gruber (eds.), *Visions of Life in Biblical Times in Honor of Meir Lubetski – A Tribute to his Scholarship, Teaching and Research* (HBM, 76; Sheffield: Sheffield Phoenix Press, 2015), pp. 47-57.

Day, J., 'The Sons of God and Daughters of Men and the Giants', *HBAI* 4.1 (2012), pp. 427-47, reprinted in J. Day, *From Creation to Babel: Studies in Genesis 1–11* (LHBOTS, 592; London: Bloomsbury T&T Clark, 2013), pp. 77-97.

Day, J., 'Whatever Happened to the Ark of the Covenant?', in J. Day (ed.), *Temple and Worship in Biblical Israel* (LHBOTS, 422; London: T&T Clark, 2005), pp. 250-70.

Day, J., 'Where was Tarshish?', in I. Provan and M.J. Boda (eds.), *Let us Go up to Zion: Essays in Honour of H.G.M. Williamson on the Occasion of his Sixty-Fifth Birthday* (VTSup, 153; Brill: Leiden, 2012), pp. 359-69; reworked as 'Where was Tarshish (Genesis 10.4)?', in J. Day, *From Creation to Babel: Studies in Genesis 1–11* (LHBOTS, 592; London: Bloomsbury T&T Clark, 2013), pp. 154-65.

Day, J., 'Why Does God "Establish" Rather than "Cut" Covenants in the Priestly Source?', in A.D.H. Mayes and R.B. Salters (eds.), *Covenant as Context: Essays in Honour of E.W. Nicholson* (Oxford: Oxford University Press, 2003), pp. 91-109, reprinted in J. Day, *From Creation to Babel: Studies in Genesis 1–11* (LHBOTS, 592; London: Bloomsbury T&T Clark, 2013), pp. 123-36.

Day, J., *Yahweh and the Gods and Goddesses of Canaan* (JSOTSup, 263; Sheffield: Sheffield Academic Press, 2000).

Day, P.L., *An Adversary in Heaven: śāṭān in the Hebrew Bible* (HSM, 43; Atlanta, GA: Scholars Press, 1988).

Deimel, A., 'Nimrod', *Or* 26 (1927), pp. 76-80.

Delcor, M., 'Le mythe de la chute des anges et de l'origine des géants comme explication du mal dans le monde dans l'apocalyptique juive. Histoire des traditions', *RHR* 190 (1976), pp. 3-53.

Delitzsch, Franz, *Neuer Commentar über die Genesis* (Leipzig: Dörffling & Franke, 5th edn, 1887), ET *A New Commentary on Genesis* (trans. S. Taylor; 2 vols.; Edinburgh: T. & T. Clark, 1888–89).

Delitzsch, Friedrich, *Wo lag das Paradies?* (Leipzig: J.C. Hinrichs, 1881).

Dershowitz, I., 'Man of the Land: Unearthing the Original Noah', *ZAW* 128 (2016), pp. 357-73.

Deurloo, K.A., 'תשוקה ›dependency‹, Gen 4,7', *ZAW* 99 (1987), pp. 405-6.

Dijk, J. van, 'Die Tontafeln aus dem *rēš*-Heiligtum', in H.J. Lenzen (ed.), *XVIII vorläufiger Bericht über die von dem Deutschen Archäologischen Institut und der Deutschen Orient-Gesellschaft aus dem Mitteln der Deutschen Forschungsgemeinschaft unternommenen Ausgrabungen in Uruk-Warka* (Berlin: Gebr. Mann, 1962), pp. 43-52.

Dijkstra, M., 'The Statue of SR 346 and the Tribe of the Kenites', in M. Augustin and K.-D. Schunck (eds.), *"Wünschet Jerusalem Frieden": Collected Communications to the XIIth Congress of the International Organization for the Study of the Old Testament, Jerusalem 1986* (Frankfurt: P. Lang, 1988), pp. 93-103.

Dillmann, A., *Die Genesis* (KEHAT; Leipzig: S. Hirzel, 3rd edn, 1886), ET *Genesis, Critically and Exegetically Expounded*, I (2 vols.; trans. W.B. Stevenson; Edinburgh: T. & T. Clark, 1897).

Dimant, D., 'Use and Interpretation of Mikra in the Apocrypha and Pseudepigrapha', in M.J. Mulder (ed.), *Mikra: Text, Translation, Reading of the Hebrew Bible in Ancient Judaism and Early Christianity* (Assen: Van Gorcum, 1988), pp. 379-419.

Doran, R., 'Pseudo-Eupolemus', in J.H. Charlesworth (ed.), *The Old Testament Pseudepigrapha*, II (2 vols.; London: Darton, Longman & Todd, 1983–85), pp. 873-82.

Dossin, G., 'Le site de Reḥoboth-'ir et de Resen', *Le Muséon* 47 (1934), pp. 107-21.

Drawnel, H., 'Moon Computation in the Aramaic Astronomical Book', *RevQ* 23 (2007), pp. 3-41.

Drawnel, H., Review of Kvanvig, *Primeval History*, in *The Biblical Annals/Roczike Biblijne* 2 (2012), pp. 355-61.

Driver, S.R., *The Book of Genesis: with Introduction and Notes* (Westminster Commentaries; London; Methuen, 1904).

Driver, S.R., 'Grammatical Notes. I. On Genesis II., 9b', *Hebraica* 2 (1885), p. 33.

Dubarle, A.M., *Les Sages d'Israël* (Lectio Divina, 1; Paris: Cerf, 1946).

Dyson, R.W., *Augustine, The City of God against the Pagans* (Cambridge: Cambridge University Press, 1998).

Ebeling, E., 'Ba'u', in E. Ebeling and B. Meissner (eds.), *Reallexikon der Assyriologie*, I (Berlin: W. de Gruyter, 1932), pp. 432-33.

Edzard, D.O., 'Kaldu', in D.O. Edzard *et al.* (eds.), *Reallexikon der Assyriologie*, V (Berlin: W. de Gruyter, 1976–80), pp. 291-97.

Eerdmans, B.D., *Die Komposition der Genesis* (Alttestamentliche Studien, I; Giessen: A. Töpelmann, 1908).

Ehrenzweig, A., 'Biblische und klassische Urgeschichte', *ZAW* 38 (1919–20), pp. 65-86.

Ehrenzweig, A., 'Kain und Lamech', *ZAW* 35 (1915), pp. 1-11.

Eichrodt, W., *Theologie des Alten Testaments* (2 vols.; Stuttgart: Klotz, 1957), ET *Theology of the Old Testament* (trans. J.A. Baker; 2 vols.; London: SCM Press, 1961).

Emerton, J.A., 'The Date of the Yahwist', in J. Day (ed.), *In Search of Pre-Exilic Israel* (JSOTSup, 406; London: T&T Clark, 2004), pp. 107-29.

Emerton, J.A., 'An Examination of Some Attempts to Defend the Unity of the Flood Narrative in Genesis', Part I, *VT* 37 (1987), pp. 401-20; Part II, *VT* 38 (1988), pp. 1-21.

Emerton, J.A., 'The Priestly Writer in Genesis', *JTS* NS 39 (1988), pp. 381-400.

Emerton, J.A., 'The Source Analysis of Genesis xi 27-32', *VT* 42 (1992), pp. 37-46.

Engnell, I., '"Knowledge" and "Life" in the Creation Story', in M. Noth and D.W. Thomas (eds.), *Wisdom in Israel and in the Ancient Near East Presented to Professor Harold Henry Rowley* (VTSup, 3; Leiden: Brill, 1955), pp. 103-19.

Eph'al, I., *The Ancient Arabs: Nomads on the Borders of the Fertile Crescent, 9th–5th Century B.C.* (Jerusalem: Magnes Press, 1982).

Epstein, I. (ed.), *The Babylonian Talmud. V. Seder Mo'ed, 'Erubin* (London: Soncino Press, 1938).

Epstein, I. (ed.), *The Babylonian Talmud. VI. Sefer Mo'ed, Pesahim* (London: Soncino Press, 1939).

Erman, A., 'נפתחים', *ZAW* 10 (1890), pp. 118-19.

Estes, D. (ed.), *The Tree of Life* (Themes in Biblical Narratives, 27; Leiden: Brill, 2020).

Ewald, H., 'Erklärung der Biblischen urgeschichte. 1, 4. Die geschlechter des ersten Weltalters', *Jahrbücher der Biblischen wissenschaft* [*sic*] (1853–54), pp. 1-19.

Fenton, T., 'Chaos in the Bible? Tohu vabohu', in G. Abramson and T. Parfitt (eds.), *Jewish Education and Learning: Published in Honour of Dr David Patterson on the Occasion of His Seventieth Birthday* (London: Harwood Academic Publishers, 1994), pp. 203-19.

Fenton, T., 'Nimrod's Cities: An Item from the Rolling Corpus', in K.J. Dell, G. Davies and Y.V. Koh (eds.), *Genesis, Isaiah and Psalms: A Festschrift to Honour Professor John Emerton on his Eightieth Birthday* (VTSup, 135; Leiden: Brill, 2010), pp. 23-31.

Fincke, J., *Die Orte- und Gewässernamen der Nuzi-Texte* (Répertoire géographique des textes cunéiformes, 10; Wiesbaden: Ludwig Reichert, 1993).

Finkel, I., *The Ark before Noah: Decoding the Story of the Flood* (London: Hodder & Stoughton, 2014).

Finkelstein, J.J., 'The Antediluvian Kings: A University of California Tablet', *JCS* 17 (1963), pp. 39-54.

Finkelstein, L., 'Some Examples of Maccabean Halaka', *JBL* 49 (1930, pp. 20-42, reprinted in L. Finkelstein, *Pharisaism in the Making: Selected Essays* (New York: Ktav, 1972), pp. 222-44.

Fischer, A. [A.K. Irvine], 'Ḳaḥṭān', in *The Encyclopaedia of Islam*, IV (Leiden: Brill, 2nd edn, 1978), pp. 447-49.

Fischer, G., *Genesis 1–11* (HThKAT; Freiburg: Herder, 2018).

Fishbane, M.A., *Biblical Interpretation in Ancient Israel* (Oxford: Clarendon Press, 1985).

Fitzmyer, J.A., *The Acts of the Apostles* (AB, 31; New York: Doubleday 1998).

Freedman, H., *Midrash Rabbah: Genesis* (London: Soncino Press, 1939).

Friedlander, G., *Pirḳe de Rabbi Eliezer* (London: Kegan Paul, Trench, Trübner, 1916).

Fröhlich, I., 'Origins of Evil in Genesis and the Apocalyptic Traditions', in S.W. Crawford and C. Wassén (eds.), *Apocalyptic Thinking in Early Judaism: Engaging with John Collins' The Apocalyptic Imagination* (JSJSup, 182; Leiden: Brill, 2018), pp. 141-59.

Gallus, T., *Die "Frau" in Gen 3,15* (Klagenfurt: Carinthia, 1979).

Gallus, T., *Interpretatio Mariologica Protoevangelii* (3 vols.; Rome: Edizioni di storia e letteratura, 1949–54).

Gardiner, A.H., *Ancient Egyptian Onomastica* (3 vols.; Oxford: Oxford University Press, 1947).

Garr, W.R., *In His Own Image and Likeness: Humanity, Divinity, and Monotheism* (CHANE, 15; Leiden: Brill, 2003).

Gaster, T.H., *Myth, Legend, and Custom in the Old Testament* (London: Duckworth, 1969).

Geiger, A., *Urschrift und Übersetzungen der Bibel* (Frankfurt: Madda, 2nd edn, 1928).

Geiger, A., *Was hat Mohammed aus dem Judenthume aufgenommen?* (Leipzig: M.W. Kaufmann, 1902).

Gelderen, C. van, 'Who Was Nimrod?', *The Expositor* (8th series) (1914), pp. 274-82.

George, A.R., *The Babylonian Gilgamesh Epic: Introduction, Critical Edition and Cuneiform Texts* (2 vols.; Oxford: Oxford University Press, 2003).

German, I., *The Fall Reconsidered* (Eugene, OR: Wipf & Stock [Pickwick Publications], 2016).

Gertz, J.C., *Das erste Buch Mose, Genesis. I. Die Urgeschichte Gen 1–11* (ATD, 1; Göttingen: Vandenhoeck & Ruprecht, 2018).

Gispen, W.H., 'Who Was Nimrod?', in J.H. Skilton, M.C. Fisher and L.W. Sloar (eds.), *The Law and the Prophets: Old Testament Studies Presented in Honor of Oswald Thompson Allis* (Nutley, NJ: Presbyterian and Reformed Publication Company, 1974), pp. 207-14.

Glassner, J.-J., *Mesopotamian Chronicles* (SBLWAW; Leiden: Brill, 2004).

Gmirkin, R.M., *Berossus and Genesis, Manetho and Exodus: Hellenistic Histories and the Date of the Pentateuch* (LHBOTS, 433; New York/London: T&T Clark, 2006).

Gnuse, R., *Misunderstood Stories: Theological Commentary on Genesis 1–11* (Eugene, OR: Wipf & Stock [Cascade Books], 2014).

Golka, F.W., 'Keine Gnade für Kain', in R. Albertz, H.-P. Müller, H.W. Wolff and W. Zimmerli (eds.), *Werden und Wesen des Alten Testaments. Festschrift für Claus Westermann zum 70. Geburtstag* (Göttingen: Vandenhoeck & Ruprecht; Neukirchen-Vluyn: Neukirchener Verlag, 1980), pp. 58-73.

Gordis, R., 'The Knowledge of Good and Evil in the Old Testament and the Qumran Scrolls', *JBL* 76 (1957), pp. 123-38.

Gordon, C.H., 'Abraham and the Merchants of Ura', *JNES* 17 (1958), pp. 28-31.

Gordon, C.H., 'Abraham of Ur', in D.W. Thomas and W.D. McHardy (eds.), *Hebrew and Semitic Studies Presented to G.R. Driver* (Oxford: Clarendon Press, 1963, pp. 77-84.

Gordon, C.H., 'Where is Abraham's Ur?', *BARev* 3.2 (June, 1977), pp. 20-21.

Gordon, R.P., '"Couch" or "Crouch"? Genesis 4:7 and the Temptation of Cain', in J.K. Aitken, K.J. Dell and B.A. Mastin (eds.), *On Stone and Scroll: Essays in Honour of Graham Ivor Davies* (BZAW, 420; Berlin: W. de Gruyter, 2011), pp. 195-209.

Goren, Y., S. Buminovitz, I. Finkelstein and N. Na'aman, 'The Location of Alashiya: New Evidence from Petrographic Investigation of Alashiyan Tablets from El-Amarna and Ugarit', *AJA* 107 (1993), pp. 233-55.

Goren, Y., H. Mommsen, I. Finkelstein and N. Na'aman, 'A Provenance Study of the Gilgamesh Fragment from Megiddo', *Archaeometry* 51 (2009), pp. 763-73.

Görg, M., 'Kain und das "Land Nod"', *BN* 71 (1994), pp. 5-12.

Göttsberger, J., 'וְשֹׁוֹא יָצוֹא in Gn 8,7', *BZ* 6 (1908), pp. 13-16.

Grant, M., *The Etruscans* (London: Weidenfeld & Nicolson, 1980).

Gray, J., *I & II Kings: A Commentary* (OTL; London: SCM Press, 1977).

Greenberg, M., *The Ḫab/piru* (New Haven, CN: American Oriental Society, 1955).

Greenfield, J.C., 'Elishah', in *IDB*, II, p. 92.

Greenfield, J.C., and Michael E. Stone, 'The Enochic Pentateuch and the Date of the Similitudes', *HTR* 70 (1977), pp. 51-65.

Greenfield, J.C., and Michael E. Stone (eds.), 'The Books of Enoch and the Traditions of Enoch', *Numen* 26 (1979), pp. 89-103.

Gregg, J.A.F., *The Wisdom of Solomon* (CBSC; Cambridge: Cambridge University Press, 1909).

Grelot, P., 'La légende d'Hénoch dans les Apocryphes et dans la Bible: Origine et signification [part 1]', *RSR* 46 (1958), pp. 5-26.

Grelot, P., 'La légende d'Hénoch dans les Apocryphes et dans la Bible: Origine et signification [part 2]', *RSR* 46 (1958), pp. 181-210.

Gressmann, H., 'Mythische Reste in der Paradieserzählung', *ArRel* 10 (1907), pp. 345-67.

Grivel, J., 'Nemrod et les écritures cunéiformes', *TSBA* 3 (1874), pp. 136-44.

Groom, N., *Frankincense and Myrrh: A Study of the Arabian Incense Trade* (London: Longman, 1981).

Gross, W., 'Die Gottebenbildlichkeit des Menschen nach Gen 1,26.27 in der Diskussion des letzten Jahrzehnts', *BN* 68 (1993), pp. 35-48.

Grossfeld, B., *Targum Onqelos: Genesis* (The Aramaic Bible, 6; Edinburgh: T. & T. Clark, 1988).

Gruber, M., 'The Tragedy of Cain and Abel: A Case of Depression', *JQR* 69 (1978), pp. 89-97.

Gruber, M., 'Was Cain Angry or Depressed?', *BARev* 6.6 (Nov./Dec. 1980), pp. 34-36.

Grünbaum, M., *Neue Beiträge zur semitischen Sagenkunde* (Leiden: Brill, 1893).

Gunkel, H., *Genesis* (HKAT, 1.1; Göttingen: Vandenhoeck & Ruprecht, 3rd edn, 1910), ET *Genesis* (trans. M.E. Biddle; Macon, GA: Mercer University Press, 1997).

Gunkel, H., *Schöpfung und Chaos in Urzeit und Endzeit* (Göttingen: Vandenhoeck & Ruprecht, 1895), ET *Creation and Chaos in the Primeval Era and the Eschaton* (trans. K.W. Whitney Jr; Grand Rapids, MI: Eerdmans, 2006).

Gutmann, J., '"Abraham in the Fire of the Chaldaeans": A Jewish Legend in Jewish, Christian and Islamic Art', *Frühmittelalterliche Studien* 7 (1978), pp. 342-52.

Hamilton, V.P., *The Book of Genesis: Chapters 1–17* (NICOT; Grand Rapids, MI: Eerdmans, 1990).

Haenchen, E., *Die Apostelgeschichte* (Göttingen: Vandenhoeck & Ruprecht, 14th edn, 1965), ET, *The Acts of the Apostles: A Commentary* (trans. B. Noble, G. Shinn, H. Anderson and R. McL. Wilson; Oxford: Blackwell, 1971).

Hall, D.J., *Imaging God: Dominion as Stewardship* (Grand Rapids, MI: Eerdmans, 1986).

Hallo, W.W., 'Antediluvian Cities', *JCS* 23 (1970), pp. 57-67.

Harland, P.J., *The Value of Human Life: A Study of the Story of the Flood (Genesis 6–9)* (VTSup, 64; Leiden: Brill, 1996).

Harrak, A., 'The Ancient Name of Edessa', *JNES* 5 (1992), pp. 209-14.

Harrington, D.J., 'Pseudo-Philo', in J.H. Charlesworth (ed.), *The Old Testament Pseudepigrapha*, II (2 vols.; London: Darton, Longman & Todd, 1983–85), pp. 297-377.

Hartman, L., 'Sin in Paradise', *CBQ* 20 (1958), pp. 26-40.

Hasel, G., 'The Genealogies of Gen 5 and 11 and their Alleged Babylonian Background', *AUSS* 16 (1978), pp. 361-74.

Haupt, P., 'The Language of Nimrod, the Kashite', *Andover Review* 2 (1884), pp. 88-98.

Hayward, C.T.R., 'Pirqe de Rabbi Eliezer and Targum Pseudo-Jonathan', *JJS* 42 (1991), pp. 215-46.

Hayward, C.T.R., *Saint Jerome's Hebrew Questions on Genesis* (Oxford: Oxford University Press, 1995).

Hehn, J., 'Zum Terminus „Bild Gottes"', in G. Weil (ed.), *Festschrift Eduard Sachau zum siebzigsten Geburtstage* (Berlin: G. Reimer, 1915), pp. 36-52.

Heidel, A., *The Babylonian Genesis* (Chicago, IL: University of Chicago Press, 2nd edn, 1951).

Helck, *Die altäyptische Gaue* (Wiesbaden: L. Reichert, 1974).

Heller, J., 'Der Name *Eva*', *ArOr* 26 (1958), pp. 634-56.

Hendel, R.S., '"Begetting" and "Being Born" in the Pentateuch: Notes on Historical Linguistics and Source Criticism', *VT* 50 (2000), pp. 38-46.

Hendel, R.S., *Genesis 1–11* (AYB, 1; New Haven: Yale University Press, forthcoming).

Hendel, R.S., 'Genesis 1–11 and its Mesopotamian Problem', in E.S. Gruen (ed.), *Cultural Borrowings and Ethnic Applications in Antiquity* (Oriens et Occidens, 8; Stuttgart: Franz Steiner Verlag, 2005), pp. 23-36.

Hendel, R.S., 'Historical Context', in C.A. Evans, J.N. Lohr and D. Petersen (eds.), *The Book of Genesis: Composition, Reception, and Interpretation* (VTSup, 152; Leiden: Brill, 2012), pp. 51-82.

Hendel, R.S., 'Nimrod', in B.M. Metzger and M.D. Coogan (eds.), *The Oxford Guide to People and Places of the Bible* (New York: Oxford University Press, 2001), p. 218.

Hendel, R.S., *The Text of Genesis 1–11: Textual Studies and Critical Edition* (New York: Oxford University Press, 1998).

Hendel, R.S., and J. Joosten, *How Old Is the Hebrew Bible?* (AYB Reference Library; New Haven, CT: Yale University Press, 2018).

Herion, G.A., 'Why God Rejected Cain's Offering: The Obvious Answer', in A.B. Beck *et al.* (eds.), *Fortunate the Eyes that See: Essays in Honor of David Noel Freedman in Celebration of his Seventieth Birthday* (Grand Rapids, MI: Eerdmans, 1985), pp. 52-65.

Herzog, R., *Punt* (Abhandlungen des deutschen archäologischen Instituts Kairo, Ägyptologische Reihe, 6; Glückstadt: J.J. Augustin, 1968).

Hibbard, J.T., *Intertextuality in Isaiah 24–27: The Reuse and Evocation of Earlier Texts and Traditions* (FAT, 2. Reihe 16; Tübingen: Mohr Siebeck, 2006).

Hibbard, J.T., 'Isaiah 24–27 and Trito-Isaiah: Some Connections', in J.T. Hibbard and H.C.P. Kim (eds.), *Formation and Intertextuality in Isaiah 24–27* (Atlanta, GA: SBL, 2013), pp. 183-199.

Hoekema, A., *Created in God's Image* (Grand Rapids: Eerdmans, 1986).

Hoffmann, D., 'Probleme der Pentateuchexegese', *Jeschurun* 1 (1914), pp. 114-19.

Holmstedt, R.D., 'The Restrictive Syntax of Genesis i 1', *VT* 58 (2008), pp. 56-67.

Hölscher, G., *Drei Erdkarten. Ein Beitrag zur Erdkenntnis des hebräischen Altertums* (Sitzungsberichte der Heidelberger Akademie der Wissenschaften, Phil.-hist. Klasse, 1944–48; Heidelberg: Carl Winter, 1949).

Holsinger-Friesen, T., *Irenaeus and Genesis* (Journal of Theological Interpretation, Supplements, 1; Winona Lake, IN: Eisenbrauns, 2009).

Holzinger, H., *Genesis* (KHAT, 1; Freiburg: J.C.B. Mohr [Paul Siebeck], 1898).

Hooke, S.H., 'Cain and Abel', *Folk-Lore* 50 (1939), pp. 58-65, reprinted in S.H. Hooke, *The Siege Perilous* (London: SCM Press, 1956), pp. 66-73.

Hoopen, R.B. ten, 'Where Are You, Enoch? Why Can't I Find You? Genesis 5:21-24 Reconsidered', *JHS* 18 (2018), article 4.

Horowitz, M.C., 'The Image of God in Man – Is Woman Included?', *HTR* 72 (1979), pp. 175-206.

Horowitz, W., 'The 360 and 364 Day Year in Ancient Mesopotamia', *JANES* 24 (1996), pp. 20-44.

Horowitz, W., 'The 364 Day Year in Mesopotamia, Again', *NABU* (1998), pp. 49-51 (no. 49).

Horowitz, W., 'The Isles of the Nations: Genesis x and Babylonian Geography', in J.A. Emerton (ed.), *Studies in the Pentateuch* (VTSup, 41; Leiden: Brill, 1990), pp. 35-43.

Horowitz, W., *Mesopotamian Cosmic Geography* (Mesopotamian Civilizations, 8; Winona Lake, IN: Eisenbrauns, 1998).

Horst, F., 'Face to Face: The Biblical Doctrine of the Image of God', *Int* 4 (1950), pp. 259-70.

Humbert, P., *Etudes sur le récit du Paradis et de la chute dans la Genèse* (Neuchâtel: University of Neuchâtel, 1940).

Humbert, P., '*Qānā* en hébreu biblique', in W. Baumgartner, O. Eissfeldt, K. Elliger and L. Rost (eds.), *Festschrift Alfred Bertholet zum 80. Geburtstag* (Tübingen: J.C.B. Mohr [Paul Siebeck], 1950), pp. 259-66, reprinted in P. Humbert, *Opuscules d'un Hébraïsant* (Neuchâtel: University of Neuchâtel, 1958), pp. 166-74.

Hurowitz, V.A., 'In Search of Resen (Genesis 10:12): Dur-Šarrukīn?', in C. Cohen *et al.* (eds.), *Birkat Shalom: Studies in the Bible, Ancient Near Eastern Literature, and Postbiblical Judaism Presented to Shalom M. Paul on his Seventieth Birthday*, I (2 vols.; Winona Lake, IN: Eisenbrauns, 2008), pp. 511-24.

Husser, J.-M., 'Entre mythe et philosophie. La relecture sapientielle de Genèse 2–3', *RB* 107 (2000), pp. 232-59.

Hvidberg, F.F., 'The Canaanitic Background of Gen. i–iii', *VT* 10 (1960), pp. 285-94.

Izre'el, S., *Adapa and the South Wind: Language has the Power of Life and Death* (Winona Lake, IN: Eisenbrauns, 2001).

Jacob, B., *Das erste Buch der Tora: Genesis* (Berlin: Schocken Verlag, 1934).

Jacobsen, T., *The Sumerian King List* (Assyriological Studies, 11: Chicago, IL: University of Chicago Press, 1939).

Jacobus, H.R., *Zodiac Calendars in the Dead Sea Scrolls and their Reception* (IJS, 14; Leiden: Brill, 2014).

Jacoby, F., *Die Fragmente der griechischen Historiker* (14 vols.; Leiden: Brill, 1923–58).

Janowski, B., 'Gottebenbildlichkeit', in *RGG⁴*, III (Tübingen: Mohr Siebeck, 2000), cols. 1159-60, ET 'Image of God', *Religion Past & Present*, VI (Leiden: Brill, 2009), pp. 414-15.

Janowski, B., and A. Krüger, 'Gottes Sturm und Gottes Atem. Zum Verständnis von רוח אלהים in Gen 1,2 und Ps 104,29f', *JBTh* 24 (2009), pp. 3-29.

Jansen, H.L., *Die Henochgestalt: Eine vergleichende religionsgeschichtliche Untersuchung* (Det Norske Videnskaps-Akademi I Oslo, II. Hist.-Phil. Klasse, 1939, No. 1; Oslo: Jacob Dybwad, 1939).

Jaroš, K., 'Die Motive der heiligen Bäume und der Schlange in Gen 2–3', *ZAW* 92 (1980), pp. 204-15.

Jastrow, M., *A Dictionary of the Targumim, the Talmud Babli and Yerushalmi, and Other Midrashic Literature* (2 vols.; New York: Pardes, 1950 reprint).

Jensen, P., *Das Gilgamesch-Epos in der Weltliteratur*, I (Strasbourg: J. Trübner, 1906).

Jensen, P., *Die Kosmologie der Babylonier: Studien und Materiallen* (Strasbourg: Trübner, 1890).

Jensen, P., Review of J.F. McCurdy, *History, Prophecy and the Monuments*, I (New York and London: Macmillan, 1894), in *TLZ* 20 (1895), cols. 508-10.

Jervell, J., *Imago Dei: Gen 1, 26f im Spätjudentum, in der Gnosis und in den paulinischen Briefen* (FRLANT, NF 58; Göttingen: Vandenhoeck & Ruprecht, 1960).

Jirku, A., 'Nimrod', *OLZ* 20 (1917), cols. 169-72.

Johnson, D.G., *From Chaos to Restoration: An Integrative Reading of Isaiah 24–27* (JSOTSup, 61; Sheffield: Sheffield Academic Press, 1988).

Joines, K.R., 'The Bronze Serpent in the Israelite Cult', *JBL* 87 (1965), pp. 245-58.

Joines, K.R., *Serpent Symbolism in the Old Testament* (Haddonfield, NJ: Haddonfield House, 1974), pp. 63-73.

Jónsson, G.A., *The Image of God: Genesis 1:26-28 in a Century of Old Testament Research* (ConBOT, 26, Lund: Almqvist & Wiksel, 1988).

Kaiser, O., *Der Prophet Jesaja, Kapitel 13–39* (ATD, 18; Göttingen: Vandenhoeck & Ruprecht, 1973), ET *Isaiah 13–39* (trans. R.A. Wilson; OTL; London: SCM Press, 1974).

Keel, O., *Vögel als Boten: Studien zu Ps 68,12-14; Gen 8,6-12; Koh 10,20 und dem Aussenden von Botenvögeln in Ägypten* (OBO, 14: Freiburg: Universitätsverlag; Göttingen: Vandenhoeck & Ruprecht, 1967).

Kidner, F.D., *Genesis* (TOTC; London: Tyndale, 1967).

Kikawada, I.M., 'Two Notes on Eve', *JBL* 91 (1972), pp. 33-37.

Kikawada, I.M., and A. Quinn, *Before Abraham Was: The Unity of Genesis 1–11* (Nashville, TN: Abingdon Press, 1985; reprinted San Francisco, CA: Ignatius Press, 1989).

Kilmer, A.D., 'The Symbolism of the Flies in the Mesopotamian Flood Myth and Some Further Implications', in F. Rochberg-Halton (ed.), *Language, Literature, and History: Philological and Historical Studies Presented to Erica Reiner* (AOS Series, 67; New Haven, CT: American Oriental Society, 1987), pp. 175-80.

Kitchen, K.A., 'Punt and How to Get There', *Or* NS 40 (1971), pp. 184-207.

Kitz, A.M., 'Demons in the Hebrew Bible and the Ancient Near East', *JBL* 135 (2016), pp. 447-64.

Knauf, E.A., *Midian: Untersuchungen zur Geschichte Palästinas und Nordarabiens am Ende des 2. Jahrtausends v. Chr.* (Abhandlungen der deutschen Palästinavereins; Wiesbaden: O. Harrassowitz, 1988).

Knohl, I., 'Nimrod, Son of Cush, King of Mesopotamia, and the Dates of P and J', in C. Cohen *et al.* (eds.), *Birkat Shalom: Studies in the Bible, Ancient Near Eastern Literature, and Postbiblical Judaism Presented to Shalom M. Paul on the Occasion of his Seventieth Birthday*, I (2 vols.; Winona Lake, IN: Eisenbrauns, 2008), pp. 45-52.

Koch, J., 'AO 6478, MUL.APIN und das 364 Tage Jahr', *NABU* (1996), pp. 97-99 (no. 111).

Koch, J., 'Ein für allemal: Das antike Mesopotamien kannte kein 364 Tage-Jahr', *NABU* (1998), pp. 112-14 (no. 121).

Koch, K., 'The Astral Laws as the Basis of Time, Universal History and the Eschatological Turn in the Astronomical Book and the Animal Apocalypse of 1 Enoch', in G. Boccaccini and J.J. Collins (eds.), *The Early Enoch Literature* (JSJSup, 121; Leiden: Brill, 2007), pp. 119-37.

Koch, K., 'P – Kein Redaktor! Erinnerung an zwei Eckdaten der Quellenscheidung', *VT* 37 (1987), pp. 446-67.

Koehler, L., 'Die Grundstelle der Imago-Dei-Lehre', *TZ* 4 (1948), pp. 16-22.

Koenig, Y., 'Les textes d'envoûtement de Mirgissa', *REg* 41 (1990), pp. 101-25.

König, F.W., *Die Persika des Ktesias von Knidus* (AfO, Beiheft 18; Graz: E. Weidner, 1972).

Kooij, A. van der, 'The City of Babel and Assyrian Imperialism: Genesis 11:1-9 Interpreted in the Light of Mesopotamian Sources', in A. Lemaire (ed.), *Congress Volume: Leiden, 2004* (VTSup, 109; Leiden: Brill, 2006), pp. 1-17.

Kooij, A. van der, *The Oracle of Tyre: The Septuagint of Isaiah XXIII as Version and Vision* (VTSup, 71; Leiden: Brill, 1998).

Korpel, M.C.A., and J.C. de Moor, *Adam, Eve, and the Devil: A New Beginning* (Hebrew Bible Monographs, 65; Sheffield: Sheffield Phoenix Press, 2014). Subsequent revised Dutch edition, *Adam, Eva en de Duivel: Kanaänitische Mythen en de Bijbel* (Vught: Skandalon, 2016).

Kraeling, E.G.H., 'The Origin and Real Name of Nimrod', *AJSL* 38 (1922), pp. 214-20.

Kratz, R., *Die Komposition der erzählenden Bücher des Alten Testaments. Grundwissen der Bibelkritik* (UTB, 2137; Göttingen: Vandenhoeck & Ruprecht, 2000), pp. 252-63, ET *The Composition of the Narrative Books of the Old Testament* (trans. J. Bowden; London: T&T Clark, 2005).

Krüger, T., 'Das menschliche Herz und die Weisung Gottes: Elemente einer Diskussion über Möglichkeiten und Grenzen der Tora-Rezeption im Alten Testament', in R.G. Kratz and T. Krüger (eds.), *Rezeption und Auslegung im Alten Testament und in seinem Umfeld. Ein Symposion aus Anlass des 60. Geburtstags von Odil Hannes Steck* (Fribourg: Universitätsverlag; Göttingen: Vandenhoeck & Ruprecht, 1997), pp. 65-92.

Kübel, P., 'Ein Wortspiel in Genesis 3 und sein Hintergrund. Die „kluge" Schlange und die „nackten" Menschen. Überlegungen zur Vorgeschichte von Gen 2–3', *BN* 93 (1998), pp. 11-22.

Kugel, J., *Traditions of the Bible: A Guide to the Bible As It Was at the Start of the Common Era* (Cambridge MA: Harvard University Press, 1998).

Kupper, J.R., 'Sutéens et Ḫapiru', *RA* 55 (1961), pp. 197-205.

Kvanvig, H., *Primeval History: Babylonian, Biblical, and Enochic: An Intertextual Reading* (JSJSup, 149; Leiden: Brill, 2011).

Kvanvig, H., *Roots of Apocalyptic: The Mesopotamian Background of the Enoch Figure and of the Son of Man* (WMANT, 61; Neukirchen-Vluyn: Neukirchener Verlag, 1988).

Lambert, W.G., 'Assyrien und Israel', in G. Krause and G. Müller (eds.), *Theologische Realenzyklopädie*, IV (Berlin: W. de Gruyter, 1979), pp. 265-77.

Lambert, W.G., *Babylonian Creation Myths* (Winona Lake, IN: Eisenbrauns, 2013).

Lambert, W.G., 'Enmeduranki and Related Matters', *JCS* 21 (1967), pp. 126-38.

Lambert, W.G., 'A New Look at the Babylonian Background of Genesis', *JTS* NS 16 (1965), pp. 287-300, reprinted in expanded format in R.S. Hess and D.T. Tsumura (eds.), *"I Studied Inscriptions from before the Flood: Ancient Near Eastern, Literary, and Linguistic Approaches to Genesis 1–11* (Winona Lake, IN: Eisenbrauns, 1994), pp. 96-113.

Lambert, W.G., 'The Qualifications of Babylonian Diviners', in S.M. Maul (ed.), *Festschrift für Rykle Borger zu seinem 65. Geburtstag am 24. Mai 1994* (Cuneiform Monographs, 10; Groningen: Styx, 1998), pp. 141-58.

Lambert, W.G., 'Trees, Snakes and Gods in Ancient Syria and Anatolia', *BSOAS* 48 (1985), pp. 435-51.

Lambert, W.G., and A.R. Millard, *Atra-ḫasīs: The Babylonian Story of the Flood* (Oxford: Clarendon Press, 1969).

Landsberger, B., and J.V. Kinnier Wilson, 'The Fifth Tablet of Enuma eliš', *JNES* 20 (1961), pp. 154-79.

Layton, S., 'Remarks on the Canaanite Origin of Eve', *CBQ* 59 (1997), pp. 22-32.

Leeuwen, N.D. van, 'Wie waren Kus en Nimrod?', *Gereformeerd Theologisch Tijdschrift* 21 (1921), pp. 18-31.

Lemaire, A., 'Tarshish-*Tarsisi*: problème de topographie historique biblique et assyrienne', in G. Galil and M. Weinfeld (eds.), *Studies in Historical Geography and Biblical Historiography Presented to Zecharia Kallai* (VTSup, 81; Leiden: Brill, 2000), pp. 44-62.

Levenson, J.D., *Creation and the Persistence of Evil* (San Francisco: Harper & Row, 1988).

Levin, C., *Der Jahwist* (FRLANT, 157; Göttingen: Vandenhoeck & Ruprecht, 1993).

Levin, Y., 'Nimrod the Mighty, King of Kish, King of Sumer and Akkad', *VT* 52 (2002), pp. 350-66.

Levinson, B., 'A Post-Priestly Harmonization in the Flood Narrative', in F. Giuntoli and K. Schmid (eds.), *The Post-Priestly Pentateuch* (Tübingen: Mohr Siebeck, 2015), pp. 113-23.

Levison, J.R., 'Is Eve to Blame? A Contextual Study of Sirach 24:24', *CBQ* 47 (1985), pp. 617-23.

Lewis, J.P., 'The Woman's Seed (Gen 3:15)', *JETS* 34 (1991), pp. 299-319.

Lewis, J.P., 'The Offering of Abel (Gen 4:4): A History of Interpretation', *JETS* 37 (1994), pp. 481-96.

Lewy, H., 'Nitokris-Naqî'a', *JNES* 11 (1952), pp. 264-86.

L'Hour, J., *Genèse 1–2,4a. Commentaire* (Etudes bibliques, NS 71; Leuven: Peeters, 2016).

Lidzbarski, M., 'Eine punische *tabella devotionis*', in *Ephemeris für semitische Epigraphik* (Giessen: J. Ricker, 1902), pp. 26-34.

Lipiński, E., 'Les Chamites selon Gen 10,6-20 et 1 Chr 1,8-16', *ZAH* 5 (1992), pp. 135-62.

Lipiński, E., 'Les Japhétites selon Gen 10,1-4 et 1 Chr 1,5-7', *ZAH* 3 (1990), pp. 40-53.

Lipiński, E., 'Nimrod et Aššur', *RB* 73 (1966), pp. 77-93.

Lipiński, E., 'Les Sémites selon Gen 10,21-30 et 1 Chr 1,17-23', *ZAH* 6 (1992), pp. 193-215.

Lieu, J.M., 'What Was from the Beginning: Scripture and Tradition in the Johannine Epistles', *NTS* 39 (1993), pp. 458-77.

Longman III, T., and S. McKnight, *Genesis* (Story of God Bible Commentary; Grand Rapids, MI: Zondervan, 2016).

Loretz, O., *Die Gottebenbildlichkeit des Menschen* (Munich: Kösel-Verlag, 1969).

Loretz, O., *Ḫabiru-Hebräer: eine sozio-linguistische Studie über die Herkunft des Gentiliziums 'ibrî vom Appelativum ḫabiru* (BZAW, 160; Berlin: W. de Gruyter, 1984).

Louden, B., 'Iapetos and Japheth: Hesiod's *Theogony*, *Iliad* 15.187-93, and Genesis 9–10', *Illinois Classical Studies* 38 (2013), pp. 1-12, reprinted in B. Louden, *Greek Myth and the Bible* (London: Routledge, 2019), pp. 37-56.

Luckenbill, D.D., *Annals of Sennacherib* (University of Chicago Oriental Institute Publications, 2; Chicago, IL: University of Chicago Press, 1924).

Macintosh, A.A., 'The Meaning of Hebrew תשוקה', *JSS* 61 (2016), pp. 365-87.

Maher, M., *Targum Pseudo-Jonathan: Genesis* (The Aramaic Bible, 2; Edinburgh: T. & T. Clark, 1992).

Maisler (Mazar), B., 'Two Hebrew Ostraca from Tell Qasîle', *JNES* 10 (1951), pp. 265-67.

Marcus, D., 'The Mission of the Raven (Gen. 8:7)', *JANES* 29 (2002), pp. 71-80.

Martin, R.A., 'The Earliest Messianic Interpretation of Genesis 3 15', *JBL* 84 (1965), pp. 425-27.

Mattfeld, W.R., *Eden's Serpent: Its Mesopotamian Origins* (n.p.; Walter R. Mattfeld, 2010).

May, G., *Schöpfung aus dem Nichts: Die Entstehung der Lehre von der Creatio ex Nihilo* (Arbeiten zur Kirchengeschichte, 48; Berlin: W. de Gruyter, 1978), ET *Creatio ex Nihilo: The Doctrine of 'Creation out of Nothing' in Early Christian Thought* (trans. A.S. Worrall; Edinburgh: T. & T. Clark, 1994).

McEvenue, S., *The Narrative Style of the Priestly Author* (AnBib, 50; Rome: Biblical Institute Press, 1971).

McFarland, L.A., *The Divine Image: Envisioning the Invisible God* (Minneapolis, MN: Fortress Press, 2005).

McKane, W., *The Book of Micah: Introduction and Commentary* (Edinburgh: T. & T. Clark, 1998.

McKeown, J., *Genesis* (Two Horizons OT Commentary; Grand Rapids, MI: Eerdmans, 2008).

McNamara, M., *The New Testament and the Palestinian Targum to the Pentateuch* (AnBib, 27; Rome: Pontifical Biblical Institute, 1966).

McNamara, M., *Targum Neofiti I: Genesis* (The Aramaic Bible, 1A; Edinburgh: T. & T. Clark, 1992).

Mendenhall, G.E., 'The Shady Side of Wisdom: The Date and Purpose of Genesis 3', in H.N. Bream, R.D. Heim and C.A. Moore (eds.), *A Light Unto My Path: Old Testament Studies in Honor of Jacob M. Myers* (Philadelphia, PA: Temple University Press, 1974), pp. 319-34.

Merhav, R., 'The Stele of the "Serpent Goddess" from Tell Beit Mirsim and the Plaque from Shechem Reconsidered', *The Israel Museum Journal* 4 (1985), pp. 27-42.

Mettinger, T.N.D., 'Abbild oder Urbild? »Imago Dei« in traditionsgeschichtlicher Sicht', *ZAW* 86 (1974), pp. 403-24.

Mettinger, T.N.D., *The Eden Narrative: A Literary and Religio-Historical Study of Genesis 2–3* (Winona Lake, IN: Eisenbrauns, 2007).

Meyer, E., *Die Israeliten und ihre Nachbarstämme* (Halle: Niemeyer, 1906).

Meyer, E., 'Miszellen. 2. Nimrod', *ZAW* 8 (1888), pp. 47-49.

Middleton, J.R., *The Liberating Image: The* Imago Dei *in Genesis 1* (Grand Rapids, MI: Brazos Press, 2005).

Milik, J.T., *The Books of Enoch: Aramaic Fragments of Qumrân Cave 4* (Oxford: Clarendon Press, 1976).

Millard, A.R., 'Ninos', in D.O. Edzard (ed.), *Reallexikon der Assyriologie*, IX (Berlin: W. de Gruyter, 1998–2001), pp. 479-80.

Millard, A.R., 'Where Was Abraham's Ur? The Case for the Babylonian City', *BARev* 27.3 (May/June, 2001), pp. 52-53, 57.

Miller, J.M., 'The Descendants of Cain: Notes on Genesis 4', *ZAW* 88 (1974), pp. 164-73.

Miller, J.M., 'In the "Image" and "Likeness" of God', *JBL* 91 (1972), pp. 289-304.

Miller, J.M., 'Ur of the Chaldeans and Interdisciplinary Research', in T.J. Sandoval and C. Mandolfo (eds.), *Relating to the Text: Interdisciplinary and Form-Critical Insights on the Bible* (JSOTSup, 384; London: T&T Clark [Continuum], 2003), pp. 307-20.

Miller, P.D., *Genesis 1–11: Studies in Structure & Theme* (JSOTSup, 8; Sheffield: JSOT Press, 1978).

Miller, R.D., *The Dragon, the Mountain, and the Nations: An Old Testament Myth, its Origins, and its Afterlives* (University Park, PA: Eisenbrauns, 2018).

Moberly, R.W.L., 'The Mark of Cain Revealed at Last?', *HTR* 100 (2007), pp. 11-28.

Moberly, R.W.L., *The Theology of the Book of Genesis* (Cambridge: Cambridge University Press, 2009).

Montgomery, J.A., *Arabia and the Bible* (Philadelphia, PA: University of Pennsylvania Press, 1934).

Montgomery, J.A., and H.S. Gehman, *A Critical and Exegetical Commentary on the Books of Kings* (ICC; Edinburgh: T. & T. Clark, 1951).

Moor, J.C. de, 'The Sacrifice which Is an Abomination to the Lord', in *Loven en geloven. Opstellen van collega's en medewerkers aangeboden aan Prof. D. Nic. H. Ridderbos* (Amsterdam: Bolland, 1975), pp. 211-26.

Murray, R., *The Cosmic Covenant* (HM; London: Sheed & Ward, 1992).

Neumann-Gersolke, U., *Herrschen in den Grenzen der Schöpfung. Ein Beitrag zur alttestamentlichen Anthropologie am Beispiel von Psalm 8, Genesis 1 und verwandten Texten* (WMANT, 101; Neukirchen-Vluyn: Neukirchener Verlag, 2004).

Nicholson, E.W., *The Pentateuch in the Twentieth Century: The Legacy of Julius Wellhausen* (Oxford: Clarendon Press, 1998).

Nickelsburg, G.W.E., 'Apocalyptic and Myth in 1 Enoch 6–11', *JBL* 96 (1977), pp. 383-405.

Nickelsburg, G.W.E., and James C. VanderKam, *1 Enoch. II. A Commentary on the Book of Enoch Chapters 37–82* (Hermeneia; Minneapolis, MN: Fortress Press, 2012).

Niebuhr, R., *The Nature and Destiny of Man* (2 vols.; London: Nisbet, 1941–43).

Nöldeke, T., *Untersuchungen zur Kritik des Alten Testaments* (Kiel: Schwers, 1869).

Nöldeke, T., Review of F. Baethgen, *Beiträge zur semitischen Religionsgeschichte*, in *ZDMG* 42 (1888), pp. 470-87.

Noth, M., *Überlieferungsgeschichte des Pentateuch* (Stuttgart: W. Kohlhammer, 1948).

Notter, V., *Biblischer Schöpfungsbericht und ägyptische Schöpfungsmythen* (SBS, 68; Stuttgart: KBW Verlag, 1974).

Nougayrol, J., *Le Palais royal d'Ugarit*, IV (Paris: Imprimerie Nationale, 1956).

Novak, D., *The Image of the Non-Jew in Judaism: An Historical and Constructive Study of the Noahide Laws* (Toronto Studies in Theology, 14; New York: Edwin Mellen Press, 1983).

Ockinga, B., *Die Gottebenbildlichkeit im alten Ägypten und im Alten Testament* (Ägypten und Altes Testament, 7; Wiesbaden: Harrassowitz, 1984).

Oded, B., 'The Table of the Nations (Genesis 10) – A Socio-Cultural Approach', *ZAW* 98 (1986), pp. 14-31.

Oden, R.A., 'Divine Aspirations in Atrahasis and in Genesis 1–11', *ZAW* 93 (1981), pp. 197-216.

Oden, R.A., and H.W. Attridge, *Philo of Byblos, The Phoenician History: Introduction, Critical Text, Translation, Notes* (CBQMS, 9; Washington, DC: Catholic Biblical Association of America, 1961).

Oederus, G.L., *Catechismus Racoviensis* (Frankfurt: J.A. Schmidt, 1739).

Ojewole, A.O., *The Seed in Genesis 3:15* (Berrien Springs, MI: Adventist Theological Society, 2002).

O'Neill, J.C., 'How Early is the Doctrine of *Creatio ex Nihilo*?', *JTS* 53 NS (2002), pp. 449-65.

Orlinsky, H.M., 'The Plain Meaning of Ruaḥ in Gen. 1.2', *JQR* 48 (1957–58), pp. 174-82.

Orlov, A.A., *The Enoch–Metatron Tradition* (TSAJ, 107; Tübingen: Mohr Siebeck, 2005).

Otto, E, 'Die Paradieserzählung Genesis 2–3. Eine nachpriesterschriftliche Lehrerzählung in ihrem religionshistorischen Kontext', in A.A. Diesel, R.G. Lehmann, E. Otto and A. Wagner (eds.), *„Jedes Ding hat seine Zeit ...“ Studien zur israelitischen und altorientalischen Weisheit. Diethelm Michel zum 65. Geburtstag* (BZAW, 241; Belin: W. de Gruyter, 1996), pp. 167-92.

Pardee, D., *Les textes para-mythologiques de la 24e campagne (1961)* (Ras Shamra-Ougarit, IV; Paris: Editions Recherche sur les Civilisations, 1988).

Pardee, D., *Ritual and Cult at Ugarit* (WBWSBL; Atlanta, GA: SBL, 2002).

Parpola, S., *Neo-Assyrian Toponyms* (AOAT, 6; Neukirchen-Vluyn: Neukirchener Verlag, 1970).

Pearce, L.E., and C. Wunsch, *Documents of Judean Exiles and West Semites in Babylonia in the Collection of David Sofer* (Cornell University Studies in Assyriology and Sumerology, 28; Bethesda, MD: CDL Press, 2014).

Pelikan, J. (ed.), *Luther's Works*. I. *Lectures on Genesis Chapters 1–5* (St Louis, MO: Concordia, 1958).

Petersen, D., 'The Formation of the Pentateuch', in D. Petersen, J.L. Mays and K.H. Richards (eds.), *Old Testament Interpretation: Past, Present, and Future. Essays in Honor of Gene M. Tucker* (Nashville, TN: Abingdon Press, 1995), pp. 31-45.

Petrovich, D., 'Identifying Nimrod of Genesis 10 with Sargon of Akkad by Exegetical and Archaeological Means', *JETS* 56 (2013), pp. 273-306.

Pinches, T.G., *The Old Testament in the Light of the Historical Records and Legends of Assyria and Babylonia* (London: SPCK, 3rd edn, 1908).

Polaski, D.C., 'Reflections on the Mosaic Covenant: The Eternal Covenant (Isaiah 24.5) and Intertextuality', *JSOT* 77 (1998), pp. 55-73.

Posener, G., *Princes et pays d'Asie et de Nubie* (Brussels: Fondation égyptologique reine Elisabeth, 1940).

Pritchard, J.B., *Recovering Sarepta: A Phoenician City* (Princeton, NJ: Princeton University Press, 1978).

Provan, I., *Seriously Dangerous Religion: What the Old Testament Really Says and Why it Matters* (Waco, TX: Baylor University Press, 2014).

Rad, G. von, *Das erste Buch Mose: Genesis* (ATD, 2.4; Göttingen: Vandenhoeck & Ruprecht, 5th edn, 1958), ET *Genesis*, Genesis (trans. J.H. Marks; OTL; London: SCM Press, 2nd edn, 1963).

Rad, G. von, *Die Priesterschrift im Hexateuch, literarisch untersucht und theologisch gewertet* (BWANT, 65; Stuttgart: Kohlhammer, 1934).

Rainey, A.F., 'Business Agents at Ugarit', *IEJ* 13 (1963), pp. 313-21.

Rainey, A.F., 'Chaldea, Chaldeans', in *Encyclopaedia Judaica*, V (Jerusalem: Keter, 1971), cols. 330-31.

Rainey, A.F., *The El-Amarna Correspondence* (2 vols.; Leiden: Brill, 2015).

Rainey, A.F., Review of O. Loretz, *Ḫabiru-Hebräer*, *JAOS* 101 (1987), pp. 31-35.

Rawlinson, H.C., 'Biblical Geography', *The Athenæum* 1799 (April, 1862), pp. 529-31.

Rawlinson, H.C., Comments made on a lecture by William K. Loftus, 'Notes on a Journey from Baghdad to Basrah with Descriptions of Original Chaldaean Remains' (Feb. 25th, 1856), in *Proceedings of the Royal Geographical Society of London* (1857), pp. 45-49.

Rawlinson, H.C., 'On the Inscriptions of Assyria and Babylonia', *JRAS* 12 (1850), pp. 401-83.

Redford, D.B., *Egypt, Canaan, and Israel in Ancient Times* (Princeton, NJ: Princeton University Press, 1992).

Reeves, J.C., and A.Y. Reed, *Enoch from Antiquity to the Middle Ages: Sources from Judaism, Christianity, and Islam*, I (Oxford: Oxford University Press, 2018).

Reicke, B., 'The Knowledge Hidden in the Tree of Paradise', *JSS* 1 (1956), pp. 193-202.

Renaud, B., *La formation du livre de Michée. Tradition et actualisation* (Etudes bibliques; Paris: J. Gabalda, 1977).

Rendsburg, G.A., 'The Biblical Flood Story in the Light of the Gilgameš Flood Account', in J. Azize and N. Weeks (eds.), *Gilgameš and the World of Assyria: Proceedings of the Conference Held at Mandelbaum House*, The University of Sydney, 21-23 July 2004 (Ancient Near Eastern Studies, Supplement 21; Leuven: Peeters, 2007), pp. 115-27.

Rendsburg, G.A., 'Gen 10:13-14: an Authentic Hebrew Tradition Concerning the Origin of the Philistines', *JNSL* 13 (1987), pp. 89-96.

Rendsburg, G.A., *The Redaction of Genesis* (Winona Lake, IN: Eisenbrauns, 1986).

Rendsburg, G.A., 'Ur Kasdim: Where is Abraham's Birthplace?', in *The Torah.com* (online, 2019).

Rendtorff, R., *Das überliefrungsgschichtliche Problem des Pentateuch* (BZAW, 147; Berlin: W. de Gruyter, 1977), ET *The Problem of the Process of Transmission in the Pentateuch* (trans. J.J. Scullion; JSOTSup, 89; Sheffield: JSOT Press, 1990).

Ridderbos, N.H., 'Gen 1:1 und 2', *OTS* 12 (1958), pp. 214-60.

Riedel, W., 'Die Gottesebenbildlichkeit des Menschen', *Alttestamentliche Untersuchungen*, I (Leipzig: A. Deichert, 1902), pp. 42-47.

Riemann, P.A., 'Am I My Brother's Keeper?', *Int* 24 (1970), pp. 482-91.

Rogerson, J., 'The Creation Stories: Their Ecological Potential and Problems', in D.G. Horrell, C. Hunt, C. Southgate and F. Stavrakopoulou (eds), *Ecological Hermeneutics: Biblical, Theological Perspectives* (London: T&T Clark, 2010), pp. 21-31.

Rogerson, J., *Genesis 1–11* (OTG; Sheffield, JSOT, 1991).

Roitman, A.D., 'The Mystery of Arphaxad (Jdt 1): A New Proposal', *Henoch* 19 (1995), pp. 301-10.

Rowley, H.H., *The Faith of Israel* (London: SCM Press, 1956).

Rubinkiewicz, R., 'Apocalypse of Abraham', in J.H. Charlesworth (ed.), *The Old Testament Pseudepigrapha*, I (2 vols.; London: Darton, Longan & Todd, 1983-85), pp. 681-705.

Rüterswörden, U., 'Der Bogen in Genesis 9. Militärhistorische und traditionsgeschichtliche Erwägungen zu einem biblischen Symbol', *UF* 20 (1988), pp. 247-63.

Rüterswörden, U., *Dominium Terrae: Studien zur Genese einer alttestamentlichen Vorstellung* (BZAW, 215; Berlin: W. de Gruyter, 1993).

Ryckmans, G., 'Ophir', in *Supplément au dictionnaire de la Bible*, VI (1959), cols. 744-51.

Saggs, H.W.F., 'Ur of the Chaldees: A Problem of Identification', *Iraq* 22 (1960), pp. 200-209.

Sanders, S.L., *From Adapa to Enoch: Scribal and Religious Vision in Judea and Babylon* (TSAJ, 167; Tübingen: Mohr Siebeck, 2017).

Sarna, N.M., *Genesis* (JPS Torah Commentary; Philadelphia, PA: JPS, 1989).

Sasson, J.M., 'A Genealogical "Convention" in Biblical Chronography', *ZAW* 90 (1978), pp. 171-85.

Sasson, J.M., 'Generation, Seventh', in *IDBSup*, pp. 354-56.

Sasson, J.M., 'Reḥōvōt 'îr', *RB* 90 (1983), pp. 96-98.

Sayce, A.H., 'Miscellaneous Notes. 10. *Irad* and *Enoch* in Genesis', *Zeitschrift für Keilschriftforschung* 2 (1885), p. 404.

Sayce, A.H., 'On Nimrod and the Assyrian Inscriptions', *TSBA* 2 (1873), pp. 243-49.

Sayce, A.H., *Patriarchal Palestine* (London: SPCK, 1895).

Scarlata, M., *Outside of Eden: Cain in the Ancient Versions of Genesis 4.1-16* (LHBOTS, 573; New York: T&T Clark, 2012).

Schellenberg, A., 'Humankind as "Image of God"', *TZ* 97 (2009), pp. 87-111.

Schellenberg, A., *Der Mensch das Bild Gottes* (ATANT, 101; Zurich: Theologischer Verlag, 2011).

Schmid, K., *Literaturgeschichte des Alten Testaments* (Darmstadt: Wissenschaftliche Buchgesellschaft, 2008), ET *The Old Testament: A Literary History* (trans. L.M. Maloney; Minneapolis, MN: Fortress Press, 2012).

Schmid, K., 'Die Unteilbarkeit der Weisheit. Überlegungen zur sogenannten Paradieserzählung Gen 2f. und ihrer theologischen Tendenz', *ZAW* 114 (2002), pp. 21-39.

Schmidt, H., *Die Erzählung von Paradies und Sündenfall* (Tübingen: J.C.B. Mohr [Paul Siebeck], 1931).

Schmidt, W.H., *Die Schöpfungsgeschichte der Priesterschrift* (WMANT, 17, Neukirchen-Vluyn: Neukirchener Verlag, 1964).

Schmitt, A., *Entrückung – Aufnahme – Himmelfahrt: Untersuchungen im Alten Testament* (FzB, 10; Stuttgart: Verlag Katholisches Bibelwerk, 1973).

Schnabel, P., *Berossos und die babylonisch-hellenistische Literatur* (Leipzig: B.G. Teubner, 1923).

Schoeps, H.-J., *Theologie und Geschichte des Judenchristentums* (Tübingen: J.C.B. Mohr [Paul Siebeck], 1949).

Schoors, A., *Jesaja* (De Boeken van het Oude Testament; Roermond: J.J. Romen, 1972).

Schrader, E., *Die Keilschriften und das Alte Testament* (Giessen: J. Ricker, 1st edn, 1872; Berlin: Reuther & Reichard, 3rd edn, 1903).

Schüle, A., *Der Prolog der hebräischen Bibel. Der literar- und theologiegeschichtliche Diskurs der Urgeschichte (Gen 1–11)* (ATANT, 86; Zurich: Theologischer Verlag, 2006).

Scullion, J.J., *Genesis* (Collegeville, MN: Liturgical Press, 1992).

Seebass, H., *Genesis. I. Urgeschichte (1,1–11,26)* (Neukirchen-Vluyn: Neukirchener Verlag, 3rd edn, 2009).

Seeberg, R., *Christliche Dogmatik* (2 vols.; Erlangen; A. Deichert, 1924–25).

Sethe, K., *Die Ächtung feindlicher Fürsten, Völker und Dinger auf altägyptischen Tongefässscherben der mittleren Reiches* (Berlin: Akademie der Wissenschaften in Kommission bei W. de Gruyter, 1926).

Sethe, K., 'Heroes and Hero-Gods (Egyptian)', in J. Hastings, J.A. Selbie and L.H. Gray (eds.), *Encyclopædia of Religion and Ethics*, VI (13 vols.; Edinburgh: T. & T. Clark, 1913), pp. 647-52.

Shanks, H., 'Is the Pope Going to the Wrong Place?', *BARev* 25.1 (Jan./Feb. 2000), pp. 16-19, 66-67.

Simons, J., 'The "Table of Nations" (Gen. X): Its General Structure and Meaning', in P. de Boer (ed.), *OTS* 10 (Leiden: Brill, 1954), pp. 155-84.

Simpson, C.A., 'Genesis', in *Interpreter's Bible*, I (New York: Abingdon-Cokesbury Press, 1952), pp. 437-829.

Simpson, St J., and S. Pankova (eds.), *Scythians: Warriors of Ancient Siberia* (London: Thames & Hudson and the British Museum, 2017).

Sjöberg, A.W., 'Eve and the Chameleon', in W.B. Barrick and J.R. Spencer (eds.), *In the Shelter of Elyon: Essays on Ancient Palestinian Life and Literature in Honor of G.W. Ahlström* (JSOTSup, 31; Sheffield: JSOT Press, 1984), pp. 217-25.

Ska, J.-L., 'El relato del Diluvio un relato sacerdotal y algunos fragment redaccionales posteriores', *EstBíb* 52 (1994), pp. 37-62, ET 'The Story of the Flood: A Priestly Writer and Some Editorial Fragments', in *The Exegesis of the Pentateuch: Exegetical Studies and Basic Questions* (FAT, 66; Tübingen: Mohr Siebeck, 2009), pp. 1-22.

Skinner, J., *Genesis* (ICC; Edinburgh: T. & T. Clark, 1910, reprinted 1930).

Smith, D.E., 'The Divining Snake: Reading Genesis 3 in the Context of Mesopotamian Ophiomancy', *JBL* 134 (2015), pp. 31-49.

Smith, G., *The Chaldean Account of Genesis* (London: Sampson Low, Marston, Searle & Rivington, 1876).

Smith, G., 'The Chaldean Account of the Deluge', *TSBA* 2 (1873), pp. 213-34.

Smith, M.S., *The Genesis of Good and Evil: The Fall(out) and Original Sin in the Bible* (Louisville, KY: Westminster/John Knox, 2019).

Smith, M.S., 'Light in Genesis 1:3 – Created or Uncreated: A Question of Priestly Mysticism?', in C. Cohen *et al.*, *Birkat Shalom: Studies in Bible, Ancient Near Eastern Literature, and Postbiblical Judaism Presented to Shalom M. Paul on the Occasion of his Seventieth Birthday*, I (2 vols.; Winona Lake, IN: Eisenbrauns, 2008), pp. 125-34.

Smith, M.S., *The Priestly Vision of Genesis 1* (Minneapolis, MN: Fortress Press, 2010).

Snaith, N.H., 'The Image of God', *ExpTim* 86 (1974), p. 24.

Soden, W. von, 'Nimrod', in H. von Campenhausen, K. Galling and W. Werbeck (eds.), *RGG³*, IV (Tübingen: J.C.B. Mohr [Paul Siebeck], 1960), cols. 1496-97.

Soden, W. von, 'Mottoverse zu Beginn babylonischer und antiker Epen, Mottosätze in der Bibel', in H.-P. Müller (ed.), *Bibel und alter Orient. Altorientalische Beiträge zum Alten Testament von Wolfram von Soden* (BZAW, 162; Berlin: W. de Gruyter, 1985), pp. 206-12.

Soggin, J.A., 'The Fall of Man in the Third Chapter of Genesis', in *Old Testament and Oriental Studies* (Rome: Biblical Institute Press, 1975), pp. 88-111.

Sommer, B.D., *The Bodies of God and the World of Ancient Israel* (New York: Cambridge University Press, 2009).

Sommer, B.D., *A Prophet Reads Scripture: Allusion in Isaiah 40–66* (Stanford, CA: Stanford University Press, 1998).

Spar, I., and W.G. Lambert (eds.), *Cuneiform Texts in the Metropolitan Museum of Art*. II. *Literary and Scholastic Texts of the First Millennium B.C.* (Metropolitan Museum of Art, New York: Brepols, 2005).

Speiser, E.A., *Genesis* (AB, 1; Garden City, NY: Doubleday, 1964).

Speiser, E.A., 'In Search of Nimrod', in M. Avi-Yonah, H.Z. Hirschberg, Y. Yadin and H. Tadmor (eds.), *Eretz Israel* 5 (Benjamin Mazar volume; Jerusalem: Israel Exploration Society, 1958), pp. 32*-36*, reprinted in J.J. Finkelstein and M. Greenberg (eds.), *Oriental and Biblical Studies: Collected Writings of E.A. Speiser* (Philadelphia: University of Pennsylvania Press, 1967), pp. 31-52, and further reprinted in R.S. Hess and D.T. Tsumura (eds.), *"I Studied Inscriptions from before the Flood": Ancient Near Eastern, Literary, and Linguistic Approaches to Genesis 1–11* (Winona Lake, IN: Eisenbrauns, 1994), pp. 270-77.

Spiegelberg,W. 'נפתחים (Gen. X, 13)', *OLZ* 9 (1906), cols. 276-79.

Spina, F.A., 'The Ground for Cain's Rejection (Gen 4): *ᵃdāmāh* in the Context of Gen 1–11', *ZAW* 104 (1992), pp. 319-32.

Stade, B., 'Das Kainszeichen', *ZAW* 14 (1894), pp. 250-318.

Stadelmann, L.I.J., *The Hebrew Concept of the World* (AnBib, 39; Rome: Pontifical Biblical Institute Press, 1970).

Stamm, J.J., *Die Gottebenbildlichkeit des Menschen im Alten Testament* (Theologische Studien, 54; Zollikon: Evangelischer Verlag, 1959).

Stavrakopoulou, F., 'Tree-Hogging in Eden: Divine Restriction and Royal Rejection in Genesis 2–3', in M. Higton, J. Law and C. Rowland (eds.), *Theology and Human Flourishing: Essays in Honor of Timothy J. Gorringe* (Eugene OR: Wipf & Stock [Cascade Books], 2011), pp. 41-53.

Steele, P.M., *A Linguistic History of Ancient Cyprus: The Non-Greek Languages and their Relations with Greek, c. 1600–300* (Cambridge: Cambridge University Press, 2013).

Steenberg, M.C., 'Children in Paradise: Adam and Eve as "Infants" in Irenaeus of Lyons', *Journal of Early Christian Studies* 12 (2004), pp. 1-22.

Steinman, A., *Genesis* (TOTC; IVP: Downers Grove, IL, 2019).

Stipp, H.-J., 'Gen 1,1 und asyndetische Relativsätze im Bibelhebräischen', in *Alttestamentliche Studien. Arbeiten zu Priesterschrift, Deuteronomischen Geschichtswerk und Prophetie* (BZAW, 442; Berlin: W. de Gruyter, 2013), pp. 5-31.

Stokes, R., *Satan: How God's Executioner Became the Enemy* (Grand Rapids, MI: Eerdmans, 2019).

Strecker, G., 'Noachische Gebote', in *RGG³*, IV (Tübingen: J.C.B. Mohr [Paul Siebeck], 1960), cols. 1500-1501.

Sullivan, J.E., *The Image of God: The Doctrine of St. Augustine and its Influence* (Dubuque, IA: Priory, 1963).

Tadmor, H., *The Inscriptions of Tiglath-pileser III King of Assyria* (Jerusalem: Israel Academy of Sciences and Humanities, 1994).

Thompson, J.A., 'Samaritan Evidence for "All of Them in the Land of Shinar" (Gen 10:10)', *JBL* 90 (1971), pp. 90-102.

Thompson, T.L., *The Bible in History: How Writers Create a Past* (London: Jonathan Cape, 1999); also published as *The Mythic Past: Biblical Archaeology and the Myth of Israel* (New York: Basic Books, 1999).

Tigchelaar, E.J.C., and F. García Martínez in S.J. Pfann *et al.*, *Qumran Cave 4. XXVI: Cryptic Texts and Miscellanies, Part 1* (DJD, 36; Oxford: Clarendon Press, 2000).

Titus, P.J., *The Second Story of Creation (Gen 2:4–3:24): A Prologue to the Concept of the Enneateuch*? (European University Studies, 23.912; Frankfurt: Peter Lang, 2011).

Toorn, K. van der, in K. van der Toorn and P.W. van der Horst, 'Nimrod before and after the Bible', *HTR* 83 (1990), pp. 1-29.

Trible, P., *God and the Rhetoric of Spirituality* (Philadelphia, PA: Fortress Press, 1978).

Tsirkin, Y.B., 'The Greeks and Tartessos', *Oikumene* 5 (1986), pp. 163-71.

Tsumura, D.T., *Creation and Destruction: A Reappraisal of the* Chaoskampf *Theory in the Old Testament* (Winona Lake, IN: Eisenbrauns, 2005).

Turner, L.A., 'The Rainbow as the Sign of the Covenant in Genesis ix 11-13', *VT* 43 (1993), pp. 119-24.

Tutu, D., *In God's Hands* (London: Bloomsbury, 2014).

Uehlinger, C., 'Nimrod', in K. van der Toorn, B. Becking and P.W. van der Horst (eds.), *Dictionary of Deities and Demons in the Bible* (Leiden: Brill, 2nd edn, 1999), pp. 627-30.

Van Beek, G., 'Frankincense and Myrrh in Ancient South Arabia' *JAOS* 78 (1958), pp. 141-52.

Van Beek, G., 'Ophir', in *IDB*, 3, pp. 605-606.

VanderKam, J.C., *Calendars in the Dead Sea Scrolls: Measuring Time* (London: Routledge, 1998).

VanderKam, J.C., *Enoch: A Man for All Generations* (Columbia, SC: University of South Carolina Press, 1995).

VanderKam, J.C., *Enoch and the Growth of an Apocalyptic Tradition* (CBQMS 16; Washington, DC: Catholic Biblical Association of America, 1984).

VanderKam, J.C., 'Enoch's Science', in J. Ben-Dov and S.L. Sanders (eds.), *Ancient Jewish Sciences and the History of Knowledge in Second Temple Judaism* (New York: New York University, 2014), pp. 51-67.

Van Seters, J., *Abraham in History and Tradition* (New Haven, CT: Yale University Press, 1975).

Van Seters, J., *Prologue to History: The Yahwist as Historian in Genesis* (Louisville, KY: Westminster John Knox Press, 1992).

Vaux, R. de, *La Genèse* (La Sainte Bible; Paris: Cerf, 2nd edn, 1962).

Vaux, R. de, *Les institutions de l'ancien Testament* (2 vols.; Paris: Cerf, 1958–60), ET *Ancient Israel* (trans. J. McHugh; London: Darton, Longman & Todd, 2nd edn, 1965).

Vawter, B., *On Genesis: A New Reading* (London: Geoffrey Chapman, 1977).

Verbrugghe, G.P., and J.M. Wickersham, *Berossos and Manetho, Introduced and Translated: Native Traditions in Mesopotamia and Egypt* (Ann Arbor, MI: University of Michigan Press, 1996).

Vermeylen, J., 'La «table des nations» (Gn 10): Yaphet figure-t-il l'Empire perse?', *Transeuphratène* 5 (1992), pp. 113-32.

Vriezen, T.C., *Onderzoek naar de Paradijsvoorstelling bij de oude Semietischen Volken* (Wageningen: H. Veenman, 1937).

Wallace, H.N., *The Eden Narrative* (HSM, 32; Atlanta, GA: Scholars Press, 1985).

Waltke, B.K., 'Cain and his Offering', *WTJ* 48 (1986), pp. 363-72.

Walton, J.H., *Genesis: The NIV Application Commentary* (Grand Rapids, MI: Zondervan, 2001).

Wasserman, N., *The Flood: The Akkadian Sources. A New Edition, Commentary, and a Literary Discussion* (OBO, 290; Leuven: Peeters, 2020).

Weinfeld, M., 'God the Creator in the Priestly Source and Deutero-Isaiah' (Hebrew), *Tarbiz* 37 (1967–68), pp. 105-32, ET *The Place of the Law in the Religion of Ancient Israel* (VTSup 100; Leiden: Brill, 2004), pp. 95-117.

Weitzman, M.P., *The Syriac Version of the Old Testament: An Introduction* (Cambridge: Cambridge University Press, 1999).

Wellhausen, J., *Die Composition des Hexateuchs und der historischen Bücher des Alten Testaments* (Berlin: G. Reimer, 3rd edn, 1899).

Wellhausen, J., *Prolegomena zur Geschichte Israels* (Berlin: G. Reimer, 2nd edn, 1883), ET *Prolegomena to the History of Israel* (trans. J.S. Black and A. Menzies; Edinburgh: A. & C. Black, 1885).

Wenham, G.J., 'The Coherence of the Flood Narrative', *VT* 28 (1978), pp. 336-48.

Wenham, G.J., *Genesis 1–15* (WBC, 1; Waco, TX: Word Books, 1987).

Wenham, G.J., 'Method in Pentateuchal Criticism', *VT* 41 (1991), pp. 84-109.

Wenham, G.J., 'The Priority of P', *VT* 49 (1999), pp. 240-58.

West, M.L., *The East Face of Helicon: West Asiatic Elements in Early Poetry and Myth* (Oxford: Clarendon Press, 1997).

West, M.L., *The Hesiodic Catalogue of Women* (Oxford: Clarendon Press, 1985).

Westermann, C., *Genesis 1–11* (BKAT, 1.1; Neukirchen-Vluyn: Neukirchener Verlag, 1974), ET *Genesis 1–11* (trans. J.J. Scullion; London: SPCK, 1974).

Wevers, J.W., *Notes on the Greek Text of Genesis* (SBLSCS, 35; Atlanta, GA: Scholars Press, 1993).

White, L., 'The Historical Roots of our Ecologic Crisis', *Science* 155, no. 3767 (1967), pp. 1203-207.

Whybray, R.N., *The Making of the Pentateuch: A Methodological Study* (JSOTSup, 53; Sheffield: JSOT Press, 1987).

Wiggins, S.A., 'The Myth of Asherah: Lion Lady and Serpent Goddess', *UF* 23 (1991), pp. 383-94.

Wildberger, H., 'Das Abbild Gottes. Gen. 1,26-30', *TZ* 21 (1965), pp. 245-59, 481-501, reprinted in H. Wildberger, *Jahwe und sein Volk: Gesammelte Aufsätze zum Alten Testament* (eds. H.H. Schmid and O.H. Steck; TBü, 66; Munich: Chr. Kaiser, 1979), pp. 110-45.

Williams, A.J., 'The Relationship of Genesis 3 20 to the Serpent', *ZAW* 89 (1977), pp. 357-74.

Williamson, H.G.M., *Israel in the Books of Chronicles* (Cambridge: Cambridge University Press, 1977).

Williamson, H.G.M., 'Micah', in J. Barton and J. Muddiman (eds.), *The Oxford Bible Commentary* (Oxford: Oxford University Press, 2001), pp. 595-99.

Williamson, H.G.M., 'On Getting Carried Away with the Infinitive Construct נשא', in M. Bar-Asher, D. Rom-Shiloni, E. Tov and N. Wazana (eds.), *Shai le-Japhet: Studies in the Bible, its Exegesis and its Language* (Jerusalem: Bialik Institute, 2007), pp. 357-67*.

Wintermute, O.S., 'Jubilees', in J.H. Charlesworth (ed.), *The Old Testament Pseudepigrapha*, II (2 vols.; London: Darton, Longman & Todd, 1983–85), pp. 35-142.

Wiseman, D.J., *1 and 2 Kings: An Introduction and Commentary* (TOTC, 9; Leicester: IVP Press, 1993).

Wiseman, D.J., *The Alalakh Tablets* (London: Occasional Publications of the British Institute of Archeology at Ankara, 1953).

Witte, M., *Die biblische Urgeschichte. Redaktions- und theologiegeschichtliche Beobachtungen zu Genesis 1,1–11,26* (BZAW, 265; Berlin: W. de Gruyter, 1998).

Wolde, E. van, *Reframing Biblical Studies: When Language and Text Meet Culture, Cognition and Context* (Winona Lake, IN: Eisenbrauns, 2009).

Wolde, E. van, 'Separation and Creation in Genesis 1 and Psalm 104, A Continuation of the Discussion of the Verb ברא', *VT* 67 (2017), pp. 611-47.

Wolde, E. van, 'Why the Verb ברא Does Not Mean "To Create" in Genesis 1.1–2.4a', *JSOT* 34 (2009), pp. 3-23.

Wolde, E. van, with R. Rezetko, 'Semantics and the Semantics of ברא: A Rejoinder to the Arguments Advanced by B. Becking and M. Korpel', *JHS* 11 (2011), article 9.

Woolley, L. *Abraham: Recent Discoveries and Hebrew Origins* (London: Faber & Faber, 1936).

Woolley, L., *Ur 'of the Chaldees'* (ed. P.R.S. Moorey; London: Herbert Press, 1982). This was a thorough revision of Woolley's *Excavations at Ur: A Record of Twelve Years' Work* (London: Ernest Benn, 1955), which in turn was a revision of his *Ur of the Chaldees* (London: Penguin Books, 2nd edn, 1950), first published by Ernest Benn in 1929.

Wright, R.M., *Linguistic Evidence for the Pre-Exilic Date of the Yahwistic Source* (LHBOTS, 419; London: T&T Clark, 2005).

Wyatt, N., 'Cain's Wife', *Folklore* 97 (1986), pp. 88-95.

Wyatt, N., 'Interpreting the Creation and Fall Story in Genesis 2–3', *ZAW* 93 (1981), pp. 10-21.

Wyatt, N., 'A Royal Garden: The Ideology of Eden', *SJOT* 28 (2014), pp. 1-35.

Yahuda, A.S., 'Calneh in Shinar', *JBL* 65 (1946), pp. 325-27.

Yamauchi, E., *Foes from the Northern Frontier* (Eugene, OR: Wipf & Stock, 1982).

Zachmann, L., 'Beobachtungen zur Theologie in Gen 5', *ZAW* 88 (1976), pp. 272-74.

Zenger, E., *Gottes Bogen in den Wolken. Untersuchungen zu Komposition und Theologie der priesterschriftlichen Urgeschichte* (Stuttgart: Katholisches Bibelwerk, 1983).

Zevit, Z., *What Really Happened in the Garden of Eden?* (New Haven, CT: Yale University Press, 2013).

Zimmerli, W., *1 Mose 1–11. Die Urgeschichte* (ZBK; Zurich: Zwingli Verlag, 3rd edn, 1967).

Zimmerli, W., *Ezechiel*, I (BKAT, 13.1, Neukirchen-Vluyn: Neukirchener Verlag, 1969), ET *Ezekiel*, I (Hermeneia; Philadelphia, PA, Fortress Press, 1979).

Zimmerli, W., 'Sinaibund und Abrahambund. Ein Beitrag zum Verständnis der Priesterschrift', *TZ* 16 (1960), pp. 268-80, reprinted in Zimmerli (ed.), *Gottes Offenbarung. Gesammelte Aufsätze zum Alten Testament* (TBü; Munich: Chr. Kaiser Verlag, 2nd edn, 1969), pp. 205-16.

Zimmern, H., 'Urkönige und Uroffenbarung', in E. Schrader (ed.), *Die Keilinschriften und das Alte Testament* (Berlin: Reuther & Reichard, 3rd edn, 1903), pp. 530-43.

Zucker, Z. (ed.), *Saadya's Commentary on Genesis* (Hebrew; New York: Jewish Theological Seminary of America, 1984).

INDEX OF REFERENCES

INDEX OF AUTHORS